Confronting Decline

Working in the Americas

UNIVERSITY PRESS OF FLORIDA

Florida A&M University, Tallahassee
Florida Atlantic University, Boca Raton
Florida Gulf Coast University, Ft. Myers
Florida International University, Miami
Florida State University, Tallahassee
New College of Florida, Sarasota
University of Central Florida, Orlando
University of Florida, Gainesville
University of North Florida, Jacksonville
University of South Florida, Tampa
University of West Florida, Pensacola

Confronting Decline

The Political Economy of Deindustrialization
in Twentieth-Century New England

DAVID KOISTINEN

Foreword by Timothy J. Minchin and Richard Greenwald

UNIVERSITY PRESS OF FLORIDA

Gainesville / Tallahassee / Tampa / Boca Raton
Pensacola / Orlando / Miami / Jacksonville / Ft. Myers / Sarasota

Funding for this publication was provided by William Paterson University.

Copyright 2013 by David Koistinen
All rights reserved
Printed in the United States of America on acid free paper

This book may be available in an electronic edition.

21 20 19 18 17 16   6 5 4 3 2 1

First cloth printing, 2013
First paperback printing, 2016

Library of Congress Cataloging-in-Publication Data
Koistinen, David.
Confronting decline : the political economy of deindustrialization in twentieth-century New England / David Koistinen ; Foreword by Timothy J. Minchin and Richard Greenwald.
  p. cm. — (Working in the Americas)
Includes bibliographical references and index.
ISBN 978-0-8130-4907-6 (cloth: alk. paper)
ISBN 978-0-8130-5408-7 (pbk.)
1. Textile industry—New England—History. 2. Textile industry—Massachusetts—History. 3. Deindustrialization—New England—History. 4. New England—Economic conditions. I. Minchin, Timothy J. II. Greenwald, Richard A. III. Title. IV. Series: Working in the Americas.
HD9857.N36K65 2013
338.4'76770097470904—dc23   2013020087

University Press of Florida
15 Northwest 15th Street
Gainesville, FL 32611-2079
http://www.upf.com

For my parents

Contents

LIST OF ILLUSTRATIONS VIII
FOREWORD IX
ACKNOWLEDGMENTS XI

Introduction 1
1. Deindustrialization in New England 10
2. Retrenchment 26
3. Federal Assistance 67
4. Economic Development 102
5. Small Business Financing in Mid-Twentieth-Century New England 139
6. Small Business Finance and Electronics Spinoff Companies along Route 128 160
7. Responses to Deindustrialization in New England during the Cold War Years 187
8. Conclusions 221

APPENDIX 1. Rates of Job Creation in Massachusetts and the United States 241
APPENDIX 2. Cotton Textile Mill Wages 243
APPENDIX 3. A Contemporary Account of Spinoff Banking at the First National Bank of Boston 245
NOTES 247
BIBLIOGRAPHY 299
INDEX 319

Illustrations

TABLES

1.1. Manufacturing Employment in Massachusetts, New England, and the United States, 1923, 1929, and 1939   15
1.2. Employment in Declining Massachusetts Industries, 1923, 1929, and 1939   16
1.3. Active Cotton Spindles in New England and the Southern States, 1859–1939   22
2.1. Assessments on Textile Corporations and All Other Taxpayers in Fall River, Massachusetts, Selected Years, 1917–1932   56
5.1. Venture Capital and Other Business Promotion Organizations Established in Boston, 1939–1946   145
7.1. Manufacturing Employment in Massachusetts, Various Years, 1923–1960   189
A.1. Gainful Workers and Employment in Massachusetts and the United States, 1880–1988   242
A.2. Wage Rates for Selected Occupations in New England and Southern Cotton Textile Mills, July 1933   243

FIGURE

3.1. Earnings distribution for southern cotton textile workers before and after imposition of the NRA cotton textile code   75

Foreword

Studies of deindustrialization, or the decline of the traditional manufacturing sector, have largely focused on heavy industries, particularly steel and automobile manufacturing in the Northeast and Midwest. In *Confronting Decline*, David Koistinen helps to address this imbalance by turning our attention to the often neglected textile industry, focusing on the cotton textile industry in New England, a region that experienced massive industrial decline as early as the 1920s. He provides a well-written and broad ranging account of an industry that played a "pioneering role" in the deindustrialization of America.

Koistinen's work is also original in other ways. Whereas existing scholarship has often focused either on the reasons why industries declined or how this painful process affected workers and communities, Koistinen instead explores the *response* of workers, manufacturers, and civic leaders to job loss. Focusing largely on the key textile state of Massachusetts, but also reflecting on deindustrialization more broadly, Koistinen aims to provide "a comprehensive picture of the impact of deindustrialization on politics and policymaking in the economic sphere—or what can be called the political economy."

The author shows that there were three principal responses to deindustrialization, terming them retrenchment, federal assistance, and economic development. Favored largely by manufacturers, retrenchment tried to cut back social legislation and taxes on business, ideas that provoked significant resistance from citizens and labor groups. In contrast, unions and their liberal allies reacted to industrial decline by calling for greater federal assistance for contracting industries, yet these efforts were bitterly opposed by big business and conservatives. The strategy of economic development, however, received broad backing, and it proved the most successful of the three. As a result, after World War II New England's economy became much more diversified, with the electronics industry growing particularly rapidly. There was also impressive growth in the service sector, partly because banks and utility companies were principal promoters of new economic development.

Although the bulk of *Confronting Decline* concentrates on the 1920s, 1930s, and early 1940s, the author also follows his story through to the post–World War II era. In the final part of the book, in particular, he reflects on America's recent—and ongoing—experience of deindustrialization, a process in which the textile industry was integrally involved. As the author shows, the number of Americans employed in the industry has fallen dramatically, tumbling from 860,000 in 1973 to about 300,000 in 2003. In all, Koistinen explores the contemporary phenomenon of deindustrialization in a fresh way and shows that it had deep historical roots. Accessible and innovative, *Confronting Decline* is a fitting addition to the "Working in the Americas" series, which aims to publish exciting research in labor history and working-class studies.

TIMOTHY J. MINCHIN AND RICHARD GREENWALD
SERIES EDITORS

Acknowledgments

I have accumulated many debts in the course of this long-running project. Dedicated reference librarians and staffers of interlibrary loan offices greatly facilitated my research. I am indebted to librarians at Yale's Sterling Memorial Library; the Widener-Pusey, Baker, Littauer, and Loeb libraries at Harvard University; the Boston Public Library; the Massachusetts State Library in Boston; Jafet Library at American University of Beirut; and Cheng Library at William Paterson University. I made extensive use of archival collections at the Harvard Business School, Harvard's Scheslinger Library, the Institute Archives of MIT, the DuBois Library at the University of Massachusetts at Amherst, and the American Textile History Museum. Devoted archivists at those and other locations provided much worthy assistance.

Alan Brinkley, Robert Johnston, and David Montgomery ably shepherded the first version of this study to completion and over the years provided valuable advice, aid, and support with revision and publication. Paul Koistinen read and commented incisively on virtually all sections of the manuscript at various times—some more than once—and assisted in multiple other ways. I am deeply grateful for his contribution. Robert Collins, Tim Minchin, and Philip Scranton each at one point read the full manuscript and offered very helpful comments. Others who provided valuable feedback and support for the study over the years include Michael Bernstein, Stacey Davis, Tomoko Furukawa, Pat Giersch, Geoff Kabaservice, Carolyn Koistinen, Janice Koistinen-Harris, John Meloy, Bruce Schulman, David Stebenne, and Salim Yaqub.

Yale University, the Harvard Business School, and the Andrew W. Mellon Foundation provided funding for the initial stages of this project. The American University of Beirut supported continuing work on the volume with a Hewlett Junior Faculty Research Grant and funding from the University Research Board and the Center for American Studies and Research. William Paterson University supported completion of the volume through the ART program and funding from the Research Center for the Humanities and Social Sciences.

Officers of what was at the time BankBoston allowed me to conduct research in historical materials in the bank's possession on the activities of its predecessor institution, the First National Bank of Boston. Paul Kennedy and Chad Gifford were key in securing access to these materials. (BankBoston later disappeared in a series of corporate acquisitions.) Officials of the Federal Reserve Bank of Boston permitted me to examine records, held at the bank, of former Boston Fed president Ralph Flanders. Anne M. Epstein, William J. McDonough, and Cathy E. Minehan made it possible to access these documents. George Paulsen generously shared with me materials in his possession from an in-house archive at the U.S. Department of Justice on the drafting of the original 1937 version of the Fair Labor Standards Act. Officers of the American Research and Development Corporation allowed me to look at materials in their Boston office relating to the history of the original ARD. Frederick Steele Blackall III permitted me to examine the papers of his father, Frederick Steele Blackall Jr. The younger Blackall as well as Charles Francis Adams Jr., Gordon Baty, Peter Brooke, William L. Brown, and Arthur F. F. Snyder kindly consented to interviews that were most useful in reconstructing elements of the New England story.

At the University Press of Florida, Meredith Babb, Sian Hunter, Sally Antrobus, and Jesse Arost provided much-appreciated assistance and support throughout the publication process. Jaehyun Kim of William Paterson University's Center for Instruction and Research Technology gave essential assistance in creating the graphic in chapter 3.

The *Boston Herald* granted permission to reproduce the article that appears in appendix 3. Much of chapter 2 appeared previously as "Reform Politics in Hard Times: Battles over Labor Legislation during the Decline of Traditional Manufacturing in Massachusetts, 1922–1928," *Historical Journal of Massachusetts* 35 (Winter 2007): 21–51. The material is reprinted here by permission.

Introduction

The decline of traditional manufacturing, or "deindustrialization," has been one of the most significant aspects of the restructuring of the American economy in the past few decades. Deindustrialization dates back to well before the contemporary era, however. As early as the 1920s, important American industries were in decline in the areas where they had originally flourished. By the 1950s, certain manufacturing cities in the Northeast and Midwest were experiencing the "hollowing-out" of their economic base.

The topic of deindustrialization has attracted significant interest from historians in recent decades, and almost all their work focuses on these earlier episodes of industrial decline. The historical scholarship can be divided into three categories. Authors writing from a labor history perspective have produced the first, and largest, group of studies. Their accounts generally concentrate on the devastating impact of plant shutdowns on workers, unions, and industrial communities and on the efforts of these groups to subsist and fashion new ways of life.[1] A second, smaller body of literature approaches the subject from the standpoint of economic and business history. These works examine the reasons established industries went into decline and the adaptations surviving firms made to stay in business.[2] A third set of more recently completed studies explores the impact of industrial decline on politics and public policy. Most of the scholars following this approach focus on attempts to generate new employment in localities hit by downsizing.[3] Others examine federal programs to aid deindustrialized areas and proposals for plant closing legislation.[4] The recent works on the politics and policy of downsizing are certainly valuable. However, none of these studies gives a comprehensive picture of the impact of deindustrialization on politics and policymaking in the economic sphere—or what can be called the political economy.[5] Providing such a portrait is the aim of the present volume.

The effects of deindustrialization on the political economy are addressed through a case study of New England, one of the first regions of the United States to experience the phenomenon when traditional industries began to collapse in the years after World War I. Deindustrialization in New England had all the traumatic characteristics of more recent instances of industrial decline. Massive plant closures created chronic unemployment and poverty in New England mill cities, initiated a long-term slowdown in the regional economy, occasioned great concern about the area's economic future, and precipitated a range of activities intended to alleviate the problem.

The volume concentrates on developments in the 1920s, 1930s, and early 1940s, when the problem of deindustrialization was new. Later episodes of industrial downsizing, in the years following World War II and during the late 1960s and 1970s, are examined as well. The study spotlights events in the commonwealth of Massachusetts, the Bay State. Massachusetts was by far the most populous New England state and the one hit hardest by deindustrialization in the era after World War I.[6] Attention focuses on cotton textiles, New England's largest troubled sector in the period between the world wars and the one declining most rapidly at that time. The establishment of cotton manufacturing in the late nineteenth-century American South set the stage for the difficulties New England fabric makers later encountered. With lower labor costs and well-honed industrial skills, Dixie cotton firms drove most northern producers out of business in the decades following World War I.

The demise of traditional manufacturing in New England resulted in a number of initiatives to address the problem, backed by a variety of interest groups. The effects of industrial decline on the political economy played out principally through these efforts. Three distinct initiatives to counter deindustrialization were advanced in New England. These can be called "retrenchment," "federal assistance," and "economic development." The study describes each effort in detail, looks at the groups supporting it, and assesses the outcome.

Retrenchment consisted of a push to reduce the government burden on the corporate sector through cutbacks in social legislation and taxes. The principal advocates of this approach were businesses, especially manufacturers, and particularly those in the declining industries. These groups tirelessly lobbied state and local officials for action on social and tax issues. Retrenchment took hold in the early 1920s, when the structural difficulties in established industries first emerged. Efforts to secure cutbacks continued from that time forward, climaxing during the periods when the region's economic difficulties seemed particularly grave. During the 1920s, Massachusetts industrialists launched a highly visible drive to roll back state regulations on the working hours of women in manufacturing. In the early 1950s, when downsizing was again acute, Bay State businesses mounted a major effort to cut back unemployment insurance. During the 1970s, as another round of downsizing occurred in Massachusetts, major battles took place over cutting back unemployment insurance and other social programs administered by state government.

Federal assistance was the second initiative for counteracting deindustrialization. The aim here was to alleviate the impact of industrial decline through decisive federal action. Unions based in the northeastern states and their liberal allies were the leading proponents of federal aid to downsizing industries and areas. The push for a national response to deindustrialization took time to get under way, since a strong, activist federal government was a prerequisite for meaningful action in this domain. Only with the New Deal's great expansion of government power were proposals put forward for a resolute federal response to deindustrialization. During the 1930s and 1940s, advocates of federal assistance to the declining textile industry of the northeastern states worked to enact comprehensive, nationwide regulation of labor standards. Such measures would equalize textile production costs in the North and South and thereby protect northeastern manufacturers. After World War II, securing federal aid for industries and areas hit by downsizing became the principal goal.

Economic development was the third initiative for countering deindustrialization in New England. The aim in this case was to compensate for losses in the declining sectors by strengthening the region's existing industries and fostering the emergence of new ones. Strong backing for this effort came from companies in the service industries, such as banks, utilities, and railroads, which were tied to the New England economy and had a vested interest in renewed prosperity. Attempts to promote growth also won significant support from the general public—important as state and local government became increasingly involved in development activities. Economic development activities got into high gear in New England in the mid-1920s, soon after the extent of difficulty in the regional economy became clear. Growth-promotion efforts continued steadily from that time forward.

The various initiatives for countering deindustrialization in New England had differing outcomes. Several of the contemplated remedies for downsizing encountered intense political opposition and were never implemented. Others were enacted but had limited impact. One initiative pursued in response to industrial decline made a substantial contribution to the region's eventual economic recovery.

The business drive to counter deindustrialization by rolling back social legislation achieved few of its aims for most of the period under consideration. Labor and reform organizations had fought hard in prosperous times to enact these social protections. The groups effectively defended their gains in repeated legislative battles as traditional industry eroded. Indeed, during the 1920s and 1930s, despite widespread plant closures, Massachusetts introduced additional social protections that further increased the expense of manufacturing in the state. The campaign of New England business groups for tax reduction achieved greater success in the period after World War I. In centers of declining industry, municipal governments acceded to manufacturers' demands that local levies be cut. After protracted effort, industrialists in Massachusetts also won state-mandated reductions in the taxes on factory machinery. The political context made retrenchment on business taxes much easier to achieve than cutbacks in social legislation. Labor and reform groups typically did not oppose reducing the fiscal burden on industry and in some instances even endorsed such steps.

Stiff political resistance also met proposals put forward in the 1930s for decisive federal action to protect threatened New England manufacturers. Union-backed legislation for strict nationwide regulation of labor standards had influential supporters in Congress and the executive branch during the New Deal years. But opposition from business and conservatives blocked passage of the far-reaching measures that would have been necessary to save vulnerable New England producers. The much weaker regulations that won approval brought few benefits to New England firms. The federal government did implement programs to aid deindustrialized locales in the 1950s and 1960s. However, antagonism to these efforts among conservatives and areas that stood to lose resources minimized the impact of the measures taken.

Efforts to ameliorate conditions in New England through economic development provoked little of the controversy that attended the other initiatives for countering deindustrialization. Few groups objected to job-creation efforts in a region struggling with chronic unemployment. The New England states thus saw a concerted development push in the 1920s and 1930s and again during periods of downsizing after World War II. In the earlier era these endeavors took place primarily in the private sector. Regional business leaders formed a special association to work for recovery and carried out a wide-ranging growth campaign. Area business people recognized that New England could not compete with less advanced regions on the basis of labor cost. As a result, their efforts aimed to capitalize on the economic advantages a developed region does possess, such as experienced management, skilled labor, numerous research facilities, and abundant financial resources. State and local government participated in the growth-promotion efforts of the 1920s and 1930s. The public role became more prominent in the years after World War II as state government set up a number of institutions to encourage development.

Most of the avenues New Englanders pursued for encouraging local economic development brought few tangible benefits. In the case of electronics, however, growth-promotion efforts contributed to the expansion of what became a key area industry. To better the prospects of new and small manufacturers in New England, development-minded business people worked in the late 1930s and 1940s to improve the financing available to such companies. They set up several venture capital organizations and sought to convince the region's commercial banks to lend on favorable terms to promising small firms. The small-business promotion efforts dovetailed nicely with events in the electronics industry. The advanced sectors of electronics produced an array of sophisticated new devices during this era. The products were often brought to market by a relatively new kind of company: the high technology spinoff. Boston was a notable center of spinoff activity in this era, but other parts of the country were initially much more important. Boston-area firms had the crucial advantage of stronger financial support, however. Venture capital organizations set up in Boston invested in a number of local electronics companies. More important, in the years following World War II, the city's commercial banks lent aggressively to the spinoff sector in a deliberate attempt to foster new regional industry. This support helped Boston's Route 128 emerge by the early 1960s as the country's foremost locus of high technology entrepreneurship.[7]

Regional leaders were the key actors in creating the various responses to industrial decline in New England. Rank-and-file workers and other area residents were the ones most directly affected by the demise of long-established industries. But the efforts to counter deindustrialization were shaped by New England leaders and the institutions they guided. The story of responses to deindustrialization is necessarily a tale of the actions of these highly placed individuals.

As New England leaders formulated responses to the demise of traditional manufacturing, they did not depart from set patterns of political and economic behavior. In confronting New England's problems, regional leaders acted in ways that fit comfortably within the established parameters of American political economy. There was thus nothing fundamentally new in the struggles over social legislation that took place as older industries declined. Deindustrialization simply intensified battles that had been going on for decades between unionists and reformers on one hand and businessmen and conservatives on the other. The efforts of New England business organizations to revitalize the regional economy beginning in the 1920s were of a piece with the "associational" activities through which corporate groups of that time advanced a diversity of aims. Attempts to protect northern textile firms through strict national controls over labor standards and to direct public aid to locales hit by plant closures were logical extensions of the expanded federal role in economic life seen in the 1930s and after. Even the endeavors of New England business leaders to encourage flexible bank lending and venture capital investments in new area companies were part of a national, mid-twentieth-century push to improve financing for small firms. What novelty there was as New England leaders forged responses to the region's deindustrialization stemmed from the nature of the situation. In confronting the disappearance of long-established and centrally important manufacturing sectors, area leaders faced a problem that was dramatically new.

From the 1920s through the 1950s, and again in the late 1960s and 1970s, New England leaders contended with the challenges of deindustrialization. There were strong continuities in the actions taken in response to industrial downsizing in these different eras. The basic approaches followed—retrenchment, federal assistance, and economic development—remained the same over time. The interest groups backing the various responses to downsizing stayed relatively constant as well.

An important discontinuity was also present. The role of government in formulating responses to deindustrialization became more pronounced as the years progressed. This was visible in all the initiatives for countering industrial decline and reflected broader changes in the public sector's place in economic life. The government role in framing responses to deindustrialization expanded in particularly dramatic fashion during and in the years after the New Deal.

Industrial decline was a central reality in the economic life of the New England states for much of the twentieth century. New England's experience was unusual in this regard. In most parts of the United States, deindustrialization has been a serious problem only since the 1970s. Because New England contended with industrial decline over such a long stretch of time, responses to the region's deindustrialization were necessarily forged during dramatically different periods of U.S. political economy. New England first saw widespread factory closures in the 1920s, a relatively conservative era. The region's deindustrialization continued during the 1930s and in the decades following World War II, when the liberal forces that emerged with the New Deal were at maximum strength. Downsizing reappeared in New England during the 1970s, when national policymaking again moved in a more conservative direction.

The shifting context of national political economy shaped the responses to deindustrialization in New England. During the more liberal decades at midcentury, policymakers pursued multiple initiatives to alleviate the impact of downsizing through strong government action. In the more conservative eras that came before and after, fewer initiatives for countering industrial decline were put forward. The proposals that were advanced in the more conservative periods relied less on government action and were more likely to involve measures in the private sector.

The responses to deindustrialization in New England have significance beyond what occurred in that one region. The broader importance of what happened in New England is explored in the book's last chapter. A number of topics are addressed. First, the three-part model of responses to deindustrialization seen in New England applies to other areas affected by industrial downsizing. The same pattern is visible in the United States at the level of national policymaking and in other developed countries. Second, the New England experience reveals important realities about the political economy of the modern United States. Most significant, events in New England and other locations show that an "industrial policy" of substantial dimensions has been pursued in the United States in recent decades—contradicting claims that steps of this sort have been entirely lacking. What occurred in New England also demonstrates the crucial place that private-sector actors can have in attempts to develop new industries. The potential of entirely private action to promote growth is largely neglected in the scholarly literature on development. Third, the New England experience permits an assessment of the responses to industrial decline undertaken there and elsewhere. Such an exercise shows that attempts to develop new area industries have been the most fruitful of the various measures for countering deindustrialization.

The responses to industrial downsizing in New England have wider import in another way as well. What occurred in New England in the middle decades of the twentieth century contrasts in an illuminating manner with events in less developed sections of the United States during the same era. Rural regions in the South, inland West, and in farming sections of the Midwest experienced structural economic decline of a different sort in the mid-twentieth century, as agricultural and resource-based sectors stagnated and mechanization displaced much of the rural work force. Seeking new sources of growth, many of these areas launched industrialization drives beginning in the 1930s, 1940s, and 1950s and continuing for decades thereafter. The efforts usually focused on attracting existing companies from the more developed parts of the country. Unions were generally weak in the areas seeking industrial growth, and the locales' recruiting pitches highlighted their open-shop, often low-wage workforce, lax labor regulations, and low taxes. Local business elites spearheaded the campaigns for industrialization, collaborating with state and local officials who were typically Republicans or conservative Democrats. What might be called a conservative political economy of growth prevailed in these places. Factory output and population expanded steadily in the newly industrializing areas, helping lay the basis for the rightward shift in national politics of the past few decades. What occurred in these regions receives significant attention in recent scholarship.[8] New England events of the same era provide a useful counterpoint to the realities portrayed in this literature.

In mid-twentieth-century New England the quest for growth did not entail a conservative approach to policymaking. To be sure, New England corporate interests sought to exploit the circumstances of industrial decline to shift economic policies in a business-friendly direction. However, these efforts had little success before the 1970s (when politics moved to the right throughout the country). Rather, reindustrialization initiatives in mid-twentieth-century New England took place in a context of strong unions and enduring welfare-state protections. Elected officials in much of the region were predominantly liberal Democrats and moderate Republicans. Low-wage sectors did flourish in some centers of declining industry, where unemployment was high. But the regionwide push for development largely involved the promotion of high-wage, skill-intensive industries. Meanwhile, at the federal level, influential New England interests agitated for new national policies to assist declining industries and locales. New England events demonstrate that structural economic decline did not necessarily lead to a conservative, low-wage, anti-union political economy. With more liberal, labor-friendly elements in power, New England responded to industrial decline by implementing policies that were essentially center-left.

The study consists of eight chapters. Chapter 1 surveys the economic and social development of New England during the generally prosperous era up to World War I; sets out the dimensions of deindustrialization in the 1920s and 1930s; considers the immediate effects of plant closures on workers and factory cities; and examines why cotton textile manufacturing went into decline in New England. The chapters that follow explore responses to New England's deindustrialization during the 1920s and 1930s. Retrenchment is examined in chapter 2, federal assistance in chapter 3, and economic development in chapter 4. Chapter 5 looks at efforts to improve financing for small New England manufacturers in the period up through World War II. Chapter 6 shows how the strong financial support available to electronic spinoff companies in the Boston area during the 1940s and 1950s facilitated the rise of the Route 128 technology complex. Industrial downsizing remained a serious concern in New England during the Cold War years. The region underwent sharp deindustrialization in the late 1940s and early 1950s and encountered another round of structural economic difficulty in the late 1960s and 1970s. Chapter 7 traces the varied responses to the Cold War–era episodes of industrial decline in the area. Chapter 8 presents conclusions based on the study of New England. Chapter 8 shows that the three-part model of responses to deindustrialization seen in the region applies at the level of national policy-making in the United States and in other developed countries. The chapter also explores what New England events reveal about the political economy of the modern United States and assesses the effectiveness of the diverse responses to deindustrialization.

CHAPTER 1

Deindustrialization in New England

> Nineteen twenty-eight, 1929, 1930, very bad. No jobs, no work, nowheres.
> NEW ENGLAND TEXTILE WORKER JOHN FALANTE,
> IN BLEWETT, *LAST GENERATION*

> It is like going through a city of the dead when you go through one of our closed mills.
> EDITH NOURSE ROGERS, U.S. REPRESENTATIVE FOR LOWELL, MASSACHUSETTS, "ADDRESS BEFORE THE COMMITTEE"

New England became one of the first parts of the United States to experience deindustrialization when textiles and other traditional sectors went into decline in the 1920s. Its pioneering role here was fitting, for the region had been the first area of the country to industrialize on a broad scale. A brief survey highlights the principal characteristics of the region's industrialization in the nineteenth century and the social and political impact of industrial growth. The dimensions of industrial decline in New England after WWI are examined and the causes of downsizing in the key cotton textile sector explored.

Industrial Growth and Social Reform in Nineteenth-Century New England

The earliest successful American experiment with the modern factory system took place in New England. Samuel Slater, a migrant from the English Midlands with knowledge of the revolutionary industrial techniques used in textile production there, teamed up with a pair of Rhode Island merchants to set up an automated cotton spinning mill in Pawtucket in 1793. Similar ventures soon sprang up across the region. Two decades later, a group of Boston merchants took the New World's industrial revolution a step farther. Introducing the automated weaving techniques developed in England shortly before, the Boston entrepreneurs integrated spinning and weaving in the same establishment. When their first works could not handle demand, they set up a series of mills at a spot along the Merrimack River called Lowell. Others invested at riverside locations elsewhere in the region. By the 1830s cotton textiles—based almost entirely in New England—had become one of the nation's leading manufacturing sectors.[1]

Other New England enterprises achieved significant advances in metalworking. The textile industry provided one stimulus to growth. Early textile manufacturers fabricated their own production equipment, but as volume increased, free-standing companies were set up to equip the mills, giving rise to an independent textile machinery sector. Momentous advances took place in the manufacture of firearms. At the federal armory in Springfield, Massachusetts, and in private shops around the region, early nineteenth-century mechanics developed innovations making possible the production of identical and thus fully interchangeable parts. Known as the American System of Manufactures, the methods were gradually adopted in other industries with a strong New England presence, including clockmaking and machine tools.[2] A highly diversified metalworking industry eventually developed in the region. Based in centers such as Worcester, Springfield, Providence, and Hartford, metalworking firms turned out steam engines, valves, motors, and countless other devices. A focus on high-precision products won New England machinists a reputation as the finest in the nation.

Additional industries flourished in New England. Entrepreneurs applied advances developed for cotton manufacturing to the production of woolen goods, and wool textiles became another of the region's leading sectors. Massachusetts had many of the largest and most advanced woolen factories in the country in the pre–Civil War period and was the nation's largest producer of woolen goods. The manufacture of boots and shoes was a major New England activity even before the introduction of modern production techniques. Artisans laboring in small workshops fabricated the elements of the shoe, with assembly operations put out to rural households. Following the development of sewing and stitching machines in the mid-nineteenth century, the locus of boot and shoe production shifted to urban factories. New England accounted for 60 percent of the value of U.S. footwear output in 1860, with Massachusetts alone fabricating half the national total. A constant stream of innovations aided the growth of the region's industries. In the middle of the nineteenth century, New England states had the highest per capita rate of patents and patents by outstanding inventors of any region in the country.[3]

Specializations in certain service industries paralleled the nineteenth-century expansion of New England manufacturing. Insurance of vessels and cargoes was an important service in the eighteenth century, when economic activity centered around trade. The demand for insurance increased as the American economy modernized, and life and property coverage evolved into important area industries in their own right, with Boston and Hartford the principal centers. New England financiers virtually invented the field of money management in the mid-nineteenth century, devising the trust fund so that regional industrialists could pass on their wealth to future generations. Management of the funds of the affluent grew from these roots into an important area specialization. The vacation industry that developed in scenic northern New England in the late nineteenth century drew crowds of well-off visitors from outside the region.[4]

New England's economic expansion in the period up to World War I progressed at a regular pace. Established industries like textiles and shoes grew steadily as demand increased. Success in one field spilled over into allied sectors and even brought into being entirely new industries, such as textile machinery and insurance. The burgeoning growth of the manufacturing sector made New England one of the wealthiest regions in the country. The area's per capita income stood 34 percent above the national average in 1880 and remained 18 percent above the national average as late as 1920.[5]

The expansion of industry in New England produced numerous social problems. Manufacturing centered in cities, which mushroomed in size. Foreign migrants searching for jobs poured into the factory districts, forming a new polyglot working class. Hours of work were long and conditions dangerous. The economic gains from industry went mostly to the property-holding classes, creating bitter antagonism among those lower on the social ladder.

New social movements emerged in New England to confront these challenges, as occurred in other places in which modern industry took hold. Since New England was the first part of the United States to industrialize, it is unsurprising that some of the earliest labor and reform agitation in the country also took place there. The commonwealth of Massachusetts, the Bay State, was at the heart of the region's economic transformation and saw a particularly high level of activity. The largely female workforce of the Lowell cotton mills carried out its first strikes in the 1830s. Massachusetts enacted restrictions on child labor in 1836, and the campaign for a ten-hour day for all commonwealth workers began in the same decade. The 1860 "Great Strike" of Bay State shoemakers was the largest walkout by workers the country had seen at that time.[6]

Labor and reform activism continued at a significant level as the industrial economy of New England matured in the decades after Reconstruction. In occupations ranging from textiles to carpentry, regional workers enthusiastically joined the era's leading union organizations, the Knights of Labor and the craft bodies affiliated with the American Federation of Labor. When the radical, western-based Industrial Workers of the World sought to establish a presence in the East after the turn of the century, they had dramatic success among the textile operatives of Lawrence, Massachusetts. Pressed by unionists and social reformers, Massachusetts in the post–Civil War era enacted a series of legal protections for workers, frequently setting precedents for the rest of the country. The Bay State passed pioneering factory inspection legislation in 1866, was the earliest to establish a state department of industrial statistics, and in 1887 approved the country's first employers' liability law. Massachusetts had one of the nation's earliest workmen's compensation systems and in 1912 enacted the first state minimum wage regulations for female workers.[7]

When traditional sectors went into decline after World War I, New England had roughly a century's experience with modern industry. The rise of manufacturing had transformed the economy; generated great wealth; given rise to burgeoning cities with large working-class populations; produced significant contention; and led to considerable social reform. In all these ways, New England constituted a classic example of the economic, social, and political impact of industrialization. The region—and the state of Massachusetts in particular—typified the complexity, conflict, and promise of industrial society.

The Decline of Traditional New England Industries after World War I

With the advent of modern manufacturing in New England at the beginning of the nineteenth century, economic growth in the region took on an apparently automatic character. Established industries developed steadily, and a continuing stream of innovations gave rise to numerous new sectors. How to manage this expansion and distribute its fruits were the central questions relating to economic life. The continuation of growth itself could seemingly be taken for granted.

Despite these appearances, the New England economy at the beginning of the twentieth century had significant structural vulnerabilities. To begin with, the region depended heavily on manufacturing. Industry accounted for a larger share of total economic activity in New England than in any other part of the country: half of all the region's wage earners earned their pay in factory work in 1920.[8] Moreover, although significant diversification had taken place since the pre–Civil War period, traditional sectors like textiles and shoes accounted for a large share of total New England manufacturing. This was problematic because the factors that had facilitated the establishment of these industries in New England (relatively simple technology, limited requirements for capital and skilled labor) made feasible their growth elsewhere, particularly in less developed regions. Heavy reliance on older sectors also left New England vulnerable to the tendency in mature industries for demand to fall off due to changes in technology and consumer taste.

New England's high dependence on traditional industries can be seen in figures on the sectoral distribution of employment and output just after World War I. At that time, cotton textiles, boots and shoes, woolen and worsted goods, and some smaller, related industries (knit goods, leather, textile finishing, and textile machinery) together accounted for 38 percent of manufacturing employment and 35 percent of manufacturing value added in New England. Reliance on these sectors was even higher in Massachusetts, where they provided 46 percent of employment and 41 percent of manufacturing value added.[9]

In the years after World War I these core sectors fell on hard times. At that point New England's generations-long record of vigorous economic growth ended, as plant closures spread across the landscape. The most severe problems occurred in cotton textiles. The largest industry in the region, with a 1919 high of 209,000 wage earners, cotton manufacturing sank into depression soon after the war as production moved to southern states with lower labor costs. In boots and shoes, with 114,000 employees in 1919, New England firms lost market share to competitors elsewhere in the United States. Stagnant demand, rather than interregional competition, plagued the woolen and worsted industry, with 106,000 wage earners in 1919. (After World War II, wool would follow cotton to the South.) Spillover effects exacerbated the difficulties in these sectors. Factory closures and the southward shift of cotton textile production reduced demand for textile manufacturing machinery, eventually leading to New England plant shutdowns in that industry. Slumping local output of boots and shoes produced significant job losses in leathermaking.

Table 1.1. Manufacturing Employment in Massachusetts, New England, and the United States, 1923, 1929, and 1939

	Workers (in thousands)		
	Massachusetts	New England	United States
1923	667	1,253	8,194
1929	557	1,099	8,378
1939	461	954	7,803
Percent change 1923–1929	-16.5%	-12.3%	+2.2%
Percent change 1929–1939	-17.2%	-13.2%	-6.9%
Percent change 1923–1939	-30.9%	-23.9%	-4.8%

Sources: Commonwealth of Massachusetts, *Report of the Special Commission Relative to Establishment of a State Department of Commerce* (December 1945), 75–76; U.S. Bureau of the Census, *Historical Statistics*, Part 2, 666. New England totals are my calculations.

Employment statistics demonstrate the cumulative impact of the difficulties in regional industry. Manufacturing employment in the New England states fell from 1.25 million in 1923 to 954,000 in 1939, a decline of 24 percent. Conditions were most dire in Massachusetts. There the number of manufacturing jobs plummeted from 667,000 in 1923 to 461,000 in 1939, a 31 percent drop. Table 1.1 presents statistics on factory employment in the Bay State, the region, and the nation during this period. Using this measure, the economic performance of Massachusetts in this era was by far the worst of the twenty-one leading industrial states in the country.[10] Available statistics on employment suggest a similarly dismal picture, as outlined in appendix 1.

Figures for Massachusetts reveal the extent of decline in particular industries. Between the years 1923 and 1939, commonwealth employment in boot and shoe manufacturing fell from 69,400 to 44,800, down 35 percent. In woolen and worsted, employment dropped from 64,800 to 44,600, off 31 percent. In the well-paid textile machinery industry, the number of workers declined from 18,700 to 8,300, a drop of 56 percent. Most dramatically, employment in cotton textiles plummeted from 116,800 to 38,900, a fall of 67 percent. Table 1.2 shows the number of Bay State factory jobs in these industries in 1923, 1929, and 1939.[11]

Firms in the troubled sectors often clustered together, concentrating the effects of industrial decline in certain New England locales. The textile manufacturing centers established along the Merrimack River before the Civil

Table 1.2. Employment in Declining Massachusetts Industries, 1923, 1929, and 1939

	Workers (in thousands)			
	Cotton Textiles	Woolen and Worsted Textiles	Textile Machinery	Boots and Shoes
1923	116.8	64.8	18.7	69.4
1929	73.7	45.7	10.6	55.1
1939	38.9	44.6	8.3	44.8
Percent change 1923–1939	-67%	-31%	-56%	-35%

Note: Figures for cotton textiles include small wares.

Sources: Commonwealth of Massachusetts, *Report of the Special Commission Relative to Establishment of a State Department of Commerce* (December 1945), 81–82; Massachusetts Department of Labor and Industries, *Statistics of Manufactures in Massachusetts, 1920–1938.*

War—Lowell and Lawrence in Massachusetts; Nashua and Manchester in New Hampshire—remained important producers into the twentieth century. In the postbellum years, coastal locations in southeastern New England, especially Fall River and New Bedford, Massachusetts, emerged as the most important cotton-making hubs. Nearby Providence, Rhode Island, and towns in the Blackstone River valley also saw significant textile output. In addition, small towns with one or two mills were scattered across the New England countryside, a legacy of the semirural labor force used by many early manufacturers. Cities such as Lynn and Brockton, Massachusetts, depended heavily on the production of shoes and boots.

In cities and towns with cotton mills, reliance on the industry was often perilously high. Cotton manufacturing accounted for 82 percent of factory jobs in Fall River and 85 percent in New Bedford. In Lowell, cotton provided a smaller but still significant part of manufacturing employment (43 percent). Moreover, with woolen and worsted, knit goods, textile finishing, textile machinery, and shoe production together occupying another 39 percent of the industrial work force, Lowell was also in a highly vulnerable position.[12]

The decline of textiles and other traditional industries beginning in the 1920s devastated local economies. In Fall River, the number of manufacturing jobs fell from 37,000 in 1923 to 20,000 in 1935, as the majority of the city's mills and some related companies shut down or moved to the South. A Works Progress Administration survey of the New Bedford labor market in 1939 found a local unemployment rate of 29 percent. Joblessness was even more extreme, at 36 percent, among New Bedford workers employed most recently in textiles. Among the area's former textile workers aged fifty-five years and above, unemployment reached a crushing 52 percent. Little wonder that a 1935 federal report concluded that textile mill closures in New England had created "large stranded populations" of operatives who would probably never work in the industry again.[13]

Visiting the mill cities of Massachusetts in late 1930, journalist Louis Adamic found "tragic towns" where depression-like conditions had prevailed since the mid-1920s. In Lowell, where joblessness was rampant, Adamic observed vacant storefronts on the main shopping streets and ill-maintained houses in the working-class neighborhoods. The city's long-term unemployed were in even worse shape:

> I saw shabby men leaning against walls and lamp-posts, and standing on street corners . . . pathetic, silent, middle-aged men in torn, frayed overcoats . . . slumped in postures of hopeless discontent . . . their eyes shifty and bewildered.[14]

With few new jobs available, many of the displaced workers ended up on public relief. In Lowell in the mid-1930s an estimated 40 percent of the population received some form of government aid. Substantial numbers moved away from mill cities to escape the depressed circumstances. Population declines of between 4 and 11 percent occurred in New Bedford, Lowell, and Fall River between the censuses of 1920 and 1930, with much of the drop taking place at the end of the decade. Migration was particularly heavy among young to middle-aged adults who could most easily find alternative work. More than a fifth of New Bedford's men aged twenty to thirty-four years in 1920 left the city before the next census.[15]

These effects were likely even more pronounced in the small, isolated towns where one or two mills provided most employment. In the central Massachusetts town of Ware (population 7,500), the Otis Company, a cotton manufacturer, had long dominated the local economy. In normal conditions the firm provided three-quarters of Ware's industrial jobs. Caught in the regional downturn of textiles, Otis's employment sank from 1,700 in 1922 to 600 in 1937, at which point the firm liquidated. According to one writer, the collapse of the town's "basic economic foundation . . . left the people of Ware in a daze."[16]

Even those who found employment in New England's depressed mill cities faced difficult circumstances. With desperate workers willing to accept low wages, and plant space available in abundance, the municipalities proved attractive to manufacturers in mobile, wage-sensitive industries looking to reduce labor costs. Scores of such employers moved to New England, particularly after the national economic downturn of 1929. Many apparently came from the New York City area. In 1932 government investigators in New Bedford and Fall River found numerous establishments in the needle trades with pay levels below the state's minimum wage guidelines. The "double lure of low rentals and a large supply of unemployed female labor" had attracted the operations from out of state.[17]

Interviews with veteran textile operatives reveal the broad-ranging impact on working-class lives of the multiple plant shutdowns of this era. A number of themes recur in these accounts. Clearly evident are the difficult and sometimes desperate circumstances for workers who lost jobs when factories closed. Equally notable is the unreliable nature of employment for operatives who had positions, since so many mills operated sporadically or on reduced hours during this period. Impressive as well is the high level of geographic mobility that occurred as displaced millworkers ranged across the region seeking textile employment. As these recollections make apparent, such difficulties appeared in the mid-1920s, when depressed conditions first took hold in New England cloth making. Circumstances grew more extreme during the Depression years of the 1930s, when joblessness was rampant across the country.

John Falante's story exemplifies the trials confronting New England millworkers. Born on the Portuguese island of Madeira, Falante immigrated to Lowell as a teenager, arriving in 1920. He found work in a textile mill, where employment was reasonably stable for several years. Then the decline of New England cloth making began, inaugurating a long period of instability and vocational and geographic movement for the young Falante:

> So when I was nineteen, around 1924, the mills started to shut down and no job. I happened to be lucky enough to go to Newmarket, New Hampshire, and I got a job there . . . in the spin room. . . . I worked nights. Then the spinning room shut down even in Newmarket, New Hampshire. They used to ship filling [yarn] out but they shut that down. . . . So I went in the weave room. . . . I worked for a few years there, and when they had a strike in Newmarket, New Hampshire, they moved [the mill] to Lowell. . . . Nineteen twenty-eight, 1929, 1930, very bad. No jobs, no work, nowheres. You couldn't get anything. . . . Thank God I always had a job. I used to go from one place to another. I had bought a little Chevrolet in New Hampshire.[18]

Joseph Golas experienced many of the same realities. Golas was from a Polish-American family who settled in the small town of Clinton, Massachusetts, west of Boston, where his parents worked as weavers in a textile mill. The plant's closure initiated a period of want for the Golases as well as geographic mobility for one family member:

> The mill went bankrupt back in 1928. They auctioned off all the [worker] hous[ing], and the place closed down. Before that, they used to have their slack periods. My father used to take off to Rhode Island or Connecticut and look for a job, and we'd be home in Clinton. If he got a job, he'd send ten or fifteen dollars depending on what he made.

By the early 1930s the family had moved to Lowell, where they labored in a silk mill. Conditions in the silk industry were difficult, and Golas recalled the unsteadiness of work at a firm that remained in operation:

> There were slack periods when you probably wouldn't be working for a month, two months, three months. You didn't look for other work, because there was no jobs around. You'd go back to the silk mill. Some of it was running; some of it was shut down. You'd wait there maybe an hour or two until the employment manager came around and says, Nothing doing today.[19]

More extreme hardship befell the millworkers of Manchester, New Hampshire. The mammoth mills of the Amoskeag Company, the region's largest textile manufacturer, provided most of the city's industrial employment. After years of difficulty the company liquidated in 1936. Virginia Erskine, from a working-class Manchester family, recalled the shock caused by the demise of the city's principal employer: "You can't imagine the impact that the shutdown had on a community like Manchester. Complete families—fathers, sisters, everyone—were all out. There was nobody that you could turn to." Lottie Sargent came from a long line of Scottish millworkers. Her father and brother worked for Amoskeag, and the closure put great strain on her family: "In 1936 the mills went out, and the world stopped for everybody. . . . There was nothing. There was no food. I really don't know how we made it. . . . I was ten or twelve, and they sent me out to work. I took care of kids, I did housework." Other millworker families, Sargent remembered, experienced worse:

> A lot of our neighbors, a lot of the men, committed suicide. . . . There was nothing else; and when [the mill] closed, everybody was desperate. One of the men who committed suicide lived two doors up from me.

He was from Sweden and there were five children. They had left the old gaslights in the corporation tenements, and he went up to the attic and gassed himself.[20]

As the tragic Manchester episodes indicate, high structural unemployment in New England's mill cities produced numerous other social problems. One study showed that crime rates in 1938 were about 50 percent higher in Brockton, where numerous shoemaking jobs had disappeared, than in Fitchburg, which had lost substantial textile and machine tool employment but had brought in new employers. The incidence of mental illness and suicide was also substantially higher in the former city. In Lawrence, which saw serious declines in cotton and wool employment during the 1920s, the Lithuanian priest reported a falling number of marriages in his congregation since young people could not afford to set up their own households. An increase in "immoral living" resulted.[21]

Trouble in the economic base of New England mill cities had serious secondary effects on local businesses and on governance. The depressed conditions devastated local real estate markets, in turn disrupting the finances of municipalities dependent on property taxes for revenue. In Lowell, the banks ended up owning numerous properties following mortgage foreclosures, and the city government held many tracts seized due to unpaid taxes. Blocks of vacant industrial and residential structures were destroyed by property owners seeking to reduce their tax burden. With a shrinking tax base and soaring relief costs, Lowell's finances tipped far into the red, leading the state government to create a Finance Commission in 1926 to recommend reductions in the city budget. The state took more drastic action in Fall River, after falling revenues and accounting legerdemain brought that city to the brink of default in 1931. A state board set up to supervise Fall River's finances for ten years eliminated services including kindergartens and the city dispensary and laid off hundreds of municipal employees.[22]

In addition to these concrete difficulties, deindustrialized mill cities and towns suffered serious problems of morale. Journalist Adamic found a sense of "general bewilderment" in Lowell. Massachusetts businessmen remarked on the "discouraging effect that has been created regarding the future" in the areas experiencing industrial decline. Speaking more bluntly, the U.S. congresswoman from Lowell declared: "It is like going through a city of the dead when you go through one of our closed mills."[23]

Deindustrialization had a similar impact on New England capitalists, lowering their morale and expectations for the region's future. Strikingly, these sentiments were evident among businessmen well removed from the centers of declining industry. One journalist found the mood of New England business leaders in 1924, after plant closures had become commonplace, to be "tinged . . . in some cases steeped with pessimism." Among those he interviewed were a prominent figure in the textile industry who agreed with the southern contention that cotton manufacturing in the region was "through" and a banker who asserted that regional money was unwilling to invest in locally based new enterprise. Another writer touring the area a year later found Boston businessmen to be fixated on the problems of the cotton and shoe industries and described the spectrum of opinion on the area's economic prospects as including "hopes for the best, fears of the worst, or just resigned and accepted gloom." Writers at one Boston newspaper seemingly pondered the prospect of the area losing all of its manufacturing, asking whether "North Carolina really hope[s] to coax all New England's industries into her waterpower valleys and leave us only the mild enterprises of a vacation-land?" Looking back on the era years later, a Rhode Island manufacturer remembered that "New England industry was languishing. A sense of defeat was upon us."[24]

Causes of the Decline of the New England Cotton Textile Industry

Cotton textile manufacturing was by far the largest troubled industry in New England and Massachusetts during the period between the world wars. It was also the sector declining most rapidly. For these reasons this study focuses on events related to cotton in examining initiatives for countering deindustrialization. A survey of the industry's development in the post–Civil War period demonstrates how and why cotton manufacturing downsized in New England in the years after World War I.[25]

The case of cotton textiles presents a dramatic example of a new group of producers disrupting the status quo in an industry and forcing sharp structural change. Manufacturers established in the South after Reconstruction upset the existing competitive equilibrium in cotton. In the years after World War I, the newer southern companies drove out of business many of the New England firms that had long controlled the industry.

For several generations following the late eighteenth-century advent of cotton manufacturing in New England, the region's firms dominated the U.S. market. Substantial output also took place in eastern sections of the mid-

Atlantic states. The antebellum years saw fitful attempts to establish textile production in the southern areas where cotton grew, but these had limited results. Things were much different after Reconstruction. The end of slavery and the depressed market for raw cotton prompted southern investors to look for new opportunities in the factory sector. Encouraged by a vigorous promotional campaign, capital flowed into the textile mills that sprang up across the hilly Piedmont section of the Southeast. Cotton manufacturing spearheaded the area's celebrated "New South" industrialization drive. Table 1.3 gives number of spindles, the standard measure of textile capacity, in the two regions. The figures show the steady, rapid growth of Dixie spindleage after 1870.

The growth of southern textiles was largely an indigenous phenomenon. Locals founded and managed almost all of the region's mills. In the words of one industry historian, "the initial impetus and driving leadership [of the southern cloth-making sector] were derived almost exclusively from native sources."[26] Textile promoters generally came from the southern business class, with personal or family backgrounds in commerce, banking, and railroads. Most of the financing for the Piedmont mills also originated locally. Available statistics indicate that southern residents provided about three-quarters of the capital invested in Piedmont textile plants in the decades after Reconstruction. Dixie mills did receive substantial financial support from the North. These

Table 1.3. Active Cotton Spindles in New England and the Southern States, 1859–1939

	Spindles (in millions)	
	New England	Southern States[a]
1859	3.9	0.27
1869	5.5	0.29
1879	8.6	0.50
1889	10.8	1.4
1899	12.9	4.0
1909	15.4	9.8
1919	17.5	14.0
1929	11.2	17.7
1939	5.4	17.1

Note: a. Alabama, Georgia, North Carolina, South Carolina, Tennessee, and Virginia

Sources: Galenson, *Migration of the Cotton Textile Industry*, 2; statistics in U.S. Department of Commerce, *Cotton Production and Distribution*.

monies came largely from textile selling houses seeking new sources of supply and textile machinery makers providing equipment on credit, rather than from cloth manufacturers based in the northern states.

Piedmont producers broke into the textile market by offering goods at low prices. The key southern advantage was labor cost. Located in a heavily populated agricultural region with few available jobs, Dixie mill managers of the Gilded Age paid wages a third to a half lower than those in New England. (Appendix 2 shows cotton textile wage rates in the two regions in 1933, when a substantial gap still existed.) In addition, organized labor was virtually absent among southern mill operatives. In New England, by contrast, unions had an important presence among the more skilled workers by the 1870s, with serious strikes breaking out on a periodic basis. The southern states also had scant labor legislation at a time when northern states were enacting rudimentary social protections. Dixie mills additionally enjoyed a small advantage in transit costs due to their proximity to the cotton fields, lower expenses for plant construction, cheaper power, and lower taxes.[27]

Southern fabric producers initially concentrated on low value-added goods requiring limited worker skill, where their labor-cost advantage was decisive. Some mills only spun yarn, usually in the lower counts, selling it to northern firms for weaving. Fabrics woven in the South tended to be in the coarsest lines, such as denim and duck cloth. Piedmont managers often shipped goods that required finishing—dyeing, bleaching, and printing—to specialized plants in the North. As entrepreneurs and operatives gained experience and mills expanded, the southern product line filled out and improved in quality. Dixie mills increasingly wove their yarn into fabric, turned out a full range of coarse goods, and broke into the higher-quality, medium-grade products that commanded steeper prices.

Yankee firms responded to the southern challenge by concentrating on higher-quality goods that required significant worker skill and managerial expertise to produce. For example, Fall River, Massachusetts, emerged after the Civil War as the key center for the manufacture of medium-grade print cloth, a popular fabric. After southern companies entered this market in the late nineteenth century, Fall River's print cloth output increasingly took the form of "odd goods," which varied in width and yarn count and necessitated repeated adjustments during the manufacturing process and close attention to consumer markets. Many Fall River mills moved into a new line altogether, producing "fine and fancy goods," which emphasized style and had elevated yarn counts. In the years before World War I a small number of New England firms responded to the new competition in a different way—by investing in southern plants. Those doing so were generally large operations with diversified product lines experiencing competitive pressures on their cheaper goods. The companies typically moved output of coarse cloth to new Dixie plants while continuing to manufacture costlier grades of fabric in their native region.

With these dynamics at work, a rough interregional equilibrium prevailed in cotton textiles through the early twentieth century. The lower-cost southern producers had higher growth and profit rates, but New England firms also fared well. Indeed, in a growing, tariff-protected national market, Yankee mill managers expanded their operations: capacity and employment at New England cotton firms peaked just after World War I. Industrial coexistence could not last indefinitely, however. As long as the South had lower manufacturing expenses, a broadening product line, and continued mill construction, a day would inevitably come when there would not be enough room at the top of the market for all New England producers. At that point, northern companies would be forced to downsize.

This juncture arrived in the 1920s. Since the higher-cost New England producers did not all retire from the market at the first sign of serious trouble, a period of excess capacity ensued, characterized by intense competition, depressed prices, and thin profit margins throughout the industry. These conditions appeared in cotton textiles in late 1923 and lasted for the better part of two decades. During this period, hard-pressed New England companies took numerous steps to enhance competitiveness. They cut wages, modernized out-of-date marketing practices, and instituted scientific management schemes to increase efficiency. For many firms, especially those fabricating the coarser grades of goods, there was no salvation in any of these steps. Dixie managers implemented similar measures and also installed new labor-saving machinery to reduce costs. Meanwhile, new mill construction continued in the South. Quite a number of New England producers responded to the challenge by setting up southern plants. Most of these were large companies with significant financial capacity. Doing so as well were some smaller firms selling brand-name goods for which there was an established customer base.

Most of the New England mills facing fierce market pressures after World War I did not have the wherewithal or competitive prospects for a move to the South. Their only alternative was to reduce capacity by partially or entirely closing plants. For the many companies with only one or two facilities, this frequently entailed "liquidation"—selling off machinery and property and dissolving the corporation. Mill liquidations spread across the New England landscape beginning in the mid-1920s and continued through the end of the following decade. In the dolorous accountings that appeared in cotton industry reports, the lists of liquidated New England firms went on for pages. In Massachusetts, the number of cotton-making establishments plummeted from 191 in 1923 to 135 in 1929 and 103 in 1933. So many New England cotton firms closed at this time that liquidation itself became a thriving industry. An active market developed in used textile machinery, and one consulting firm placed advertisements in the trade press offering "advice and counsel from experts" to help companies achieve "scientific liquidation."[28] As table 1.3 demonstrates, New England's cotton spindleage in 1939 stood at less than a third of its level twenty years before.

CHAPTER 2

Retrenchment

> Labor in this state is watching, watching closely what is going to happen to the 48-hour law. Labor put that law here. Labor is going to fight to maintain it.
>
> MASSACHUSETTS UNION OFFICIAL ON PROPOSALS TO EASE THE STATE'S STRICT LIMITS ON WORKING HOURS, *REPORT OF HEARING*, 1928

Beset by low-wage southern competition and additional ills, textiles and other established New England industries experienced dramatic downsizing beginning in the 1920s. Regional leaders launched a number of initiatives to counter industrial decline. The first response to the area's deindustrialization can be called "retrenchment."

Retrenchment entailed a push by business interests to reduce the government burden on industry by rolling back social legislation and cutting taxes and public spending. Executives of manufacturing corporations spearheaded this effort, with managers in declining industries like cotton textiles taking a particularly prominent role. Pressure for retrenchment commenced in the early 1920s, as the textile sector began to downsize, and continued thereafter. In Massachusetts—the focus of this chapter—business groups launched repeated high-profile drives for cutbacks in the 1920s and 1930s. Bay State business achieved mixed results in its push for retrenchment during these years.

In regard to social legislation, Massachusetts manufacturers' drive to reduce the regulatory burden was completely frustrated. Restrictions on the working hours of women in factories were a prominent and contentious issue in the politics of the deindustrializing Bay State. Throughout the 1920s and into the following decade, manufacturers sponsored bills in the state legislature to roll back the commonwealth's strict limits on female working hours. Industrialists insisted that such action was necessary to improve the competitiveness of the state's textile plants. Legislators rebuffed these claims, keeping the existing hours of work regulations in place. Lawmakers maintained the status quo due largely to pressure from unions and reform organizations. These groups had lobbied hard during more prosperous times to enact the labor hours restrictions and worked vigorously to protect these achievements during an era of industrial decline.

There was much misleading rhetoric in industrialists' campaign to repeal the Massachusetts hours of work statutes. Although manufacturers argued that the laws were a key handicap to cotton production, close analysis of factory operating rates shows that in the depressed market conditions of the time the regulations had little impact on the state's cotton makers. Certain producers were probably affected, but even these in many cases likely found ways to sustain output while complying with the restrictions. Why then did manufacturers make altering the hours of work laws such a major issue? Some industrialists apparently wanted to take advantage of an opportune moment to overturn statutes that did not presently affect them but could prove more restrictive in the future. Longstanding antagonism between capital and labor may help explain management's enthusiasm for overturning workplace restrictions cherished by the union movement. That industrialists had such motives for seeking to change the hours of work statutes make labor's determination to protect the status quo all the more understandable.

Massachusetts business interests also fared poorly during this era in the fight against broad social programs that affected all industries. The burden on commonwealth manufacturing became more onerous in the years up to 1930, despite corporate opposition and the conservative tenor of 1920s national politics. The state legislature liberalized workmen's compensation benefits and initiated a system of old age pensions for the indigent, disregarding claims that these steps would further damage the competitiveness of Massachusetts industry.

On fiscal issues the outcome for commonwealth manufacturers was happier. Efforts to hold down ballooning municipal spending achieved little. But in the late 1920s and early 1930s, textile industrialists won sharp reductions in the local tax assessments on company property. Furthermore, the state government in 1936 altered the taxation system in a way that significantly reduced the levies on all manufacturing corporations. Manufacturers succeeded in cutting their taxes in part because labor and reform groups did not oppose such action. Indeed, commonwealth unions endorsed tax reduction as a worthwhile step for increasing the competitiveness of the state's industries.

The outcome of battles over Massachusetts social legislation in the 1920s and 1930s contrasts with the results of similar struggles in the more recent era. During the periods of economic difficulty and industrial decline in the 1970s and 1980s, business groups again agitated for cuts in government regulations and taxes. The later efforts at retrenchment achieved substantial success. The authors of *The Deindustrialization of America*, writing in 1982, found that private-sector demands in the preceding years for a "good business climate" resulted in "the weakening of pro-labor, pro-consumer regulations on industry," together with tax breaks and business subsidies. Amidst the economic stagnation of the 1970s, asserts David Vogel, business groups halted a push for enhanced legislative protections for consumers, labor, and the environment and then won cuts in existing restrictions in these areas.[1]

There is no definitive explanation for the divergence in outcomes on the retrenchment question between the early twentieth century and the more recent era. The successful drive for cutbacks in the late twentieth century probably reflects the diminishing political influence of labor and reform groups and the growing power of business interests. The change in results certainly highlights the importance of distinguishing between agendas and achievements. Considering the effort expended, the retrenchment drive of Massachusetts business in the 1920s and 1930s achieved paltry gains.

The Push to Enact Legislative Protections for Massachusetts Workers

Laws restricting the working hours of women in manufacturing were a prime target of the business campaign for retrenchment in 1920s Massachusetts. At that time, the Bay State permitted women to work only 48 hours per week in industry and forbade female labor after 6:00 p.m. in textile plants. The commonwealth's laws on female work hours were stricter than the regulations in other cloth-making jurisdictions. The statutes were important because a significant portion of the textile labor force was female.

The Massachusetts hours of work laws that proved so contentious in the 1920s were the fruit of a long campaign by organized labor and its social reform allies for legal limits on working times.[2] Agitation on this subject first occurred in the 1840s and took place on a sustained basis after the Civil War. The main impetus for legal restrictions on hours came from the more skilled employees in textiles, who were usually English-speaking men. Their unions, first the Knights of Labor and later craft groups affiliated with the American Federation of Labor (AFL), led the push for state laws limiting the work week in manufacturing. A legislative strategy for hours reduction was key due to the uneven union presence in Bay State textiles. In the leading southeastern Massachusetts production centers of Fall River and New Bedford, the more skilled workers had strong organizations. Unionism was much weaker in the commonwealth's other textile mills, which were scattered in a rough arc around Boston. Since labor did not have sufficient strength to secure uniformly reduced hours through shop-floor action, the legal route offered the best chance of success. Advocates of reduced working times sought legislation that applied only to female operatives for purely tactical reasons. It was believed that the period's gendered attitudes facilitated the approval of measures that would protect a seemingly vulnerable group of employees. Furthermore, after the Supreme Court's *Lochner* decision of 1905, workers knew that judges would disallow hours of labor laws affecting male operatives. Unionists calculated that since females accounted for a sizable segment of the textile labor force, limits on the employment hours of women would apply in a de facto manner to their male counterparts.[3] Workers received important support in the fight for restricted laboring times from middle-class reformers calling for an eight-hour work day.

In pressing the case for shorter hours, advocates organized rallies, circulated petitions, forged alliances with sympathetic politicians, and campaigned to defeat hostile candidates for office. Most legislators from the Bay State's minority Democratic Party backed hours reduction—not surprising since the party drew the bulk of its urban vote from Irish Catholic residents, who were often working class and generally pro-union. Support also came from Republican legislators representing working-class constituents in import-sensitive industries who adhered to the Republican Party primarily due to its backing for protectionist tariffs. Reform-minded Republican lawmakers provided additional backing. Manufacturing interests vociferously opposed reductions in legal working times, and the conservative, usually Republican legislators with whom they aligned fiercely resisted hours restrictions. The labor-reformer coalition made slow but significant progress on the work hours issue during the Gilded Age. The commonwealth enacted a 60-hour week for female workers in manufacturing in 1874; closed a loophole preventing effective enforcement of the restriction in 1879; and lowered the limit to 58 hours in 1892.

In the early twentieth century, advocates of shorter hours shifted their attention to the related question of restricting night work. Textile manufacturers in the preceding years had evaded the intent of the existing 58-hour law by hiring one group of women employees for the permitted time during the day and a different set of female operatives for several additional hours of labor at night. Male employees were pressured to serve on both the regular and the extra shift, resulting in an extremely long mill day for the men. To prevent such maneuvers, the unions resolved to eliminate the possibility of night work by banning the labor of women in textiles after 6:00 p.m.[4]

A multi-year drive to secure passage of the law ensued. The unions demonstrated impressive political clout in the course of this fight. The measure eliminating female labor in textiles after 6:00 p.m., which was known at the time as the Overtime Bill, passed both houses of the state legislature in 1904 but was vetoed by the governor. Unionists campaigned hard that autumn against the governor's bid for another term, and he was defeated. In 1905, and again in 1906, the bill won approval in the state House of Representatives but was halted in the more conservative Senate. Unionists then decided on an all-out push for the legislation. A leading opponent of the measure held the state Senate seat for Lowell. To deny his bid for reelection, the Massachusetts AFL coordinated with the Lowell Central Labor Union. The state organization's former president was dispatched to Lowell for a week to ensure that "no stone would be left unturned." The incumbent lost. A Boston senator who had opposed the Overtime Bill received a barrage of hostile union attention and failed in his campaign for a seat in the U.S. Congress. In all, six state senators who had voted against the measure or absented themselves from the chamber while it was being considered did not win reelection in 1906. The Overtime Bill passed easily at the next legislative session, encountering only one dissenting vote in the Senate, and was signed into law by the governor.[5]

Unionists' attention then returned to securing further reductions in the work week. In the reformist atmosphere of the Progressive Era, advances were quickly achieved. Massachusetts cut the limit on laboring times for women in manufacturing to 56 hours in 1908 and 54 hours in 1911.[6]

Further pressure from labor and reform organizations brought about passage of the 1919 bill implementing a 48-hour work week for women in Bay State manufacturing. Massachusetts textile unions did not participate in the legislative phase of this campaign. The groups had pledged several years earlier, as a condition of 54-hour law approval, to refrain from continued efforts aimed at legally limiting Massachusetts working times until restrictions in other cotton-producing states came into line with those in the commonwealth. The initiative in seeking lower legal caps on the work week passed, as a result, to a network of reform groups. Spearheading the effort was the local branch of the Women's Trade Union League (WTUL), a national organization bringing together reform-minded middle- and working-class women, founded in Massachusetts in 1903 under the partial sponsorship of the state AFL. The WTUL introduced 48-hour bills in the state legislature beginning in 1916 and organized an impressive list of women's organizations in support. These included the Consumers League of Massachusetts, the local affiliate of the National Consumers League; the Women's Educational and Industrial Union, a Boston-based organization that sought to aid female workers; the Federation of Women's Clubs; and the Women's Suffrage Association. The state branch of the AFL, not bound by the textile workers' pledge to abstain from further agitation for legal limits on laboring hours, also sponsored 48-hour proposals during this period.[7]

The drive for shorter hours received added support in late 1918 when the United Textile Workers of America (UTW), the sector's leading union, announced its intention to impose the 48-hour week through shop-floor action in all the industry's plants. A heavy majority of the mills in Massachusetts adopted the shorter schedule in early 1919, with a downturn in the demand for textile goods making them more willing to do so. Manufacturers' organizations put up a spirited fight against writing the new limit into Bay State law. But with most textile concerns operating only 48 hours, their exertions had little effect. The 48-hour bill passed both houses of the legislature by crushing majorities that spring and was signed into law by Republican governor Calvin Coolidge.[8]

Massachusetts was not alone in enacting legal protections for workers during this era. However, in the period up through World War I, social legislation was more advanced in the commonwealth than in the other major textile-producing jurisdictions. The Bay State's earlier industrial start and more developed unions and reform organizations doubtless accounted for its leading position in this field. As a result, when the northern textile industry went into decline in the years after the war, the hours of work laws in Massachusetts were more stringent than those in competing states. The legal limit on the work week of women stood at 54 hours in Maine, New Hampshire, and Rhode Island in the early 1920s, and 55 hours in Connecticut. These laws remained unchanged into the 1930s, despite periodic efforts in various New England jurisdictions to move to 48 hours. No other New England state had anything nearly as strict as the Massachusetts ban on work by women in textiles after 6:00 p.m. In the textile-producing areas of the Southeast, regulations on female working hours were even laxer in the early 1920s. South Carolina enforced a 55-hour week, Tennessee permitted 57 hours, North Carolina and Georgia allowed 60 hours, and Alabama had no limit. All southern states permitted night work by women, and in the years after World War I Dixie mills commonly ran a full second shift with ample numbers of female employees.[9]

Battles over Repeal of Massachusetts Hours of Work Laws during the 1920s

In leading the fight to retain existing work hours limits during the 1920s, organized labor benefited from a significant Massachusetts presence. Union membership in the state stood at 272,000 in 1922, equal to about 15 percent of the work force.[10] By the standards of the era, this was a relatively strong position. In textiles, the largest organizations were still in Fall River and New Bedford. The more skilled workers there had established stable collective bargaining arrangements with employers by the early twentieth century.[11] Only about a third of textile operatives in Fall River and New Bedford were organized in the 1920s, but all employees benefited from the union role and recognized its importance.[12] The Textile Councils of Fall River and New Bedford coordinated the activities of the unionized mill workers in the two cities. Labor remained much weaker in most of the state's other textile centers. With a few exceptions, only the most highly skilled workers in those municipalities belonged to unions—typically locals of the AFL-affiliated UTW. Outside of Fall River and New Bedford, the unorganized, moderately skilled, usually "new immigrant" operatives who accounted for the bulk of the textile labor force periodically mounted militant actions with guidance from radical activists. The most notable of these were the great Lawrence strikes of 1912 and 1919. Divisions emerged even among the established textile organizations. In 1915 most Fall River and New Bedford operatives left the UTW and set up their own union. Other Bay State industries with a weighty union presence in this era included construction, railroads, street railways, printing, cigarmaking, shoemaking, metalworking, and ironmolding.

The state branch of the AFL served as an umbrella group for Massachusetts labor. Set up in 1887, the organization spearheaded the lobbying efforts of unions on questions of commonwealth policy. The function was important, since workers had a stake in numerous subjects regulated at the state level, including working times, injunctions, mandatory school attendance, factory safety, and workmen's compensation. Central to the lobbying effort of the Massachusetts AFL was the organization's legislative agent. This individual was a constant presence at the statehouse when the legislature was in session, testifying at hearings and conferring with lawmakers and sympathetic reformers. The agent later reported to the state AFL's annual convention on the disposition of the many pieces of legislation on which the organization had taken a position. The Massachusetts AFL was weakened by the reluctance of many labor organizations to affiliate and pay the requisite dues. The group had a membership of 53,000 in 1925, two-thirds of whom were in good standing.[13]

Institutional weakness did not prevent Massachusetts unionists of the 1920s from presenting a united front in defense of the commonwealth's hours of work laws. At legislative hearings on proposals to ease the statutes, the state AFL's legislative agent typically headed labor's defense of the existing restrictions. Appearing in support were representatives of the UTW and of the Textile Councils in Fall River and New Bedford. Members of unions with no direct stake in the legislation also turned out on some occasions to back the status quo.

The drive by Massachusetts business interests to roll back the state's hours of work laws began in 1922.[14] That year, and annually thereafter until 1928, industrialists sponsored bills in the commonwealth legislature to return to a 54-hour week. Proposals were also introduced in several years to modify the ban on work by women in textiles after 6:00 p.m. On every occasion representatives of business argued that the existing restrictions handicapped Massachusetts industry and discouraged continued cotton manufacturing in the state. Businessmen and conservatives talked endlessly about the issue and numerous publications dealt with some angle of the controversy.[15] The battles attracted increasing public attention. By the end of the decade, hours of work had become one of the leading public policy questions in the commonwealth.[16]

Textile executive Ward Thoron played a central role in the efforts of Massachusetts manufacturers to secure cutbacks in social legislation and taxes. The son of a prominent northeastern businessman and a graduate of Harvard Law School, Thoron practiced law in Washington, D.C., before moving into textile management. In 1920, he became treasurer, the chief executive position, at the Merrimack Manufacturing Company. Merrimack Manufacturing was one of the leading fabric producers in Lowell, Massachusetts, and maintained a second plant in Alabama. Thoron quickly emerged as a leading figure in the cotton industry's business associations. He filled various posts at the National Association of Cotton Manufacturers (NACM), the sector's principal trade group in the Northeast. He also served as president of the Arkwright Club, a second textile trade association. Thoron was an outspoken and determined advocate of retrenchment, appearing repeatedly before state legislative committees to call for easing labor laws and reducing mill taxes. The Merrimack executive often employed extreme rhetoric to support his position. He clashed with other business executives whom he regarded as insufficiently firm on the retrenchment question.[17]

The 1924 session of the legislature saw a serious effort to weaken the state's restrictions on laboring times. A number of Massachusetts cotton mills had permanently ceased operations by this point, making clear the gravity of conditions in the industry. Measures introduced that year on the manufacturers' behalf would raise the weekly ceiling on working hours of women in all industries to 54 hours and alter the night work ban so that women could labor in textile factories until 11:00 p.m.

The fabric-making interests vigorously pressed the case for change. Robert Amory, president of the textile trade group NACM, bluntly laid out how the existing laws discouraged further production in the state. At a public debate on the measures in early 1924, Amory stated:

> A mill can legally be run by women in Massachusetts only 48 hours per week. In other States they are permitted to run 110. Suggestions have been made that we use more automatic machinery. Why put it there if you can only use it 48 hours a week, when you can take it somewhere else and run it longer?[18]

The legislature referred the proposals to its joint Committee on Labor and Industry. At hearings of this panel the mill men offered further arguments for passage. Ward Thoron, treasurer of Lowell's Merrimack mills, gave a lengthy survey of the deteriorating position of cotton manufacturing in New England. He demonstrated that southern producers had taken over more and more product lines in recent decades and noted that New England–based companies, including his own, had begun to invest in the South. Thoron favored confrontational rhetoric and concluded his testimony with a bald threat. If the Massachusetts labor laws were not changed, he asserted, manufacturers would construct no new facilities in the state. As existing mills became obsolete, "we shall rebuild them in the South and move our machinery there." NACM president Amory hit a positive note in his testimony, arguing that the ability to run a night shift would enable Bay State manufacturers to reduce costs and make quicker deliveries on rush orders.[19]

A delegation of unionists appeared at the hearing to argue equally forcefully for the maintenance of existing labor standards. Charles Hodsdon, legislative agent of the state AFL, asserted that watering down the state's laws would not reverse the decline of cotton manufacturing in the commonwealth. Abraham Binns of the New Bedford Textile Council claimed that the existing statutes had broad public support and did not hamper the competitiveness of Massachusetts mills. Representatives of shoe workers, carpenters, machinists, and municipal employees also spoke against the proposed changes, as did a "score" of officers from women's unions.[20] Members of the latter organizations likely saw the issue in terms of preserving protections for women workers. The carpentry and machining sectors had no female employees. Unionists from those industries presumably appeared at the hearing to demonstrate solidarity in defense of labor's past legislative gains. The union position prevailed. The Committee on Labor and Industry reported unfavorably on the bills.[21] Both houses approved the recommendation, bringing the matter to a close.

Changes during this era that undermined the Republicans' longstanding dominance of Massachusetts politics added to the difficulties of those seeking to alter the hours of work laws. The Republican Party (Grand Old Party, or GOP) had controlled most elected offices in the commonwealth since the nineteenth century, based on strong backing from Protestants of British and northern European extraction. Bay State Democrats did well in the anomalous circumstances of 1912 and succeeding years, but Republicans reasserted their dominance soon thereafter. GOP candidates won every race for Massachusetts governor from 1916 through 1928 and controlled both houses of the state legislature by wide margins during that period.[22] Although some Republican officeholders of the post–World War I era supported reform, most sympathized with business and followed a laissez-faire approach to policymaking. The nativist currents that appeared in Massachusetts, as elsewhere, during the 1920s threatened the GOP's predominant position in commonwealth politics. Migrants from southern and eastern Europe had poured into Massachusetts in the preceding decades. Particularly numerous were Italians, Jews, Poles, and Portuguese as well as French Canadians who had moved from north of the border. In the period after World War I resentment of these newcomers grew. Prohibition and immigration restriction found strong support among the commonwealth's white Protestants; the Ku Klux Klan established a sizable presence in the state; and a Massachusetts court headed by a Yankee judge railroaded Italian immigrant radicals Sacco and Vanzetti. In the face of this hostility, new immigrants who had previously voted Republican or abstained from the polls increasingly leaned toward the newcomer-friendly Democrats. Plant shutdowns in textiles and shoes created additional problems for the GOP. The Republicans had earlier won strong backing from working-class voters in those industries through support for the high tariffs that seemingly facilitated prosperity. The party's protectionism proved less compelling amid the depressed conditions in the fabric and shoemaking sectors.[23]

An episode from the 1926 legislative session demonstrates the pressures that could be brought to bear in this political context and indicates why legislators were so reluctant to alter the existing hours of work laws. That year the Arkwright Club, an organization of New England cotton mill executives, sponsored a measure to extend the work week in Massachusetts manufacturing to 54 hours. Ward Thoron was then president of the Arkwright Club. He appeared in February before the legislature's Committee on Labor and Industry to urge passage of the bill. Thoron's public appearances generally displayed little finesse. On this occasion, a Lowell Democrat on the committee cornered Thoron into conceding several awkward points. The Arkwright president admitted that "quite a number" of mills owned by Senator Butler belonged to the Arkwright Club and that the Butler companies favored "some modification" of the 48-hour law.[24]

The mill owner in question was U.S. Senator William Butler, leading Republican and president of a number of Massachusetts cotton companies. Butler had been appointed to the Senate two years earlier, filling the post left open by the death of Henry Cabot Lodge. He would have to defend his seat in elections in the coming November. His likely opponent in the forthcoming race was veteran Democratic politician David Walsh. Of working-class origin, Walsh was the first Irish Catholic to hold statewide political office in Massachusetts, winning two terms as governor and election to the U.S. Senate in 1918.[25] Walsh lost the senatorial seat six years later in a tight race against a challenger who shared the Republican ticket with President Calvin Coolidge, the highly popular native son. Walsh had consistently supported social legislation during his stints as governor and senator, backing stronger labor laws, university extension courses for workers, old age pensions, and aid to mothers with dependent children.[26] Given the numerous difficulties confronting the Massachusetts GOP, Walsh would clearly present a tough challenge to Butler in the 1926 Senate race.

With a likely Walsh-Butler electoral clash looming, the story of Butler's seeming opposition to the 48-hour law at the February 1926 legislative hearing attracted considerable attention. On the evening of the hearing, the late edition of one Boston newspaper featured a lengthy account of Thoron's travails at the session under the large-font headline "Senator Butler's Mills Favor 48-Hour Change." The Arkwright Club moved quickly to contain the fallout. The organization issued a statement the same evening in which Thoron asserted that he had misunderstood the lawmaker's question and believed that Butler did not favor the proposed change. Butler himself addressed the issue the following day. From Washington, D.C., the senator declared his opposition to any change in the 48-hour statute and made the highly questionable claim that he had worked within the Arkwright Club to head off efforts to alter the law. (Four years earlier, Butler had urged repeal of 48 hours before another committee of the state legislature.)[27]

This series of events, and especially Butler's high-profile reversal of position on the 48-hour law, is revealing. With the votes of new immigrants and textile and shoe workers increasingly up for grabs in the mid-1920s, Democrats saw advantage in painting their opponents as enemies of labor legislation. Mainstream Republicans, meanwhile, viewed support for easing work hours restrictions as politically risky—even when it could be argued that such action would help the struggling industries of Massachusetts. The proposal for 48-hour repeal made little progress in the 1926 legislative session.[28]

Advocates of easing the hours of work statutes came closest to achieving a success in 1928. The textile interests played no formal role in that year's legislative fight, having apparently abandoned hope of modifying the restrictions after being stymied at the statehouse for years in a row. This left organizations representing a broad spectrum of business interests to take the initiative in 1928. The Associated Industries of Massachusetts (AIM), the lobby for all Bay State manufacturers, actively supported altering the laws. So did the Massachusetts section of the New England Council, a business group founded several years earlier to work for recovery of the regional economy. Council leaders from Massachusetts were increasingly worried by the regulatory and tax burden on struggling commonwealth industries and had been pushing for some time for retrenchment in these areas.[29]

Bay State business associations found a receptive audience for their views in Republican governor Alvin T. Fuller. After entering politics in the previous decade as a Progressive, Fuller drifted to the right during the 1920s. The economic problems of the commonwealth deeply concerned the governor. On taking office in 1925, he called for the burdens on industry to be eased. Years of inaction on this agenda exasperated Fuller. He wondered aloud in his opening address to the 1928 session of the legislature whether the situation had not gotten so extreme that business would be driven from the state:

> It is an open question whether we have not traveled so far in the protection we give labor, and in the . . . taxes that we . . . exact from [manufacturing that] our industries have not reached a position where there is nothing left for a good many of them to do but quit.

Developments in textiles seemed to support the governor's view. Another wave of mill closures swept through the industry, causing statewide employment in cotton goods to slump from 91,000 in 1927 to 65,000 in 1928. Continued downsizing obviously ratcheted up the pressure to ease regulations on fabric producers.[30]

With the governor and a spectrum of business groups agitating for change, a 1928 bill to ease the night work ban by permitting women to labor in cloth-making factories until 10:00 p.m. came somewhat close to passage. (A companion measure easing the 48-hour law made little progress that year.) The commonwealth's night work law was particularly stringent and furthest out of line with restrictions in competing states.[31] Anticipating a struggle in the 1928 legislative session, the state AFL convened a conference of officials from the Fall River and New Bedford Textile Councils and the UTW's Massachusetts locals to "plan . . . for an active fight" to defend the current regulations. Representatives of these and numerous other labor and reform organizations appeared at February 1928 hearings to oppose altering the statutes.[32] Business groups advocating change made a forceful showing at the session. The legislature's labor and industries committee reported favorably on the proposal to permit night work by women in textiles, although nearly half the joint panel's lower house members dissented. The bill then moved to the Senate, where it prevailed in March by a 20–11 vote.

Everyone involved knew that the real battle would take place in the more liberal House of Representatives, and furious lobbying began the next day. The New Bedford Cotton Manufacturers Association pressed members of its House delegation to permit "fair play" for the industry. The Joint Committee on Industrial Conditions for Women and Children in Massachusetts, which brought together representatives of the WTUL, the Consumers League of Massachusetts, and numerous other reform groups, wrote to each member of the lower chamber opposing changes to current law. At the previous month's hearing, the manager of a textile finishing firm from southeastern Massachusetts had appeared with a group of young female operatives from the fabric mills of Taunton who affirmed their support for legal changes permitting late work. Labor leaders charged that the women had been coerced into taking this position. The industrialist returned with a similar delegation as the House took up the night work question. This time the unions were ready. Officers of the Fall River and New Bedford Textile Councils arrived at the statehouse that day accompanied by young female workers from their cities. The women made the rounds among legislators, pressing for retention of the current regulations. Members of the House debated the late work proposal before galleries packed with onlookers. After lengthy and sometimes heated addresses from the floor, the bill failed on a roll call, with 90 representatives in favor and 116 opposed.[33]

An analysis of the "no" vote on this measure provides a good window on how, in the generally conservative 1920s, defenders of the hours of work laws mustered the legislative support necessary to maintain the status quo.[34] The Massachusetts House of Representatives had 240 members at this time. Given the habitually high level of legislator absenteeism, it was likely that somewhat more than 200 representatives would be present and voting on repeal of the night work ban. To defeat the measure, opponents thus had to mobilize slightly more than 100 negative votes. Constituting a hard core of support for the night work law was a bloc of legislators who might be termed reform stalwarts.[35] Several political elements made up this group. Accounting for the largest numbers, and representing heavily Irish Catholic, mostly working-class constituencies, was the relatively small Democratic House contingent. (There were 63 Democrats in the 1927–28 House, not all of whom appeared to vote on the night work bill.) Present as well was a cluster of Republican "labor representatives" elected by working-class voters toiling in tariff-dependent industries who adhered to the GOP principally because of the party's protectionist stance.[36] Finally, there were a number of Republicans representing more affluent or nonindustrial districts who supported social reform out of personal conviction. Of similar political complexion to the stalwarts was a smaller group of representatives who inclined strongly in favor of reform causes but occasionally voted against labor's position.[37] On the critical day, the stalwarts accounted for 66 "no" votes and those who leaned heavily in favor of reform added another 15. Moderates—mostly Republicans whose votes on labor issues were about evenly divided between support and opposition—plus a few representatives with such poor attendance records that no pattern was discernable, added another 15 voices to the negative column. This brought the number of representatives opposed to the measure to 96.

What put the anti–night work cause over the top, and indeed gave it a secure margin of victory, were the 20 "no" votes from Republican members of the House with records of strong opposition to labor-backed measures. Why did these legislators depart from their usual position to support the existing restrictions on working hours? A few came from outlying nonindustrial parts of greater Boston. In such suburban areas, the gendered rhetoric of reformers about the hazards of late factory work for women might have had some appeal. Most of the surprising opponents of late work represented districts in manufacturing cities.[38] Fear of the consequences of countering labor on this issue likely motivated these lawmakers. Massachusetts Republicans were losing ground in the late 1920s among new immigrants and workers in declining industries. The state's relatively strong unions mounted a vigorous defense of the current restrictions on laboring hours, and feelings on the subject likely ran high in blue-collar districts. In these circumstances, some Republican legislators from manufacturing centers who generally opposed reform probably calculated that a vote to permit night work might end their political careers. Even GOP lawmakers representing industrial cities who had favorable prospects for reelection may have worried that taking an anti-labor position on this prominent issue could cost their party's candidates crucial votes in upcoming statewide races.[39]

After the failure of 1928, no more proposals to repeal or ease the statutes on working hours of women came before the legislature for several years. Even in the unpromising atmosphere of repeated plant closures, Massachusetts unions and reform groups had defended with complete success the state's advanced hours of work laws.[40]

Manufacturers' Motivations for Seeking to Change the Hours of Work Laws

What motivated Massachusetts cotton manufacturers to press so insistently during this era for easing of the state's hours of work statutes? The question is more complex than it might appear since careful analysis of statistics and other information on the industry's operating rates in the 1920s demonstrates that the restrictions had only a limited effect on the competitiveness of commonwealth producers.

In principle, the impact of the laws should be significant. Longer running times allowed companies in other locations to spread the fixed expenses of mill buildings and equipment over a larger quantity of output, lowering overall production costs and raising profit rates.[41] In the style goods market that was increasingly important for some Bay State mills, the inability to run enough hours to turn out fabric quickly could lead to the loss of time-sensitive orders. Business advocates put forward precisely these arguments in pressing for the regulations on working times to be eased.

Although sound in theory, these claims did not apply well in practice given the realities prevailing in Massachusetts cotton textiles. On the question of daylight operating times, from the early 1920s onward most of the state's factories did not even run all the hours permitted under existing law due to the depressed condition of the industry. Statistics on operating rates for the Bay State cotton textile sector as a whole show that, on average, mills ran considerably less than 48 hours per week.[42] The figures are somewhat misleading because they are industrywide aggregates. Operating rates appear to have varied dramatically from company to company, with some firms running full schedules despite the generally dire state of the market.[43] Those mills that could secure enough business to operate for all the permitted hours were the ones that might have suffered competitive harm from the commonwealth's strict limits on working times.

Massachusetts manufacturers potentially hindered by the 48-hour statute could avoid any restraints stemming from the law by operating a second shift at night. Late work enabled mills to accommodate surges in demand for standardized products. Night running also permitted rush orders for style goods to be turned out quickly. As a representative of Massachusetts cotton manufacturers put the matter in 1928, late operations were desirable "when you have a business which is sporadic, which requires for a month or two months, or a week or a few days, the operation of a night shift in order to complete rush orders, or to complete an unusual volume of business which has come in suddenly on the mill."[44] Bay State textile managers could not employ women for night work due to the commonwealth's 6:00 p.m. law, even though females normally accounted for a substantial segment of the textile labor force. The personnel on second shifts therefore had to be all male.

Employers insisted that it was not possible to hire adequate numbers of male operatives for the typically short-lived stints of night work.[45] Labor leaders contested these claims. They asserted that with high levels of joblessness in the industry, mill managers could find sufficient employees to run all-male shifts at night.[46] Union representatives at a 1928 legislative hearing insisted that certain Massachusetts mills were operating late shifts at that very point in time.[47] There were similar reports in earlier years, not all of them originating from labor-friendly sources.[48] Such work could only have been carried out with male-only crews, given the ban on employment of female operatives after 6:00 p.m. At least some of the reported instances of night operation seem to have been of short-term duration. It appears, at a minimum, that certain Bay State mills were able to carry out night work on a sporadic basis with a labor force of men.

The picture that emerges taking all these details into account is not entirely clear. Massachusetts' hours of work laws did not constrain the cotton industry *as a whole* in the 1920s. Particular firms were potentially hindered, although certain of these could apparently circumvent the problem by running all-male shifts at night. It seems likely that the hours of work laws significantly limited the operations of *some* Bay State cotton manufacturers. It is easy to understand why such employers would press vigorously for modification of the statutes. More difficult to explain are the vociferous calls for change coming from manufacturers on whom the laws had no substantive effect. *Most* of the firms in the industry were probably in this position. Yet all seemed to support the push for repeal of the restrictions with equal enthusiasm. In particular, the existing regulations almost certainly had no impact on the company managed by Ward Thoron, the principal spokesman for easing the working time laws.

Thoron's Merrimack Manufacturing Company had begun operations at Lowell, Massachusetts, in the early nineteenth century. In the years after World War I the firm produced high-grade fabric at the Lowell plant. Thoron was the leading advocate among Massachusetts cotton manufacturers for changing the hours of work laws, and the issue seemingly obsessed him. Four times during the 1920s, Thoron appeared before committees of the state legislature to testify on behalf of easing the statutes. His lengthy 1924 testimony was published twice—in pamphlet form and as an article in a trade periodical. The text of his 1925 talk on the subject to Lowell civic groups was also distributed as a booklet.[49] In business circles behind the scenes, Thoron agitated on the hours of work question with a determination matching his public rhetoric. At mid-decade, he delayed by eighteen months publication of a Boston Chamber of Commerce study of cotton textile manufacturing in New England because he felt it did not take a strong enough position against the Massachusetts hours of work laws.[50]

Despite the determined, years-long, public and private effort that Thoron mounted against the Massachusetts hours of work restrictions, the records of Merrimack Manufacturing demonstrate that the statutes had no significant impact on the firm. Indeed, due to low rates of capacity utilization and the maintenance of large inventories, the Bay State's laws on working times probably had no effect whatsoever on company operations throughout the 1920s. Nor from early 1923 to the end of the decade was there ever a reasonable basis to expect that the laws would constrain Merrimack's functioning in the near future.[51]

Why then did Thoron expend so much energy seeking repeal of Massachusetts' restrictions on work times and particularly the 48-hour limit? A careful reading of the manager's statements from the period offers an explanation. Despite the constant rhetoric about the intolerable burden the regulations created in the current depressed state of the industry, it seems that Thoron's true concern was the constraints the laws would impose in some future period when prosperous conditions returned.

The Merrimack executive's 1925 address on cotton textiles to Lowell civic organizations demonstrates that he anticipated a relatively bright future for northeastern manufacturers of quality goods, such as his company. Thoron observed in the speech that although southern mills controlled the market for cheaper fabrics, northerners still dominated the production of quality cloth. Thoron expected this to remain the case. The labor-cost advantage of southern firms was narrower on the higher grades of goods, he commented, and even the present differential would lessen over time due to increases in Dixie pay rates that were the "necessary consequence of increasing prosperity." In Thoron's view, northern and some southern producers, all paying approximately the same wages, would eventually contest the market for quality cotton textiles.[52] In these circumstances the 48-hour law could create substantial problems for Merrimack. The company would have to spread its fixed costs over 48 hours' worth of output, while producers elsewhere spread their expenses over 54 hours of production.[53] Merrimack would likely have higher costs and lower profits as a result.[54]

Massachusetts cotton manufacturers found themselves in a palpably ironic situation in the 1920s with respect to the state's hours of work laws. The mill men mounted a major effort to ease the statutes as their industry downsized. They doubtless knew that the current harsh conditions improved their chances of receiving a sympathetic hearing from the legislature. The actual effect of the restrictions was limited at that time, since average operating hours were so low and male labor for overtime shifts was so plentiful in the industry's ongoing depression. The laws could have a substantial impact if and when conditions improved. However, as the manufacturers surely appreciated, during prosperous times the legislature was much less likely to ease the statutes.

The longstanding antagonism between capital and labor in cotton textiles may have been another factor motivating Thoron and other manufacturers unaffected by the hours of work laws to campaign for their repeal in the 1920s. Industrialists in cotton had ample reason to resent the labor movement, its leaders, and its accomplishments. Over the years Massachusetts had seen numerous clashes on the shop floor and in the streets as textile workers sought an organized voice, better working conditions, and higher wages. Actual or threatened textile strikes in 1919, 1922, and 1928 were but the latest episodes in a decades-old history of clashes.[55] The industry's employers and workers battled it out even more frequently in the halls of government. Leaders of the two groups crossed horns over laboring times and other questions specific to cotton making in almost every year until the 48-hour law passed in 1919. The work hours issue aside, the political struggle between capital and labor in textiles continued during the post–World War I years within a broader context. Cotton workers belonged to a union alliance that fought business interests led by the state manufacturers association (AIM) for government protections in a range of areas. On a number of these issues, the unions prevailed. Against this backdrop of conflict, manufacturers may have seen the campaign to roll back the hours of work laws as a chance for revenge—an opportunity to strike at a cherished accomplishment of the labor movement at what seemed a propitious moment.

Manufacturers certainly appeared to have a low opinion of the union movement and its aspirations and allies. In 1925 Thoron headed the NACM committee on tariffs and taxation. That year the panel's report featured the sharp rhetoric repeatedly employed by the committee chair. The report critiqued the "Utopia of short hours and high pay" achieved by labor since the world war, which "has brought in its train high costs and high prices" and a "wasteful and expensive . . . standard of living." The editor of the *American Wool and Cotton Reporter*, a trade journal, may have spoken for many in management ranks when he characterized the supporters of the 48-hour standard as "the 'bleeding hearts,' the socialistic propagandists, and the labor-union-terrified members of the Legislature."[56]

Even if animus against labor did not motivate business interests to press for repeal of the work hours statutes, the legislature's refusal to change the regulations allowed manufacturers to blame the laws for the industry's demise. Mill interests repeatedly asserted that legal restrictions accounted for the sector's woes. Such claims became more commonplace as downsizing proceeded. Editorializing in 1924 about proposals to ease work hours restrictions in Massachusetts, the leading textile trade publication asserted that "cotton, knit goods and shoe plants . . . have been driven out of the state by existing illiberal laws." In a 1926 letter to stockholders, the treasurer of Everett Mills, a cotton manufacturer in Lawrence, Massachusetts, cited "labor troubles, restrictive legislation, and high labor costs [that] have hampered the company in competing with southern mills" to explain the dire conditions at his firm. Commenting on the millions of cotton spindles lost to Massachusetts by 1931, another industry periodical held that "this drying-up of the textile business . . . is certainly due to the 48-hour law and to no other condition." In a 1934 letter to members, the secretary of the NACM claimed that the "forty-eight hour law and other restrict[ive] legislation . . . has reduced the spindles in Massachusetts by over one-half in the short space of ten years."[57]

In making such assertions, the textile interests engaged in either duplicity or self-deception. The decline of cotton textile manufacturing in Massachusetts emerged out of a complex interplay of factors. The central reason was the rise of new competitors in the southern states who could produce fabric more cheaply due to the lower wage rates in that region. Industry journalists, company managers, and trade association executives were as aware of these realities as anyone. They were thus in a position to know that it was totally unjustified to ascribe the decline of the industry in Massachusetts solely to the state's hours of work laws. Even the more nuanced statement of the Everett Mills manager contained serious distortions. He cited labor troubles as one reason for the company's problems although Lawrence had not seen a serious strike in years. "Restrictive legislation" could not have limited the company's competitiveness at the time of writing, as the firm had operated at an average of 36 percent of single-shift capacity during the two preceding fiscal years.[58]

What makes the quoted statements even more extraordinary is that they were directed to an audience of industry insiders and thus cannot have been part of an effort to convince the public at large that the Massachusetts labor laws needed changing. Textile executives comprised the main readership of the trade publications cited; the Everett Mills manager was addressing his stockholders; and the letter from the NACM director would not have been seen by anyone outside the organization. Commonwealth cotton manufacturers had apparently chosen to believe—or at least consistently to assert—that the state's labor laws accounted for the bulk of their woes.[59] Of course, in blaming the statutes for their problems, industrialists by implication pinned responsibility on the unionists, reformers, and politicians who favored keeping the restrictions in place.

The fight over the hours of work laws in the context of industrial decline created an ideal situation for executives in the cotton sector of Massachusetts. If the legislature eased the laws, the mill men would marginally improve their competitive situation and gain the satisfaction of seeing the removal of restrictions that been thrust upon them after years of political struggle. If lawmakers refused to act, manufacturers could blame the regulations and their supporters for the decline of textiles in the commonwealth. Whatever the outcome, the mill men gained something.

Labor's Motivations for Opposing Change to the Hours of Work Laws

What of the defenders of the existing hours of work laws? Why did unionists, the primary supporters of the statutes, and their reformist allies fight with such determination to maintain the status quo? The question is particularly interesting because it seems that the laws probably had some impact on certain Massachusetts cotton manufacturers, resulting in at least a slight decrease in the employment and earnings of Bay State textile workers at a time when joblessness and reduced wages haunted the mill towns. Examination of the arguments put forward by officials of labor and reform organizations shows that they acted as they did for a range of reasons. The published transcript of a 1928 legislative hearing on altering the hours of work statutes is a particularly useful source for illuminating the thinking of union and reform leaders.

The unionists opposing change to the hours of work laws clearly did not believe that much economic benefit would come from easing the present restrictions. Labor leaders repeatedly pointed out that many Massachusetts cotton firms were not operating during all the hours permitted under current law. They argued as well that companies in neighboring New England states with less restrictive legislation were also performing poorly. Abraham Binns of the New Bedford Textile Council observed during testimony in 1928 that "Rhode Island is not better off than Massachusetts. Mills are shut down, mills are threatening to go South, and some of them, although they could run their mills night and day, are running three days a week."[60]

Union resistance to raising the cap on the work week was spurred by the belief that altering the statutes would produce lower hourly wages rather than higher total earnings. As a result, operatives might end up receiving the same total pay for 54 hours of work that they had previously received for 48. UTW official Francis Gorman alluded to this possibility in 1928 testimony, stating that proponents of change "lose sight of the fact that wages and hours go together. If shorter hours make higher wages, then longer hours tend to decrease wages."[61]

Unionists also feared that easing Massachusetts' statutes on working times might lead competing states to alter their regulations in the same fashion. If this occurred, the competitive position of the commonwealth would not improve, while working conditions would decline for operatives in all locations. A union representative from Fall River discussed this possibility in terms of a recent pay cut by the mills in his city that producers elsewhere had tried to replicate:

> I know from a city where a 10 per cent reduction has been in effect that it was the opinion of the majority of the mill owners that it would do the mills some good, but before it went into effect the reduction passed on to someone else. . . . This repeal of these laws . . . I consider . . . the same way.[62]

Widespread among worker advocates was the belief that the solution to the problems of textile operatives lay in shortening the hours of all who toiled in the mills. This position had forceful logic. Overcapacity, stemming from the growth of southern factories that often operated at night, was the root problem in the cotton industry. Cutting work hours would effectively reduce capacity and bring production back into balance with consumption. A New Bedford unionist articulated this view at the 1928 hearings, stating that "the only remedy is to run 48 hours, and if all the mills in the country were running 48 hours we would have enough production for the whole of the country." Another labor witness pushed this reasoning even farther, arguing that "instead of working 48 hours we should be working 44, or 40 would be plenty, because there are so many people out of work."[63] If the difficulties in textiles could indeed be resolved by shortening the hours of labor, then lengthening Massachusetts working times as employers demanded was clearly the opposite of what was needed.

Bay State laws on adult labor hours applied only to women for the pragmatic reason that drafting the legislation in this manner made it easier to pass. Protecting female operatives was not a prime motivation for the workingmen who led the campaign for these measures. Defenders of the statutes nevertheless cited the welfare of women as one reason for preserving the status quo. Male unionists deployed such arguments for rhetorical effect, but the views expressed by female employees and reformers concerned with women's issues were clearly genuine. At the 1928 hearing, the president of the Consumers League of Massachusetts (CLM) cited "the principle of restrictive and welfare legislation for the women in industry" as a reason to retain the existing limits. A male representative of the unionized operatives at the Naumkeag Steam Cotton plant in Salem, Massachusetts, reported that female employees there "bitterly opposed" the prospect of night work.[64]

The long battle against the manufacturers that had been necessary to win approval of the hours of work laws clearly motivated unionists to defend the status quo. Labor leaders remembered both the heated nature of these fights and the lengthy span of time over which the struggles had taken place. During a 1927 legislative debate on easing the 48-hour law, New Bedford representative John Halliwell, a lifelong textile worker and vociferous defender of the existing standards, attacked the association of industrialists sponsoring the proposal. For him, the identity and legislative record of this group was reason enough to reject the measure: "This is an *organization of manufacturers*, and I defy any man who intends voting for this bill to point to a single instance when this Arkwright Club has come here and favored any piece of humanitarian legislation for women or any other textile workers." At the 1928 hearing, Martin Joyce, legislative agent of the state AFL, recalled the lengthy struggle that had been necessary to enact the standards under dispute. He observed that the bill to abolish the night work law "carries my thoughts back to a little over twenty years ago when this present petition was . . . called an overtime bill." Now, two decades later, the manufacturers "are coming back . . . asking you to establish the same conditions . . . we had" before the measure passed.[65]

Another political factor that surely entered the calculations of those defending the hours of work statutes was the interactive nature of state labor legislation. With social reform in this era occurring almost entirely below the federal level, a vanguard dynamic had arisen. The most liberal states, such as Massachusetts, enacted laws that put their industrialists at somewhat of a disadvantage in relation to producers elsewhere. Other locations then matched the higher standards. Through this process, conditions improved for workers everywhere. Catch-up by the less progressive states also allowed advanced jurisdictions such as Massachusetts to enact further reforms with minimal competitive damage to their own industry. In reversing itself on a key item of reform legislation such as the hours of work, Massachusetts would upset the established pattern. One possible outcome would be to endanger further progress on social legislation in all locations. Speaking on behalf of the 48-hour law at the 1928 hearing, the CLM president referred to the vanguard logic just described: "having arrived at the 48-hour week, *which . . . is the peg on which the country is now tenting . . .* it would be a step in the wrong direction if you should now step back and extend the hours."[66]

Even if they thought about Bay State politics in isolation, defenders of the existing hours of work laws undoubtedly recognized that acceding to the repeal of the statutes would contradict their longstanding reform strategy. The established pattern was for unions and activist groups to secure a gain, protect it against any attempt at reversal that might arise, and then start the fight for additional advances. Unionists and their allies had won numerous past victories in this manner, and they sought further action in the 1920s on a range of issues. Permitting a backward move would contradict the time-tested approach of pressing relentlessly forward with the reform agenda. Activists may even have feared that success in rolling back the hours of work laws would encourage business interests and conservatives to attack other legislative achievements. A CLM official referred to this possibility in the early 1930s as employers again pushed to ease the hours of work laws, writing to a colleague that a "backward step [on labor hours] . . . would be only the first step in a much wider attempt to break down other regulations."[67]

In defending Massachusetts labor standards that were more stringent than the regulations in other states, unionists insisted that considerations of competitive harm to commonwealth industries could not be allowed to undercut what had been achieved. According to this view, any loss of jobs to jurisdictions with less advanced legislation was the necessary, and acceptable, price of social progress. Labor leaders backing the existing hours of work laws in the early 1920s expressed this idea in stark language. At a committee hearing in 1923, legislator and textile worker Halliwell argued that the state's mills could successfully compete against those of the South with the present work time restrictions in place. He added that "if the textile industry cannot succeed in this State on a 48-hour basis the citizens will lose nothing by its removal to the South." Union officials told a legislative committee the following year that if commonwealth mills could not remain competitive without harm to female and child workers, "let them go."[68] The dismissive tone of this rhetoric disappeared in later years as Massachusetts cotton manufacturers "went" in increasing numbers. But labor's standpoint did not change. At the 1928 hearing, William Batty of the New Bedford

Textile Council eloquently articulated the same concept, albeit in more restrained terms:

> My view . . . is that the plea of commercial necessity is inadequate to change legislation of this kind. Once you admit the principle that commercial necessity should be sufficient to scrap social legislation . . . then everything that is intended to promote human welfare is at stake. You can scrap your Workman's Compensation Act under the same excuse . . . [and] all your safety laws. . . . There is no stopping once you begin to recognize that as an adequate cause.[69]

Taking all of the foregoing into account, it is apparent that advocates of the existing hours of labor statutes had numerous social and political reasons to resist any modification of the current standards. They expected any benefits from easing the restrictions to be slim and directed to those who needed the assistance least. Given this balance of factors, staunch defense of the laws unionists and reformers had struggled long years to enact was the only position they could have been expected to take.

The individuals speaking at legislative hearings on the hours of work laws were almost all men in leadership positions with unions or reform organizations. Their testimony offers little sense of how rank-and-file workers viewed the hours restrictions. Evidence on this point is available from the 1928 hearing, where two former millworkers and one current operative spoke. All three were women, which additionally allows us to hear the opinions of those for whom the hours of work statutes had supposedly been enacted. Such views were seldom aired in public debates.

None of the female witnesses at the 1928 hearing explicitly challenged prevailing views of women's subordinate social role. All saw the hours of work restrictions as specifically intended to improve conditions for women and viewed this special protection as worthwhile. (The original aim of the legislation was shortening hours for all millhands, not safeguarding women workers in particular.) The female witnesses advanced a number of arguments in defending the present limits on hours. A repeated theme was that laboring in a textile mill was difficult, dirty, and dangerous—and that having to do so more than 48 hours per week, or after 6:00 p.m. at night, would make a bad situation even worse.

Bertha Reisroff, who had toiled in the cloth mills for seven years, framed her support for the existing hours of work laws in terms of broad social progress. A "people can be judged as to what stage of civilization and culture they have attained by the treatment they give their women," Reisroff asserted. "In olden times . . . in primitive society," she continued, women had been obliged to do hard physical labor. Even in the contemporary era, the demands on women could be significant. In textile factories, female workers had to contend with heavy, dust-filled air, the roar of machinery, and "nerve-straining work." Requiring female operatives to toil even longer hours in such conditions, concluded Reisroff, would constitute "further exploitation of women."[70]

Mary Thompson had worked for twenty years in the textile mills and was active in the Women's Trade Union League, a group that fought for the interests of factory women. Thompson, too, saw the hours of work laws as promoting social progress. Class and gender consciousness also infused her views. Thompson noted how much "misery and suffering there is among our people . . . the working people." She emphasized the health hazards of breathing the dust-laden mill air. She evoked as well the double shift confronting female workers, who after long days at the factory were responsible for "taking care of you men folks . . . and . . . of the children." Rolling back the Bay State's hours of work laws in these circumstances would be tantamount to "going back to the old times," Thompson stated. Conversely, by maintaining the present restrictions "we in Massachusetts . . . can well keep on . . . leading the way so far as humane conditions pertaining to women and children in industry are concerned."[71]

Flora Durant, who worked at the time in a mill in Salem, Massachusetts, defended the existing hours of work laws through a somewhat contradictory mix of women's domestic role and women's rights. Class resentments and the demands of factory labor also figured prominently in her thinking. Durant endorsed the prevailing belief that women's place was in the home, holding that only the low wages received by men made female jobs like her own necessary. She clearly resented the dirty nature of textile labor, describing in vivid terms the effects of the omnipresent cotton dust. Durant was keenly aware that women of higher social classes did not have to do this kind of work. "We are the ones . . . furnishing the money" that allowed wealthy females to "dress . . . up nice and pretty," she asserted. Durant saw the existing laws as promoting women's rights, stating that the regulations were justified "because the women are entitled to freedom as much as the men." She conceived of this liberty in rather limited terms, arguing that the hours restrictions freed up time for female operatives "to do their home work, and other things they have to take care of." Durant closed by describing the health risks of cotton dust and the fast pace of mill labor. She concluded: "Forty-eight hours is long enough for women to work under those conditions."[72]

Expansion of the Massachusetts Welfare State in the Era of Textile Decline

Laws on female working hours in manufacturing were just part of the network of social protections enacted by Massachusetts in the industrial era to shield its residents from the pressures of the market economy. Despite the sagging manufacturing base and the costs that social measures imposed on producers, the commonwealth's nascent welfare state continued to develop in the period after World War I. Social protections were bolstered in a range of areas. Unions and social reformers were the prime advocates of such expansive government action.

In the field of workmen's compensation, Bay State lawmakers broadened coverage in at least sixteen of the twenty-one legislative sessions between 1911, when the program was established, and 1934. Some of the most important additions occurred during the program's early years, but reforms continued after World War I. Changes in 1923 and 1924 reduced the period after injury during which workers received no benefits from ten days to seven and then, in serious cases, to none. A 1926 law allowed for workmen's compensation payments to certain parents upon the death of a minor child. In 1927 the legislature substantially increased the maximum benefit. A 1929 change gave added leeway to dependents of deceased workers seeking full benefits in cases where an earlier injury later resulted in death. Additionally, rulings during this period by the courts and by the state board overseeing compensation extended coverage to the effects of occupational diseases as well as accidents.[73]

Protections expanded in other areas as well. The Bay State's social efforts entered a new domain with the enactment of old age pensions. After considering various proposals for public relief of indigent retired persons in the 1920s, the legislature in 1930 established a limited system of payments to "deserving citizens" seventy years and older who had resided in the state for twenty years.[74] Massachusetts additionally emerged as a national leader during the Depression years in the effort to cushion the blow of cyclical unemployment. Special state commissions studying this issue proposed scheduling state construction projects to counteract economic downturns and then compulsory unemployment reserve funds to be maintained by employers. A third commission was at work on a plan for a full-blown state unemployment insurance program when Congress enacted national jobless insurance guidelines as part of the Social Security Act of 1935.[75]

Business interests fought hard in this era against each accretion in the Massachusetts welfare state. Lobbying against such programs in the state legislature was the principal mission of the manufacturers' organization AIM. In making the case against further social legislation, business interests unfailingly pointed out the additional burdens these measures would impose on the state's struggling industries.[76] On the whole, the corporate sector's efforts fell short. AIM lobbying did succeed in limiting the increase in the maximum workmen's compensation benefit to 12.5 percent, rather than the 25 percent jump many expected, during a 1927 overhaul of the system.[77] But the overall trend, even in the conservative 1920s and despite the decline of manufacturing in Massachusetts, was toward a broader system of social protection, with new programs, more inclusive coverage, and higher levels of benefits.

National Implications of Battles over Social Legislation in 1920s Massachusetts

Massachusetts battles over social legislation have implications for assessing the national labor movement of this period. Bay State unions of the 1920s mounted a potent defense of existing labor hours protections and on this issue seemingly provided decisive leadership for the working class. Moreover, virtually all of the unionists at the forefront of the fight were affiliated, then or previously, with the craft-based, exclusionary AFL. The vitality Massachusetts labor displayed in the political arena during this period seems at odds with the portrait of a weak and dispirited AFL-led union movement that appears in earlier and more recent labor scholarship on the 1920s.[78] The Bay State experience suggests that the established picture of 1920s American unions as completely moribund may require some modification.

Events in the commonwealth may also throw added light on the oft-remarked reluctance of most old-line unionists to capitalize on the conducive environment for organizing of the early New Deal years. This lack of enthusiasm ultimately led frustrated industrial unionists in the AFL to break away and set up a new group, the CIO, which aggressively sought increased membership.[79]

The union impulse originates in workers' desire to improve conditions at the place of employment. But channeling the political potential of the working class to shape government policy in a favorable manner has always been a key additional goal of the labor movement. Massachusetts in the 1920s looked like unfavorable terrain for achieving union policy aims, given the dramatic downsizing of traditional industries and the dominance of state government by the business-oriented Republican Party. Yet on the hours of work, and other issues such as workmen's compensation and old age pensions, Bay State unionists of the 1920s got their way. In the eyes of established labor leaders, this may have been an additional reason, beyond the craft pride, antipathy to radicalism, and ethnic condescension commonly cited by scholars, for indifference to organizing. From the standpoint of achieving policy goals, an expanded labor movement might not have seemed necessary to these officials. As events had demonstrated, desired results could be secured with unions of modest size.

Business Demands for Tax and Spending Reduction in Massachusetts

Corporate taxes and public spending were another domain in which business groups pushed for retrenchment as the Massachusetts economy slipped into difficulty in the 1920s. Government levies on manufacturing corporations rose sharply during this era, and business groups insistently campaigned for reductions in these taxes. Local levies accounted for the bulk of Massachusetts taxes paid by business at this time, and demands for tax reduction focused at the local level. The property taxes paid by textile firms and other manufacturers were the locus of attention. The period's tax increases were driven by ballooning government expenditures, particularly by municipalities. In response, business interests also sought to enact controls over local spending.

The campaign by Massachusetts business for tax and spending reduction encountered numerous obstacles in the years following World War I. Repeated attempts to put formal controls on local government expenditures failed completely, and efforts to cut taxes encountered numerous rebuffs. In the end, however, business achieved signal successes on fiscal questions. Cities that had sharply raised property tax assessments on textile companies during and after World War I cut them drastically in the latter part of the 1920s. In some municipalities hit by plant closures, low levies on manufacturing became a central component in the drive for recovery. Additionally, the state of Massachusetts heeded a longstanding demand of cotton textile makers and in 1936 took the important step of exempting manufacturing machinery from local property taxes. The retrenchment drive launched by business in response to industrial decline was thus much more successful in securing tax cuts than in rolling back or containing the growth of social legislation.

A prime reason this was so was that efforts to cut taxes faced much less resistance than moves against social legislation. Particular interest groups did oppose changes to the tax system that threatened to increase the levies they would pay. Nevertheless, the push to reduce taxes on manufacturing faced nothing like the determined mobilization of unions and reform groups in defense of the hours of work laws. Indeed, unionists in at least one mill city supported reduced assessments on textile firms, and the bill exempting manufacturing machinery from local taxation had the endorsement of the Massachusetts AFL. Labor saw reductions in the taxes on manufacturing as a worthy means to help revive failing industries. By contrast, business efforts to place additional controls on local expenditures encountered firm resistance from representatives of the municipalities concerned. The proposed spending limits did not come close to implementation.

Sharp increases in public revenue and expenditures during and after World War I set the stage for the corporate drive for tax and spending reduction in the 1920s. State and local expenditures doubled in Massachusetts between 1916 and 1926. Since government at this time was largely a parochial affair, the preponderance of the fiscal burden fell at the local level. Massachusetts counties and municipalities (mostly the latter) collected $237 million worth of taxes in 1926, far outweighing state tax collections of $41 million. Moreover, local taxes increased more rapidly in this period, jumping 106 percent between 1916 and 1926, while state levies rose 75 percent. With most of the tax burden falling at the municipal and county level, the local tax payments of commonwealth manufacturers in 1929 were almost three times larger than their payments to state government. The fiscal take in Massachusetts was large compared to other American states. Only three jurisdictions had higher state and local taxes in 1922 on a per capita basis. In 1929, after years of agitation on the issue, the commonwealth's tax bite was still the sixth highest in the country.[80]

Dramatic increases in the services provided by local government drove the large tax hikes of this era in Massachusetts. Jumps in expenditures were particularly dramatic in education, where spending more than doubled in the ten years up to 1925 due to great expansion of the public schools. Growing use of automobiles also pushed up budgets as local governments made large outlays for roads, highways, and bridges and to motorize police departments. Significant increases in public spending occurred in many U.S. locations in the 1920s, and the rising tax burden of state and local government provoked political resistance across the country.[81]

During and after World War I, taxes on Massachusetts textile manufacturers increased by at least as much as overall levies in the state. Taxes on a representative sample of Bay State cotton mills jumped to more than two-and-a-half times their previous level in nominal terms, rising from 25.3 cents per spindle in 1915 to 68.5 cents per spindle in 1920. Levies remained at that elevated level into the late 1920s.[82] In the cotton manufacturing center of Fall River, city officials increased the property taxes due from textile companies through inflated mill assessments. (In Massachusetts, as in most states, all property owners in a jurisdiction were taxed each year at the same rate. The value assigned to a piece of property by local assessors was thus the key variable in determining the taxes due.) The total assessment on the mills of Fall River rose from $43 million in 1917 to $101 million in 1921. The assessed valuation of the nontextile corporations and individually owned properties making up the rest of the Fall River tax base did not increase to nearly the same extent.[83] Assessments on the Fall River cotton firms declined in the following years, but remained relatively high, and even increased by $10 million in 1926. Table 2.1 shows assessments on cotton companies and other city property owners during this period. Fall River cotton firms paid their taxes under pro-

Table 2.1. Assessments on Textile Corporations and All Other Taxpayers in Fall River, Massachusetts, Selected Years, 1917–1932

	Total Assessment on Textile Corporations ($ million)	Total Assessment on All Others[a] ($ million)	Number of Textile Spindles (millions)
1917	43.1	67.2	3.79
1919	60.0	72.2	3.76
1921	100.6	91.5	3.81
1923	89.9	98.0	3.76
1925	75.1	131.4	3.65
1926	85.4	128.7	3.71
1927	71.3	117.6	3.67
1928	54.7	107.0	3.35
1930	43.9	105.1	2.68
1932	17.0	95.4	1.95

Note: a. Non-textile corporations and all individually owned businesses and residences.

Source: Calculated from figures in Donahue, *Causes of the Financial Breakdown*, 32.

test in this era. In a court case decided in 1925, the mills won refunds of $1 million on previously paid taxes, with additional refunds ordered in ensuing years. A city official involved in these cases later admitted that the Fall River mills had been "overassessed."[84] Similar realities apparently transpired in the mill city of New Bedford. There the share of total city assessments accounted for by cotton firms rose from 35.4 percent in 1910 to 47.3 percent in 1920.[85]

The taxes paid by the state's manufacturers was an important question in Massachusetts politics even before traditional New England industries entered a spiral of decline in the early 1920s. The issue drew increasing attention as the decade progressed. AIM, the association representing all commonwealth manufacturers, campaigned during the early 1920s for cuts in state spending and taxes. Under a succession of Republican governors, the state government reduced outlays and limited the commonwealth's debt.[86] Austerity at the state level brought little benefit to manufacturing, however, since most of the Massachusetts tax burden emanated from local government. At mid-decade the focus of business lobbying thus shifted to reducing the local tax bite. Property taxes—the principal source of revenue for local government—were the principal issue. Demands for lower levies on the property of the troubled textile mills attracted particular attention. In 1926 AIM kicked off a drive to reduce local levies on industry. The organization's weekly journal declared that rapacious municipal officials were driving the "gold-egg hens" of industry out of the state. AIM published tables comparing property tax rates in cities across the commonwealth and lauded the efforts of local finance commissions, usually made up of businessmen, to restrain spending.[87] The Massachusetts section of the New England Council went into action on the local tax question the following year. A panel at the organization's summer 1927 meeting highlighted methods of reducing municipal levies and expenditures. At a conference that September John Tinsley, executive of a textile machinery manufacturing firm and chairman of the New England Council's Massachusetts section, reported that high taxes constituted a distinct obstacle to economic development. Tinsley asserted that the Bay State was generally believed to have "exceedingly burdensome" levies on industry and that this view was having "a weighty influence with industrial managements as to the wisdom of planning future growth in this section, or even continuing operations at all."[88]

The demands of business associations for lower local taxes on manufacturing became entwined during the late 1920s in a broader effort to reform the entire Massachusetts taxation system. Observers concurred that the state's patchwork of levies, the result of repeated legislative tinkering, was arbitrary and unwieldy. State taxes on corporations and personal income were poorly conceived, and local government raised too much of its revenue from the property tax.[89] Beginning in 1927 and continuing every year through 1931, special legislative commissions investigated the tax system and tried to formulate solutions. Despite five years of effort, little was accomplished.[90] Tax reform is always a dicey political proposition. Few interest groups willingly accede to the tax increases required to offset reductions in unduly onerous levies. In addition, the impact of proposed changes is often unclear, leaving many parties fearful that they will pay more under the new system than had previously been the case.

The drive to cut levies on manufacturing crossed paths in the latter part of 1927 with the push to overhaul the state's taxation system. As the first special commission on tax reform gathered evidence, the NACM, lobby for the cotton manufacturers, mounted its own campaign to reduce the fiscal bite of local government. Ward Thoron of the Merrimack Manufacturing Company, point man in the drive to ease the state's hours of work laws, chaired the NACM committee on tariffs and taxation and spearheaded this effort as well. To bolster its case, the NACM issued a report on the local taxes paid by Massachusetts cotton producers. The study highlighted the steep increases in municipal levies on Bay State mills in recent years and asserted that textile firms in the South paid local taxes that were from 28 to 57 percent lower. The report claimed that high taxes had contributed to the widespread closures of Massachusetts cotton firms in the preceding years: "Mills have been forced out of business due partly to heavy taxation in competition with other mills in localities where the taxes are [significantly] less."[91]

To alleviate the burden, the cotton manufacturers renewed longstanding requests for a change in the way they were taxed. Under the existing system, corporations paid local property taxes on their real estate and machinery, with the latter accounting for more than half of the total assessment. The cotton makers wanted manufacturing equipment exempted from local taxation, so that companies would pay local levies only on their buildings and land. To make up the lost revenue, Thoron proposed an increase in the state tax on corporate income, with the proceeds to be distributed to municipalities that had lost property tax revenue.[92] The idea of reducing the local tax burden of textile manufacturers won some support outside the industry at this time. The association of local Massachusetts assessors called for the property taxes of the state's textile producers to be cut by one-third to increase competitiveness and considered a more far-reaching proposal to reduce property taxes on textile machinery to a fraction of the current rates.[93]

The legislature's 1927 special commission on tax reform evinced little sympathy for the proposals to reduce levies on cotton mills or on all manufacturing corporations. The panel's report conceded that assessments on textile mills had risen "beyond all reason" in the era of wartime prosperity, and that in the present depressed state of the industry these valuations were "out of all proportion" to the actual value of company property. The commission nevertheless declared itself unwilling to endorse the NACM's "radical" proposal to exempt manufacturing machinery from local taxation. The panel's report voiced what appeared to be striking indifference to the hardships of textile producers:

> Excessive taxation is only one of the causes that is driving the textile industry from Massachusetts. It may have been one of the important factors bringing about the decline, but at the present time no reduction in taxes can give any substantial relief to the industry as a whole.... [The proposed tax reduction] would save but a comparatively few of the mills that are going to the wall.[94]

Manufacturers could find something to like in the work of the 1927 special commission.[95] Though mandated only to investigate taxes, panel members maintained that taxes and spending were inextricably linked and devoted considerable energy to examining government expenditures, especially at the local level. In preliminary conclusions, the commission endorsed the oft-expressed (and well-grounded) contention of business and conservatives that local spending was out of control. Its report cited "the recognized tendency of school boards ... to spend all the money they can lay their hands upon" and "the wastage which seems to be inherent in our municipal form of government."[96] The panel recommended that the legislature mount a separate inquiry into municipal expenditures, alongside the continuing study of taxes. AIM and the Massachusetts division of the New England Council lobbied with enthusiasm for the proposed spending investigation, doubtless believing that it could lead to meaningful state action to hold down city budgets.

The legislature approved the formation of a special commission on municipal spending. But any hopes of business groups that the investigation would inaugurate a new era of austerity in city finances were grievously disappointed. The expenditures commission refused to recommend the elimination of, or even reductions in, the spending for any item in local government budgets. Its report focused instead on ways of streamlining city outlays through modern techniques such as pooled purchasing and improved budget procedures. Business groups undoubtedly favored the adoption of up-to-date methods in city finances, but they had clearly hoped that this investigation would result in more hard-hitting proposals to rein in spendthrift local officials. To make matters worse, the legislature refused the expenditure commission's request that its work be continued for another year, halting for the time being the possibility of state action to limit municipal spending.[97]

Business interests had little more success in the further iterations of the state's tax investigation. The 1927 special commission's strong opposition to exempting manufacturing machinery from local levies killed that issue for years to come. The 1929 special commission showed considerable interest in less dramatic reductions in the taxes on industry. Its plan for a one-third cut in the state corporate excise would have afforded manufacturers some relief. The proposal ran into opposition from various interest groups, however, and was in the end tabled.[98]

Pressure to reduce taxes and municipal expenditures in the commonwealth continued to build during the early Depression years. The Massachusetts Industrial Commission, a newly established state development agency, called in 1930 for reductions in taxes on manufacturing and for fairer assessments of textile mills. A 1931 consultant's study carried out for the Industrial Commission affirmed the views of numerous corporate executives that heavy taxes on industry were a significant "impediment to industrial progress in this State." The New England Council also stepped up its activity on fiscal issues. In 1930, the Massachusetts division of the New England Council helped organize the Massachusetts Tax Association (MTA), which brought together business and a range of other interest groups. The MTA planned to investigate whether commonwealth industries were overburdened by taxes and to reopen the vexed question of limiting municipal expenditures. Although the Depression led to increased demands for fiscal reforms, in other ways the slump eased pressures for change. Massachusetts business groups increasingly worried as the economy worsened that alterations to the tax code could further disrupt commercial conditions. State-level agitation on fiscal issues therefore focused on a renewed push for action to limit municipal expenditures.[99]

An important move in this direction took place when the MTA called for Massachusetts to emulate steps taken elsewhere and set up a state agency to regulate municipal spending. The MTA proposed to the 1931 special commission on taxation that such an entity be established. The powerful body, to be called the Board of Municipal Finance, would investigate plans for certain types of city borrowing. It would also hear taxpayer appeals against "extravagant or unwarranted" appropriations, cutting those found lacking in merit. The 1931 special commission approved the proposal, although the usual unanimity could not be mustered. Two of the panel's seven members opposed the plan, including a Democrat from heavily Irish Catholic South Boston who was doubtless steeped in the area's patronage politics.[100]

A bill to establish the Board of Municipal Finance was introduced in the 1932 legislative session. At hearings before the committee on municipal finance, speakers from the MTA headed the testimony on behalf of the bill, with one tax expert asserting that the measure was necessary to rein in "heedless" city spending. Representatives of AIM, the Boston Chamber of Commerce, the Massachusetts Chamber of Commerce, and the Boston Real Estate Exchange also appeared in support. Opposition came from several Boston city officials who deemed the proposal to be unworkable and denied that municipal budgets were out of control. A municipal finance committee member representing Worcester also voiced doubts, arguing that the public was sufficiently protected against unwarranted local spending through its power to vote offenders out of office. The panel referred the proposal to the following year's legislative session, where it was killed.[101]

Cotton manufacturers did win reductions in their local property taxes beginning in the later 1920s, even as proposals for systematically limiting municipal spending and cutting levies fell short. Table 2.1 demonstrates the dramatic fall in assessments on the cotton mills of Fall River in the latter part of the decade. After soaring during the years after 1917 and remaining at elevated levels in the mid-1920s, assessments on the city's cotton mills dropped steadily beginning in 1927. Although the change stemmed in part from the decline in Fall River spindleage as mills went out of business, the remaining cotton firms saw sharp drops in their assessed valuations.[102] Table 2.1 also demonstrates that assessments on the mills of Fall River dropped by a far greater extent than assessments on the city's nontextile property. Textile companies in other cities saw similar declines in their assessed valuations.

The decline in cotton company assessments in Massachusetts was consistent with the findings of the Fall River courts that valuations of that city's mills had been inflated. The drop in assessments also reflected the fall in the real value of mill property as depressed conditions and plant shutdowns spread through the New England textile industry. More than this was at work, however. Numerous textile cities reduced valuations as a means of aiding the cloth-making companies that remained in business and also as a way to attract new industry. In 1927 the New Bedford Board of Assessors announced a "complete realignment" of assessments on textile machinery. The new approach was expected to lead to significant tax reductions for the city's mills in the years to come. New Bedford also abated the tax bills of some companies for preceding years on the basis of the reduced machinery valuations. Tax abatements became a central element in the New Bedford redevelopment strategy, a policy supported by business owners and unionists alike. The city's mayor stated in the late 1930s that abatements were granted to manufacturers in exchange for guarantees that a certain number of workers would be employed for a stated period. Similarly, Lowell by early 1927 elected a mayor on a platform of lowering municipal taxes to stem further losses in manufacturing. Soon afterward the city reduced assessments on its textile companies by more than $6 million.[103] Lower assessments on existing textile firms, together with mill shutdowns that eliminated formerly important taxpayers, severely strained the finances of New England mill cities.[104]

Cloth-making companies, along with all other Massachusetts manufacturers, received a tax break of significant magnitude in the mid-1930s, on top of the reductions in property tax assessments granted by individual municipalities. Efforts that had begun in 1927 to overhaul the state taxation system sputtered out in the early 1930s. Little activity on fiscal reform took place in the ensuing years of deep economic depression. As recovery took hold in 1935, the issue resurfaced. With the governor calling for action and a raft of bills introduced on various tax questions, the legislature that year authorized another special commission on taxation. The NACM approached the panel, again calling for manufacturing machinery to be exempted from local property taxes. This time the idea found a warm reception. The commission endorsed the proposal, declaring in its January 1936 report that high levies had played an "important" part in the state's industrial decline over the last fifteen years.[105]

A bill to enact the change went before the state legislature soon afterward. The original proposal called for replacement revenue to be raised by extending the property tax to the inventories of nonmanufacturing corporations. Retailers turned out in force to oppose this plan. An alternative was then adopted whereby industry machinery would be removed from local assessors' rolls but added to the "corporate excess" that was taxed by state government. The corporate excess consisted of company assets not subject to local duties; the levy on it was part of the state's excise tax on corporations. The state rate on the corporate excess was $5 per $1,000 of valuation, as compared to local rates on property, including manufacturing machinery, that averaged $37.60 per $1,000 of valuation in the mid-1930s.[106] The precise degree of relief manufacturers would receive under the plan varied with local tax rates but would be dramatic in all cases. NACM estimates showed that a mill in Holyoke, Massachusetts, where the rate was $27.50 per $1,000, paid local taxes on machinery of $10,390 in 1935 but would have faced a state machinery levy of only $1,890 with the change in place. The proportional reduction would be even greater in Fall River, with a local rate of $42.00 per $1,000. There a company with local machinery taxes of $38,420 in 1935 would have owed the state only $4,570.[107] The proposed reform called for the funds raised through the state machinery levy to be distributed to municipalities where property taxes had been reduced. Since the new state tax would bring in less revenue than the local levies it replaced, manufacturing cities would experience a fiscal shortfall after these monies were distributed. Additional state transfers would help make up the difference during an interim period, and federal spending at the local level brought about by New Deal programs gave municipal officials some scope to reduce outlays. Still, in the long run the affected municipalities would likely be forced to cut spending or raise tax rates. The latter solution would result in higher levies on the residential and nonmanufacturing business real estate that made up the remainder of the local tax base.[108]

The modified tax reform proposal won support from a broad spectrum of interest groups. Representatives of AIM and the state AFL testified jointly in support of the bill at a legislative committee hearing. The legislative agent for the state AFL later explained that his organization supported the measure because it would "encourage manufacturing in Massachusetts," thereby producing "more employment and . . . increased pay-rolls." Witnesses from the NACM also spoke in favor of the measure at the hearing, and "scores" of manufacturers attended to express their support. State tax commissioner Henry Long, a longstanding advocate of reducing local taxes on industry, told lawmakers that the change would make a substantial contribution to the industrial revival of Massachusetts. No one appeared at the hearing to oppose the measure. The bill passed both houses of the legislature and was signed with enthusiasm by Democratic governor James Curley, a steadfast liberal.[109]

Massachusetts thus saw a striking turnaround on business taxation in the space of eight years. While the special commission of 1927 had rejected out of hand a plan to exempt manufacturing machinery from taxation, the special commission of 1935 strongly supported the idea. The proposal passed in modified form soon afterward, even though it included no permanent provision for replacing all the lost revenue. Continued structural decline in Massachusetts industry probably explains the reversal. The state's total manufacturing employment in 1927 stood at 578,000, with cotton textiles and shoes together accounting for 147,000 jobs. By 1936, the number of factory jobs had fallen to 481,000, with cotton textiles and shoes employing only 88,000. The Depression accounted for some of these losses, but many positions in textiles and shoemaking had disappeared permanently. Industrial decline clearly affected the thinking of members of the 1935 special commission on taxation. In recommending a sharp cut in the taxes on manufacturing, the panel's report stated that "idle factories and abandoned mills are the silent and convincing evidence of the disaster that has come upon our people."[110]

Conclusion

During periods of economic difficulty and industrial downsizing in the late twentieth century, U.S. corporate interests were able to secure tax reductions and favorable changes in government regulation. Of business-government relations in the years 1960–88, David Vogel concludes that "business has tended to lose political influence when the economy was performing relatively well and has become more influential when the performance of the economy deteriorated."[111] During the 1920s and 1930s in Massachusetts, the link between deindustrialization and retrenchment was less direct. Bay State business groups in the earlier period energetically demanded cuts in taxes, public spending, and social legislation as traditional industries downsized. Capital did not necessarily achieve the desired results, however. Manufacturers did win reductions in their taxes after lengthy effort. But attempts to roll back restrictions on the working hours of women and enact new controls over local government spending failed completely. Meanwhile, social programs such as old age pensions and workmen's compensation were introduced or expanded despite business opposition. The key factor in determining whether corporate pressure for retrenchment succeeded in post–World War I Massachusetts was the degree of resistance confronted. Where opposition was substantial, as with social legislation or efforts to limit municipal spending, cutbacks did not occur. Where resistance was limited and diffuse, as in reductions in the taxes on manufacturing, retrenchment took place. Thus, the relationship between the competitive strength of the economy and the political power of business does not appear to be fixed, as Vogel suggests, but instead contingent. Even in the context of economic decline, capitalists can secure changes in public policy only by mobilizing politically in a more effective manner than their opponents.

Business groups argued in the years after World War I that retrenchment in taxes and social legislation was necessary to restore competitiveness to Massachusetts industry. As a means of halting downsizing, such steps could do little. Despite substantial reductions in the taxes on manufacturing, traditional industry in the Bay State continued to decline. Fall River significantly reduced property tax assessments on textile firms beginning in the late 1920s. Local cotton companies nevertheless continued to close their doors, with the city's spindleage plummeting from 3.67 million in 1927 to 1.95 million in 1932. Among the cotton manufacturers that went out of business in neighboring New Bedford during the 1930s were two firms that made great efforts to remain in operation and received "heavy abatements" on their local tax bills.[112]

That the decline of cotton textiles proceeded despite reductions in the industry's taxes is not surprising. Government levies accounted for such a small part of overall mill costs that reducing them could not substantially aid beleaguered New England producers. Taxes amounted to approximately 3 percent of total production costs at northern mills, according to calculations performed at the time.[113] Even the radical and completely unrealistic step of abolishing all state and local levies on New England cotton producers would not have restored the region's mills to competitiveness. Nor would easing social legislation, such as limits on the hours of work, have substantially helped New England cotton makers. Most Massachusetts cotton manufacturers in the 1920s were unaffected by the state's stringent laws on working times. The hours of work restrictions in the other New England states did not differ dramatically from the limits in certain southern jurisdictions.

Of course, as examination of the motives of manufacturers seeking to roll back the hours of work laws shows, improving conditions for struggling textile firms was not necessarily a principal aim of the retrenchment campaign. Many of the corporate managers involved took advantage of public concern over realities in the industry to push for legal changes that had little bearing on the current competitive situation of their firms. It seems that they did so either to improve the position of their companies in a future more prosperous time or as an expression of hostility toward longtime adversaries in the labor movement.

A similar opportunism characterized the drive by Massachusetts manufacturers for reductions in taxes and local government spending. Producers from a wide range of sectors pushed for these steps, and the 1936 change in the Bay State's tax law exempted the machinery of all industrial firms from local taxation. Companies in troubled areas like cotton textiles got some small benefit from the resulting reduction in levies. However, much of the tax relief went to firms in fields such as metalworking that were in relatively good condition in this era and faced no grave competitive threat. In essence, manufacturers in the Bay State's prosperous industries piggybacked onto those from the struggling sectors to take advantage of public concerns over industrial decline. They won substantial unneeded tax relief as a result.

While retrenchment in taxes and social regulation could do little to ameliorate conditions in the troubled cotton textile industry of New England, federal intervention to equalize wages and hours at northern and southern producers had much greater potential to aid New England firms. Unionists and liberal activists worked to halt the erosion of northern industry through such action. Their efforts are examined in the next chapter.

CHAPTER 3

Federal Assistance

> Under Abraham Lincoln it was said that America cannot be half free and half slave. I think we could well paraphrase this phrase today and, particularly in the textile industry, we can say that America cannot remain half union and half sweatshop. You must defeat the sweatshop or the sweatshop will defeat you. You must bring up the standard of wages and hours in the South or the South will tear down the standards in the North.
>
> HENRY ELLENBOGEN, U.S. REPRESENTATIVE FROM PENNSYLVANIA, "ADDRESS TO HOSIERY WORKERS," 1937

Federal government assistance to industries and areas affected by factory closures was a central response to deindustrialization. Representatives of New England and of other locales hit by downsizing spearheaded efforts to secure federal aid.

New England leaders pursued a range of initiatives in response to the decline of textiles and other established industries. Seeking economic assistance from the federal government was the second of these efforts. Union officials and liberal activists had a central role in the drive to obtain government assistance and worked for far-reaching forms of federal aid.

Attempts to secure meaningful federal assistance for downsizing industries began during the New Deal, well after the other responses to deindustrialization were initiated. The delay was no accident. In the 1920s, when Republicans sympathetic to laissez-faire controlled national policymaking, there was no possibility of serious federal action to counter industrial decline. With Franklin Roosevelt and reform-minded Democratic legislators firmly in power in the mid-1930s, strong federal measures addressing deindustrialization could finally be considered.

During the 1930s, the push for federal assistance to the troubled cotton textile industry of New England focused on national regulation of labor standards. New England cotton manufacturers were being undercut at this time by open-shop southern producers that paid lower wages and had more onerous working conditions. Federal restrictions that created nationwide uniformity in wages and working hours would reduce and potentially eliminate the competitive advantage of Dixie's low-cost fabric manufacturers. Such action would save the remaining textile firms of New England and other northern locations.

Cotton manufacturers took the first steps toward harmonizing labor standards in textiles. Attempting to stabilize markets in their depressed industry, the manufacturers, beginning in the late 1920s, sought to implement voluntary controls over working conditions. These efforts were unsuccessful. But they laid the groundwork for the mandatory regulation of minimum labor standards under the National Industrial Recovery Act (NIRA), the Roosevelt administration's 1933 program for restoring industrial prosperity. NIRA controls improved conditions in cotton textiles to an extent. The Supreme Court's spring 1935 decision voiding the NIRA left a regulatory vacuum.

Union leaders and liberal officials then stepped forward with proposals for comprehensive regulation of labor standards in textiles and other industries. Prompted by textile union officers, liberal U.S. representative Henry Ellenbogen introduced several bills in Congress beginning in August 1935 for strictly regulating labor standards in the cloth-making sector. The original version of the Fair Labor Standards Act (FLSA), presented in 1937, embodied a similar approach on a more sweeping scale. Authored by prominent Roosevelt administration liberals and backed by the president, the measure would have applied the tight controls Ellenbogen envisaged to any industry where low labor standards at some producers threatened to undermine better conditions elsewhere. Both the Ellenbogen bills and the original version of the FLSA would have stabilized conditions definitively in cotton textiles, thereby protecting the remaining manufacturers of the North. The decisive role of union officials in initiating the Ellenbogen plan reflected the greatly enlarged influence of labor in the New Deal era.

The Ellenbogen bills and the original 1937 draft of the FLSA encountered strong opposition from southerners and conservatives and did not win approval. The version of the FLSA that passed in 1938 set only minimum labor standards and had a limited impact on the textile industry. In the absence of comprehensive federal regulation of working conditions, low-cost producers in the South continued to undercut beleaguered northern cloth manufacturers. Ongoing mill shutdowns took place in the North as a result.

Manufacturers' Voluntary Efforts to Stabilize the Cotton Industry

The ongoing southern takeover of cotton textiles created the conditions that made schemes to stabilize the industry appear necessary. With low wages and a steadily expanding product line, manufacturers in the Piedmont section of the southeastern states claimed a growing share of the American market for cotton cloth in the decades after Reconstruction. In the 1920s, Dixie firms began to force the long-established, higher-wage fabric manufacturers of the North out of business. The majority of northern firms remained in operation, at least initially, in the face of the southern challenge. As a result, cotton textiles had excess capacity for most of the period between the world wars, leading to surplus output of cloth and savagely competitive markets. Conditions were worst in the North, but even southern cotton manufacturers were hurt by persistently low prices and profits.[1] Overcapacity and falling demand plagued other sectors of the textile industry during the 1920s and 1930s, including knit goods, wool, and silk and rayon.

In response to the poor conditions in cotton textiles, leading manufacturers sought to stabilize markets for cotton cloth through coordinated action that would restrict output and force up prices. Improving labor standards in cotton mills was the prime means of stabilization pursued. Manufacturers' efforts ended up demonstrating both the potential of uniform labor standards to bring order to a highly competitive industry and the inability of voluntary restrictions to accomplish this end.

A new national trade group spearheaded the stabilization effort in cotton textiles. Until the 1920s there had been two principal organizations of cotton manufacturers, reflecting the regional division of the industry. The National Association of Cotton Manufacturers (NACM) represented New England firms and the small number of cotton producers in the mid-Atlantic states. Companies based in the South came together in the American Cotton Manufacturers Association (ACMA). As the cotton sector's post–World War I slump continued, leading manufacturers worked to bring the rival wings of the industry together for united action. This was accomplished in 1926, when representatives of the NACM and the ACMA set up a third organization, the Cotton Textile Institute (CTI), which was national in scope.[2]

The CTI initially sought to strengthen the market for cotton goods through statistical exchanges. This was a stabilization device seen frequently in the era. Under the CTI plan, manufacturers exchanged statistics on output, inventories, and orders. When the numbers indicated a surplus, companies were supposed to cut back production until supply came into line with demand. The program had little success. Even when the data indicated overproduction, many operators did not reduce output. Moreover, participation in the statistical exchanges was far from universal. Indeed, many companies did not initially join the CTI. Firms controlling only 63 percent of the industry's spindleage had become members by 1929, despite energetic recruiting.[3]

The efforts of cotton textile manufacturers to resolve their problems through a new national business association exemplified the "associational" ideals of the 1920s. Promulgated by Commerce Secretary Herbert Hoover and widely popular among corporate leaders, associationalism held that the cooperative activities of groups of capitalists could successfully address most social and economic problems.[4] Hoover saw CTI activities as embodying this philosophy and supported the organization's work. He publicly saluted the creation of the CTI and maneuvered behind the scenes to shield the group from any possibility of an anti-trust challenge.[5]

Backing private-sector efforts was as far as top Republicans were willing to go in addressing the troubled circumstances in cotton. Hoover and the other GOP officials who controlled national policymaking after 1920 were determined to constrain the activities of the federal government. Leading Republicans therefore did not consider more far-reaching measures to address the cotton industry's problems that would have entailed significant federal intervention.

The difficult conditions in cotton textiles that led to the CTI's creation significantly worsened with the onset of the Great Depression. As the overall level of economic activity declined, consumers and industrial buyers cut back on purchases of cotton fabric. The CTI responded to the deepening crisis by stepping up its market stabilization efforts. Pursuing a new strategy, industry leaders sought to establish uniform labor standards as a means of reducing output. First came a plan to cap working hours. In 1930 the CTI proposed limiting factory operations to 55 hours per week on the day shift and 50 hours at night. The scheme would reduce to a degree the long running times seen in southern plants. By early 1931, after months of lobbying manufacturers to go along, the limitation in hours was achieved in much of the industry. Market conditions continued to deteriorate, however. CTI leaders then pressed for a more ambitious program of ending night work by women and children. The arrangement was expected to reduce output on the night shift run by many mills. Following a lengthy campaign to secure manufacturers' participation, the night work restriction plan went into effect in 1931 and continued the following year. Once again, the significant efforts had little impact. Second-shift production continued unabated in many Dixie mills as managers substituted male workers, widely available during the Depression, for women and children. In late 1932, due to a drop in manufacturer participation, the plan was formally abandoned in key segments of the industry. Herbert Hoover, who by this time was U.S. president, continued in the early 1930s to back CTI efforts. He and Commerce Secretary Robert Lamont sought to help CTI leaders carry out the association's program by repeatedly endorsing the organization's work.[6]

The unwieldiness of the textile industry was one obstacle to CTI efforts to stabilize cotton cloth markets through coordinated, voluntary action. With hundreds of producers scattered along the eastern seaboard, a great deal of effort was required to put *any* stabilization plan into effect. Incomplete adherence to CTI programs was another serious difficulty. Participation was never universal in any of the stabilization schemes. At all times a hard core of resisters refused to take part in joint control programs. Louis Galambos, author of the definitive study of the CTI, calls such individuals "nonconformers." Contemporary observers and fellow industrialists knew them by the less charitable term "chiselers."

Several groups made up the nonconformer element in cotton textiles. In the South many of the nonconforming companies were small and had been established relatively recently. Such firms were likely to be located in quasi-rural towns.[7] These operators were the low-cost producers of Dixie and accounted for much of the region's recent growth in capacity. Determined individualism seemingly accounts for the behavior of another set of nonconformers who were present in both regions. Elliot Springs, a major southern manufacturer who reveled in his abstention from market-stabilizing schemes, probably represented well the mentality of these textile makers. Years later Springs sketched out a three-part taxonomy of the sector's managers. Included were the insider, who "sits . . . on the platforms of all [trade association] banquets and will always agree to shut down for the good of the industry"; and the incompetent, who "runs his plant at capacity until his warehouse is full of cloth . . . then . . . makes speeches about cutthroat competition and . . . clamors for everyone else to shut down." Springs the nonconformer placed himself in a third category: "the Bastard, First Class . . . [who] runs his mills twenty-four hours a day . . . makes the finest cloth in the market . . . [and] has never curtailed for the good of the industry."[8]

"First Class Bastard" individualism probably motivated most of the nonconforming cloth manufacturers of the North. The region's companies seemingly had everything to gain from the CTI's voluntary stabilization plans. Many firms in the area could not land enough orders to necessitate a night shift or even to run all the daytime hours permitted under the 55–50 plan. A strong CTI made it more likely that competing southern mills would face the same constraints. Nonetheless, quite a few northern companies declined to join the CTI when it first formed. Galambos reports that a "surprisingly large" number of the northern region's mills refused to participate in the program banning night work by women and children.[9]

With a fringe of nonconformers producing a steady flow of low-price fabric that undercut voluntary stabilization efforts, bringing order to the cotton industry would clearly require stronger action. Future programs would need legal standing that would compel nonconforming mills to respect the will of the majority. An effective stabilization scheme would also have to regulate more aspects of the manufacturing process, including wages. After years of ineffective CTI efforts, leading industry voices began calling for just such steps. In 1932, the president of the New England–based NACM endorsed the idea of congressional action to limit working hours, establish a minimum wage, and ban female and child labor on the night shift. The head of the ACMA, representing southern fabric makers, similarly declared that "we must have some form of economic control" and called for federal legislation to make this possible.[10]

The National Industrial Recovery Act

Passage of the National Industrial Recovery Act (NIRA) in the first months of the Roosevelt administration gave textile industry leaders the opportunity to put these aims into practice. The NIRA was the new president's principal program for ending the Depression. It sought to bring about industrial recovery through a business planning approach in which trade associations would set mandatory controls over prices, wages, and output. The strategy had broad support in the corporate sector. The legislation's principal concession to labor and reform forces was section 7(a), which guaranteed workers the right to organize and select collective bargaining agents of their own choosing.[11] The NIRA suspended the anti-trust laws for two years and authorized the president to approve codes of fair trade practice drawn up by trade associations for their individual industries. The legislation required each industrial code to include provisions for maximum hours, minimum wages, and acceptable working conditions. Other forms of control, such as restrictions on prices and output, were neither authorized nor outlawed.[12] The NIRA entailed an unprecedented level of public-sector intervention in the peacetime economy. The program reflected the great enthusiasm among Roosevelt administration officials for government action that would address national economic ills.

Cotton industry representatives had an active role in the events leading to the NIRA's passage. CTI officers touted the benefits of mandatory self-regulation to national business leaders beginning in 1931. After the 1932 election, they lobbied Roosevelt's advisers for some form of mandatory action, worked on early drafts of what became the NIRA, and met with FDR to discuss the issue. Diverse New England interests also weighed in on behalf of strong government measures. Massachusetts textile unionists joined with the state's cloth manufacturers in a March 1933 resolution calling on Roosevelt to take "emergency action to bring about uniform hours of labor and elimination of the employment of women and minors at night in the textile industry." John S. Lawrence, past New England Council president and an FDR acquaintance, wrote to the chief executive to urge "suspen[sion] of the Sherman Anti-Trust law" and government authority "to enforce curtailment in any industry." Roosevelt, in turn, had the plight of the cotton industry prominently in mind as the recovery legislation took shape. In public statements in the spring of 1933, he repeatedly cited the example of cotton textiles to illustrate the larger problem of nonconforming, or "unfair," employers and the necessity of legally enforced cooperative arrangements to stabilize industrial conditions.[13]

Eager to get a model industrial code into operation, administration officials asked cotton textile leaders to begin writing one weeks before the NIRA received final congressional approval.[14] An industry committee made up of manufacturers from the North and South and other business representatives had a draft code ready days after the NIRA became law in June 1933. The proposal was scrutinized at a hearing held by the National Recovery Administration (NRA), the agency set up to supervise implementation of the act. Critiques from unionists and reformers led to a number of changes. The revised code was then submitted to Roosevelt and implemented by executive order in July 1933.

The new cotton textile code limited the industry's mills to two 40-hour work shifts per week. This 40–40 plan, as it was known, represented a sharp decrease in the hours run by many southern mills, and a cut from the voluntary 55–50 schedule earlier promoted by the CTI. The code also established minimum wages. Drafters were aware that fully eliminating the gap in pay between the factories of the North and South "would have sparked a revolt by southern management" and thus settled on a one-dollar weekly differential. Wage minimums were eventually set at $12 for a full 40-hour week at southern mills and $13 in the North. To prevent increases in manufacturing capacity, the Code Authority that would administer the regulations had to approve the installation of new machinery. As required by the NIRA, the code included a clause guaranteeing textile workers the right to organize and bargain collectively. The industry committee that had drafted the code and essentially represented the CTI was designated as the Code Authority that would enforce the regulations.

The cotton code at first looked like a powerful tool for recovery, as a miniboom in the summer of 1933 bolstered output and employment throughout the industry. Cotton mills took on tens of thousands of new workers, with employment reaching an all-time high of 466,000 in September 1933. The turnaround was particularly dramatic in New England, where cloth factories saw the best conditions since just after World War I. In Massachusetts the employment index for cotton textiles rose 54 percent between May and November 1933.[15] Unfortunately the upturn did not signal a permanent improvement in markets but was rather a temporary surge in demand spurred by the enactment of New Deal recovery programs. Observers expected the wage increases fixed by the cotton code to push up manufacturing costs and prices for finished cloth. A new processing tax on raw cotton due to take effect in August 1933 under the Agricultural Adjustment Act (AAA) would further raise the expense of cotton goods. Buyers therefore rushed to place orders before the anticipated increases occurred.[16]

While implementation of the cotton code did not bring about a permanent recovery in textile markets, the fact that New England mills met so much of the temporary increase in demand stemmed directly from the more equal labor standards the code established in the two producing regions. The code's relatively high wage minimums forced firms in both sections to raise pay levels significantly. Even with the higher minimum in the North, the effect was more dramatic in the South. Between July 1933, on the eve of the code's imposition, and August 1934, average hourly earnings rose 56 percent in northern cotton mills but 80 percent in the South. As a result, the differential between wages at northern firms and wages at mills in the South narrowed over this period from 39 percent to 18 percent, the latter being the lowest figure in the

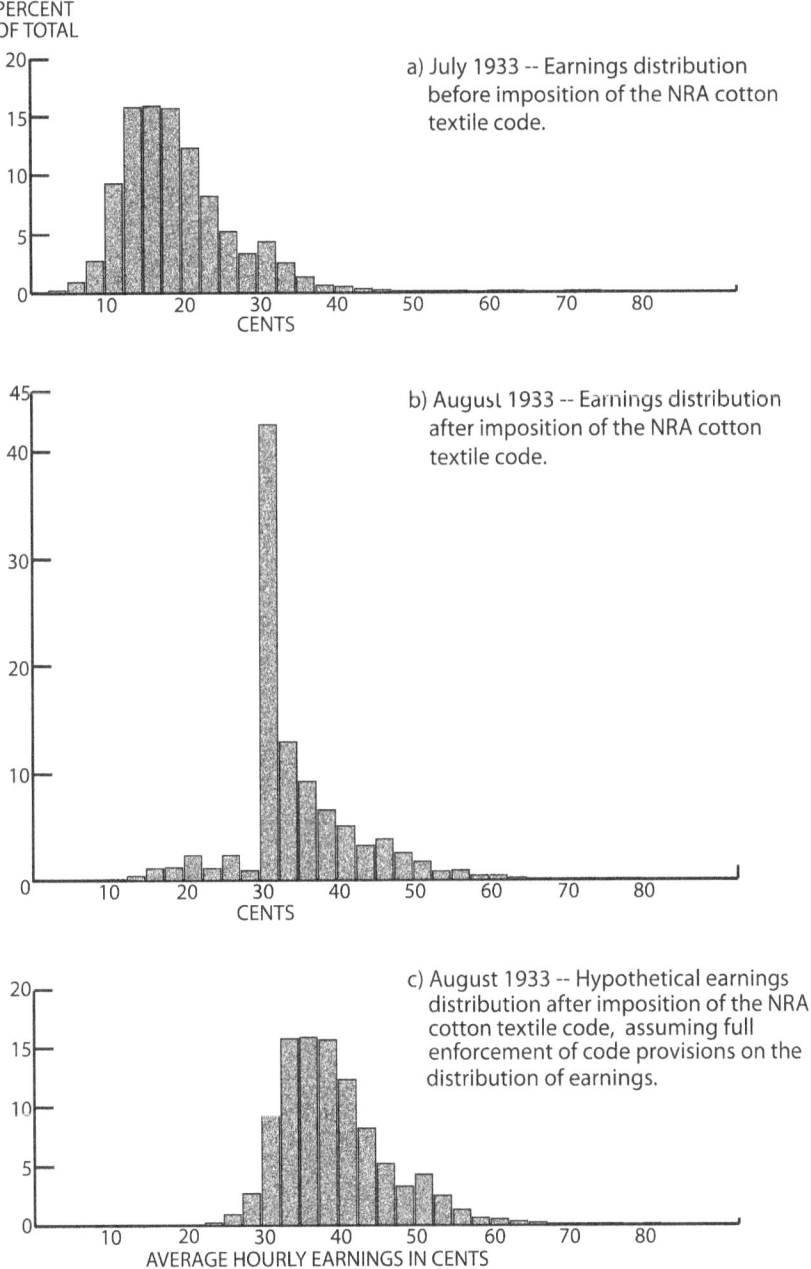

Figure 3.1. Percentage distribution of average hourly earnings for cotton textile workers in the South, before and after imposition of the NRA cotton textile code. *Source*: Hinrichs, *Wages in Cotton-Goods Manufacturing*, 118–19. Chart created by Jaehyun Kim and the author.

industry's history. Charts of the wage distribution for cotton textile workers in the South show a bell-shaped curve before the code but a large pile-up at $12 a week (30 cents an hour) afterward, as most hands saw their pay pushed up to the minimum. Panels (a) and (b) of figure 3.1 illustrate this effect.[17] The 40–40 restriction on work hours probably also aided New England firms. Numerous southern manufacturers had run their plants more than 100 hours a week prior to the code. The drop in their output resulting from the reduced operating times necessarily freed up space in the market for the products of other mills that had earlier run shorter schedules.[18]

The cotton industry's artificially induced recovery did not last long. In late 1933 demand fell off and inventories began to accumulate. In response the cotton Code Authority ordered 25 percent curtailments in working hours. As a result, the industry actually operated on a 30–30 schedule for several months in late 1933–early 1934 and again in spring 1935.[19] Overproduction and continuing weak demand brought on a renewed slump throughout the industry in late 1934. As competitive pressures closed in on the higher-cost New England mills, another wave of plant shutdowns swept through the region. The governor of Massachusetts estimated in March 1935 that cotton employment in his state, which had reached 45,000 in 1933, presently stood at 36,000. In Rhode Island the textile sector saw a "tidal wave of liquidations and removals."[20]

New England mills would have fared better in this period had all parts of the NRA cotton code been enforced. Mill owners seem to have respected code provisions relating to minimum wages and working hours—the sections most important to the industry leaders controlling the Code Authority. But other parts of the code that would have aided northern manufacturers vis-à-vis their competitors in the South were routinely ignored.

One important issue was the prohibition on increases in individual workloads that appeared in the code. During the 1920s, textile managers had frequently imposed heavier individual job responsibilities, the so-called "stretchout." When the NRA cotton code sharply increased wage costs, southern mill men sought corresponding increases in productivity. This generally meant a further intensification of the work process, since there were strict limits on the installation of new machinery. Stretchout "is the constant cry of the workers," one investigator reported from the Piedmont in 1934. The panel set up to investigate violations of the cotton code, known as the Bruere Board after chair Robert Bruere, did little to halt the increase in southern mill workloads.[21] A stronger response to Piedmont complaints about stretchout would have increased production expenses in Dixie, further narrowing the cost gap between northern and southern plants.

The Bruere Board disregarded another provision of the NRA cotton code that had key implications for the interregional dynamics of the industry. In the executive orders implementing the code, Roosevelt administration officials added a clause stating that the "amount of differences existing prior to [the code's imposition] between the wage rates paid various classes of employees receiving more than the established minimum wage were not to be decreased." This convoluted language meant that the pile-up of southern mill wages at the $12 a week (30 cents an hour) minimum described earlier should not have occurred. Instead, mill managers should have increased pay levels by the same amount for all southern workers, so that the wage distribution shifted upward while maintaining its original shape. (Appendix 2 demonstrates the wide variation in the wages received by different categories of textile workers before the NRA regulations took effect.) Thus, as mill workers previously receiving $10 a week were moved up to the weekly code minimum of $12, those who had earlier received $12 should have moved to $14, those earlier at $15 to $17, and so on. Panels (b) and (c) of figure 3.1 show the actual wage distribution at southern mills after the imposition of the cotton code and the hypothetical distribution that would have resulted if this provision had been implemented. NACM officials directed northern mill managers to adjust pay scales upward, as the regulations specified, when the cotton code took effect. The region's firms appear to have carried out these instructions. Wage increases along the same lines in the Piedmont would obviously have brought manufacturing costs at southern mills even closer to the levels prevailing among northern producers, improving the latter's competitive position. There seems to have been no attempt to enforce in Dixie mills the cotton code's provisions on the distribution of wages.[22]

Yet another provision of the NRA cotton code ignored by the Bruere Board was the protections for union organizing assured by section 7(a) of the NIRA and included in the code. Lack of action on this issue was crucial, as unions could have made a key contribution to resolving the problems in cotton textiles.

Unionization would have done a great deal to bring the labor standards of southern textile workers up to the levels prevailing in the Northeast, thereby stabilizing the industry. Indeed, unions could have accomplished this end much more effectively than the quasi-governmental regulation of the NRA. This is so because union contracts typically specify the pay levels of workers at each skill classification within a plant and often touch on issues such as individual workload as well. (Appendix 2 demonstrates the variation in cotton textile wages according to the level of worker skill.)

In industries with a large number of producers, such as cotton textiles, equalizing labor standards is central to the entire union effort. Companies in these sectors have a strong incentive to seek competitive advantage by lowering standards to reduce costs. To foreclose this possibility, unions in these industries strive to impose exactly the same terms of production on all companies. The collective bargaining arrangements of the textile craft unions of southeastern Massachusetts, the strongest in the industry before World War II, demonstrate the point. In New Bedford, the Textile Council represented all unionized workers and negotiated a single contract with the New Bedford Cotton Manufacturers Association. Wages and working conditions were thus identical at the dozens of city firms covered by the agreement.[23] Even with a powerful union presence in the South, labor standards would probably not have been completely uniform at all American textile mills.[24] But a strong national textile workers union would certainly have sought to bring standards in southern mills as close as possible to those in the North.

Leaders of the northern textile unions were well aware that collective bargaining could compress the cost advantage of southern firms by equalizing labor standards. Despite the conservative, localistic, craft-centered mentality of the AFL-affiliated United Textile Workers, it and several smaller, northern-based textile labor organizations fitfully attempted to organize Piedmont operatives. Union drives in the South during and after World War I and in 1929–30 had some successes but secured few lasting gains.[25]

During the early New Deal years, a union breakthrough in southern textiles appeared to be a serious possibility, despite the earlier setbacks. Like other American workers, Piedmont millhands took the collective bargaining protections spelled out in section 7(a) of the NIRA as a government endorsement of unionism. In the summer of 1933 southern cotton workers poured into union ranks in a largely spontaneous surge. By June 1934 the UTW claimed a nationwide membership of 250,000, more than six times the figure of a year earlier. Many of the new members were southerners.[26] Most Dixie textile manufacturers remained deeply hostile to organized labor and acted to repress the growing union presence. Southern managers ignored demands for collective bargaining, harassed and fired worker activists, and made pledges of nonmembership a condition of employment. The panel set up to adjudicate workplace disputes under the NRA cotton code (the Bruere

Board) had responsibility for investigating complaints about union organizing. The board received scores of grievances on the subject but took few steps to rein in mill managers.[27]

Enraged by these and other abuses, Piedmont operatives pushed the United Textile Workers into the ill-fated 1934 General Strike in textiles. In September 1934 the UTW called for a nationwide walkout of cloth-making workers, setting off one of the largest labor confrontations in U.S. history. The UTW mounted an impressive effort in the southern mills where the strike centered, despite a skeletal organization in the region and depressed market conditions that left manufacturers with bales of unsold cloth. Hundreds of mills across the South ceased operations, at least temporarily, due to strikers' efforts. But local and state officials in Dixie came down forcefully on the side of industry, deploying the National Guard in several states to keep plants open. Faced with this resistance, operatives returned to the mills without winning any of their demands. In the strike's aftermath union loyalists across the South were purged from factory payrolls. Textile unionism would never again see this level of strength in the region.[28]

Despite the defeat of the 1934 textile strike, the fact that such a broad-based labor uprising happened at all was significant. Particularly impressive was the wide support for the walkout in the southern Piedmont, an area notoriously hostile to organized labor. These developments testified to the growing power of American unions during the early New Deal years, even before the breakthroughs of the late 1930s in northern industry.[29]

The cotton textile industry experienced significant instability during the two years when NRA controls were in effect. The outlook worsened in spring 1935 when the Supreme Court's *Schechter* decision struck down the NIRA. The Court's ruling removed all aspects of compulsion from NRA cotton code guidelines, sharply reducing the federal government's ability to improve conditions in the industry. The manufacturers who had established the Cotton Textile Institute and sponsored the cotton code responded to the code's demise by returning to the voluntary market stabilization efforts that had preceded the NRA. Following the court decision, the CTI called on mills to respect central code provisions of two 40-hour shifts, minimum wages, and a ban on child labor. The effort received broad support. CTI surveys showed that 90 percent of cotton firms were adhering to the code guidelines at the end of the summer. This figure of course confirmed that the nonconforming group had swiftly reemerged, with 10 percent of cotton producers eschewing the CTI program. Some mills went to three-shift operations the moment the

Court voided the NRA. By late 1935 rumors of growing abandonment of the standards swept the industry. In fall 1936 the CTI formally called off the voluntary effort.[30]

Strict Federal Regulation of Textile Labor Standards: The Ellenbogen Bills

With the NIRA overturned, the drive to unionize southern textile workers defeated, and a new voluntary stabilization drive by cotton manufacturers unlikely to succeed, the long-term prospects of northern textile producers were not favorable. Without some means of imposing uniform national labor standards, the industry would almost certainly continue to experience overproduction and depressed markets, leading to further liquidations of higher-cost northern mills.

Confronted with these realities, textile union leaders and their liberal supporters came forward with an audacious new plan to stabilize the industry and protect northern jobs. Under the sponsorship of Representative Henry Ellenbogen, Democrat of Pennsylvania, unionists put before Congress a series of proposals for strict federal regulation of labor standards in textiles. In addition to setting a floor on wages and a ceiling on hours, these bills allowed for national wage minimums for each occupation in cloth-making plants. The provisions, if strongly enforced, would have eliminated completely the historic pay differential that had driven textile production to the Piedmont. The remaining fabric manufacturers of the North would have been safeguarded as a result. The legislation envisaged a level of public sector intervention in the free-market economy that would have been unthinkable a few years before. That union leaders and liberals proposed such far-reaching measures demonstrated the great faith of these groups in government action following several years of New Deal reforms.

The labor standards legislation was a joint effort of Ellenbogen and UTW vice president Francis Gorman. Born in the English woolmaking center of Bradford, Gorman as an adolescent migrated with his family to Providence, Rhode Island. There he found work in a woolen mill. He later joined the UTW, serving as an organizer, president of his union local, and head of the Providence Central Labor Union. Gorman became a full-time union staff member in 1922. He assumed the rank of UTW vice president in 1928, emerging as the key lieutenant of longtime union president Thomas McMahon. Gorman had a flair for battlefield strategy, which was demonstrated during the 1934 national textile strike. He oversaw the overly ambitious walkout from an office in Washington, D.C., and in many ways made the best of a bad situation. Gorman directed strikers in the use of "flying squadrons," caravans of picketers who drove from town to town calling on employees to leave work. The technique shut down hundreds of southern mills in the first days of the strike. Through an effective radio publicity campaign, Gorman created the impression of a more organized national walkout than was actually taking place.[31]

The highly idealistic representative Ellenbogen presented a distinct contrast to the pragmatic Gorman. Ardently liberal and very hardworking, Ellenbogen was born into a middle-class Jewish family in Vienna. He completed legal studies there by age nineteen before joining family members who had earlier migrated to Pittsburgh. Attending night school while working during the day, Ellenbogen earned an American law degree within four years of arrival in the United States. He then set up a private legal practice, defending unions, workers, and immigrants, while publishing articles on social and economic questions. Moved by the plight of the Depression-era jobless, and angered by President Herbert Hoover's opposition to federal unemployment relief, Ellenbogen challenged the sitting U.S. representative for Pittsburgh in the 1932 elections. This was a bold step. A conservative Republican machine had long controlled Pittsburgh politics, and Ellenbogen's application for U.S. citizenship had not yet received final approval. The young lawyer won election as part of the year's Democratic sweep. In Congress he vigorously supported liberal causes including unemployment insurance, old age pensions, public housing, and government-guaranteed home mortgages.[32]

Soon after the Supreme Court struck down the NIRA in May 1935, the UTW leadership resolved to sponsor a bill that would recreate, and expand on, the protections in the textile codes.[33] Gorman was given responsibility for the legislative project. The UTW's membership was badly depleted due to layoffs and employer hostility. With limited influence in Washington, union officials must have had difficulty finding a lawmaker to carry the measure. They turned to the fearless and idealistic Ellenbogen. The representative's adopted Pennsylvania home had a sizable textile sector, but the cloth plants were in the eastern part of the state, far from Ellenbogen's Pittsburgh base. The young legislator was thus initially "reluctant" to take on the challenge. He explained that with "no textile mill in my Congressional District . . . it would take a lot of time . . . effort . . . and heartaches . . . to get anywhere with such a bill and it would benefit nothing to me personally." Ellenbogen eventually relented, believing that "we could develop a model bill that would benefit not only the textile worker, but the entire labor movement."

An intensive drafting effort took place in the months that followed. The UTW had originally sought legislation that would only apply to cotton-making, but the measure was soon broadened to address the situation in other branches of the troubled textile industry, including wool, silk, and hosiery. Ellenbogen and Gorman consulted with dozens of individuals in Washington while drawing up the bill, including lawyers, textile experts, and officials of the still extant National Recovery Administration, which had administered the NIRA. Ellenbogen discussed the legislation with President Roosevelt and claimed that it had FDR's approval. Entitled the National Textile Act but known as the Ellenbogen bill, the measure was submitted to Congress in August 1935. The collaboration in writing the legislation between the industrial unionist Gorman and the passionately liberal Representative Ellenbogen personified the strong labor-liberal alliance that emerged during the New Deal era.[34]

The bill drafted by Ellenbogen and Gorman was a wish-list of labor demands. It created a Federal Textile Commission that would regulate the industry and license all firms engaging in interstate commerce. Cloth-making firms that did not uphold the strictures of the law would have their licenses revoked. Among the requirements were freedom for union organizing and the assent of employees to changes in workload (i.e., stretchout). The bill outlawed child labor, limited the work week to 35 hours, and fixed a weekly minimum wage of $15 that would apply throughout the country with no regional differential. It gave the textile commission the power to curtail output in case of overproduction. These provisions were far-reaching, but rather obscure language in the middle of the act went much further. If the commission found that

> equitable and proper ... differentials of wages above the minimum ... are not being maintained, or that *competition in or directly affecting interstate commerce is tending to reduce such proper wage differentials above the minimum* ... it shall have power ... to establish minimum wages for various classifications of occupations.

In other words, the commission could set wage minimums to be effective throughout the country for each occupation in cotton manufacturing all the way up the hierarchy of skill in the plant. (Appendix 2 shows the wide dispersion in the wages received by different categories of textile workers.) The bill did not set parameters for determining these minimums. But under robust enforcement they would likely be set at the levels prevailing among the best-paid workers in the industry—the unionized operatives of the North. The National Textile Act would thus give the federal government the power to fix industrywide wage scales at a relatively high level: precisely what occurs in a strong union contract. Such an arrangement would eradicate the longstanding regional wage differential in textiles, dramatically improving the competitive outlook of the beleaguered northern manufacturers.[35]

Hearings on the Ellenbogen proposal took place in early 1936 before a highly sympathetic subcommittee of the House Committee on Labor. In an opening statement, Ellenbogen outlined how his bill would stabilize the industry and end competition on the basis of labor cost:

> The bill contemplates the regulation of fair trade practices for the purpose of protecting the honest employer against chiseling fellow employers and establishes minimum standards of labor, so that one of the chief evils in the textile industry, the competition between employers at the expense of labor, will be eliminated.

The UTW had launched a national campaign for passage of the legislation, and union representatives appeared in force at the hearings. Their carefully balanced presentation projected the broadest possible support for the bill. In addition to top officers Thomas McMahon and Francis Gorman, unionists appeared from most branches of the industry, including cotton, wool, hosiery, silk, and synthetics. The major centers of production—New England, the mid-Atlantic states, and the South—were all well represented.[36] A number of liberal Democratic politicians from the Northeast testified on behalf of the measure, including the lieutenant governor of Massachusetts, a representative of Rhode Island Governor Theodore Greene, and Pennsylvania's Governor George Earle. Even Wilbur Cross, the moderate Republican chief executive of Connecticut, dispatched an official from the state labor department to speak in favor of the bill. (Cross qualified this endorsement by also backing the appearance of Connecticut textile executive John Nickerson, who testified in opposition.) Several officials from the U.S. Department of Labor appeared as well, offering guarded support for the legislation's aims.[37]

Labor activists from across the Northeast were among those who spoke at congressional hearings on the Ellenbogen bill. Some of these individuals still worked in the textile mills. Their testimony gives an indication of how rank-and-file operatives viewed proposals for sweeping federal regulation of textile labor standards.

The labor activists came from different branches of the cloth-making industry. Their views were shaped by the recent experience in textiles, which varied from sector to sector. Common themes nevertheless emerged in the activists' statements. Workers remembered the harsh conditions of the late 1920s and early 1930s, before the onset of National Recovery Administration regulation. Most said that circumstances had improved during the NRA period, despite the numerous shortcomings of the program. All saw significant potential in the tighter restrictions to be enacted by the Ellenbogen bill.

Harold Daust worked as a weaver in a cloth-making mill and headed the Massachusetts Textile Council, a small organization representing operatives in wool, cotton, rayon, and other branches of the industry. Daust held that NRA regulation had been a "blessing" for the industry. He viewed the Ellenbogen proposal as essential for ending competitive turbulence in textiles: "We know that Federal legislation is necessary for the stabilization of the industry and to eliminate the cutthroat competition."[38]

Harry Jennings shared most of these sentiments. Jennings labored in a New Hampshire woolen mill and served as an officer in the UTW's division for woolen and worsted workers. He believed that circumstances had improved during the NRA period, despite continuing problems such as speeded-up machinery and short working hours stemming from insufficient demand. In Jennings's view, only the stronger regulation proposed in the Ellenbogen measure could definitively better conditions in the industry: "Federal legislation will have to do it. . . . We know that it is the means of saving the industry from the deplorable conditions such as existed before the enactment of the N.R.A."[39]

Labor representatives from full-fashioned hosiery were a forceful presence at hearings on the Ellenbogen bill. Organized labor had made significant inroads among that industry's highly skilled workers, but the union position was undercut during the 1920s by low-wage, open-shop competitors in the North and South. Strong regulation during the NRA period decisively improved circumstances in the unionized sector. Manufacturers and union leaders jointly wrote the NRA hosiery code, which fixed industrywide wage minimums for each category of mill labor.[40] By setting the wages of all workers at the levels of pay received by unionized millhands, the hosiery code provided a model for the comprehensive wage setting that the Ellenbogen measure envisaged for all textile plants.

Joseph Burge was one of the hosiery representatives testifying at the congressional hearings. He toiled in the full-fashioned mills of Philadelphia, an important production center. Burge gave a detailed account of the "indelibly bitter" experience of the city's hosiery workers as the favorable conditions of the late 1920s disintegrated under the pressure of low-cost competition. At the outset, Burge recalled, "Almost all of us who were knitters in 1928 were buying our homes. . . . Our wages were above the average of the textile industry and we were all dreaming middle-class dreams of a decent home, a car, and an education for our children." The expansion of full-fashioned output by low-wage producers dramatically altered these realities:

> The accumulated effects of overexpansion began to be felt in the spring of 1929, even before the general depression . . . set in. And from the spring of 1929 to the summer of 1933 we were pushed steadily downward. During that dark period at least 18 knitting companies in our section were liquidated. . . . We accepted five wage reductions . . . in the vain hope of establishing parity between the union and non-union sections of the industry in the matter of labor costs. . . . We lost our homes, our cars, our dreams, and we stalked the streets in droves.

NRA regulation reversed this situation, Burge explained. The NRA hosiery code imposed the labor standards prevailing in the unionized mills on the industry's other producers:

> [Through the hosiery] code . . . we were able to negotiate two small, but badly needed increases in the organized mills, and to push up the rates in the open shops to our level—which meant an increase of 100 percent in some cases. [The union's] wage scale, which had been observed by barely 20 percent of the employers before the N.R.A., became the standard in 85 percent of the industry. . . . The stretch-out . . . tended to disappear. The 12-hour day, which had been endemic in 80 percent of the industry, gave way to the 8-hour day.

After the Supreme Court invalidated the NRA codes, the poor standards of the previous era began to reappear:

> [Following] the Supreme Court's decision . . . conditions slowly but surely began to decline. We in Philadelphia, who had not had a strike in 20 months, found it necessary to declare five strikes in the last half year . . . to maintain code conditions. . . . More mills are shut down in Philadelphia right now than at any time since the summer of 1933. And the terrifying specter of liquidation, banished by the code, is again among us.

Only passage of the Ellenbogen measure, Burge asserted, would prevent the return of the dire conditions seen before 1933: "We feel that unless this bill is enacted we workers will lose all the benefits we gained during the N.R.A.; that a series of liquidations will sweep the industry; and that widespread unemployment, enormous suffering, and desperate industrial conflicts will be inevitable."[41]

Textile manufacturers appearing at congressional hearings on the Ellenbogen measure emphatically resisted the strong federal intervention called for by the legislation. Most vociferous were officials of the Southern States Industrial Council. The organization represented the small, low-cost manufacturers of the South who depended most heavily on cheap labor.[42] The group's president excoriated the act as "the greatest threat to the development and continued prosperity of [the southern] textile industr[y] that has yet been faced," claiming that its effects on Dixie industry would be "almost murderous." Determined opposition also came from more established cotton manufacturers, who in the early 1930s had worked to stabilize the industry through federally enforced improvements in labor standards. The Cotton Textile Institute, which represented producers in the North and South, apparently appointed a special "strategy committee" to defeat the measure. Its officers gave harshly critical testimony before the congressional subcommittee. CTI president Claude Murchison claimed that the bill would change the character of the industry "so radically as to be in opposition to everything that we have heretofore thought of as being the traditional American method of doing business." His assistant called the commission that would administer the act "dictatorial."[43] Established manufacturers such as those of the CTI objected to the very broad range of management activities to be regulated by the bill, including all wages and individual workloads. They were put off as well by the presidentially appointed commission that would oversee the new restrictions. It was unlikely that industrialists would dominate this panel in the way they had controlled the cotton textile Code Authority. The CTI's Murchison actually expressed cautious support for more limited legislation that would deal only with standards targeted by the NRA cotton code, such as maximum hours, minimum wages, and child labor.[44]

New England textile manufacturers also testified against the Ellenbogen legislation.[45] The manager of a New Bedford cotton mill appeared on behalf of the New England–based NACM. He denounced the bill as "pregnant with fallacious provisions" and asserted that its effect on textiles would be to "disrupt conditions to an extent that we have not yet experienced."[46] John

Nickerson, who worked for a Connecticut silk manufacturer and spoke as the representative of the diversified textile makers of his state, also argued against the proposal. Yankee mill managers opposed the Ellenbogen measure even though the bill would strengthen their firms vis-à-vis lower-cost producers in the South. The seeming illogic of this stance made a strong impression on some of those present at the hearing. A labor-friendly backer of Ellenbogen's proposal who sat on the congressional panel castigated Connecticut manufacturers' representative Nickerson for resisting a measure that would help industrialists in his state hold off southern competition.

An appreciation of the political and business environment inhabited by New England textile makers renders their resistance to the legislation somewhat more comprehensible. For decades the region's textile magnates had battled encroaching state regulation of hours of labor and other working conditions. Their highly decentralized industry continued to resemble traditional visions of laissez-faire. The opposition of these men to the Ellenbogen bill was thus consistent with long-established patterns. The episode is nonetheless a striking demonstration of the power of entrenched political-economic viewpoints. New England fabric manufacturers faced two options at this juncture: industrial stability under the close supervision of independent federal regulators, or untrammeled competition that was likely to force eventual company shutdowns. Given the choice, the vast majority of the region's producers preferred to take their chances with the free market.

A cross section of manufacturers from other branches of the textile industry rounded out the employers' presentation at hearings on the Ellenbogen measure. Representatives of woolen and worsted, hosiery, and textile finishing all testified against the legislation, and the underwear manufactures submitted a statement critiquing it.[47]

After these contentious hearings, the original proposal underwent considerable redrafting. The chairman of the subcommittee considering the measure wanted a bill that was less overtly favorable to labor, and there were also concerns about the proposal's constitutionality. Revised legislation emerged following numerous conferences among the subcommittee chairman, Ellenbogen, and textile union leaders. The primary change was the elimination of special protections for union organizing in textiles, which in any case largely duplicated provisions of the recently approved National Labor Relations Act (Wagner Act). Other key sections of the original measure remained intact. In preparing the final legislation, drafters consulted with mill owners, who evinced little more enthusiasm for the reworked version than for the original.[48]

The rewritten bill won the backing of the full House Labor Committee. That body's report in favor of the measure did include a stinging minority statement by Representative Fred Hartley Jr., the conservative New Jersey Republican who would cosponsor the 1947 Taft-Hartley Act restricting union activities. Hartley charged that even the revised Ellenbogen proposal constituted "a permanent scheme of Government regulation on a selected group of American industries more sweeping and drastic than Congress or any State has ever before attempted to impose." Particularly offensive, Hartley declared, were the provisions of the act allowing the government to set minimum wages for all occupations in textile manufacturing.[49] The revised bill was apparently held up by the House leadership, as it did not come to the floor of the chamber before the congressional session ended.

After the November 1936 elections, textile union leaders announced plans to try again in the next session of Congress. Ellenbogen introduced a new version of the measure in early 1937. Another round of hearings took place in May of that year, with similar results. Before further action could be taken, the House Labor Committee "pigeon-holed" the Ellenbogen bill to make way for the omnibus Fair Labor Standards Act. That legislation would regulate working conditions in all American industries, including textiles.[50]

Although the Ellenbogen measure did not pass, the creation and progress of the bill were telling. The textile unions believed the political environment of the mid-1930s to be sufficiently receptive to warrant pursuing a legislative effort. Labor leaders found a determined congressional sponsor for the measure and mobilized a notable level of support for it. These were all signs of the increased economic and political influence of the nation's unions during the New Deal period.

The Fair Labor Standards Act

The Fair Labor Standards Act, eventually approved in 1938, was the most important social legislation of the later New Deal. The FLSA put in place for the first time permanent national standards on wages, working hours, and child labor—issues that had been regulated on an emergency basis under the NIRA. Passage of the FLSA was a landmark achievement for the measure's liberal and labor supporters.[51]

The legislation enacted was nevertheless much less ambitious than what had originally been proposed. In its final form the FLSA regulated only minimum labor standards. The initial draft of the bill, by contrast, called for comprehensive government control over the wages of many low-income workers. Had the original version of the FLSA passed and been strongly enforced, the wage advantage of southern textile producers would have been erased, stabilizing the industry and affording northern manufacturers a new lease on life. Given the political strength of liberal forces in late 1936 and early 1937, approval of the original bill looked likely for a time. The shifting fortunes of the Roosevelt administration in early 1937 opened the door to strong congressional resistance to the more interventionist vision of federal labor standards, leading to the abandonment of this approach.

Substantive proposals for federal labor standards legislation first arose within the Roosevelt administration in early 1935. The NIRA appeared vulnerable to legal challenge at this time, endangering the wage and hour guidelines in the industry codes. Secretary of Labor Perkins accordingly supervised the drafting of a bill that would maintain existing labor standards in the absence of the NIRA. The proposal was quickly put aside.[52] After the Supreme Court decision voiding the NIRA, administration officials sought to craft a new recovery program that would retain labor standards and other elements of the NRA codes while winning the approval of business and the courts. These efforts came to nothing. As a stopgap, Congress in 1936 approved the Walsh-Healey Act, which regulated wages and hours at companies receiving large government contracts. The measure upheld the principle of federal labor standards regulation but applied to only a fraction of the country's employers. The Democratic Party made the need for wage and hour legislation an issue in the 1936 campaign. Further steps in this area were a major priority for President Roosevelt, who spoke repeatedly on the subject during late 1936 and early 1937.[53] Amid initial attempts to draw up legislation, Roosevelt himself handwrote a skeleton one-page wage and hour bill.[54]

Work on a detailed labor standards measure began in various parts of the administration in late 1936. The Council on Industrial Progress, successor agency to the NRA, advanced a number of plans, and Department of Labor officials crafted a separate bill. Members of Congress put forward other ideas. Roosevelt asked attorneys in the Department of Justice to assess the various proposals, a task directed by Solicitor General Stanley Reed. Department of Justice attorneys found the various measures deficient and began drafting their own legislation, albeit at a halting pace. With leading administration figures doubtless frustrated at the slow speed of work, Thomas Corcoran and Benjamin Cohen were brought into the bill-writing process.[55]

Thomas Corcoran and Benjamin Cohen were among the most prominent of the gifted, hard-driving young men who worked in the burgeoning federal agencies of the New Deal, and they had an essential part in implementing the era's reforms.[56] Cohen, the older of the two, was born into a well-off Jewish family in Indiana. He graduated from the University of Chicago in 1914 and earned law degrees there and at Harvard Law School. Cohen's outstanding performance at Harvard brought him to the attention of Felix Frankfurter, esteemed law school professor and later a key confidant of Franklin Roosevelt. Cohen served with the U.S. Shipping Board during World War I, then as counsel for the American Zionist movement. He entered private practice in 1922 while doing legal work on a voluntary basis for the National Consumers League. At Frankfurter's recommendation, Cohen went to Washington, D.C., in 1933, where he held several legal positions at the Department of Interior. Cohen continued at the department until 1941. Thomas Corcoran was the son of prosperous Irish-American parents from Rhode Island. He studied at Brown University and then at Harvard Law School, where he too earned the admiration of Frankfurter. Corcoran completed his legal studies in 1926, clerked for Supreme Court justice Oliver Wendell Holmes, then worked for five years as a securities lawyer on Wall Street. In 1932 he joined the legal staff of the newly created Reconstruction Finance Corporation. He retained this post under the new Democratic president and remained with the agency until 1940.

Corcoran and Cohen exercised far greater influence in the Roosevelt administration than their midlevel posts would indicate. The two, who became close friends, were trusted advisors on domestic political issues. Corcoran emerged as a leader of the energetic young men who took federal government positions in the 1930s. Working as a team, Corcoran and Cohen helped author key pieces of New Deal legislation. They gained familiarity with the question of wage regulation when, in 1932, on behalf of the National Consumers League, they assisted in writing a model state minimum wage law for female workers. The two played a central part in drafting the Securities Act of 1933, the Securities and Exchange Act of 1934, the Public Utilities Holding Company Act of 1935, and the Rural Electrification Act. By assigning the Fair Labor Standards Act to Corcoran and Cohen, administration officials confirmed that the issue had high priority and signaled their impatience with the delays in preparing a bill.

With Corcoran and Cohen involved, work on the labor standards measure shifted into high gear. It also moved in new and more ambitious directions. While many in the administration favored varying standards tailored to conditions in individual industries, Corcoran and Cohen preferred an omnibus approach, in which the same restrictions applied throughout the economy. The two men also sought a government role in setting standards above the minimum for some workers, a position Department of Justice attorneys supported. Under the measure Corcoran and Cohen drew up, Congress would fix a firm floor for wages and a ceiling on hours. Conditions below these levels would be deemed "oppressive" and banned outright. Additional regulation could occur in certain industries that routinely saw poor conditions above the minimums. In sectors where the low standards of some workers threatened to undermine higher norms for others, the lower standards would be deemed "unfair." The Labor Standards Board set up to administer the act would then order mandatory "fair" standards for all employees in the industry. In the affected sectors, this would likely entail wage minimums for each occupation that applied throughout the country. The Labor Standards Board could not impose a work week shorter than 35 hours, nor weekly wages above an annual income of $1,500 ($30 per week). Since Congress was expected to set the absolute weekly minimum wage far below this level, at $16, the proposal meant that the board could end up directly regulating conditions for a substantial segment of the working population. The Corcoran-Cohen draft also contained a total ban on child labor and protections for union organizing beyond those in the Wagner Act.[57] Like the Ellenbogen acts, the legislation authored by Corcoran and Cohen would use federal power to stabilize industries where competition was creating geographic shifts in production and lowering the working conditions of all employees. The end result would again be government-imposed wage scales that resembled union contracts. Assistant Attorney General Robert Jackson later asserted that although the measure did not seek to preempt collective bargaining, it was intended to aid workers who did not receive the benefits of collective bargaining.[58]

President Roosevelt kept tabs on the evolving proposals for labor standards legislation. In a diary entry from mid-April 1937, Attorney General Homer Cummings noted that disagreements on certain points between Corcoran and Cohen and Department of Justice attorneys likely constituted "a matter the President himself will ultimately have to pass upon." Five days later, Roosevelt hosted a White House meeting on the subject attended by Cummings, Reed, Corcoran, Cohen, and others. Word soon came down that the Corcoran and Cohen approach should be followed. Draft legislation based on their template was completed by April 30 and circulated within the administration.[59]

Corcoran and Cohen modified the April 30 proposal in several respects in response to critiques. The arrangements for the Labor Standards Board were altered, and the ceiling up to which the board could set wages was reduced to $1,200 a year ($24 a week). But the essence of the legislation did not change. In May the bill was handed to Senator Hugo Black and Representative William Connery, chairs of the labor committees in the two chambers and veteran fighters for federal labor standards legislation. The measure was then introduced in both houses as the Black-Connery Act, or Fair Labor Standards Act.[60] The bill's drafters saw the provisions for regulating labor standards above the minimum as a central feature of the legislation. Cohen highlighted these sections in an internal memo explaining key aspects of the final proposal. For the act's backers within the administration, according to a journalist, elimination of the language fixing standards above the minimum would result in a "failure . . . as complete . . . as if the entire bill were killed."[61] That Roosevelt administration officials authored such sweeping legislation demonstrated how far top Democrats were willing to go by 1937 in regulating the market to secure reform goals.

Political alignments for and against the proposed Fair Labor Standards Act closely resembled what had been seen earlier with the Ellenbogen measures. In hearings on the proposal in June 1937, leading liberals and textile unionists expressed strong support. New Deal economist Leon Henderson backed the act as a means of redistributing income and thereby aiding economic recovery. Isador Lubin of the Bureau of Labor Statistics offered evidence on the wide extent of low earnings among American workers. Sidney Hillman gave the bill an enthusiastic endorsement. Hillman was longtime president of the Amalgamated Clothing Workers and leader of the recently launched textile organizing drive by what would become the Congress of Industrial Organizations (CIO). He thus had extensive background in industries where labor-cost differentials and unionism had led to major geographic shifts in production. This experience had clearly shaped his outlook. Explaining why he considered provisions for regulating standards above the minimum to be one of the "most valuable features" of the bill, Hillman stated:

> In those industries with which I have had to deal, where new units are not infrequently deliberately established in places most difficult for the unions to reach effectively, it is vitally necessary that the law should recognize and protect fair labor standards. . . .
>
> [Furthermore,] it is difficult to induce employers to enter into collective bargaining agreements when the unions are not in [a] position to protect the employers from the undercutting of labor costs in other areas.

An officer of the International Ladies' Garment Workers' Union also testified in favor of the measure. The bill received added support from several reform-minded industrialists.[62]

Even in the reform camp, the measure did not command unanimous backing. Many in the AFL leadership harbored longstanding fears that federal wage setting would supplant collective bargaining, thus robbing unions of their function. They worried as well that government boards would impose caps on earnings. AFL President William Green's attitude toward the bill had vacillated for weeks. In testimony before Congress, he made his support conditional on numerous amendments that would blunt the measure's impact. Surprisingly, John L. Lewis also voiced fears that an extensive federal role in wage fixing could replace collective bargaining. Lewis was the longtime head of the coal miners' union and, along with Hillman, a top CIO leader. The coal chief endorsed minimum standards but recommended dropping entirely the provisions for pay regulations above the minimum. Lewis's desire to shield his miners from unwanted government intervention perhaps outweighed any desire to improve conditions among workers in textiles, apparel, and other industries where the union presence was geographically restricted. Secretary of Labor Perkins also offered only half-hearted support for the bill. Although strongly backing the principle of labor standards regulation, she and other Department of Labor officials saw the powerful Labor Standards Board envisaged in the act as a bureaucratic rival. Perkins additionally opposed minimum standards that would apply throughout the economy, preferring instead specific restrictions for each industry, to be set by panels attached to her department.[63]

Most in the business world strongly resisted the proposed extension of federal power into another realm of economic life. An officer of the National Association of Manufacturers submitted a list of forty-one industrial organizations opposed to the bill and attacked the broad powers granted to the Labor Standards Board. The U.S. Chamber of Commerce also denounced the measure. Members of the Department of Commerce's Business Advisory Council, which generally represented liberal corporate views, backed the concept of a labor standards bill but opposed fixing wages above the minimum.[64]

The position of cotton textile executives on the new legislation followed the lines established previously on the Ellenbogen bills. John Edgerton of the Southern States Industrial Council, the lobby for Dixie's low-wage manufacturers, denounced all federal attempts to regulate labor standards. CTI President Claudius Murchison opposed regulating wages above the minimum and the broad powers granted to the Labor Standards Board. But he supported regulations that would keep the industry's low-cost producers in check. Murchison backed a 40-hour limit on working hours, urged action against plants running a third shift, and expressed great eagerness to halt child labor. The NACM did not send a representative to testify before Congress but took a stance similar to that of the CTI. The New England–based organization continued its strong opposition to comprehensive government regulation of wages, even though such action would greatly strengthen the competitive position of northern mills. In an internal memorandum, the NACM president described the original draft of the FLSA as a "serious legislative threat" that would "give a commission power to set all wages, not only the minimum." The NACM did favor steps that would raise costs at southern competitors, including a wage floor with no regional differential. This would ideally be set "at any point below the minimum wage . . . already prevailing in New England" so that payscales at northern firms would not be affected.[65] Managers from other branches of the textile industry took positions resembling those of the main cotton operators.[66]

Observers anticipated quick passage of the original FLSA. The shifting political context badly hurt the bill's prospects, however. The biggest difficulty was the fallout from Roosevelt's plan to pack the Supreme Court. Sentiment against the Court had been strong during the 1936 campaign due to decisions overturning key New Deal reforms. But the president's proposal to add as many as six undoubtedly liberal justices to the panel resonated with traditional fears of unrestricted executive power. His attempts to force an unwilling Congress to act on the issue made matters worse. With FDR's previous invincibility shaken, his popularity dropped markedly during the first half of 1937. Taking the initiative, conservatives in both parties mobilized against the administration's most important proposal before Congress—the wage and hour bill—directing much of their fire at the far-reaching provisions regulating labor standards above the minimum. As a final blow, House Labor Committee Chair William Connery, a cosponsor of the measure, died as hearings were held on the legislation.[67]

President Roosevelt publicly opposed alterations to the administration proposal during June 1937 hearings on the FLSA. Senator Black, the measure's other sponsor, vowed to "keep this bill clean." But in the face of broadening opposition, congressional liberals cut their losses. In July, Black's committee reported out revised legislation that jettisoned the provisions for comprehensive wage setting and instead established only minimum standards. These included a 40-hour week, a weekly wage floor of $16, and a ban on child labor. Even this watered-down proposal met significant resistance from southerners and conservatives opposed to any government regulation of wages. The economic downturn that began in June 1937 further diminished FDR's popularity, bolstering congressional opponents of administration-backed measures. Reform advocates, meanwhile, split over the considerable discretionary powers granted to the Labor Standards Board that would enforce the act. Amid byzantine maneuvering, the bill passed in the Senate but was recommitted in the House. A somewhat revised measure setting minimum standards, including a minimum wage, finally passed in June 1938. The new national wage floor would be introduced in stages and reach $16 a week (40¢ an hour) in all industries by 1945.[68] In textiles, a transitional minimum wage of 25¢ an hour would take effect in 1938, going up to 32.5¢ an hour the following year. Imposition of this floor did raise the pay of many southern workers but was not sufficient to eliminate the wage gap between northern and southern mills. By the time the 40¢ an hour minimum went into effect in 1945, most southern cloth factories were already paying above that rate due to wartime inflation. According to a leading textile labor scholar, no Dixie mills ever closed due to wage increases imposed under the FLSA.[69]

Later Efforts to Regulate Textile Labor Standards and Organize Southern Workers

During and after World War II, unionists and their liberal allies continued to push for strong federal action that would equalize labor standards in the two wings of the textile industry. The Textile Workers Union of America (TWUA) spearheaded this effort. Affiliated with the CIO, this dynamic union had by the early 1940s organized most northern textile workers, although its inroads in the South remained limited.[70] The TWUA repeatedly sought rulings from the National War Labor Board, the federal agency regulating wartime labor issues, to eliminate the wage gap between Dixie fabric manufacturers and the unionized producers of the North. The effort was unsuccessful. In 1945 reformers introduced a bill in Congress to raise the wage floor in the original Fair Labor Standards Act to compensate for wartime inflation. The measure included language that required companies bringing base pay levels up to the new floor to maintain "reasonable" differentials in the wages of more skilled workers, with no cap on the rates to which this requirement would apply. Union backers of the legislation clearly had large ambitions for it. Testifying in support of the bill, TWUA research director Solomon Barkin argued that the wartime record demonstrated that federal regulation of all wages in an industry was feasible. Barkin pointed out that other developed countries had systems similar to what was being proposed. In those foreign locations, labor standards fixed by union contract in one part of an industry were imposed on all the sector's producers. No amendment to the FLSA passed in 1945, nor in the Republican-dominated session that followed. The amendment to the FLSA approved in 1949 set only minimum wages, with no regulation of higher levels of pay.[71] The conservative southern Democrats who chaired important congressional committees during this era were a significant obstacle to reform measures, such as strong amendments to the FLSA.[72]

With the legislative route blocked, unionizing Dixie workers was the alternate available method for bringing southern textile wages into line with those of the North. The TWUA and other northern-based unions made determined efforts in this regard in the years after World War II, although their endeavors met little success.[73]

The CIO mounted the largest organizing push. Dubbed "Operation Dixie," the drive concentrated on textiles, the South's largest industry. The TWUA was at the forefront of the effort. Operation Dixie began with great fanfare in mid-1946 but quickly confronted difficulties in southern textile towns. Employers fired pro-union employees, while police officers and vigilantes attacked organizers and sympathetic workers. Anti-union forces capitalized on Cold War and southern racial concerns, charging that the CIO was infiltrated by communists and favored race mixing. Paternalistic labor practices made workers at numerous firms reluctant to unionize. Troublesome as well was the fact that the organizing drive occurred in an era when wartime wage increases and postwar prosperity had created the most favorable conditions ever seen by southern textile operatives. TWUA organizers signed up only 11,000 new members during the first five months of Operation Dixie. Southern fabric-making then employed 400,000. The CIO scaled back the expensive organizing push by late 1946. The drive continued at a lower level through 1953 but with little additional effect. The AFL also launched a postwar southern organizing effort. It too had scant success. Most of the advances unions realized in the South during this era occurred in industries other than textiles. In the cloth-making sector, organized labor actually struggled to hold onto gains achieved in the favorable circumstances of World War II. Strikes at numerous textile firms in the late 1940s and early 1950s destroyed locals established during the war.

Organizing efforts persisted in the South after the mostly unsuccessful ventures of the immediate postwar years. The united AFL-CIO gave high priority to unionizing southern factories. Ongoing employer opposition ensured that little was achieved. The TWUA did realize some success in its long-running, high-profile campaign against J. P. Stevens, a major employer. In the 1970s, the union complemented traditional organizing techniques by mounting a boycott of Stevens products, accompanied by a public relations campaign. Company managers tired of the negative publicity and in 1980 recognized the union at a number of Stevens plants. The vast majority of southern textile workers remained unorganized at this time, however, and the Stevens victory occurred much too late to be of any assistance to northern textile workers.

In the immediate post–World War II years a substantial interregional gap in labor costs continued to characterize the textile industry. The unionized mills of the North still paid higher wages than their mostly open-shop southern counterparts.[74] Union contracts also provided northern workers with "fringe benefits" such as paid vacations and health insurance that added to employer expenses and were not available in much of the South. Workloads were generally lower at unionized northern mills than at southern facilities, which contributed to the disparity in labor costs.

Eliminating the North-South wage differential was essential for the survival of textile manufacturing in the northern states during the post–World War II era. Establishing robust Dixie unions was one way to accomplish this outcome. Enacting strong federal regulation that significantly raised wages at southern mills was another means of achieving the same end. In the absence of either step, the sizable cloth-making sector that remained in New England at the end of the war was doomed. Many of the region's cotton mills shut down during an early 1950s slump in the industry. Long-established northern wool manufacturers invested heavily in new Piedmont mills after the war while downsizing their facilities in the Northeast. This led to a spectacular crash of the woolen sector in Massachusetts.[75] The attempts of unionists and reformers to shore up textile manufacturing in the North had failed.

Conclusion

The push to establish uniform national labor standards in cotton textiles and other industries was a long effort spanning several particularly turbulent decades in American economic life. Within this complex chronology of events a number of points stand out.

First, uniform labor standards were clearly the most effective instrument for stabilizing the depressed market for cotton textiles. In other industries, stabilization schemes (whether legal or in violation of anti-trust laws) generally focus on fixing prices or limiting output. But in textiles, efforts to bolster the market concentrated on controlling the conditions under which goods were produced: the presence or absence of child labor, the length of the work week, and the wages paid.[76] All attempts to remedy the depressed conditions in textiles, from the voluntary programs of the Cotton Textile Institute to the most ambitious plans for federal regulation, aimed at establishing uniformity in these areas.

Second, over time, those connected with the industry sought steadily more comprehensive controls over labor standards as less restrictive ones failed to solve the problem. Thus, the Cotton Textile Institute tried initially to stabilize the market through the relatively modest steps of limiting the work week to 55 hours on the day shift and 50 hours at night and banning night labor by women and children. Then the cotton code enacted under the NIRA shortened the working week to twin shifts of 40 hours and instituted wage minimums that forced significant increases in millhands' pay. And the Ellenbogen bills and the original draft of the FLSA went well beyond minimum standards, envisaging controls over the wages of virtually every textile worker so as to equalize labor costs at all producers.

Third, while the earlier, more moderate efforts were not sufficient to stabilize conditions in the industry, the far-reaching proposals of unions and liberals would have accomplished this goal. Low wages constituted the key advantage of southern textile manufacturers. Action that eliminated the interregional gap in pay levels would have permitted the remaining New England producers to stay in business. Such measures were never enacted. The New England textile industry continued to downsize as a result, with widespread plant closures taking place in the years before and after World War II.

Fourth, forceful federal regulation of labor standards did not take effect due to determined political resistance. Unions and liberals were the principal advocates of this type of legislation. These groups had long been enthusiastic backers of strong government intervention in many areas of the economy. As plant closures swept through the New England textile industry, they looked to the federal government for decisive action to remedy the problem. Opposition to such steps came from several directions. Congressional conservatives saw the proposals as dangerous interference with private-sector prerogatives. Southern industrialists fiercely resisted measures threatening the low labor costs that gave them a decisive competitive advantage. Even New England textile manufacturers fought thoroughgoing regulation of labor standards, although such steps afforded their firms the best chance for long-term survival. This opposition presumably stemmed from the traditional laissez-faire ethos of the industry.

While proposals for strong federal regulation of labor standards were defeated, one can imagine similar legislation winning approval under somewhat different circumstances. A significant union presence in southern textiles might have decisively shifted political alignments in the industry, laying the groundwork for the passage of measures such as Representative Ellenbogen's bill. Stronger southern unions would have acted as a vocal lobby in Dixie for strict federal regulation. They might also have won some Piedmont textile manufacturers over to their side. Dynamics of this type played out in bituminous coal, where the miners' union established a strong position during the 1930s in pits of the North and South. After the demise of the NIRA, the industry came under comprehensive federal regulation with the support of the union and many mine operators.[77] It is also not difficult to envisage a situation in which something resembling the original draft of the Fair Labor Standards Act won approval. Observers anticipated this outcome as the legislation went before Congress. The marked drop in Roosevelt's popularity during the first half of 1937 largely explains the failure of the bill in its initial form. If he had moved more adeptly, the legislation might have passed.

Enactment of a system of comprehensive federal wage setting of the kind contemplated in the Ellenbogen bills and the original FLSA would have permitted the continued existence of the remaining New England textile mills. It is important to recognize, however, that government intervention of this magnitude would have produced a new series of complications for the industry, especially in the South.

To begin with, administering such measures would have presented a significant challenge, particularly in the Piedmont where the impact would have been heaviest. Giving a government board the power to fix wages for virtually all of an industry's workers would have constituted a major increase in federal power. The law would have required comprehensive enforcement to be effective. Government inspectors would have needed full access to employment and wage records and job descriptions on an ongoing basis. They would undoubtedly have had to stamp out subterfuges such as the fraudulent reclassification of workers into low-paying job categories by which Piedmont employers evaded the demanding requirements of the NRA cotton code. In the South, such intrusive federal activity would have aggravated regional sensibilities long adverse to strong central government intervention. The result would have been loud complaints, and perhaps organized resistance, from manufacturers and many local residents.

Furthermore, enactment of such a system would have increased the vulnerability of all U.S. textile makers to import competition. As government regulation forced wages upward, labor costs in the industry would have risen, resulting in substantial increases in the price of finished fabric. But textile manufacturing in this period was increasingly global in nature. Cheap Japanese imports emerged as a serious problem in a number of U.S. product lines in the mid-1930s, despite substantial tariff protection.[78] A significantly higher wage scale in American textiles—with corresponding increases in prices—would have increased the opportunities for sales in the United States by foreign producers.

Additionally, enforced wage equity throughout the industry would have hurt some Piedmont manufacturers badly. There had always been a zero-sum aspect to the North-South competition in textiles. Since the market could only accommodate a finite number of producers, gains for the manufacturers of one region necessarily entailed losses in the other. The established Piedmont companies that accounted for the bulk of national output in cotton textiles by the 1930s could probably have adapted to a regime of higher wages without severe disruption. The same could not be said for the small rural mills that paid the lowest wages within the South. Cheap labor was the essential advantage of these firms. Many lacked the capital and managerial talent to stay competitive on any other basis. The imposition of a uniform national wage scale in textiles would probably have forced a significant number of these companies out of business. This would have produced a round of deindustrialization in the rural South, with the same painful effects this phenomenon created in New England.

Finally, North-South wage equity would largely have halted the ongoing shift of textile production to Dixie. This would have detracted from southern growth and hurt the region's working population. In the late 1930s a significant number of cotton plants continued to operate in New England and the mid-Atlantic states. The northern regions retained a strong position in other textile lines as well, most notably the large woolen sector, almost all of which was based in the North at the outbreak of World War II. In the years after the war most fabric production—in cotton, wool, and other fibers—moved to the Piedmont states. The shift badly damaged textile-making locations in the North. But it produced substantial benefits in the South, creating tens thousands of jobs in the region's expanding cloth mills. The positions were primarily filled by poor, mostly white southerners pushed out of agriculture. Without the new employment in textiles, economic growth would have been less rapid in Dixie. Displaced southern farmers would likely have migrated north in search of work, a forced move that would have caused significant social disruption.

On the other hand, the imposition of higher wages would have had positive effects in the South. Textile operatives from shuttered rural factories who found employment at the region's remaining mills would have received significantly larger paychecks. Moreover, as is true elsewhere, higher rates of pay would have led all southern textile manufacturers to assess carefully their management techniques, search for efficiencies, automate certain tasks, and devote increased resources to training and research and development. Put another way, the imposition of higher wages would have led southern textile manufacturers to take steps that enhanced the competitiveness of their companies.

The decline of established industries had similar effects in New England, as the next chapter demonstrates. In the third response to deindustrialization in the northern region, business and government launched a wide-ranging development drive that sought to increase the competitiveness of existing area industries and foster the establishment of new ones.

CHAPTER 4

Economic Development

> There has been much discussion . . . about the disadvantageous position of some of our leading industries, such as textiles and boots and shoes, in meeting competition from other parts of the country and abroad. . . . *We must bend our efforts towards inaugurating a new era of enterprise and skill in management,* so that we can meet and overcome competition.
>
> FREDERICK H. CURTISS, CHAIRMAN OF THE FEDERAL
> RESERVE BANK OF BOSTON, *ADDRESSES BEFORE THE
> STOCKHOLDERS*, 1924 (EMPHASIS ADDED)

In the decades after World War I New England elites campaigned to strengthen the area's existing industries and foster the emergence of new ones. Regional leaders pursued a range of initiatives in response to the decline of textiles and other established industries. Encouraging the growth of area industries was the third of these efforts. The endeavor is known here as "economic development."

New England's growth drive began in the mid-1920s, soon after the difficulties in the regional economy became evident. Development efforts took place on a continuous basis for decades thereafter. The private sector dominated New England's growth push of the post–World War I decades, with business associations directing most development ventures.

The key organization in this regard was the New England Council, a regionwide business association formed in 1925 with the aim of reviving the area economy. The group functioned according to the principles of "associationalism," which emphasized private-sector action and had great influence on U.S. political economy during the 1920s. The New England Council drew strong support from service-sector companies with tight links to the region. Manufacturers of metal goods also played a prominent role in the organization's work. The New England Council was extremely active in the years from its founding through World War II. It pursued a multifaceted development program, with activities that varied from publicizing the strengths of the area economy to aiding in the recruitment of new manufacturers to advertising regional vacation spots. The New England Council aimed to strengthen the area economy as a whole. The organization therefore encouraged employment growth in all parts of New England, not just in the locales hit by downsizing.

State and local government also took part in New England's development push of the pre–World War II era, although the private sector dominated. An early development effort involving government took place in the 1890s, when regional textile firms first confronted competitive difficulties. In response, state and local authorities in Massachusetts provided key backing for the establishment of textile schools offering advanced training for future managers of that industry. As widespread factory closures took place in the 1920s and after, state governments in New England set up agencies to work for economic development. In the cities and towns hit hardest by industrial decline, municipal officials had a hand in recovery attempts, usually cooperating with business groups that were trying to bring in new employers. All the while New England government continued the traditional public-sector function of providing infrastructure to facilitate growth.

An outstanding characteristic of the public and private recovery efforts in New England was a heavy emphasis on the use of research, expertise, advanced technology, and up-to-date managerial techniques as instruments of economic development. This was the approach Boston bank chairman Frederick Curtiss had in mind in calling for "a new era of enterprise and skill in management" to revitalize the area economy. Development initiatives reliant on research and expertise in the period through World War II included the establishment of Massachusetts textile schools; attempts to convince area manufacturers to analyze and streamline their operations in a systematic way; the encouragement of laboratory research to develop new products and processes; and the establishment of a regional industrial research foundation to provide expert advice to those investing in innovative products. Working to improve the flow of finance to new and small manufacturers in New England was a related effort of great importance. It receives extensive treatment in the chapters that follow.

As the decline of traditional manufacturing became more widespread in the last decades of the twentieth century, other areas adopted recovery strategies that similarly emphasized research, technology, small business finance, and new product development. In the United States, activity of this type has been particularly prominent in the states of the old Northeast-Midwest industrial belt. The trend has captured the imagination of contemporary writers on economic policy. Noting that the approach encourages the growth of an area's existing business potential, these authors have labeled it "entrepreneurial." The method is hailed as a major departure from what is deemed to be the traditional regional growth strategy of offering inducements to outside employers, a technique derisively labeled "smokestack chasing."[1] While the expertise-based nature of recent development efforts is to be lauded, the New England experience shows that the claim for their novelty is unfounded. Generations earlier, in one of the first regions to experience the decline of traditional manufacturing, business and government leaders mounted a recovery campaign that was highly "entrepreneurial."

That New England growth-promotion efforts proceeded in this manner was not fortuitous. The region's economic elites were acutely aware that competing locales were more favorably situated and had lower labor costs, making it impossible for New England products to prevail on the basis of price. They also knew that the developed status of the area economy gave it important advantages, such as experienced management, ample skilled labor, numerous researchers, and abundant finance. By adopting a growth strategy based on knowledge and expertise, regional leaders were playing to their strengths. In a stiffly competitive environment, the approach held the greatest promise for generating new sources of prosperity.

Economic development efforts pursued in response to industrial decline have received considerable attention from historians in recent years. Most studies focus on attempts to create new manufacturing employment in the locales where industrial downsizing has occurred.[2] The role of public officials in development endeavors receives the bulk of the attention in these accounts. The promotional campaign launched at the regional level in New England was clearly of a significantly different nature—both in its largely private-sector nature and in its emphasis on generating compensating growth throughout the region, not just in locations where factories had closed.[3] Recognizing that this kind of redevelopment drive took place as well is crucial for a full appreciation of deindustrialization's impact on the political economy.

Aid for a Troubled Industry: Establishing Textile Schools in Massachusetts

Steps to strengthen New England's competitiveness by improving managerial expertise occurred even before area factories began closing in the years after World War I. A dramatic example occurred in Massachusetts in the 1890s. The first signs of structural difficulty in cotton textiles appeared during this era. In response the commonwealth founded several schools of textile engineering to provide comprehensive training for the industry's future managers. The institution set up in Lowell eventually became one of the premier centers of textile education in the country. Efforts in the private and public sectors brought the Massachusetts textile schools into being. Influential individuals linked to the cloth-producing sector pressed for the establishment of the schools, while state and local government provided essential financing.

Leaders of the New England textile industry had at various points in the late nineteenth century called for specialized training of aspiring mill managers. Such preparation would make possible improvements in productivity and allow American firms to compete with European manufacturers of the finest goods. The Lowell School for Practical Design in Boston and the Rhode Island School of Design in Providence, both established in the 1870s, helped fill the gap. The former institution operated for just a short period, however, and the latter focused only on product design and initially had no concentration in textiles. The Philadelphia Textile School, which opened in 1884, became the first American institution to offer training in all aspects of textile manufacture. This left New England, the nation's leading center of cotton and wool production, without a textile school of its own.[4]

The competitive pressures facing the region's manufacturers at the end of the nineteenth century changed this situation. The initiative came from James T. Smith, a Lowell native who returned to his home city in 1887 after a long career at the U.S. Treasury. Smith took the position of secretary of the local Board of Trade. The textile manufacturers who dominated this organization were deeply concerned by the emerging competitive challenge from recently established southern mills and were eager to identify remedies. Smith quickly focused on the benefits of establishing an institute of textile education of the kind that existed in Philadelphia and in foreign centers of the industry. Such an institution, he believed, would foster skills allowing Massachusetts manufacturers to break into the market for high-quality, high-price goods, a market currently dominated by European producers. Smith first worked to establish a training center affiliated with a local professional association or housed at the Massachusetts Institute of Technology (MIT). When these efforts fell short he turned to government, seeking city and state financing for a textile school at Lowell.[5]

With the competitive difficulties of New England mills made worse by the depression of 1893, the idea proved widely popular. A number of sites competed to host the new institution. A state legislator who edited a local textile trade publication vigorously supported the proposal; he preferred a Boston location.[6] Manufacturers in Fall River and New Bedford also favored government-supported textile education. Each group wanted the school in its own city. A compromise reached in 1895 authorized a state grant of $25,000 to any of the four leading textile centers in the commonwealth that would provide matching funds. Lawrence interests were amenable to a location in nearby Lowell, and the government of the latter city provided the necessary subsidy. Smith had a key role in the administration of the new Lowell Textile School, and numerous leading figures in the fabric-producing industry sat on the board of directors. Schools were also set up in Fall River and New Bedford.

Over the years the schools developed demanding programs of textile instruction. This applied particularly to the institution at Lowell. The Fall River and New Bedford schools concentrated on night classes, for the most part educating upwardly mobile operatives who were moving into the lower rungs of mill management. Night instruction also took place at the Lowell Textile School, but its directors were determined to establish an elite institution that would provide an engineer's training to high school graduates who would serve as the industry's future leaders. To realize this goal, the Lowell school offered a rigorous day curriculum that grew steadily broader over time. The original choice of concentrations in cotton manufacture, wool manufacture, chemistry and dyeing, and design was widened in 1905 to permit a specialization in textile engineering. The three-year diploma program was modified in 1912 to allow four-year degrees, and the institution began offering classes in the liberal arts. In 1935 the school began granting master's degrees, and in 1949 it set up an exchange program with MIT. The textile schools also became fully public during this period of expansion.[7]

In addition to a steadily widening curriculum, the Lowell institution became an important center of textile research. In its early days, the school set up a "special service" that allowed faculty members to carry out paid testing, consulting, and research for private companies. A number of new products and processes were developed at the school under this program. Textile chemistry and dyeing emerged as a particular strength, and in 1921 a Lowell professor founded the American Association of Textile Chemists and Colorists. A major research effort in this field later took place at the school, with financial backing from the association. Over time the reputation of Lowell Textile seems to have at least matched that of the older institution in Philadelphia. The sizable numbers of Lowell students in the 1920s from developing textile centers in India, China, and Latin America testified to the institution's international standing. A 1928 change of name to the Lowell Textile Institute symbolized the school's growing stature.[8]

Private-Sector Economic Development: The Formation of the New England Council

The corporate sector dominated economic development efforts in New England between the world wars. This was so despite the key role of government in the earlier establishment of Massachusetts textile schools and in other growth-promoting activities during the 1920s and 1930s. Of the private-sector organizations that mounted development campaigns in response to the decline of traditional manufacturing, the most important by far was the New England Council.[9] This regional business association was set up in 1925 with the mission of countering the area's economic difficulties. Formation of the New England Council represented the culmination of a series of efforts by business leaders to address the looming troubles in the New England economy. The Boston Chamber of Commerce played a central role in these preliminary events.

The Boston Chamber was one of the oldest and most prestigious municipal trade organizations in the country.[10] By the early twentieth century, the group had become thoroughly professionalized, with a full-time staff, a regular periodical, and standing committees dealing with a broad spectrum of issues. The Boston Chamber was able to draw on the area's leading businessmen and professionals to fill its rotating executive positions and staff the committees.[11] Chamber efforts to strengthen the industrial sector of Boston in the years before World War I gave the organization's leaders important experience with growth-promotion issues.[12]

The Boston Chamber early on addressed issues relating to regional prosperity, in addition to questions of municipal development. The organization had members all over Massachusetts and in other New England states and saw its field of concern extending throughout the area. In 1911, during an early bout of concern over New England's prospects, the chamber published a book-length survey of the possibilities for future regional growth. For a time, the organization's periodical was entitled *Chamber of Commerce News and Advance New England*. That the Boston Chamber would take an active interest in the prosperity of the entire region made sound economic sense. The city was the transportation and financial hub of New England, and its fortunes were closely tied to the demand for goods produced in the hinterland. As one Boston-area businessman put the matter some years later, "There is no question but what if New England prospers Boston can not help but prosper."[13] The failure of other groups to take action probably helped account for the Boston Chamber's broad perspective. For example, Massachusetts, like other jurisdictions, had a state chamber of commerce, but the organization was weak and had almost no involvement with substantive policy questions.[14]

The Boston Chamber's concern with New England conditions deepened as industrial decline set in during the 1920s. In response the organization first sought to strengthen troubled manufacturing sectors. The initiative came from Howard Coonley, chamber president and head of a Boston metalworking firm. Noting New England's slipping market share in goods such as cotton and shoes, Coonley proposed in June 1923 that the chamber conduct a study to determine the extent of decline, the reasons for it, and "what can be done to enable New England to maintain her industrial and commercial supremacy."[15] In an address to chamber members that autumn Coonley underlined the grave realities confronting the region and the necessity for remedial action:

> New England has for generations been a leader in industrial activities, and she is today, but . . . not . . . by as large a margin as she was a few generations ago. . . . It is time that we recognize that fact and do something about it. . . . Here in New England we seem in part to have forgotten that after all, industrial success is the basis of all progress and that no community can prosper unless its commerce and its industry is prosperous.

Refining his plans, Coonley recommended that the chamber organize studies on the position of principal area industries and possibilities for improvement. A group of past and present chamber leaders warmly endorsed the proposal, stating that the competitiveness of regional manufactures was "the biggest issue facing New England."[16]

A committee was formed to oversee the industry studies, with Coonley serving as chair. Other members included Charles F. Weed, an attorney and former Boston Chamber president currently working for the First National Bank of Boston, the region's leading lender; W. P. G. Harding, president of the Federal Reserve Bank of Boston; and Robert Amory, textile sales agent and manufacturer and leading figure in the association of regional cotton mills.[17] The Boston Chamber supervised the publication of a series of New England Industrial Surveys in the years that followed. Reports appeared on cotton textiles, shoes, metalworking, fishing, and agriculture. Each study examined conditions in the industry and recommended steps for improving efficiency.[18]

The local economic situation meanwhile worsened as layoffs in core industries spread across New England. The Boston Chamber assembled another panel, this time of merchants and manufacturers from around the region, to formulate a response to the aggravated circumstances. The idea had arisen in the past of a commercial fair featuring New England products. With serious slumps in key sectors, the time seemed propitious for an event spotlighting the area's quality manufactures. Increasing sales of goods from regional factories was one aim. Generating favorable publicity for local industries was another. The proposed fair would "boom New England" and, its promoters hoped, persuade area residents and those elsewhere that the region's economy remained vital, despite the current difficulties.[19]

Planning for the event took place under the guidance of John S. Lawrence, partner in a textile commission house with offices in Boston and New York. Lawrence had a good reputation in business circles and held quite conservative political views, which were downplayed when organizational efforts required.[20] Lineage was one of the man's most important personal characteristics. A direct descendant of the Lawrence brothers who founded the Merrimack Valley manufacturing center that bears their name, Lawrence was a Boston Brahmin. The most select social circle in the United States, the members of these forty Boston families had for a century played a central role in the area's political, social, and cultural life.[21] Despite this glorious past, John Lawrence at this time confronted the same business difficulties as regional manufacturers. For decades the family commission house, Lawrence and Company, had handled the sales of products from leading New England textile mills. By the mid-1920s the industry's troubles had begun to hurt his firm. A consolidation of regional cotton makers in which Lawrence and Company had an interest faced soft markets and paid no dividends in 1925. The following year, unable to make payments on outstanding loans, the consolidated company began selling off constituent units. Lawrence and Company itself confronted more serious difficulties later in the decade. A string of client mills went out of business or set up their own sales departments, a common reform in textiles during this period. Bereft of customers, the Lawrence and Company partnership liquidated in early 1930.[22]

John Lawrence headed the planning effort for the regional commercial fair, which took place in September 1924. Dubbed New England Week, the event featured exhibitions of the region's goods, public meetings, factory tours, and radio and motion picture features on area industries. The goings-on received intensive coverage in the regional press.[23]

The week of events went off so well, and the need for some sort of ongoing response to the area's economic problems was so widely felt, that organizers contemplated setting up a permanent association to promote the region and its products. Uncertainty existed about how to proceed toward this goal. As Lawrence explained to Coonley of the Boston Chamber of Commerce, the task of advocating on behalf of the economic interests of New England fell logically to the chambers of commerce of the region's larger cities. However, given the "present jealousy" among these organizations, it was not clear which group or groups would call the initial meeting, nor whom should be invited.[24] Lawrence did not spell out the substance of these rivalries, but it is not hard to imagine how they would arise. The various chambers often competed with one another to attract new industry, and organizations in outlying locales generally feared domination by those based in Boston and Massachusetts.[25]

A solution was found by turning to the region's political leadership. The New England governors had scheduled a conference for June 1925. It was arranged that from this venue, the governors would call on regional business leaders to create an organization to tackle the area's economic problems.[26] To lay the groundwork for the new body, each governor appointed three representatives to a planning committee. The eighteen members of the panel (three from each of the six New England states) were all corporate executives or trade association officers. On the Massachusetts delegation, in addition to John Lawrence, sat the president of the Jordan Marsh department store and the president of the United Drug Company. Representing Rhode Island were an executive of machine tool maker Brown and Sharp, the secretary of the Providence Chamber of Commerce, and the president of the Rhode Island Textile Association.[27]

Having the New England governors ask corporate leaders to set up a regional development organization may have been necessary to circumvent local jealousies in the business world. The arrangement also neatly served purposes of legitimation. With elected officials publicly calling for action and appointing the members of the planning committee, it was easier to ignore the question of why business leaders alone were selected to address the region's economic problems, with no formal input from other interested parties, such as unions, reformers, professional groups, and academics, not to mention state and local government. In later years, when the proposed association had taken shape as the New England Council, its leaders carefully maintained the mantle of official approval for their activities. The approved version of the organization's beginnings, frequently retold, held that the original initiative came from the governors. Council officers were consistently at pains to keep state officials involved in the group's work. An informational brochure issued by the organization in the mid-1930s even claimed formal approval for ongoing activities. After giving the standard account of the group's genesis—"The New England Council was created in 1925 at the joint suggestion of the Governors of the New England States"—the pamphlet went on to assert that the organization "has since enjoyed *the official sanction* and cordial cooperation of the succeeding Governors."[28] Business domination of the nascent New England development organization typified the conservative politics of the 1920s. With reform forces on the defensive in this era, corporate leaders played an active role in the formation of public policy. Indeed, the "associational" program championed by U.S. Commerce Secretary Herbert Hoover held that coordinated action by businessmen, with minimal guidance from government, could resolve all the social and economic problems of the day.[29] In this context, it was not surprising that New England political leaders called on corporate representatives alone to address the region's economic difficulties.

With John Lawrence as chair, the eighteen delegates appointed by the New England governors worked intensively through the summer of 1925. By the end of the season they had produced a detailed outline for the proposed development organization. A September 1925 address by a member of the committee of eighteen provides the best available account of planners' intentions.

The new entity was to be called the New England Conference. Concluding that the business world did not need another highly centralized association focused on advocacy and research, planners instead envisaged a loosely organized federation. Membership would be limited to existing business associations such as chambers of commerce, farm groups, industry-specific bodies like the National Association of Cotton Manufacturers, and umbrella organizations such as the Associated Industries of Massachusetts. Each group could send as many as three delegates to the New England Conference, which would hold one large annual meeting. The conference would set "broad policies," which would be referred to the member organizations for discussion and implementation. During the conference, delegates from each state would elect twelve representatives to a state council. The seventy-two representatives (twelve from each of the region's six states) would together constitute a New England Council, which would act as the "executive and deliberative body of the Conference," with final authority on all decisions. Since most of the work of the new body would take place among the member associations, planners saw no need for "elaborate machinery" of administration. They anticipated that a "part-time [executive] secretary with a small office and stenographer" would be sufficient to take care of the organizational details, and "if the time ever came when some great project had to be carried on for the benefit of New England, it was assumed the Council would set up the machinery for raising a special fund to carry on this special work."[30] Although organizers designed a detailed structure for the New England Conference, they left open the specific aims of the group, on the grounds that the conference should set its own agenda. Planners stated only that the organization should seek "united action" for the "promotion of New England Agriculture, Commerce, Industry, Transportation, Public Utilities and other matters of common concern."[31]

The inaugural meeting of the New England Conference took place in November 1925 in Worcester, Massachusetts. The Bay State's Governor Alvin Fuller formally opened the meeting. In a typically low-key introductory address, John Lawrence declared: "We have come here to discuss . . . New England's problems and see if we cannot come at a way to solve some of them." Speakers included Owen D. Young, the famed chairman of General Electric; Dr. Julius Klein, director of the U.S. Commerce Department's Bureau of Foreign and Domestic Commerce; and Martin Insull of the Chicago-based Insull power conglomerate, which had large holdings in northern New England. Commerce Secretary Hoover did not attend but sent a message declaring that "the solution of regional problems such as yours is dependent upon larger cooperation among all industries." He also characteristically counseled the elimination of economic waste as a means of restoring competitiveness. In a rousing address that brought down the house, Governor Ralph Brewster of Maine declared that "the turn of the tide has reached New England. California and Florida have had their boom. Everything indicates that the next boom coming is a New England boom." With a flag-draped rostrum, a long program of speakers, and fervent calls to believe (in the area's future), the conference reminded one observer of both a political convention and a revival meeting.[32]

The conflicts among regional interest groups feared by New England Conference organizers were clearly in evidence at the meeting. Farm associations attacked the regional power companies, demanding lower electric rates for rural areas and assailing the mergers then commonplace in the industry. Trouble also broke out at the meeting to select the twelve Massachusetts representatives to the New England Council, as demands arose for greater representation of farmers, labor, and the less developed western section of the state. After debating past midnight, delegates rejected two candidates on the original slate of twelve to make way for a central Massachusetts farmer and a unionist. Conference participants also chose acting executive officers for the organization, with John Lawrence named temporary chair.

New England Council Operations

As its founders had hoped, the new organization soon became the leading force in the drive for economic recovery in New England. Little of the uniquely decentralized structure originally mapped out for the association was translated into reality. The yearly New England Conference, initially intended as a focal point of activity, quickly devolved into an ordinary annual meeting where ongoing work was reported on and approved. The plan to limit membership to trade associations was abandoned, and by 1930 an associate membership category existed, so that all companies and individuals "believing in New England" could join.[33] Since the organization took a regional approach to most issues, the twelve-person state councils, for which an important role had been foreseen, had little to do, although the Massachusetts Council did at times lobby the state legislature. The most durable effect of the group's original structure turned out to be the name. Since the annual New England Conference had little weight and the seventy-two-person New England Council exercised executive power, the entire organization became known as the New England Council (hereafter Council or NEC).

Planners had originally anticipated a small headquarters overseen by a part-time administrator, but a much larger operation was soon in place. The Council set up offices in the Stadtler Building, a prestigious Boston business address, and by the end of the 1930s had a budget raised from member dues that approached $100,000. Operations were overseen by an elected president, usually a corporate executive, who served an unpaid two-year term. A salaried executive vice president supervised day-to-day matters. The latter position was filled by Dudley Harmon, a former Washington correspondent who had previously served as assistant to the president of the Connecticut Manufacturers Association. Harmon took the NEC job in 1926 and carried it out with solid competence for the next twenty-five years.[34] He had the assistance of a sizable staff, which included some accomplished people. The Council's industrial department was for years headed by Ray Hudson, who had previously run the Division of Simplified Practice in Secretary Hoover's Department of Commerce. After World War II, rising Massachusetts politico and future Watergate felon Charles Colson served as the group's Washington representative. Issue-specific committees had not even been foreseen in the original NEC structure, but a full complement of these soon existed and carried out much of the organization's work. By 1930 the Council had panels dealing with research, industry, community development, power, the recreation sector, agriculture, and forestry.[35] With a strong central office, a professional staff, busy committees, and a largely inactive membership, the initial vision of an innovative structure faded, and the NEC ended up operating much like the Boston Chamber of Commerce and other business associations.

As with most voluntary organizations, to be effective the Council had to attract skilled people to serve as officers and fill out the committees. The group performed impressively in this area. John Lawrence, NEC founder and first president, enjoyed a high reputation in New England, and in the ensuing decades individuals of like caliber and prestige served in leadership roles. They included manufacturers James Hook and Frederic Blackall Jr., who were active in national trade associations and ran successful businesses; attorney Charles Weed, former president of the Boston Chamber of Commerce and vice president at the region's largest bank; Lincoln Filene, co-manager of the famed Boston department store and noted political reformer; Karl Compton, president of MIT; Ralph Flanders, a successful industrialist active in trade associations and moderate reform politics who later served as president of the Federal Reserve Bank of Boston and as U.S. senator from Vermont; and Richard Bowditch, head of a regional oil and coal firm and future president of the U.S. Chamber of Commerce.

Farmers and unionists took part in Council activities, as did professionals, educators, and politicians, but the organization was made up overwhelmingly of businessmen. The group's membership was thus quite homogenous. The participants were exclusively male. The great majority were of Northern European Protestant, and often Anglo, extraction. Brahmins like John Lawrence were an active presence, although they did not overshadow other participants. Conversely, some of those working hard to boost New England had arrived in the region relatively recently. Howard Coonley, the Boston Chamber of Commerce president who initiated the activity leading to the NEC's establishment, was born and raised in Chicago and moved to New England in 1913. Karl Compton, who would do important work for the Council in the late 1930s, was originally from Ohio and spent years at Princeton before coming to Massachusetts in 1930 to take up the presidency of MIT.[36]

Council members came from throughout the business world, but support for the organization was strongest among regional service-sector companies that served a local customer base. This included firms in banking, water and power, transportation, communications, and hospitality as well as newspaper publishers and retailers. The prospects of these companies depended on the overall level of economic activity in New England. They had, as a result, a strong vested interest in the return of regional prosperity. Thus, the twenty-four members of the Massachusetts and Rhode Island state councils in 1930 included four officers of regional utilities, two bankers, one hotel manager, and one executive who apparently headed a regional shipping line.[37] As the work of the NEC got under way, the National Shawmut Bank, the second largest lender in Boston, took out large newspaper advertisements supporting the organization. When Council leaders sought during the 1940s to raise funds for a regional industrial research foundation, they looked primarily to the area's banks, phone companies, utilities, and railroads.[38]

The Council also drew notable backing from small and medium-sized manufacturers of precision metal products. In 1930 the Massachusetts and Rhode Island state councils together included officers of three such companies—a tap and die firm, a machine tool maker, and a producer of textile manufacturing equipment. Among the key leaders of the NEC in the 1930s and 1940s were Ralph Flanders, Frederick Blackall Jr., and James Hook, managers of machine tool companies in Vermont, Rhode Island, and Connecticut, respectively. It is not completely apparent why manufacturers of precision metal products supported the Council so warmly. A likely explanation is that these companies perceived a vested interest in maintaining New England's reputation as a producer of quality goods. In addition, the strong trade associations in these industries, particularly notable in machine tools, may have predisposed metalworking executives to support an endeavor like the Council.[39]

Companies in other sectors of the New England economy were notable for their relative absence from Council activities. The most important manufacturer in New England, General Electric, participated to only a limited extent in the organization's work. As a large employer with operations in numerous states, GE had little riding on the economic welfare of a particular locale. The textile and shoemaking firms that were disappearing from the economic map of New England similarly had little stake in the region's future and, aside from the exceptional involvement of John Lawrence, a restricted role in Council doings.

Almost all participants in the NEC had some vested interest in regional economic recovery, but this was not their only motivation. Loyalties to the area were strong. Whether they were old-line Yankees or successful newcomers, New England had done well by these men, and many seemed to feel a corresponding obligation to aid the region as it passed through a difficult period. Political legitimation was another motive for participation. The collapse of established industries entailed great working-class hardship, challenging the image of capitalism as a system creating prosperity for all. The return of regional prosperity, conversely, would improve perceptions of the free-market economy. John Lawrence discussed these issues in a 1924 address before a business audience. Management would be blamed for the unemployment arising from plant shutdowns, Lawrence asserted. The refusal of capitalists to take responsibility for the well-being of their communities, he continued, had been "the main cause of the Russian revolution."[40]

Although the political orientation of NEC members varied, the dominant strain could be described as conservative but pragmatic Republican. Council members enthusiastically supported the associational philosophy ascendant in the 1920s. Commerce Secretary Hoover was received with reverent enthusiasm when he attended an NEC conference in 1926. As the New Deal brought dramatic change to American political life in the 1930s, circumstances obviously became less accommodating for an association of mostly conservative capitalists. Like many in the business world, Council leaders complained frequently about the new restrictions on corporate behavior and the vast increase of federal power. In the wake of Franklin Roosevelt's landslide reelection in 1936, a shocked James Hook, then NEC president, wrote to a colleague that the result of the poll "forewarns a serious time ahead.... Only Roosevelt, by abandoning his proclaimed Fascist theories and advisors, can avert it." In the end, however, most in the NEC adopted a strategy of accommodation and containment toward the new political realities, rather than the outright resistance seen among many American businessmen. The Council enthusiastically backed a 1937 proposal for an industrial relations center at MIT that would work to solve regional labor disputes. Speakers at the group's 1939 annual meeting included left Keynesian economist Alvin Hansen and Congress of Industrial Organizations (CIO) leader Sidney Hillman.[41]

Finally, for all its members' conservatism, the very existence of the Council entailed a departure from the strictest formulations of laissez-faire, in which private actors pursue their individual interests in a wholly uncoordinated manner. Moreover, in working to revive the New England economy, the NEC tacitly acknowledged that conditions in the world of enterprise affected the entire community. Certain NEC leaders openly talked of business as a kind of public utility. Council activist Ralph Flanders told a 1945 seminar on regional affairs:

> We have been accustomed to think of business profit as private profit. It is much more than that. A profitable expanding business is an asset to the Commonwealth. It increases employment, supports trade and agriculture, and helps carry the burden of state and local taxes. The unprofitable business fails in all of these public services. When business ownership allows ... management to decay, it is failing in its responsibilities to its employees, its fellow citizens, and the region.[42]

Capitalists are generally loath to concede, particularly in times of economic difficulty, that business has such responsibility for the general welfare.

Economic Development Initiatives of the New England Council in Research and Technology

In seeking to counter the effects of industrial decline, leaders of the New England Council determinedly pursued a broad range of development initiatives—in essence, every possibility they could think of. Much of this activity focused on manufacturing, which all recognized as the heart of the regional economy. To bolster area industry, the NEC urged regional manufacturers to streamline their operations, sought to induce large industrial corporations to set up branch plants in New England, and worked to help local entrepreneurs bring new products to market. The Council attempted to strengthen other facets of the regional economy as well, endeavoring to upgrade power and transportation systems, develop the vacation and recreation industry more fully, modernize agriculture, improve public perceptions of economic conditions in the area, and help bring new employers into towns hit by factory closures.

As it acted to revitalize the New England economy, the NEC put great weight on research, expertise, advanced technology, and the use of up-to-date managerial methods as instruments for encouraging growth.[43] The Council's focus upon expertise and technique was most clearly apparent in efforts of the 1920s and 1930s to promote industrial research and new product development. The initiatives were among the most important pursued by the NEC and received great attention within the organization and from the public at large.

In highlighting the importance of expertise and technique, New England business leaders were soundly within the mainstream of contemporary American economic and social thought. New technologies and innovative managerial practices accounted for much of the dramatic growth the country had experienced since the late nineteenth century. Contemporary observers did not have the benefit of the modern scholarship that has illuminated the contributions of technological and organizational change to the era's industrial progress.[44] There was nonetheless a basic appreciation at the time of how these forces had propelled growth. Indeed, enthusiasm about advances originating in the business world was so great that many advocated using them to confront social and political problems. Numerous Progressive Era reformers worked to rationalize governance by applying corporate methods of gathering and analyzing information to questions of public policy and administration. Using the principles of engineering to rectify socioeconomic problems was a prime tenet of Herbert Hoover's associationalism.[45] In looking to revitalize the local economy through expertise and technique, New England corporate leaders therefore sought to harness forces that commanded the respect of businessmen and others everywhere to address a challenge that was specific to their locale.

Emphasizing expertise and technique as a path to recovery was a sound approach. New England business leaders correctly understood that the competitive advantage of their region lay in these domains. Other areas had more central locations, more plentiful raw materials, and cheaper labor. But New England had the economic advantages of a developed region, including skilled labor, experienced management, numerous educational and research institutions, and plentiful finance. A development strategy that sought to maximize the gains from these assets made good sense. Indeed, given the fierce competition from elsewhere confronting New England industries and the economic strengths the region did possess, an approach to revitalization based on expertise and technique was arguably the only route that had a plausible chance of success.

The NEC push to promote expertise and technique began with the work of the Research Committee, which was formed to considerable fanfare during the organization's first year. Boston department store executive A. Lincoln Filene chaired the group. Filene was eminently qualified to head the Council effort in this area, as his family's company had pioneered in applying the techniques of research and scientific management to the retail sector.

Lincoln Filene was born in Boston in 1865, the son of an immigrant shopkeeper. His father William ran a number of moderately successful stores that sold specialty goods in northeastern cities. In 1881 the father, together with Lincoln's older brother Edward, organized a new venture in central Boston. Lincoln joined the business soon afterward. The two young men took control of the store upon the father's 1891 retirement, naming it William Filene's Sons. Astutely managed, the business thrived. The brothers broadened the product line, expanded floor space, and introduced retailing innovations such as quick turnover of stock and emphasis on customer service. They were among the first to address problems of retail distribution using the methods of scientific management. Collaborating with other department stores, Lincoln set up one organization to research retail questions and a second to purchase jointly from manufacturers. Lincoln was active in business associations operating beyond the retail sector. He headed a committee on trade relations for the U.S. Chamber of Commerce and participated in the work of the American Arbitration Association and the International Chamber of Commerce.

The Filene store was known for its progressive personnel policies. These were introduced beginning in the late nineteenth century and eventually included arbitration of employee complaints, profit sharing, minimum wages for female workers, and paid vacations. The Filene brothers' concern with the well-being of their employees was part of a broader engagement with social welfare issues. Edward Filene was a leading early twentieth-century advocate of social and political reform, and Lincoln Filene was also interested in reform questions. In 1931–32 Lincoln represented Massachusetts on an interstate commission that recommended the creation of state programs of unemployment insurance. He lent support to the New Deal in the following years, serving on the Industrial Advisory Board of the National Recovery

Administration and the Business Advisory Council of the U.S. Department of Commerce.⁴⁶

Working with Lincoln Filene on the NEC Research Committee were several high-powered business executives, including the vice president of New Haven–based Southern New England Telephone and the president of Rhode Island's Blackstone Valley Gas and Electric Company. An attorney and officers of companies manufacturing shoes and boxes rounded out the committee membership.⁴⁷

Under Filene's dynamic leadership the Research Committee pursued an extremely active agenda in the late 1920s. The philosophy guiding the panel's work was that regional manufacturers could become significantly more competitive by systematically analyzing their operations through the "scientific" or "research" method. Members of the committee saw potential gains from research in every phase of business activity, including product design, manufacturing, advertising, sales, and the development of export markets.

To demonstrate the benefits of this approach, the committee arranged for a survey of successful applications of the research technique at various New England companies. The resulting publication, *Better Business through Research in New England Industry*, gave countless examples of improvements in efficiency resulting from the careful analysis of operations. Investigators determined, for example, that one manufacturer's salesmen spent much more of their time traveling or waiting for meetings than actually conferring with potential customers. By reorganizing the itineraries of sales people to minimize the distance between stops and targeting areas where the buying season was at a climax, the firm nearly doubled its salesmen's contact time with clients.⁴⁸

The Research Committee emphasized to New England manufacturers the benefits of tapping the expertise at the region's institutions of higher learning. As in other parts of the country, many New England colleges and universities would for a fee carry out research for private parties. MIT had a nationally recognized program of "industrial cooperation," and the Manufacturers Association of Connecticut set up at this time an exclusive research arrangement with the Sheffield Scientific School at Yale. Contract research generally involved scientific inquiries in the laboratory, although many institutions would also make available personnel in the business and social science departments for topics related to management, markets, industrial psychology, municipal government, and public health.⁴⁹ To encourage more New England businesses to set up collaborations with universities, the NEC Research Committee published a directory of institutions in the region where such arrangements could be established. In a foreword to the guide, the committee asserted that there was a "direct ratio between profits and the application of the research method." For New England business not to take full advantage of the research facilities at the region's institutions of higher learning, the committee continued, would be akin to "neglecting the vast copper deposits in the mining regions of Arizona and Montana." The directory listed twenty-eight educational institutions to which problems for investigation could be addressed, ranging from MIT and Yale to the International YMCA College in Springfield, Massachusetts.[50]

The economic development efforts of regional service companies were another field the Research Committee examined. Utilities, railroads, and banks in New England had for years promoted economic expansion in their service areas, usually through assistance to manufacturers. Equivalent firms in other parts of the country had similar programs, and these efforts were everywhere intensifying in the early twentieth century as the interregional competition for industry heightened. The NEC Research Committee arranged for a number of studies to determine if the development programs of New England service providers were sufficiently energetic. The report on commercial banks concluded that lenders in the region engaged in about the same level of activity as their counterparts elsewhere. In contrast, the study of power companies found that local efforts lagged behind what "progressive" firms in other regions were undertaking. The NEC helped design a follow-up program to step up the development activities of power producers. Studies were also conducted of the promotional work of New England railroads and gas companies.[51]

The marketing practices of New England manufacturers facing strong competitive challenges were a key concern of the Research Committee. To increase awareness of this issue, the committee invited well-known design expert Henry Creange to address a quarterly meeting of the Council. Creange outlined his "3-phase system for the mass production of style goods," which enabled firms to avoid debilitating competition and price cutting through careful attention to market trends and the strategic introduction of new designs. Creange's approach to marketing accorded with that of the Research Committee. The subtitle of his talk, "A Plan for Lifting New England Manufactures out of Price Competition," epitomized what the NEC panel sought to accomplish for the region's embattled industries.[52]

To address the problems of declining New England industries directly, the Research Committee commissioned studies of marketing procedures in shoes, knits, and the style-oriented cotton products known as dress goods. The research was directed by Sanford Thompson, consulting engineer and officer of the Taylor Society, an association promoting scientific management. The resulting reports highlighted the possibilities for enhanced competitiveness through innovations in marketing. The studies recommended that manufacturers increase contacts with distributors and retailers to gain better information on demand; monitor market trends more closely; introduce new styles in a more systematic manner; and increase advertising. The use of scientific management to increase production efficiency was also advocated. One outgrowth of these studies was the establishment of cooperative arrangements among New England knit goods and shoe manufacturers for continuing research on production and sales problems.[53]

As revealing as the content of the Research Committee's marketing reports were the subjects left out. Executives of New England cotton and shoe firms generally blamed the difficulties of their industries on cost disadvantages resulting from high taxes, strict labor laws, and restrictive union work rules. Most businessmen in the area endorsed this conclusion. Indeed, at about the time that the Research Committee's marketing studies appeared, the Boston Chamber of Commerce issued separate reports on the cotton and shoe industries of New England that counseled cutbacks in taxes, labor laws, and work practices as a way of restoring competitiveness.[54] The Research Committee, by contrast, paid conspicuously little attention to these controversial issues. The panel's paper on cotton dress goods did acknowledge that differentials in labor cost gave southern producers an edge. But none of the committee's studies in any way supported manufacturers' demands for retrenchment. Moreover, in a presentation on the marketing studies delivered at an NEC annual meeting, committee members averred that it was unclear whether higher labor costs were truly a "serious handicap" to regional industry.[55] For the Research Committee, the path to the economic regeneration of New England lay through investigation, analysis, and expertise—fields where a developed region, with its universities, consultants, and experienced business managers, had significant advantages. Social retrenchment would do little to improve competitiveness, members of the panel apparently believed, and led to unnecessary political conflict besides.

Lincoln Filene's Research Committee was active for only a few years, but its work had a permanent impact on the NEC's mode of operations. According to a summary of Council activities published some years later, the Research Committee not only brought about studies of direct value to important New England industries, but also, through its brilliant achievements in the field of research, impregnated the whole organization with the firm belief in the research method which has characterized it ever since.[56]

Considering that Filene's liberal approach to the social side of business questions contrasted sharply with the outlook of almost the entire Council membership, this was high praise indeed.

The Research Committee paid some attention to the economic benefits of technical inquiries in the laboratory but concentrated principally on the ways systematic analysis could improve corporate management. Other NEC efforts highlighted the potential gains from scientific investigation of industrial problems, particularly as a means of developing new products and production processes. New England had an abundance of technical institutions and personnel that could contribute to the push for growth. The region was host to four Ivy League universities, the nation's foremost school of engineering (MIT), many small private colleges, and six state universities. Many of these educational institutions carried out applied research for industry, as exemplified by the Technology Plan at MIT and the arrangement between the Connecticut Manufacturers Association and the Sheffield Scientific School at Yale. In addition, the area had numerous consulting engineers with laboratory facilities working on a contract basis for industry, including Arthur D. Little, Inc., the industry's pioneering firm. Finally, a complement of the larger manufacturers in New England maintained proprietary research laboratories, including Dewey and Almy (a chemical company) and the United Drug Company (pharmaceuticals).[57]

Such a concentration of laboratories is not unusual for a developed region. A large technical research capacity with close ties to industry is one of the signal characteristics of advanced industrial societies. National directories of research facilities from the period show that other industrial states in the Northeast and Midwest also had significant numbers of educational and corporate laboratories and that installations of this type were increasingly present on the Pacific Coast.[58] Beginning in the 1920s, however, New England's research base was scrutinized with an intensity not seen elsewhere as regional development advocates looked for ways to harness this capacity to advance the goal of economic revitalization.

As New England Council leaders worked to promote the use of laboratory research in business, one area of sustained concern was ensuring that the small manufacturing firms typical of their region carried out this kind of activity. Aside from textiles and shoes, New England had few mass production industries; most manufacturers were relatively small, producing limited runs of specialized goods. In 1937, 87 percent of the region's plants averaged one hundred or fewer employees. The NEC feared that limited resources would prevent these firms from pursuing the kind of technical research programs that had become common among large manufacturers, as epitomized by the famed laboratories at General Electric and AT&T. Deprived of the resulting stream of new products and processes, sales at small New England companies would erode. Council leaders repeatedly cited cases such as that of the Reed-Prentice Corporation to illustrate the dangers of a static product line and the possible remedies available through research. A regionally based machine tool maker, Reed-Prentice confronted a precarious situation as demand for its traditional products stagnated. Through a research program the company effected a dramatic turnaround, developing a high-quality injection molding machine that soon accounted for the bulk of sales.[59]

During the 1930s, the NEC mounted a number of initiatives aimed at increasing the use of technical research among the region's smaller manufacturers. In 1930, the Council drew up a detailed proposal for a new center at MIT that would conduct industrial research for small New England firms unable to hire their own technical personnel. Planning for the center reached an advanced stage, eventually falling apart when arrangements for financing could not be settled.[60] The Council organized a New Products Day in 1932. This event highlighted the importance of a well-planned development program for bringing new products to market and included a tour of the research laboratories at MIT. In 1936, the NEC was at work on another proposal for a New England industrial research institute, although here again the plans did not culminate in any concrete action. To encourage research by small manufacturers, the Council in 1938 inaugurated Research Week. This annual series of events, organized with the assistance of the New England branches of the national engineering societies, featured laboratory visits and exhibits of new products.[61]

Related to the NEC's promotion of industrial research was an effort to identify emerging, and often technologically advanced, industries in which New England firms could begin production. One initiative along these lines took place in the late 1920s, when the Council assembled a Committee of New England Research Consultants to provide expert advice on technical questions. Samuel Stratton, then president of MIT, chaired the group. Some of the leading consulting engineers in the region participated. The committee of research consultants began its work by examining the possibilities for aircraft production in New England. Aircraft was one of the principal new "high technology" sectors of the era, although with limited demand, uncertain government support, and scores of small producers scattered across the country, it was unclear how the industry would develop. After studying the situation, the consultants' committee issued a report identifying possibilities for area manufacturers in various stages of aircraft production. The study also recommended greater investment in the industry by local capital and more regional airfields to encourage aviation. "Airplane manufacture is on the threshold of tremendous expansion," the report stated in highlighting the possibilities for regional production in this sector, "and New England needs the new industry."[62]

Council efforts to promote technical research and identify promising new industries for the region reached a climax during the late 1930s in the work of the New Products Committee. NEC president Charles Weed set up this body in 1938 with the aim of "stimulat[ing] the development and manufacture of new products in New England." Weed saw the move as a crucial initiative on behalf of the regional economy. Although his background was in law and finance, he told an associate that "it would be difficult . . . to over-state my belief in research and new product development as essentials to the future preservation, growth and prosperity of New England's industries."[63] In a major coup, Weed recruited Karl Compton, president of MIT, to chair the group.[64] Compton was an exceptionally savvy choice to head the New Products panel. After attaining prominence as a physicist, Compton during the 1930s was in the midst of a highly successful career as a science administrator.

Karl Compton was born in Ohio, the son of a professor at the University of Wooster. Karl's younger brother Arthur became a highly acclaimed physicist. Karl Compton completed undergraduate and master's degrees at Wooster, earned a Ph.D. in physics from Princeton in 1912, and began teaching at the institution several years later. There he conducted what were viewed as groundbreaking experiments on the interaction between electrons and gases. He published a prodigious number of papers on this and other subjects. Compton became chair of Princeton's physics department in 1929 and soon afterward was offered the presidency of MIT. He took the job and the accompanying mandate to upgrade the institution's graduate and research programs. Compton remade MIT in the years that followed, dramatically raising its research profile. During World War II, he had a major role in the National Research Defense Committee, which guided the nation's investigations of new technologies with military applications.[65]

Compton was deeply interested in social and political issues, apart from his accomplishments in science. He established a Division of Humanities at MIT and over time became involved in public policy questions ranging from peaceful uses of the atom to alleviating traffic in central Boston. As science and technology drew increasing blame for Depression-era unemployment, Compton became a leading spokesman for the optimistic viewpoint. He argued that technological advance, rather than being a net destroyer of jobs, had vast potential to create new industries and new sources of employment.[66] His public stands on this issue helped convince Compton to accept the chairmanship of the NEC New Products Committee. As Compton told a former NEC officer:

> I do not know whether anything can be done effectively, but I am sure that there are possibilities and I have talked so much about this subject that I would feel like a "quitter" if I did not make at least a serious effort to deliver something along this line.[67]

Drawing on a wide range of connections, Compton assembled a highly capable New Products Committee of more than thirty people. Members included a number of prominent New England industrialists; the deans of science or technology at several regional universities; Harvard Business School professor Georges Doriot; Earl Stevenson, president of Arthur D. Little, Inc.; and Carroll Wilson of the New York–based Research Corporation, which administered the patents of MIT and other research universities. MIT arranged to pay the salary of a full-time staffer to support the committee's work. In a little more than a year of intensive effort, the panel examined numerous possibilities for fabricating new products in the region.[68]

Four main avenues of new product development were pursued. One was a continuation of the Council's longstanding efforts to encourage increased industrial research among small manufacturers. To this end the committee worked to expand the Research Week program inaugurated by the NEC some years before. Meetings adapted to the needs of local industry and intended to "indoctrinat[e] ... industrialists with the spirit of research" were held around the region.[69] A second effort involved New England's mineral resources. New Products Committee members believed that the area's reputation for being mineral poor was exaggerated, since surveys conducted in the nineteenth century had ignored substances for which industrial uses had since been found. They believed that a new canvass would reveal previously ignored mineral deposits and worked with regional geologists to organize such an undertaking. Identifying new manufacturing opportunities for the region was a third route explored by Compton's committee. Attention turned first to finding unexploited ideas that could be developed into marketable products. To identify such possibilities, panel members considered soliciting proposals from independent inventors and scanning government registers for patented ideas that were not in production. Eventually deciding that these efforts would bear little fruit, the committee attempted instead to bring existing industries into New England. This would be accomplished, as in other regions, by persuading national manufacturers to set up local branch plants. Here again, attention focused on resource-based industries. As possible growth areas, committee members targeted staple rayon, which would draw on the forest resources of northern New England, and glass making, for which the region's sand deposits would be an input. The fourth field examined by the New Products Committee was the availability of financing, or "venture capital," to support the development and marketing of new products. For a time the committee considered starting a venture capital fund to back promising projects.[70] Since several venture capital groups were set up in Boston around this time, committee members concluded that adequate finance existed to support deserving ventures. The key issue, the panel decided, was providing proper technical analysis to guide investors' decisions.

The New Products Committee wrapped up its work by recommending that a permanent organization be set up to provide this kind of advice. The body would evaluate the technical feasibility of investment proposals that were under consideration. The service would be available to established New England manufacturers expanding their product lines, national corporations considering branch plants in the region, and venture capital groups. The organization would have only a small full-time staff but could provide authoritative recommendations by consulting with experts at regional universities and in private industry. The agency would also continue to propagate the "gospel of research" among small companies and would coordinate a new survey of the region's mineral resources. With Compton spearheading the campaign, the New Products Committee won the NEC's endorsement for creating such an entity and set about putting the plan into effect.[71]

Committee members envisaged the organization as a nonprofit foundation that would eventually support itself through fees for its advisory services.

128   Confronting Decline

Planners anticipated that the agency would require two years to become self-sufficient, and that $100,000 would be needed to support operations during the startup period. This amount would be raised through donations. Under Compton's guidance, a finance committee mapped out a strategy for approaching area business leaders to seek contributions. The bulk of the funds would come from regionally based firms with an "over-all interest in New England," such as banks, utilities, and railroads. Large manufacturers with a "broad stake" in the area and a few "public spirited citizens" would provide the balance.[72]

The ensuing fund-raising campaign had mixed results. The Boston banks, a principal target, responded positively. After wrangling over the relative size of their donations, the First National Bank of Boston and the National Shawmut Bank, the city's largest commercial lenders, exceeded their quota, putting in more than $13,000. The telephone companies and a few other utilities came through with the hoped-for amounts. On the other hand, Godfrey Cabot, scion of a prominent Boston family and a leading industrialist, turned down Compton's appeal for support, and other sectors made contributions far smaller than the quantities sought. In the end only two-thirds of the desired funds were raised. To get the project under way, MIT and the NEC picked up some of the costs of staff. The new organization went into operation in 1942 as the New England Industrial Research Foundation. An important initial success was recruiting the associate director of Pittsburgh's Mellon Institute, a leader in industrial research, to head the body.[73] Despite this auspicious start, in the end little came of the foundation's work, for reasons described later in this chapter.

Other New England Council Development Efforts

Although the NEC devoted great energy to sophisticated recovery efforts emphasizing research, technology, and new products, there were many other facets to the organization's development push in the years before World War II. The Council sought to improve public perceptions of economic conditions in the region, bring new manufacturers into the hardest-hit industrial communities, improve infrastructure, modernize farming, and promote tourism, among other endeavors. In these domains, as in others, attention to expertise and the use of up-to-date techniques often characterized the association's work.

Publicity was an important element of the NEC development drive. The economic problems of New England received intensive attention in the news media. Council leaders feared that this coverage created negative impressions of the region that might make a bad situation even worse. This would occur if potential outside investors avoided putting money into an area where capitalist energies had seemingly stagnated. To counteract this possibility, the NEC gave high priority to creating a more positive perception of the region's economy. Through the "ceaseless iteration and reiteration of the facts about New England" the Council worked to foster the impression that despite problems in some industries, the area as a whole was prosperous, forward-looking, and a "good place in which to live, work, and play." The Council's public relations department churned out material highlighting such positive themes and closely monitored its reproduction in media outlets.[74]

Helping to secure new sources of employment in individual communities directly hit by factory closures was an important aspect of the Council's work. This activity often fell under the heading of "community development."

Industrial development efforts in individual municipalities took place principally at the local level. Community business leaders acting through local chambers of commerce typically spearheaded these endeavors, with city government playing a supporting role. Cities and towns tried a variety of strategies to attract new employers. If businessmen in an area had good contacts, some prospects could be located through informal inquiries. Many cities advertised their advantages as sites for manufacturing. The desperate mayor of New Bedford at one point formed an Industrial Development Legion and declared war against the city's high unemployment. Municipalities frequently established industrial development corporations that sold or leased vacant mill space at low cost to new employers. Regional leaders repeatedly condemned the use of giveaways to attract jobs, but some New England municipalities did offer tax exemptions, moving subsidies, and other inducements to incoming manufacturers.[75]

Several NEC committees worked to facilitate local efforts to attract new manufacturing.[76] As one Council publication expressed the philosophy behind this endeavor, "The so-called 'New England problem' is largely a community problem. There cannot be a prosperous New England unless New England's communities are prosperous." In the late 1920s the Council's Committee on Community Development urged municipalities to conduct comprehensive surveys of their industrial assets and liabilities and prepared a primer on growth techniques for city leaders. Relatively high municipal taxes on manufacturing were a concern of the NEC community development committee from the outset. As straitened local finances forced up levies in the early 1930s, the panel encouraged the formation of local taxpayers' councils that would press for reductions in city spending.[77] In the mid-1930s the NEC set up an Industrial Development Committee to invigorate the effort on behalf of regional manufacturing. There was an important town-level component to the committee's agenda, and the panel worked closely with local chambers of commerce.

Compiling regional economic data was an important development activity of the NEC and one that contributed to the recovery efforts in individual towns. Gathering and distributing economic information and statistics is an essential growth-promoting step in any industrialized area. Government departments typically carry out this task, but the region's public development agencies were weak and underfunded in the period between the world wars. The NEC picked up the slack, assembling a sophisticated set of economic data and indicators. The organization calculated a monthly index of regional business activity and kept a master file of vacant industrial properties. Beginning in 1937, the Council published statistical profiles of every community in New England, with data on population, labor force, income, and transportation links that would be useful to industrialists seeking new plant sites.[78]

Providing strong infrastructure for economic activity is a time-tested means of regional development, and the NEC was active in this area as well. From the time of its establishment through World War II, the Council worked to draw attention to the issue, conducted numerous studies of New England's transportation and power systems, and participated in the planning for a number of important public works projects.[79]

The NEC acted in a variety of ways to promote the well-being of the region's farm sector. Agriculture accounted for a limited portion of total business activity in New England, but it still played an important role in the economic life of rural areas. Moreover, farm interests were an important Council constituency, since the organization's avowed aim was to represent all producers in the region. Like industry, regional agriculture faced serious structural difficulties in this period, as local farmers producing perishable goods such as milk and eggs lost market share to more efficient western producers. The NEC's Agriculture Committee worked to ameliorate farm conditions. A crucial initiative was the establishment of standardization and grading systems that would recapture consumer loyalties. The Council spearheaded a multi-step farm marketing program to put these reforms in place.[80] In later years the NEC devoted considerable attention to management of natural resources, particularly forests, which was another important issue in rural New England.

The Council worked diligently to promote the region's vacation and recreation sector. The area's historic sites and scenic coasts and mountains provided the basis for this industry, which constituted an increasingly vital component of the New England economy in the years after World War I. The sector was particularly important as an alternative source of income in rural areas experiencing long-term declines in farming and extractive industries. The NEC early on formed a Recreation Committee to address problems in the vacation sector. Advertising quickly emerged as a key issue. The Council committee worked to bring coherence to a regional advertising message muddled by the competing efforts of numerous state and local organizations. The group also called for systematic inventories of the area's recreational resources and conducted its own promotional campaigns, in particular promoting winter sports as a complement to the established summer vacation trade.[81]

The NEC performed a number of general functions on behalf of New England that are worthy of note, in addition to the efforts on behalf of particular sectors. At times this work had a political element.

The organization repeatedly served as a kind of catalytic agent, spurring other groups into action on regional issues. It was at the urging of the Council, for example, that the executives of the region's states formed the New England Governors Conference and began meeting regularly to coordinate policy on issues of common concern. For years Council staff provided administrative support to the governors' conference, acting as its de facto secretariat. Other regional roundtables were established at the Council's behest, including conferences of state officials with responsibility for labor, education, industrial development, and aviation.[82]

In the absence of another business association representing all of New England, the NEC functioned as the region's representative on diverse economic issues. In the 1930s the group served as a regional clearinghouse for administering the National Industrial Recovery Act and helped write codes for certain industries. During World War II it handled many responsibilities relating to economic mobilization. The Council also spearheaded lobbying on national economic questions that could affect the area. The NEC opposed the equalization of U.S. freight rates, which would have reduced costs for southern shippers, and agitated against a proposal to "freeze" World War II defense plants in the Northeast and Midwest while turning those in less developed parts of the country over to private owners.

Finally, in conflicts between economic interest groups within the region, the NEC repeatedly played the part of honest broker, mediating settlements on difficult issues. After conflict between farm groups and regional power companies almost disrupted the organization's inaugural meeting, the Council set about finding common ground. Agreement was finally reached at an NEC-sponsored conference in 1927. Following a "very frank, open, and wholehearted" exchange of views, power and farm interests set up a "strong joint committee" to formulate remedial action.[83] During the New Deal years the NEC often brought warring Massachusetts leaders of industry and labor together on issues of mutual concern. The Council organized joint support for what became the National Industrial Recovery Act and arranged a dramatic dual endorsement for a successful Bay State proposal to reduce property taxes on manufacturing.[84]

Government Economic Development Efforts in New England: The Establishment of State Development Agencies

Government directly participated in New England's recovery campaign in the period between the world wars. This was so despite the private sector's domination of regional growth-promotion efforts and the relatively limited powers and capacities of the public sector at this time. An important and innovative development initiative was the establishment within state government of agencies to encourage growth. Massachusetts was a leader here, setting up a state Industrial Commission in 1929.[85]

The push to establish a government development agency in Massachusetts began in early 1929 when Republican governor Frank Allen called for such action in his annual address to the legislature. State government, Allen told lawmakers, should "lend . . . every assistance to the industries within her borders, and . . . extend . . . every inducement to new ones to locate here." The governor envisaged a commission of five unpaid members that would conduct research and coordinate the activities of voluntary organizations already dealing with economic questions. In backing the creation of the new agency, Allen clearly had the grim economic realities of recent years foremost in mind. "To bring to the Commonwealth new industries to replace those which move away is highly important," he declared.[86]

Allen recommended the creation of a public development body even though he was a businessman with a rather conservative political philosophy. The gravity of the state's industrial situation evidently led the governor to brush aside any hesitations he might have had about this expansion of government's economic role. Allen did recognize that the proposed agency might be seen as contradicting laissez-faire ideals. To counter such concerns, he later asserted that establishing the commission constituted a method of "putting the state into business without in any way competing with private enterprise."[87]

To assure support for the proposed agency, steps were taken to broaden its appeal. Although the decline of manufacturing had obviously motivated the governor, he suggested that the new body deal with agricultural concerns as well, with the commissioner of agriculture and also the commissioner of labor and industries sitting as ex-officio members of the new state development commission. The initial draft of the measure creating the panel, drawn up by a legislative committee, went even further. The agency's purview was expanded to include promotion of the recreational sector as well as industry and agriculture. To forestall the impression that industrial interests would dominate, the draft bill specified that one of the commission's five members always represent labor. The powers of the proposed commission became more extensive as the measure moved through the legislative process, indicating the seriousness with which its mission was viewed. In addition to conducting research and coordinating the activities of other organizations, the final version of the bill authorized the agency to publish publicity materials and hire a small staff.[88]

The fleshed-out measure commanded support across the political spectrum. At committee hearings in April 1929, business turned out heavily in favor of the bill. Local chambers of commerce were particularly supportive. The membership of these groups included many service-sector firms with business prospects that were linked to the overall condition of the area economy. The past president of the Cambridge Industrial Association led the presentation on behalf of the development agency, submitting letters and telegrams from thirty chambers of commerce and boards of trade across the state. Representatives of the chambers of commerce of Boston, Lowell, Lawrence, and Brockton, among other municipalities, appeared in person to back the measure. Also testifying favorably were John Lawrence of the NEC, the president of the Boston and Maine Railroad, and a representative of the state's hotel associations. The proposal won backing from the liberal end of the political spectrum as well. Two officers of the state AFL spoke in favor of the development agency, as did several liberal state legislators. No one appeared in opposition. The measure was approved by both houses and signed by the governor. The Massachusetts Industrial Commission began operations that summer.[89]

The new organization's approach to economic development resembled that of the larger and more influential New England Council. The commission began its work with numerous studies of the state economy. At the direction of the legislature it investigated conditions in textiles and means for dealing with unemployment in that and other sectors. It hired a consultant to report on why manufacturing was faring worse in Massachusetts than in the other New England states. The commission also examined the industrial development efforts under way in numerous municipalities; studied possibilities for increased local production of agricultural goods; inventoried the state's recreational facilities; and carried out a mineral survey to identify possible inputs for new industries.[90] Like the NEC, the Industrial Commission attached great importance to public perceptions of local economic conditions. To counter "pessimistic propaganda" that was "disparaging in its import and damaging in results," the agency mounted a significant publicity effort highlighting the industrial advantages of Massachusetts.[91] Overly earnest efforts in this direction at times produced unintended effects.[92]

Like the NEC, the state commission focused much of its energy on seeking new industries to replace those that had disappeared. But while the NEC devoted great attention to fostering the growth of indigenous enterprise, the commission concentrated on inducing manufacturers based elsewhere to set up new plants in Massachusetts. This mirrored the strategy pursued by developing areas in the South and West. To attract outside investment, the commission distributed promotional material, maintained information on the industrial possibilities in each municipality, and on at least one occasion direct-mailed manufacturers in neighboring states about the advantages of transplanting to Massachusetts.[93] The Industrial Commission also played the same role of attempting to mediate private-sector disputes that was occasionally carried out by the NEC. In 1930–31 the commission held a series of meetings with business and union leaders to discuss the decline of the state's industries and steps that could be taken to make them more competitive. The primary topics were the by then familiar issues of taxes on manufacturing, labor laws, and the costs of social insurance. Nothing of substance emerged from the parleys, although the effort was "commended by those who have attended."[94]

Other state government entities participated in Massachusetts development efforts, although the Industrial Commission's work was most visible.

The activities of other agencies for the most part entailed a continuation of the public sector's traditional role of providing infrastructure to facilitate growth. Aviation was an important new means of transportation in this era, and a number of New England states, including Massachusetts, created commissions to deal with aviation issues. Their work related mostly to the planning and construction of airfields to handle the new traffic. Particular effort was devoted to the establishment of a fully equipped international airport at Logan Field near Boston. The poor condition of the Boston port was another important transportation concern. A number of state entities worked on this question in the 1930s, laying the groundwork for major renovations carried out after World War II.

While the work of state economic development agencies had greater visibility, municipal government also had a hand in the efforts to bring replacement industries into the cities and towns hardest hit by the decline of traditional manufacturing. Local officials generally cooperated with business leaders in recruiting new employers and readying abandoned mill space for new users. Working the political system could at times do as much as promotional efforts to bring in new jobs. U.S. Representative Edith Nourse Rogers of Lowell claimed that she devoted "many months of hard work, made up of hundreds of conferences, thousands of dollars in long distance calls," before federal officials agreed to locate a Remington munitions plant in that city during World War II.[95]

Assessing Economic Development Efforts in New England

In response to the decline of traditional manufacturing in New England, private-sector organizations such as the New England Council and state and local government mounted a wide-ranging campaign to revitalize the area economy. Many of the growth-promoting initiatives sought to maximize the competitive advantages typical of a developed region, including a large research apparatus and abundant managerial expertise. Others resembled the growth strategies seen in developing parts of the country, such as advertising the suitability of particular locales for manufacturing and recruiting potential new employers. All of this activity raises an important question: what difference did it make? Did the development push result in concrete gains for the New England economy? A precise answer is not possible, as we cannot know how the area would have fared in the absence of these efforts. Some informed estimates can nonetheless be made.

It is clear that the growth drive was not a swift and overwhelming success. Economic conditions in the area remained seriously troubled at the end of the 1930s, fifteen years after the decline of traditional manufacturing had begun and at a time when the nation was recovering from the Depression. This is not to say that development efforts in New England made no difference. On the whole, the initiatives undertaken probably boosted regional production and employment to some extent, although not by much. In making a more detailed assessment, it is useful to divide growth-promoting endeavors into three categories. The first group consisted of activities that were well thought-out and likely had some success. Those in the second group were also sound but failed to produce benefits for reasons of circumstance. Activities in the third category were thoroughly misconceived and could not under any conditions have aided the regional economy.

Most of the development initiatives pursued in New England in this period probably fell into the first group—well-designed efforts that likely had a degree of success. An example for which some hard evidence exists is the establishment of the Massachusetts textile schools. Surveys of Lowell Textile School graduates conducted in the 1950s showed that most alumni made their careers in New England textiles, with significant numbers rising to leadership roles in the industry.[96] It seems a reasonable assumption that the rigorous training these individuals received at Lowell enabled them to perform more effectively than would otherwise have been the case in the executive, sales, engineering, and research positions they filled. Their work probably helped some of the region's struggling textile companies stay in business as long as they did. All of this was just as the school's founders had intended. Establishing the schools would thus seem to have been moderately successful. Steps to promote industrial research, improve the marketing of agricultural and manufactured goods, and bring order to the recreation industry's advertising probably produced incremental gains for those sectors as well.

The fate of the New England Industrial Research Foundation, which emerged in the early 1940s from the work of the NEC New Products Committee, exemplifies the second category of development efforts—those that were well-conceived but for reasons of circumstance had scant success. The concept of a nonprofit entity that would provide expert advice to investors considering new industrial endeavors was a promising one. However, the foundation began operations in early 1942, just as war mobilization disrupted normal business conditions. The industrial researchers who would have worked with the organization were suddenly in great demand, while the market for new products without military applications evaporated. The foundation ended up scrambling for a place in the mobilizing economy. It helped some companies organize their research programs and secure defense contracts, but income from fees never reached a level sufficient to cover costs (a potential problem even in peacetime). When the director took another position in 1944, the foundation was essentially shut down, with remaining activities taken over by the NEC.[97]

The third category of growth efforts were those that were badly conceived and never had a chance of success. An example is an emphasis on regional self-sufficiency that occasionally surfaced in the thinking of growth advocates. For instance, the report on aircraft manufacturing issued in the late 1920s by an NEC-affiliated panel of experts called for new aircraft factories that would "supply New England's requirements with New England–made products."[98] Similarly, an early NEC newsletter lamented the fact that delegates to a Council meeting would be wearing name badges produced elsewhere in the country and concluded that "there would seem to be a field for the manufacture of low-priced badges in New England."[99] Such assertions thoroughly misconstrued the area's economic history and future prospects. New England manufacturers had prospered in the past by selling quality goods in well-defined markets to buyers around the country and even abroad. To recover, the region needed to develop other specialized products that would achieve similarly broad sales. Attempting to compete with lower-cost producers of standardized goods or falling back on a regional version of autarchy offered no solutions to New England's problems.

The experience of the NEC and other growth advocates demonstrates that promoting economic development is not an easy task. Industries locate in particular areas on the basis of concrete competitive advantages, such as availability of materials, proximity to markets, and access to the appropriate labor force. Trying to tilt the balance toward a locale that has not been selected through the free play of market forces means surmounting the built-in advantages that exist elsewhere. Even a group of talented and determined people, like the individuals at work with the NEC, will encounter repeated frustration when confronting such a challenge. Moreover, incremental gains—like those from the first category of well-designed and partially successful development efforts—accomplish little. An area losing a sizable chunk of its economic base requires sectors with dramatic growth prospects that will create broad swathes of new employment.

Expansion of this sort took place in a number of New England industries in the years after World War II. In one case the development efforts of regional business facilitated success. Attempts to improve the financing for small regional companies were centrally important here. Through these measures, significant funds were made available to small New England businesses, as the following chapter demonstrates.

CHAPTER 5

Small Business Financing in Mid-Twentieth-Century New England

A campaign for economic development was one of the principal responses to the demise of textiles and other established industries in New England. Regional leaders encouraged the expansion of existing industries and the emergence of new ones, thereby seeking to create jobs to replace those lost in declining sectors. Business elites initially headed New England's drive for growth. The private sector's development push began in the mid-1920s with the formation of the New England Council and continued steadily in the years thereafter.

In seeking to stimulate growth in New England, development advocates engaged in a wide range of activities. Most of the development possibilities that were pursued had little impact. In one domain, however, the push for growth achieved significant results. This was an attempt to improve the financing available to the region's new and small companies. Efforts to improve small business financing in New England started in the 1920s, shifted into high gear in the late 1930s, and continued during the 1940s.

The shortage of finance for small business was an important concern of the American corporate sector as a whole in the early twentieth century. Private-sector initiatives to address the problem were mounted throughout the country beginning in the 1920s. A desire to legitimate capitalism and prevent the long-term stagnation of the national economy motivated most of those working on the issue. The need for added employment in New England gave the small business finance question greater urgency there. To make more money available to small firms, New England businessmen conducted studies on the sources of financing, established some of the country's first venture capital organizations, and pressed local commercial banks to provide additional small business loans. Small New England companies obtained significant new financing as a result of these efforts. The increased availability of small business finance contributed in important ways to the area's subsequent economic growth.

The Nationwide Shortfall in Financing for Small Businesses

Beginning in the 1920s, small companies throughout the United States confronted significant difficulties in obtaining adequate finance. Established firms with a record of profits and a sound credit history could generally raise needed funds from banks and the securities markets. Smaller companies, by contrast, faced obstacles in attracting both equity and debt financing. The problems were particularly grave for small firms that had been established recently or that sought to expand. The trouble on the equity side stemmed from a shortage of what was known as venture capital—funds that would take an ownership stake in risky but potentially very profitable enterprises. On the debt side, difficulties arose because commercial banks and other lenders were reluctant to provide sufficient credit to smaller borrowers, who were perceived as unduly risky. Lenders were particularly wary of giving small firms longer-term loans that could be used to pay for equipment or the expense of developing new products.

The shortfall of finance for small companies generated considerable concern in national business circles in the 1920s and would become much more worrying, and highly controversial, in the years that followed. Attempts to alleviate the problem produced a range of experimental initiatives that laid the groundwork for the modern venture capital industry—a key innovation in twentieth-century capitalism.

The shortage of finance for American small business was a byproduct of the country's economic modernization and first became apparent in the years after World War I. Before that time, long-established, usually local arrangements seem to have provided a sufficient flow of funds to small companies. One veteran of the New England machine tool industry recalled that before World War I numerous firms had been set up by "young men with energy and ideals who received the backing of local capital in amounts ranging from a few tens to a few hundreds of thousands of dollars." The establishment in the 1920s of Massachusetts chemical company Dewey and Almy exemplified the traditional routes of small business finance that were in decline during this period. According to one of those involved, to raise startup equity the company's backers "practically passed the hat around among 20 people and asked for $5,000 or $10,000 apiece and got it." The investment banks scattered across the country were an important avenue for securing this kind of financial backing. The institutions often raised funds for promising local entrepreneurs or gave references to people who could provide the needed money. In some places, banks and chambers of commerce maintained lists of wealthy individuals willing to invest in local industry. Commercial banks themselves were a significant source of support, providing de facto long-term finance to trusted customers by repeatedly rolling over ostensibly short-term loans.[1]

In the 1920s, structural changes in the financial markets constricted the traditional flow of venture capital to small companies. Securities listed on the stock exchanges saw enormous growth in popularity during this period. Rather than investing money in small local businesses, wealthy individuals increasingly purchased listed stocks. Listed securities were highly liquid and, since only well-established firms were listed, seemingly more secure. In addition, a great deal of money flowed into the newly developed investment trusts (mutual funds), which avoided the riskier small stocks. These developments reshaped the investment banking industry. As informal local markets for the securities of small firms dried up, influence shifted to the more established investment banks in the big cities that concentrated on large issues.[2]

The increasing scarcity of finance for small firms caused alarm in financial circles during the 1920s. The era saw at least one instance of voluntary private action to address the problem. Under the leadership of Brice Disque, a financier and sometime progressive reformer, forty Wall Street veterans in 1928 put $25,000 each into a special loan fund. Known as the $1,000,000 Small Issues Corporation, the fund aimed to serve small companies that wanted to expand their operations but could not obtain the necessary financial backing. The timing for the venture could not have been worse. All of the small companies to which loans were extended went under in the Depression, and the forty backers of the experimental corporation lost their entire investment.[3]

The shortage of finance for small companies worsened during the Depression years. In the face of sizable loan losses and stiffer regulation, commercial banks became stricter about granting loans to smaller business borrowers. Studies in the mid-1930s found banks in Chicago pressing small firms to pay off outstanding long-term loans and institutions in Connecticut demanding extensive collateral before lending to even the most reliable small business customers. In the meantime the flow of equity capital to new businesses dropped off even further. The scars of the stock market crash and the higher federal taxes to be paid on the eventual profits led wealthy individuals to shun risky equities, while investment banks avoided small issues.[4]

Squeezed for finance, and facing strong competitive pressure from corporate America, small business mobilized in the 1930s. Groups such as the Conference of Small Business Organizations and the National Federation of Independent Business, and locally the Smaller Businessmen's Association of

New England, lobbied for strong federal assistance to small business. Their program included rigorous anti-trust enforcement, protection from large corporate competitors, and financial and technical assistance. The small business insurgents had a high-profile spokesman in future Commerce Secretary Henry Wallace and a number of other key allies. These included Brandeisian liberals who feared corporate domination of the economy, interventionist liberals who favored government intervention to revive growth, and developmentalists from the South and West who believed that northeastern monopolists were retarding the expansion of their regions. The battle of small business against corporate America lasted through World War II and well into the 1950s and featured seemingly endless congressional investigations of the difficulties confronting smaller companies. While corporate domination of the economy was never seriously challenged, small business advocates achieved some institutional successes. These included the establishment of a Small Business Advisory Committee to the U.S. Department of Commerce during the New Deal; the formation of the Smaller War Plants Corporation to steer World War II contracts to small firms; and the creation of an Office of Small Business, later the Small Business Administration, in the commerce department.[5]

Federal financial assistance to small firms was an important component of the small business agenda. Government had taken on an important role in private-sector financing during the Depression through the activities of the Reconstruction Finance Corporation and the regional Federal Reserve Banks, which used their authority under section 13(b) of the Federal Reserve Act to make industrial loans. Small business advocates repeatedly proposed that the government financing function be expanded and targeted to smaller companies. In 1939 Senator James Mead of New York introduced one bill providing for public insurance of small business loans and a second that would set up a small business lending arm within the Federal Reserve System. Versions of the loan guarantee and loan provision ideas were reintroduced in Congress toward the end of World War II. Securities and Exchange Commission staffer Rudolph Weissman proposed to go even further. In a 1945 book that attracted widespread attention, Weissman called for the establishment of a government venture capital system that would invest public funds in the equity of small companies.[6]

Proposals for an expanded, permanent government role in financing private business horrified conservatives already reeling before the scale of New Deal intervention in the free market. "Nationalize [banking and finance]," one business leader warned, and "you have pretty nearly reached that last long mile down the road to a complete socialist economy."[7] Ideological hostility was compounded by financiers' fears that government agencies providing loans and investment capital would compete with their own private institutions. To preempt government intervention and help revitalize an economy dogged by depression, business leaders urged the financial industry to provide better funding to small business. New England industrialist James Hook told an audience of bankers in 1938 that to avoid "further government control and disbursement of the nation's credit," banks had to provide increased support for entrepreneurial activity. When "groups and individuals feel the urge to borrow money for constructive long pull ventures into the future," Hook stated, "proper facilities to aid them must be at hand."[8]

Pressured by small business and facing federal encroachment, the financial industry took a number of steps in the late 1930s and 1940s to increase the flow of money to small firms. To deflect charges that commercial banks were not doing enough for their smaller borrowers, a commission of the American Bankers Association recommended that banks establish regional credit pools that would make loans to small and medium-sized businesses that had been refused funds by individual lenders. Twenty-three banks in New York City participated in the first pool, pledging $100 million in small business credit. Bankers' groups in Connecticut, Massachusetts, and other states quickly followed suit.[9] Life insurance companies also moved to include smaller firms in their business lending programs.[10]

More dramatic steps took place regarding the provision of equity for small business, as the country's first venture capital funds were established. These organizations had the sole aim of investing in new and small companies. The venture capital firms had expert staff members who sifted through myriad solicitations, selecting a promising few in which to invest. As important as the capital provided was the management advice venture capitalists gave to managers of the companies in which they took positions. Many investments were expected to fail, but it was anticipated that a few would turn out so successfully that the entire endeavor would realize a profit. Numerous venture capitalists preferred to invest in technically innovative products and processes, though others favored more conventional businesses. The first venture capital organizations appeared before World War II and included the Shaw-Isham Company, founded in Chicago in 1936, and Enterprise Associates, established in Boston in 1939. Other funds were set up during a flurry of activity in the initial postwar years.[11]

The money for most early venture capital organizations came from wealthy individuals and families with a sense of social responsibility. Some of the best known operations set up in the postwar years include J. H. Whitney and Company and Payson and Trask, founded in New York by siblings of the Whitney family; a fund established by the Rockefeller brothers, also in New York; and a Pittsburgh organization set up by the Mellon family.[12] There were also attempts to channel monies managed by insurance companies and investment trusts into the venture capital field. A group of Chicago businessmen tried to set up such a fund in the late 1930s, and the American Research and Development Corporation was established along these lines in Boston after the war.[13]

Two other types of organizations established during this period pursued different routes for bringing new products to market. One set of companies carried out laboratory development work on promising but unexploited ideas. If a viable product resulted, it was licensed to an existing manufacturer. The National Research Corporation, which moved into this field after opening in Boston in 1940, was an early example of this kind of operation. Others were the Hodges Research and Development Corporation, set up in San Francisco in 1947, and the Rand Development Corporation, established in Cleveland in 1948 by an heir to the Remington-Rand fortune.[14] Another type of organization acted as a referral service and broker, seeking to bring together inventors with ideas for new products and industrial firms seeking diversification, which could do the manufacturing. The New Products Research Corporation was active in this field in Boston in 1946, as was the National Foundation for Science and Industry in Chicago.[15]

Of the three kinds of organizations working to aid small business and boost innovation, the venture capital firms would eventually prove the most successful. But it was not apparent at the time that this would be the outcome. Moreover, the activities of the three types of organizations occasionally intertwined, confirming that they were pursuing different means to similar ends. Thus the venture capitalist Whitney family invested in Hodges Research and Development, a development laboratory, and American Research and Development in 1953 set up a broker arm to bring proposals it found promising but did not wish to invest in to the attention of interested manufacturers.[16]

Many of the small business promotion organizations of the 1930s and 1940s were based in areas (such as New York, Chicago, and Detroit) that had experienced prosperous conditions until the Depression hit. These promotional groups were founded to advance national aims, such as preserving and legitimizing capitalism and assuring future national growth. In regions facing underdevelopment or structural economic decline, revitalizing the local economy was an additional—or even the primary—motivation. Spurring development in the troubled Pittsburgh region was one aim of the Mellon family's venture capital body. The three small business organizations set up in the San Francisco area were doubtless linked to northern California's development drive.[17] And the need to foster new industry in New England helped spur the formation by 1946 of no fewer than seven Boston organizations promoting the growth of small firms. Table 5.1 lists the small-business development entities set up in Boston during this era.

Table 5.1. Venture Capital and Other Business Promotion Organizations Established in Boston, 1939–1946

Organization	Year Created	Activity	New England Council (NEC) Role in Organization?
Enterprise Associates	1939	Venture capital	No. Although revitalizing the regional economy was an avowed goal of some of those involved.
New England Industrial Development Corporation	1940	Venture capital	Yes. Founded on the initiative of Lincoln Filene, chair of the NEC Research Committee, to aid the growth of small local manufacturers, which the committee had identified as essential to regional development.
New England Industrial Research Foundation	1942	Advise venture capitalists and others considering investment in the region	Yes. Set up at the recommendation of the NEC New Products Committee.
Venture Research Company	by 1942	Locate and investigate opportunities for venture capital investment by Venture Research clients	Some indirect role. Several leading NEC figures became involved in the organization's work.
New Products Research Corporation	1942	Match inventors with manufacturers seeking new products to fabricate	Unknown.
New Enterprises, Inc. (reorganization of prewar Enterprise Associates)	1946	Venture capital	No. (But see Enterprise Associates above.)
American Research and Development Corporation	1946	Venture capital	Yes. Founded on the initiative of leading NEC member Ralph Flanders, who drew heavily on the findings of the NEC Committee on the Financing and Ownership of New England Business Enterprises.

Note: Table summarizes events described in chapters 4, 5, and 6.

Initial Efforts to Improve Small Business Finance in New England

The New England businessmen spearheading the 1920s push for regional economic recovery looked into finance questions soon after their development campaign began. The first issue to arise in this connection was whether the area's commercial banks provided sufficient support to local industrial companies. The New England Council Research Committee, headed by Lincoln Filene, assembled a group of bankers in 1926 to investigate the matter. An officer of the First National Bank of Boston, the largest lender in the region, chaired the bankers group, which included representatives from around New England. The lenders in turn hired consultants who conducted a national study of the services banks provided to their business customers. Investigators interviewed scores of bankers in New England and other regions.[18]

The consultants' report documented a wide range of activities undertaken by banks to assist their industrial customers. One institution maintained a corps of engineers and accountants to advise borrowers. Others helped customers install modern budgeting, bookkeeping, and marketing systems. Enlightened self-interest lay at the root of these advisory activities, concluded the consultants conducting the study. The banks providing extensive services to industrial borrowers sought rapid expansion. By aiding the growth of customers and the local community, the lending institutions aimed to increase their own volume of business.[19] The study's authors found that New England banks were, on average, as supportive of local manufacturing as institutions elsewhere. The report noted a wide variation in the level of promotional activity from bank to bank, both within New England and in other regions. In an introduction to the study, Filene's Research Committee stated hopefully that if New England institutions could do "a better job for industry than banks in any other section of the country, then no one would have much cause to fear for New England's industrial future."[20]

Soon after the study was complete, Filene and some of his collaborators launched an early initiative in venture capital. In their investigations of regional industry, members of the Research Committee had concluded that small manufacturers would play an essential role in the future development of the New England economy. Working with a group of financiers, committee members sought to identify steps that could be taken to aid the small firms. A leading recommendation was to establish a public interest industrial development company that would stimulate private investment in small manufacturers. Filene and some of his fellow investigators set about organizing such a corporation. They were apparently ready to start operations under the name New England Industries, Inc., when the 1929 stock market crash abruptly foreclosed the possibility of increasing equity investment in any kind of company.[21]

The possibilities for improving the flow of finance to New England small business were limited during the worst years of the Depression. As the economy recovered in the mid-1930s, proposals for accomplishing this goal again circulated. At a 1936 meeting of the New England Council (NEC) one speaker called for the creation of a $5 million industrial development corporation to foster new manufacturing in the region. The same year, the NEC's Industrial Development Committee investigated methods of financing new industry and examined the difficulties small firms faced in securing equity and long-term loans. As the 1930s ended, the NEC's New Products Committee again examined the venture capital question. Committee members considered setting up their own equity fund but concluded that recent developments made this step unnecessary. Following years of discussion and frustrated plans, two venture capital organizations began operating in the region at this time.[22]

One of the new groups represented the revival of a venture capital project first contemplated in the late 1920s. As economic conditions improved in 1939, Lincoln Filene and his colleagues dusted off their decade-old plan for an organization that would provide investment capital and management advice to small New England manufacturers. The principals spent a year circulating proposals, publishing treatises on the need for venture capital, and consulting with regional leaders including NEC officer Ralph Flanders, MIT president Karl Compton, and Oscar Hausserman, attorney and former president of the Boston Chamber of Commerce. The organization finally opened its doors in Boston in late 1940, eventually taking the name New England Industrial Development Corporation (NEIDC). Filene and several other individuals provided startup funds, on the assumption that the corporation would eventually become self-supporting. William Stoddard, Filene's assistant, acted as the body's president. Sitting on the board of directors in 1943 were Henry B. Cabot, a wealthy lawyer and descendant of one of Boston's most esteemed families, and a number of attorneys and industrialists. The corporation's large advisory committee included Powell Cabot, head of the public Massachusetts Development and Industrial Commission, officers of several of the smaller Boston commercial banks, and a number of other attorneys. The NEIDC directed its aid to small manufacturers in routine lines of business; as a matter of policy, the corporation would not support "patented devices in their embryonic or experimental stages."[23]

Another group of financiers, businessmen, and technical experts set up a separate venture capital organization in Boston in 1939 under the name Enterprise Associates.

Aiding the regional economy was very likely the goal of Enterprise Associates, as was true of the NEIDC.[24] The prime mover behind Enterprise Associates was William A. Coolidge, member of an old Boston business family and relative of the recent U.S. president. Coolidge epitomized the wealthy, well-connected, idiosyncratic individuals who pioneered in venture capital. Coolidge graduated from Harvard College and worked at the Boston investment banking firm Jackson and Curtis before deciding to pursue an interest in law. He attended Harvard Law School and joined the old-line Boston firm of Ropes and Gray. A friend later described Coolidge as being full of novel ideas, never wanting to work in a mold, and possessed of a sense of noblesse oblige. About twenty other individuals participated in Enterprise Associates, among them investment bankers Charles F. Adams Jr., and Henry I. Harriman; William Rand, an executive with the Monsanto chemical company; and Daniel Comstock, co-inventor of technicolor and owner of a Boston commercial laboratory. Each contributed to the group's pool of investment money and stood to gain from the eventual profits. Comstock's associate Stanley Livingstone helped with the organization's staff work, and Georges Doriot, professor and assistant dean at the Harvard Business School, advised on investments.[25]

Enterprise Associates had a technological orientation, seeking "research developments and inventions which show good promise of industrial importance." This contrasted with the NEIDC's focus on assisting small firms in established industries. Enterprise Associates must have announced publicly its formation, because hundreds of investment proposals had been received by 1940. The group apparently acted on only one, putting $50,000 into a firm set up by MIT graduate Richard Morse to pursue the possibilities of manufacturing in a high vacuum environment. In the research-intensive economy of World War II, Morse's National Research Corporation (NRC) proved an enormous success. NRC made notable advances in the production of penicillin and realized a major breakthrough by vacuum-coating glass to prevent glare, which facilitated the manufacture of bombsights. The firm also devised a vacuum technique to produce frozen orange juice concentrate that was licensed to what later became the Minute Maid corporation. NRC was probably the first overnight success story in the Boston area technology industry. In 1949, the company had 150 employees, enjoyed sales of $1.4 million, and occupied offices in a handsome building along the Charles River near MIT.[26]

After making one landmark investment, Enterprise Associates seems to have gone on hiatus during the war years. Staff member Stanley Livingstone apparently left the organization and by 1942 had set up a third vehicle to aid in financing new firms, known as the Venture Research Company. Little is known of this group, which was also headquartered in Boston. Sitting on the board of directors in 1942, in addition to Livingstone, were Frederick Roberts, an investment banker, and Thomas Nelson Perkins Jr., the son of an eminent lawyer. MIT president Compton assisted in launching Venture Research, and by 1945 former NEC president Ralph Flanders had "a finger" in its work.[27]

Although several venture capital organizations were set up in New England in 1939–42, area business leaders still worried that the new manufacturers who could help revive the local economy were not receiving sufficient financial support. Efforts to improve financing for small business in the region therefore continued during World War II, resulting in comprehensive studies of the problem and additional steps to rectify it.

Edward E. Chase provided the impetus for this activity. Chase was a highly successful businessman with a deep interest in politics and public policy. He was a pillar of the business and political establishment in his native Maine, yet acted, in his own words, as a "rebel, off and on."[28]

Chase was born into a locally prominent family from the northern Maine coast. He graduated from the University of Maine in 1913, served in local government, then became a clerk for the Maine state legislature. In 1919 Chase joined a securities firm in Portland, Maine's largest city. By 1926 he was the organization's vice president. Two years later he opened his own business, the Maine Securities Company. The venture prospered. By the mid-1930s the firm regularly participated, along with leading Boston and New York investment houses, in stock and bond issues for the largest Maine companies. These deals would have brought Chase into contact with executives of the power, banking, and manufacturing firms that dominated the political and economic life of Maine. Chase retained a vital interest in politics and public affairs throughout his life. In 1926 he was elected (as a Republican) to the first of two terms in Maine's House of Representatives. He was active in the securities industry's trade associations, participated in the New England Council's New Products Committee, and became president of the NEC in 1942. Chase was elected to several more terms in the Maine legislature beginning in 1946.

Although he held conventionally Republican views, Chase periodically defied the party leadership. He opposed the GOP's 1924 gubernatorial nominee, who had Ku Klux Klan backing, and campaigned in 1932 to end state party support for Prohibition. In 1953 he antagonized Maine manufacturers by calling for higher state taxes on industrial firms. Chase long advocated local control of Maine resources. He bemoaned the era when outside investors controlled the state's principal railway. Advertisements for his securities company proclaimed that the firm offered "facilities for intelligent employment of Maine capital in Maine enterprises." With a background in finance and politics, dedication to local business, and a readiness to challenge the status quo, Chase was ideally suited to pressure New England financiers for better support of regional industry.

Chase, then president of the New England Council, reopened the question of small business finance with a panel discussion on venture capital at an NEC meeting in September 1943. Chase initiated the proceedings with an address calling for a "financial policy suited to New England" that would make possible a "sound and stable economy based primarily upon a strong industrial [sector]." Representatives from the various sectors of the New England financial industry were then asked to comment on what their institutions could do to increase the availability of finance to new and small firms in the region.[29]

Rather than generating useful ideas, the session underscored the extent of the problem. Speaking on what the region's commercial banks could do to increase the supply of "permanent risk-capital," Charles Spencer, president of the First National Bank of Boston, claimed that government regulations limited the ability of banks to make available such money, and that the mission of institutions like his own was to provide loans rather than investment capital. New England banks were meeting the credit needs of area businesses, Spencer continued—although long-term loans could only be granted to established companies. Chase then turned to the savings banks (akin to savings and loans), suggesting that since these institutions made long-term real estate loans and were permitted to hold certain kinds of stock, they could provide some aid to small manufacturers. The industry's representative, an officer at a Boston savings bank, demurred. The desires of depositors were paramount, he stated, and since these individuals valued security above all, savings banks were unlikely to begin purchasing riskier corporate equities.

The session continued in this vein. The speaker for the insurance companies cited government regulations and the need for liquidity as reasons for investing only in the stocks of large companies, and opined that in insuring the risks of small firms his industry was doing its part for small business in the region. The representative of the investment trusts conceded that firms in his sector generally invested only in the securities of large companies and asserted that this policy was unlikely to change. Major industrial corporations such as GE and AT&T might be a promising source of venture capital, he suggested. The speaker for the trust funds declared that although these institutions had sizable holdings of the stock of smaller New England manufacturers, government regulations definitely ruled out providing capital to new enterprises. In closing remarks, an exasperated Chase stated that the session had spotlighted the problem of "inhibited capital." Several weeks later, he admonished those attending a convention of New England commercial bankers that the financial problems of New England required "something better than a 'Someone Else Policy' that does not identify the 'Someone.'"

Under Chase's guidance, the NEC then set out to identify additional sources of finance for small regional companies. Appointed for this purpose was a Committee on the Financing and Ownership of New England Business Enterprises. A Harvard Business School professor headed the thirty-member group, which had representatives from numerous banks and insurance companies, several prominent regional manufacturers, the AFL and CIO, and academia. Among the latter was the former dean of the Harvard Business School.[30] As in other NEC endeavors, the committee initially focused on gathering authoritative information. Members mapped out an ambitious research agenda that included inquiries into the amount of New England capital available for investment each year; the extent of demand for new money at small firms in the region; and the laws, regulations, and other restrictions on investments in effect at different types of institutions. The panel's research agenda also called for an examination of "long term credits" (essentially bank loans) to New England firms.[31] The NEC committee investigated the availability of finance for New England small business throughout 1944. At the close of the year, Chase, whose term as New England Council president had ended, took over leadership of the panel. Incoming NEC president Frederick Blackall Jr. called for Chase to direct the work of the group, by this time known as the Committee on Ownership and Finance, away from research and toward convincing regional financiers to pony up more money for small business. "Unless we can convince the lenders of their own self-interest in making venture capital available, our researches will have been of little avail," Blackall stated.[32]

Efforts to persuade businessmen to do more to advance regional economic development were likely to receive a warm reception during the last years of World War II. As bad as New England conditions had been in the 1920s and 1930s, there were indications that things would worsen after the conflict ended. War mobilization had led to the construction of a vast amount of industrial plant, much of it federally financed, in the underdeveloped West and South. When this capacity was converted to peacetime use, New England manufacturers would face even stiffer competition from other parts of the country. Partisans of underdeveloped regions even floated proposals to "freeze" war plants in the northeastern industrial belt while privatizing those elsewhere, which would bolster these developmental effects. In addition, the demand for industrial growth outside the traditional centers crescendoed during the war years. In 1944 an official of the Federal Reserve Bank of Boston noted "everywhere . . . an eagerness on the part of different regions to move forward, to develop their local resources and to promote business expansion in their own communities." Legitimation for this industrialization drive came from sources such as the widely read 1946 book *The Revolt of the South and West*, which attacked "the economic aggression by the Eastern corporate oligarchy" against the country's less developed regions.[33]

With the competitive threat from other regions rising, New England saw a whirl of economic development activity during the war years. In Massachusetts, business and government leaders mounted a significant postwar reconversion planning effort, slated a major renovation of Boston's crumbling port facilities, and proposed to set up a state Department of Commerce to guide future development efforts. An October 1945 letter from two leaders of the Boston financial community to Harvard Business School professor and Enterprise Associates advisor Georges Doriot, then working at the Pentagon, captured this energetic developmentalist spirit. Boston had become "a very ambitious city," the letterwriters declared, noting "the great interest which all leaders in the city are now taking" in economic development.[34]

An important change in personnel occurred at a leading Boston financial institution while these events were taking place. In 1944, Ralph Flanders, past member of the New England Council's New Products Committee and former president of the NEC, became president of the Federal Reserve Bank of Boston.

Ralph Flanders was a self-made man with significant accomplishments in a range of fields. Flanders was born in Vermont in 1880, the oldest child in a large, poor farm family. Completing high school at age fifteen and unable to afford college, he entered the apprenticeship program of a machine tool firm. He excelled at machining, supplementing his skills with night and correspondence classes in mechanical drawing and engineering. By age thirty, Flanders had worked as a machinist, machine designer, and engineer; invented improvements in machining process; written extensively on machine design; and served as associate editor of *Machinery* magazine. In 1911 he married the daughter of the chief executive of Vermont's Jones and Lamson Machine Company. He went to work for the firm, becoming its chief executive in 1933. During the 1920s Flanders was active in the machine tool industry's trade associations. The onset of the Depression drew his interest to broader socioeconomic questions. He published books and lectured widely in the ensuing years, advocating measures to stabilize production levels and raise living standards for workers. Flanders's devout Protestant faith, which emphasized social justice, bolstered his view that the capitalist system required significant reform. Flanders served on a number of federal panels during the New Deal, including the Department of Commerce's Business Advisory Council and the National Recovery Administration's Industrial Advisory Board. He was president of the New England Council in 1941–42 and held posts in the World War II economic mobilization apparatus. A moderate Republican, Flanders was appointed to an empty seat in the U.S. Senate in 1946. He won election to the position several times, serving in the Senate until 1958.[35]

Flanders was a dynamic individual committed to maintaining the social viability of capitalism. His background and interests made him well suited to address the small business finance question. In becoming president of the Federal Reserve Bank of Boston in 1944, he gained an ideal position from which to agitate for increasing the funds available to small companies.

Soon after taking charge of the Boston Fed, Flanders launched an inquiry into the contribution that the area's commercial banks could make to regional development. He assembled two committees of bank officers to look into the issue. One group focused on ways of aiding New England agriculture. The other took up questions related to commercial lending that had been under examination by the NEC for some time. Means of financing new and small businesses received particular attention from the second committee. Flanders told the 1944 annual meeting of Boston Fed member banks that these efforts would "largely occupy the attention" of the Reserve Bank's officers and directors in the coming year. At the following year's meeting he reported progress on the agricultural issue. The committee looking at the vexed question of commercial lending had achieved fewer concrete results, he stated, although this remained "a matter of continuous and active concern."[36]

The NEC Committee on Ownership and Finance, which had worked throughout 1944 on small business financing questions, published two reports in 1945, as Flanders carried on his efforts at the Boston Fed. The NEC panel's reports included numerous recommendations for increasing the flow of finance to small companies in New England. The committee described its goal as the development of a stable economy of diversified industries which were "firmly anchored" to the region and "fortified and reinforced by venture capital which will finance the constant creation of the new to replace the inevitable obsolescence of the old." To realize these aims, committee members counseled steps in each of the financial sectors that had been represented at the 1943 NEC conference panel on venture capital.[37] For commercial banks, the committee advised changes in regulations and practice to permit a greater flow of credit, especially longer-term loans, to small business. For savings banks, insurance companies, and trusts, panelists advocated measures that would allow institutions to lend to or invest in the securities of small companies. Committee members apparently saw great opportunity in the monies controlled by investment trusts. Their report called for the NEC to hold a conference with leading regional organizations in that sector to discuss increasing purchases of the stocks of New England companies, especially smaller firms.

NEC leaders communicated the findings of the Committee on Ownership and Finance at a regional commercial bank conference in late 1945. Boston Fed president Flanders was on the program, and his address pressed the argument that area banks should do more to assist local industry. In doing so, Flanders presented the audience of bank officers with the unusual spectacle of a high official of the Federal Reserve System urging member institutions to make more risky loans. On certain types of loans to new and small businesses, Flanders asserted, the usual tools for assessing creditworthiness, such as company financial statements and credit history, did not apply. In these cases bankers had to rely on their personal judgment of an applicant's "character and abilities." For the good of the region, Flanders stated, all New England banks should make such loans: "there should be a reasonable percentage of these marginal cases in each bank portfolio if the bank is to be of the greatest service to its community."[38]

Some New England financiers resisted the idea that they should provide greater assistance to area industry. Flanders's proposals for increasing the number of marginal loans attracted considerable heat from the audience of bank officers at the 1945 meeting. NEC President Frederick Blackall Jr. reported on the same occasion that some of the bankers who had read a draft of the since-published report of the NEC Committee on Ownership and Finance "almost resented" the group's work for being "critical of . . . existing banking procedures."[39]

On the other hand, leading figures in Massachusetts finance were by the end of World War II eager to support new business in the region. The two Boston financiers who wrote to Georges Doriot in October 1945 were obviously supportive of development efforts in the city. They described prominent figures at two of the city's principal investment banks—Neal Rantoul, president of F. S. Mosely and Company, and James Minot, a senior partner at Paine, Webber, Jackson and Curtis and a veteran of the NEC New Products Committee—as "keenly aware and anxious to do everything possible for new enterprise in this locality."[40] Some in the financial world had probably always felt this way. The investment bank Jackson and Curtis, a predecessor of Minot's firm, seems to have long been a center of pro-development sentiment. William Coolidge and Charles F. Adams Jr., two of the leading figures in the pioneering venture capital organization Enterprise Associates, both worked there. It does appear, however, that minds had been changed in financial circles by the repeated calls for greater support for small local business. At the 1943 NEC conference on venture capital, Charles Spencer, president of the First National Bank of Boston, had rebuffed the idea that his institution could do more for the area's small firms. But in 1945, the writers of the letter to Doriot singled out Spencer as one of the individuals anxious to aid the growth of new enterprise in the Boston area.

Establishment of the American Research and Development Corporation

Following the publication in 1945 of the reports of the NEC's Committee on Ownership and Finance, the drive by regional business leaders to improve the financing available to small local companies focused on creating a large new venture capital organization in the area. After a year of intensive work these efforts culminated in the establishment of the American Research and Development Corporation (ARD). The firm would emerge as a landmark institution in the nascent venture capital industry and a significant investor in New England technology enterprise. Due to a highly successful 1957 investment in fledging computer maker Digital Equipment Corporation (DEC), ARD also became extremely profitable. The fund attained legendary status within the twin worlds of venture capital and the Boston-area technology industry, and the story of its establishment has repeatedly been told in print. Many of the previous accounts greatly underemphasize the regional concerns motivating the fund's founders.[41]

The idea of setting up a large new venture capital fund was in the air amid the intense pro-development spirit flourishing in Boston toward the end of World War II. The initial report of the New England Council's Committee on Ownership and Finance, issued in the first half of 1945, noted proposals circulating locally for a $5–10 million "investment fund of a promotional character."[42] In the summer of 1945, the issue caught the attention of Boston Fed president Flanders, later identified as the "prime mover" in the formation of ARD.[43] Flanders secured copies of a report on venture capital that had been prepared by the national Federal Reserve System and set up a study group in the Boston Federal Reserve Bank to examine the matter further.[44]

Flanders, like the members of the Committee on Ownership and Finance, was impressed by the volume of investment money in New England controlled by fiduciaries—institutions that manage the funds of others. Key fiduciaries included insurance companies; trusts, which were pioneered in Boston in the nineteenth century; and investment trusts (mutual funds), a 1920s innovation of the region's money managers. Studies conducted in the 1930s estimated that New England fiduciaries had $10–13 billion under supervision. None of this money was invested in small, innovative companies. As Edward Chase's 1943 NEC panel on venture capital had shown, these funds were "inhibited"—restricted by habit and government regulation to conservative investments in well-established firms. Like Chase and others before, Boston Fed president Flanders saw in the accumulated money a means of achieving economic recovery. Flanders believed, according to a contemporary, that a regional turnaround could be accomplished by "bringing New England's declining industry and its swollen institutional reserves together."[45] Flanders spoke publicly during the summer of 1945 on the possibilities for venture capital and consulted with local experts, such as Harvard College treasurer William Claflin and Donald David, dean of the Harvard Business School. David had recently discussed this topic with Merrill Griswold, president of a leading Boston investment trust and an authority on inhibited capital. Griswold had helped shape the Investment Company Act of 1940, which governed the investment trusts, and knew that a clause in the act permitted investment trusts to put a small fraction of their holdings into funds providing venture capital to small business.[46] David, Flanders, and Griswold met at the end of the summer and resolved to establish a "development capital company" that would invest the monies of fiduciaries in small New England businesses.[47]

As they pursued this effort during the remainder of 1945 and early 1946, the initial group of three drew on the advice and assistance of a widening circle of business and financial leaders. Participants in these consultations included NEC president Frederick Blackall Jr.; Bradley Dewey, president of the Boston-based Dewey and Almy Chemical Company and national director of wartime rubber production; MIT president Karl Compton; MIT treasurer Horace Ford; Ira Mosher of the Associated Industries of Massachusetts; and a number of investment bankers. Georges Doriot, Harvard Business School professor and advisor to the prewar venture capital group Enterprise Associates, and Paul Clark, president of John Hancock Mutual, the largest Massachusetts insurance company, were kept apprised of developments.[48] The projected firm was to be organized as an investment company with initial funds raised through the sale of stock to fiduciaries and individual investors. Numerous regulatory obstacles had to be overcome before plans could be finalized, and securing the needed startup money also proved challenging.

On the regulatory side, modifications and exemptions from state and federal restrictions on investment companies were required before the firm could begin operation. Shady practices in the early days of the investment trust industry had led several states to bar the trusts from holding the securities of companies less than three years old. Such rules blocked the participation of entities such as Merrill Griswold's Massachusetts Investors Trust in the proposed corporation. New England promoters pushed for easing of the state restrictions. To achieve that end, Flanders addressed a convention of state securities regulators in November 1945. Declaring that "American business, American employment, and the prosperity of the citizens of the country . . . cannot be indefinitely assured . . . unless there is a continuous birth of healthy infants in our business structure," Flanders asked that the investment trusts be allowed to invest a small percentage of their holdings without restriction.[49] The response was positive. The commissioners unanimously approving a resolution calling on states to amend their regulations in the desired manner. The New Englanders then contacted the state commissions with tough restrictions, sending endorsements of the sought-after changes from Flanders, dean David of the Harvard Business School, prominent scientist Vannevar Bush, and other notables. Regulators in Ohio, Minnesota, and New Hampshire altered their rules as requested. Then word arrived that the highly conservative Wisconsin commission was preparing further restrictions on the holdings of investment trusts. Extended negotiations with bureaucrats at the Wisconsin commission ensued, including a trip to the state by Flanders, before a compromise was reached that allowed plans for the investment company to go forward.[50]

Regulatory obstacles also existed at the federal level. The organizers planned to establish the corporation under section 12(e) of the Investment Company Act of 1940. However, they proposed to contravene some technicalities of the law—for example, by having institutions other than investment trusts purchase stock in the company. Exemptions from the Securities and Exchange Commission (SEC) were necessary to proceed in this manner. Obtaining them did not prove difficult, as the Democratic presidential administrations of this era strongly backed efforts to improve financing for small business. Members of the SEC were "outspoken in their desire to cooperate in every possible way" at an April 1946 meeting with a delegation from Boston. The commission granted the necessary exemptions that summer.[51]

The organizers of the planned company worked to raise the necessary money, in addition to battling regulatory obstacles. It was decided that the corporation needed startup capital of $3 million. This amount would be raised by selling stock, with fiduciaries such as investment trusts and insurance companies taking at least half the total. Early in the process, Griswold's Massachusetts Investors Trust agreed to put $500,000 into the corporation if other investment trusts participated. The John Hancock life insurance company likewise committed to investing a sizable sum, provided that other insurers followed suit. To find the needed additional investors, an intensive process of recruitment took place in the early months of 1946. Griswold arranged for Rupert Maclaurin, a business professor at MIT with expertise in the economics of technology, to give a talk on the need for venture capital to an "investment group" in Boston. Flanders, Compton, and Griswold hosted a luncheon to convince other New England insurers to join the John Hancock company in supporting the corporation. And Compton and MIT treasurer Horace Ford sought the approval of the MIT governing board for a purchase of stock in the new corporation by the institute's endowment.[52]

These exertions were fully worthwhile, as raising sufficient capital proved to be a struggle. Of the six New England insurance companies other than John Hancock present at the investment luncheon, only State Mutual, a relatively small firm based outside Boston, agreed to put in money. Numerous investment trusts declined to buy stock. Even the MIT governing board was wary of taking a stake in the new organization, despite the deep involvement in the project of the institute's president and treasurer as well as several professors. After months of concerted salesmanship, a last-minute purchase of stock by a foundation controlled by Sears magnate Lessing Rosenwald was necessary to meet a self-imposed deadline for raising the $3 million in startup funds.[53]

Once the corporation, by this time known as American Research and Development, had secured sufficient funds, a single problem remained: the organization needed a president. Flanders had filled the position during the summer of 1946, but this was a stopgap. After months of consideration the search finally settled on Harvard Business School professor Doriot. David, Griswold, and Doriot confirmed this decision at a meeting in November 1946, putting the organization on a firm footing at last.[54] Commenting on the experience several years later, Merrill Griswold opined that ARD had succeeded thanks only to the "the prodigious efforts and enthusiasm of a very limited number of individuals and institutional investors."[55]

The saga of ARD's founding—and contemporaneous attempts to convince New England commercial bankers to provide better support to small local business—point to the same conclusion. On one hand, leaders of business and finance are generally conservative. Many doubt that anything can be done to change existing realities and some oppose making the effort. On the other hand, there may exist a small group of highly motivated people who are convinced that action must be taken and are willing to go to extraordinary lengths to advance their agenda. Through creativity and persistence, the latter group as often as not achieves considerable success.

The financing made available to small New England companies in the years after World War II facilitated the growth of recently established electronics producers in the Boston area. How this occurred is described in the next chapter.

CHAPTER 6

Small Business Finance and Electronics Spinoff Companies along Route 128

> Financing a venture like ours is a lot easier here in Boston than in many other places.
>
> MANAGER OF A BOSTON-AREA HIGH TECHNOLOGY SPINOFF COMPANY, CIRCA 1966, IN DEUTERMANN, "SEEDING SCIENCE-BASED INDUSTRY"

A concerted campaign to stimulate the growth of the New England economy was one of the principal responses to the decline of textiles and other established industries in the region. From the mid-1920s until the early 1950s, the private sector dominated the area's development drive. Growth advocates pursued many possibilities for encouraging economic expansion during this era, most of which had limited success. More fruitful were attempts to improve the financing available to new and small companies in New England. To achieve this goal, area promoters set up venture capital organizations and worked to convince commercial banks to provide additional loans to small business customers. The small business financing efforts, in tandem with events in the electronics sector, laid the basis for the dynamic expansion of an important new regional industry.

Electronics was a key growth sector in the American economy of the mid-twentieth century. The development of the industry's technologically advanced segment gave rise to a new kind of company: the high technology spinoff. These firms were set up by technical personnel leaving established research organizations to go into business for themselves. The non-union status of these small firms contributed to their growth potential. The large-scale electronics research taking place at the Massachusetts Institute of Technology, in affiliated government laboratories, and at a number of established local companies provided a launching pad for numerous Boston-area spinoffs in the 1940s and after. Initially, however, the city was a spinoff center of only secondary importance. By the early 1960s, in contrast, the explosive growth of electronics and computer spinoffs made Boston's "Route 128" the best-known locus of technologically advanced industry in the world.

Spinoff companies near Boston were able to outpace their competitors in other parts of the country due in part to the greater support they received from local financiers. New England venture capital organizations made a number of prominent early investments in area spinoffs. More important, Boston commercial banks lent on easy terms to small local electronics firms and extended other forms of assistance. Financiers' willingness to provide this backing stemmed from the earlier decline of traditional New England industry. As regional development advocates pressed for increased small business lending, bank executives became more willing to support newly established, innovative companies. Bankers came to see the great growth potential of the electronics spinoffs as providing an opportunity to revitalize the New England economy—while reviving the flagging prospects of their own institutions.

The Emergence of Small Research-Based Companies in the Electronics Industry

A new type of small company with enormous growth potential emerged in the mid-twentieth century, just as New England business leaders worked to increase financial support for small firms in their region. Bigness had been the central characteristic of American business for decades, as consolidation produced an economy dominated by large corporations. Developments in the electronics industry and allied sectors during the 1930s and 1940s upset this general pattern. There a new group of entrepreneurs started to establish small companies that came to be known as spinoffs—firms that could benefit greatly from the kind of financial assistance New Englanders were trying to generate for small business.

Electronics was one of the key growth industries of the twentieth century.[1] Emerging with the invention of radio out of the electrical equipment industry, electronics in subsequent years saw continual technological advances leading to an endless assortment of new products.[2] Consumer electronics was the largest subsector within the industry. In the period between the world wars, this primarily meant the burgeoning market for home radio sets. Television was the key consumer electronics product of ensuing years. As in many industries, a welter of small firms produced consumer electronic goods during an initial period of explosive growth. As the market matured, the technology stabilized and a limited number of large producers came to dominate.

A very different situation prevailed in a less prominent sector of the industry, which can be called "advanced electronics." The principal products here were sophisticated, customized devices such as radar, scientific instruments, industrial controls, and navigation, guidance, and targeting systems for aircraft and missiles. Continuing innovation in the field led to the first electronic computers. In the 1940s and for several decades thereafter, the Pentagon and other federal agencies were the principal buyers of advanced electronics.[3] Devices purchased by federal officials equipped the World War II and Cold War arsenals and had a central place in the space program. The high level of military spending in the 1940s, 1950s, and 1960s greatly increased the demand for advanced electronic products, hastening the sector's development. Private-sector markets also existed, particularly for producer goods like scientific instruments and industrial controls. Business demand for computers grew steadily, too, as the machines became easier to handle. Closely related to advanced electronics and catering to similar buyers was a sector known at the time as "nucleonics," which can also be called "applied physics." Included here was equipment making use of physical phenomena such as radiation, ultrasound, and microwaves.

In addition to devising a continual stream of new products, the advanced electronics and applied physics industries gave rise to a radically different kind of firm. This was the science-based spinoff company or, in today's terminology, the high technology startup.[4] The spinoff company represented the latest permutation in the evolving system of developing and commercializing new technology. Until the later nineteenth century, technological innovation remained largely independent of science. Most key advances were realized by mechanics and "tinkerers," who often had limited education and worked independently. By the early twentieth century a dramatic shift had taken place. Science and technology had become closely related, and most new products and processes were developed by technically trained personnel working in university and private-sector laboratories. One Boston patent attorney reported in 1940 that the place of the independent inventor had steadily decreased in importance during his thirty years in the field, so that 90 percent of his firm's work at the time was on behalf of companies. The highly organized research and development facilities maintained by the leading firms in electronics and other technically sophisticated industries were the most visible sign of the move toward science-based technological advance. The laboratories of General Electric and AT&T were universally recognized as the models for corporate R&D.[5]

Commercially oriented laboratory research increasingly concentrated in large firms in the early twentieth century. But in advanced electronics and applied physics, things moved in the opposite direction. In these sectors, small companies vaulted into importance as researchers left, or "spun off," from corporate and university laboratories to set up their own firms. Isolated examples of spinning off took place during the 1920s. At that time, MIT professor Vannevar Bush and several partners formed the Raytheon Corporation near Boston to produce sophisticated radio components.[6] As the economy recovered from the Depression, spinoffs appeared in noticeable numbers. By 1940, Richard Morse, an engineer with experience in Eastman Kodak's research laboratory, had established the National Research Corporation to pursue advances in high vacuum technique. During the same era, Stanford engineering graduate students Bill Hewlett and David Packard, one of whom had worked in the research division of GE, set up a company to build electronic instruments. The firm still bears their names.[7] High wartime demand for radar and other advanced products created a favorable environment for continued company formation. After the war, spinoffs were established at a rapid and steadily increasing pace.[8] Information from various sources shows that two dozen electronics spinoffs had been set up in the Boston area by 1951, and this is doubtless an incomplete tally. A Massachusetts electronics directory published in 1957 lists approximately two hundred such firms.[9] Defense expenditures facilitated the launch of many spinoffs.[10]

The motivations of those establishing spinoffs varied. Some had always harbored entrepreneurial ambitions and started their own business at the first opportunity. Others valued working independently and set up a firm to escape the hierarchical environment of the large laboratories. Numerous companies were established by former leaders of research teams at major labs who left in frustration, often with subordinates in tow, when their projects were placed on the back burner. The desire to make a fortune played a markedly less important role than it does in today's technology industry. Markets for early advanced electronic goods were quite narrow, so that few firms in this early era achieved the mega-million-dollar sales and stock valuations seen repeatedly in later years. Whatever their motives, spinoff entrepreneurs almost never worked alone: a small group of "principals" formed the core of virtually all companies.

The nature of the advanced electronics industry was conducive to the formation of spinoff firms. Technical expertise was the essential asset, allowing companies to get under way without large amounts of capital or equipment. Due to rapidly advancing technology, new market niches opened up at a steady rate. If a fledgling firm did not immediately have products to sell, which was often the case, it was usually possible to secure consulting work from larger companies and research organizations as a stopgap. Some spinoffs consulted permanently, never bringing out their own products.

Like most small businesses, the great majority of spinoffs achieved limited success. Many folded. Some became viable but remained small in size. A good number established a respectable market presence and were acquired by larger firms. A few broke through to become leading producers. Examples of the latter include Hewlett-Packard, which emerged as a major manufacturer of scientific instruments and later of computers; High Voltage Engineering, a 1940s Boston-area spinoff that wrested an important share of the market for particle acceleration equipment (used in medicine and science) away from large producers like GE; and Digital Equipment, the first computer maker to challenge seriously IBM's domination of the market with a minicomputer brought out in the 1960s.

The presence of an ever-shifting cast of spinoffs had important effects on the development of the U.S. advanced electronics industry. Spinoffs often brought new kinds of products to market more quickly than did established companies. They provided an outlet for the energies of researchers who did not work well in large organizations or who had unorthodox ideas their supervisors did not wish to pursue. Even unsuccessful spinoffs, by their very presence, heightened competitive pressures, thereby speeding the pace of innovation. The technology industry of the United States was for decades almost uniquely open to the spinoff form of enterprise, in contrast to technology sectors in the developed countries of Europe and Asia. This undoubtedly helps account for the fact that even today American firms dominate the more innovative segments of the electronics, computer, and software industries. Employees at virtually all spinoff companies were not unionized, at least during the firms' early phases. The absence of union restrictions on work practices added to the companies' growth potential.[11] Spinoffs flourished during the Cold War years despite the higher taxes and greater regulation of investors put in place during the New Deal.[12] Those enactments tended to inhibit the emergence of new industries by reducing the amount of capital available for investment and by restricting investors' behavior.[13]

For all their dynamism, spinoff firms faced some of the same hurdles that confronted more conventional small businesses. Finance was a constant area of difficulty. The startup money for most spinoffs came from the personal funds of the principals, with outside investors known as "angels" at times putting in moderate amounts in exchange for a share of the business. A narrow equity base constrained the growth potential of many spinoffs. Retained earnings were generally insufficient to finance expansion. Paying for the research and development needed to ready products for market and the expenses of starting up manufacturing often necessitated repeated injections of capital or long-term loans. If such support was not available, opportunities could be lost in fast-moving markets. Simply bringing in sufficient funds to maintain normal operations could be a challenge. Like small firms in many industries, electronics spinoffs were at the mercy of larger buyers that often delayed payments for products beyond the dates specified in the contract. Even firms selling directly to the Pentagon experienced this problem.[14]

Financiers treated the spinoffs with circumspection, despite the firms' need for financial support. Most spinoffs had been in business for a limited time, and financiers are wary of new companies without proven track records. The spinoffs presented added reasons for caution. Their products were arcane, based on technology that was incomprehensible to the layman. Because of the unusual rhythms of the electronics industry, the balance sheets of small firms in sound condition typically looked terrible by conventional measures. Most spinoff companies also suffered from a shortage of management expertise, since their principals had technical backgrounds and were often ignorant of business fundamentals. At the time they set up shop, more than one spinoff manager would later say, they did not know a stock from a bond, let alone how to establish a smooth-running corporate organization. To deal with the spinoffs, financiers needed a basic understanding of the advanced electronics industry; an appreciation of the companies' unique growth potential; and a willingness to commit significant time and energy to customers who, at least initially, operated on a small scale.

Location of Original Spinoff Enterprise

The "Route 128" complex of electronics and computer companies surrounding Boston was the first area to gain widespread recognition as a center of spinoff enterprise. Although the San Francisco Bay Area's Silicon Valley later achieved greater prominence, Route 128 remains one of the principal hubs of technology-related spinoffs in the United States and the world. The emergence of Route 128 gained widespread attention from scholars and the media by the 1960s and has inspired a number of histories. These accounts take it as a given that from the beginning, Boston was the leading center for this type of activity. The presence of the Massachusetts Institute of Technology is repeatedly cited as the Boston area's great advantage. In particular, it is claimed that MIT had a uniquely encouraging attitude toward entrepreneurial activity by faculty and graduates. Analysts also point to the large MIT-affiliated federal research facilities as a source of electronics spinoffs. These include the Radiation Laboratory during World War II, and others, such as the Lincoln Lab and the Instrumentation Lab, in the years that followed.[15] A great deal of government-financed weapons research took place at these institutions in the early phases of the Cold War.[16]

MIT and related laboratories were important foci of electronics research and spawned numerous companies. The accounts of Route 128's rise are nonetheless misleading. Startup firms in advanced electronics and applied physics tended to cluster together, but there were many U.S. centers of spinoff enterprise after World War II, and Boston was far from the most important. The New York City metropolitan area, including adjoining New Jersey, was initially the leading spinoff center. The second most important locale was Los Angeles. Numerous spinoffs existed in the industrial Midwest, especially around Chicago, and in Philadelphia as well as Boston. The San Francisco area saw only a trickle of activity during the early era.

Industry directories demonstrate the early geographic distribution of advanced electronics firms. A 1952 buyers' directory for broadcasting and related equipment from an electronics trade journal lists manufacturers throughout the country in a range of fields. Included are listings for three areas—aviation, servo and telemetering, and point-to-point microwave—that are unequivocally the kind of advanced domains under discussion here. Tallying the number of firms in each specialty by geographic area shows the following distributional pattern: companies in New York City and environs accounted for 38–40 percent of all producers; firms in Southern California 12–20 percent; Illinois 4–16 percent; and Massachusetts, 5–11 percent.[17]

Contemporary accounts confirm this picture. New York City is often mentioned as a principal locale of the industry, as is Southern California. A study of electronics from the late 1950s held that "in military and industrial electronics . . . the New York Metropolitan Region . . . has consistently been the nation's leading center [of production] by a wide margin." Surveying the West Coast electronics industry in 1952, one observer noted the tendency in the "specialized electronic" sector for the "ambitious and competent young man to start a company of his own, rather than taking even quite a good job with an established outfit." As a result, the writer continued wittily,

> you can scarcely throw a horseshoe over your shoulder anywhere in Los Angeles County without injuring the vice-president of a small electronics firm, usually one with ambitions to apply the information-processing techniques of modern electronics to the clerical and control problems of business and industry.[18]

Spinoff firms came into existence as technical personnel left large research organizations to go into business for themselves. A concentration of established institutions conducting advanced electronics research was therefore necessary for a significant number of spinoffs to exist in a given place. New York City and Los Angeles were both major centers of electronics research in this era. In or near New York were Columbia University and New York University, each with distinguished engineering programs; AT&T's Bell Labs, where the transistor was invented and other important advances took place; corporate research facilities of IBM, GE, and RCA; a U.S. Army Signal Corps research lab at Fort Monmouth, New Jersey; and on Long Island, leading aircraft and aviation instrument producers including Grumman, Republic, Fairchild Camera and Instrument, and Airborne Instruments. Aviation, the most important industry in Los Angeles, was the locus of electronics research in that city. Each of the large Southern California aircraft firms maintained sizable electronics R&D staffs; Hughes Aircraft had a particularly advanced program. In addition, the Hollywood movie studios pursued innovative electronic techniques for recording and reproducing sound and video. Research also took place at Caltech, a leading engineering school in nearby Pasadena.

Furthermore, MIT's encouraging attitude toward entrepreneurship by faculty, staff, and students—much discussed by other writers—was not unique to educational institutions in the Boston area. Engineering schools and departments throughout the country maintained cooperative research arrangements with private-sector companies.[19] Many educational institutions were also open to the idea of faculty members and other affiliates establishing their own companies. An extreme example occurred at the Brooklyn Polytechnic Institute, a New York engineering school of local importance. The president of the institute was also chief and apparent founder of Polytechnic Research and Development, a commercial laboratory that did extensive work in electronics.[20]

Technological Focus of Later New England Efforts to Encourage Small Business Finance

Many of the New Englanders who had worked since the 1920s to revitalize the regional economy did not immediately recognize the growth potential of the spinoff sector. Electronics spinoffs formed in noticeable numbers during the late 1930s in Boston and other parts of the country. Yet members of the New England Council's New Products Committee, active at the end of the 1930s, seemingly did not perceive the spinoffs' promise, even though MIT president Karl Compton chaired the panel. As it sought to identify new industrial possibilities for the region, the panel considered and rejected several avenues of fostering technologically advanced sectors. In the end, the panel fell back on a growth strategy seen in less developed areas—seeking to convince national manufacturers to build local branch plants. By contrast, the Boston investment bankers who in 1939 set up the venture capital group Enterprise Associates appeared cognizant of the spinoffs' potential. Enterprise Associates only considered proposals involving innovative technology. The organization's one investment was in National Research Corporation, an applied physics spinoff active in high vacuum manufacturing. New England growth advocates became increasingly aware of the possibilities in research-oriented industry as the years passed. The war research effort, in which the Boston area played a major role, apparently accounted for much of the shift. In 1946 MIT president Compton described how the war experience had highlighted the industrial potential of laboratory research:

> The accomplishments of research during the war provided a dramatic demonstration of the effectiveness of planned investigation. Many people who had been skeptical of the power of research or who had identified it as an activity engaged in by long-haired scientists remote from the problems of industry are now aware of what it can accomplish.[21]

The war economy also provided concrete local examples of the potential contribution of electronics to regional economic development. After winning an important government contract for radar components, the Raytheon Corporation, based near Boston, became a major producer of advanced electronics, with thousands of employees. During the same period, the National Research Corporation parlayed innovative ideas and entrepreneurial drive into a flourishing enterprise with a handsome headquarters adjoining MIT. Regional growth advocates had been working for twenty years to bring about such business success stories in the area. No wonder that a Boston newspaper's 1946 survey of the region's economic prospects found local observers fixated on the gains that could be achieved through the "greater practical, dynamic, use of the 'gold mines' of research facilities here."[22]

The increased awareness of the potential of science-based industry and spinoff companies was evident in the business development organizations set up in New England just after the war. One example was New Enterprises, Inc., the postwar incarnation of the Enterprise Associates of the late 1930s. The earlier venture capital operation was revived under a new name in 1946 with the same leadership, a more formal structure, and increased funds available for investment.[23] New Enterprises had an even stronger technological orientation than its predecessor. One New Enterprises brochure stated that the organization would only consider projects of "pronounced technical characteristics—a new process, a new or improved technique."[24] Another Boston organization in operation by 1946 also had a technological orientation. Rather than providing venture capital, the New Products Research Corporation served as a kind of innovation broker. The firm scrutinized new products and processes submitted by inventors and brought those believed to have commercial potential to the attention of interested manufacturers.[25]

The growing appreciation among New Englanders of the possibilities of technology and spinoff enterprise is most apparent in the case of the American Research and Development Corporation (ARD), the Boston venture capital fund set up after long effort in 1946. The company's organizers specified that investments would only be considered in companies with "some new product or process that is of scientific importance . . . some invention or laboratory discovery." In the near term, the "mass of new developments coming out of our war activity" was seen as a prime source of investment possibilities. The MIT professors who served as technical advisors on the project expected future proposals to come from "the many new discoveries being made in university laboratories, and inventions made by professors and research men." An investigator who interviewed many of the company's founders at the time ARD went into operation observed that in speaking of "new enterprise," development advocates in the South and the West generally meant "the application of some established and familiar technique." By contrast, this observer found, the organizers of ARD "apparently took it for granted that a new enterprise implied a new invention or a new business idea."[26]

The possibilities for spinoff enterprises in advanced electronics were articulated by Rupert Maclaurin, an MIT economist with a longstanding interest in the economics of technology who had carefully monitored developments at the wartime Radiation Laboratory. In early 1946, Maclaurin spoke to a group of Boston investors as part of the effort to raise startup capital for ARD. His address highlighted the opportunities that were emerging as researchers established their own firms. Maclaurin explained that many of the young men who had worked at the Radiation Laboratory during the war would have liked to set up their own firms to pursue ideas developed there. Lacking the financial wherewithal to do so, most had joined the research staffs of industrial firms. The major corporations hiring these men would carry out much of the important technological research of the future, Maclaurin continued. However, large organizations needed to focus their efforts and inevitably become bureaucratic, so that "the radical notion and the new risk-taking approach are frequently not exploited." As a result, "there will be important opportunities in the coming years for scientists and engineers who are interested in the . . . practical applications [of their research] to start new enterprises of their own."[27]

Spinoff Lending by the Boston Commercial Banks

American Research and Development and the other venture capital organizations set up in New England in the 1930s and 1940s made some contribution to the growth of the region's spinoff firms. Enterprise Associates had a key early investment in an applied physics company, setting the stage for that firm's meteoric growth. New Enterprises, Inc., the successor to Enterprise Associates, also put money into several technologically advanced firms. ARD similarly invested in Boston spinoff companies. Of the latter fund's three initial investments, two were in the local applied physics firms Tracerlab and High Voltage Engineering. Tracerlab became another high-profile success story in the late 1940s, beating out much more established competitors to secure a federal contract to reprocess radioactive material. High Voltage Engineering grew at a more deliberate pace and eventually proved an even bigger winner. ARD made a number of other investments in Boston-area spinoffs in the years that followed.[28]

The very existence in Boston of organizations like ARD that were ready to back small, risky, science-based companies doubtless heartened local researchers thinking about establishing their own firms. The much-publicized success of area companies like the National Research Corporation and Tracerlab that received venture capital backing was probably more encouraging still. The support Boston venture capital firms could provide to local spinoff companies in the formative years of Route 128 was necessarily limited, however. The city's venture capitalists were few in number, they had limited funds available for investment, and a major portion of this money went to companies in other industries or in other parts of the country.

Another segment of the local financial industry devoted sufficient resources to the electronic spinoffs to have a major impact. This was the Boston-based commercial banks. Boston bankers enthusiastically cultivated the spinoff sector, avidly seeking customers, providing indefinitely renewed loans that functioned as the equivalent of venture capital, advising on management questions, and helping entrepreneurs bring in additional equity when this was needed. In doing so, the bankers contravened their own repeated claims that their institutions could not provide venture capital and had to be very cautious about extending loans of any kind to risky small borrowers. Bank managers acted as they did because they understood the dynamic growth potential of the spinoff firms, believing that these companies could help revitalize the regional economy—and their own banking business in the process. The strong support for local spinoffs from Boston-area commercial banks had a significant effect, facilitating the growth of the electronics firms.

The Boston-based banks were the dominant commercial lenders in New England. The world of Boston banking was a cozy one. As in other major cities, early twentieth-century consolidations had reduced a once highly competitive market to a limited number of participants. Towering over other area lenders was the First National Bank of Boston, which in 1940 had assets of nearly $900 million. The National Shawmut Bank was the city's second largest institution, with assets in that year of $270 million. A cluster of smaller lenders with 1940 assets of less than $130 million rounded out the Boston-based industry. These included the Merchants National Bank, the Second National Bank of Boston, the State Street Trust Company, and the New England Trust Company.[29]

The businessmen seeking to revitalize the New England economy worked hard to convince area banks to take the kind of supportive approach toward regional industry that eventually occurred with the electronics spinoffs. In the 1920s, the Research Committee of the New England Council commissioned an in-depth study of banking practices as a means of encouraging lenders to support local business. The aid commercial banks could provide to small area companies was one of the topics raised at the NEC's 1943 panel on venture capital. On assuming the presidency of the Federal Reserve Bank of Boston in 1944, Ralph Flanders assembled a committee of bankers to examine ways of better serving the credit needs of new and small companies in the region. Increased bank lending to small firms was one of the subjects addressed by the New England Council's 1945 report on the ownership and finance of local industry. Flanders and NEC leaders reiterated the findings of this report at the 1945 meeting of regional bankers—the venue at which Flanders told bankers that they were doing an insufficient job for the local economy if their portfolios did not contain some "marginal" loans to small firms.

The banks had powerful reasons of their own for supporting regional industry, in addition to these external pressures. The Boston lending institutions had historically conducted a great deal of business with the area's textile and shoe manufacturers. In 1948, after many New England mills had closed, textiles still accounted for 9 percent of large commercial loans at the First National Bank of Boston.[30] As companies in traditional industries shut down or left the region, much of this business was lost. The fate of the Second National Bank of Boston, one of the city's smaller commercial lenders, demonstrated how serious this problem could be.

For nearly a century, members of one family headed the Second National and a predecessor institution. Managers fiercely maintained the bank's independence, repeatedly spurning offers to merge with larger entities. By 1953, however, a dangerous situation had developed. The bank had lost some of its biggest and best commercial borrowers as firms in traditional sectors shut down or moved away. The list of former Second National customers was a roll call of New England's vanished prowess in traditional industries and included prominent textile makers American Woolen, Pacific Mills, Wamsutta Mills, Bourne Mills, and Hathaway Manufacturing. To remain viable in these circumstances, bank executives decided that it was necessary to combine with another lender. A careful search was made for a candidate of like size, so that a "merger . . . of two equal institutions" could take place. The Second's managers finally settled on the State Street Trust Company, a Boston lender with a Massachusetts charter. Legal complications upset these plans, as federal regulators would not approve the combination of a state and a nationally chartered institution. The proud managers of the Second then acceded to a humiliating liquidation of their institution, with the State Street Trust taking over the outstanding loans and accounts.[31]

Larger and nimbler banks could compensate for the disappearance of traditional customers through diversification. As restructuring took hold in the region, the First National Bank of Boston launched a multifaceted campaign to develop new kinds of business, much of it outside New England. The bank became an important lender to the motion picture and petroleum industries, was active in financing mergers and acquisitions and arranging corporate turnarounds, and expanded branch operations set up in Latin America during World War I. The First National even held on to a significant share of the textile lending business as production shifted to the South. It did so by becoming one of the first banks in the country to offer factoring, a traditional means of textile finance.[32] The First National also worked to find new business in its home region. In 1939, a New Business Committee, formed at the request of bank president Charles Spencer, designed a program to retain existing New England customers and find new ones. The strategy was to systematize and fully document the bank's calling effort—the regular visits lending officers make to present and prospective customers—to ensure that each was visited regularly and received complete information on available services.[33]

Locating new clients outside the region and building up the local customer base were both viable strategies for offsetting a decline in traditional business. But the latter approach had a powerful advantage. A bank can only lend out and make a profit on money that has been deposited with it. Customers are thus as valuable for the deposits they bring to an institution as for the interest they pay on loans. Decline in the New England economy meant potential erosion of the deposit base as well as the disappearance of traditional borrowers. Moreover, since government regulations forbade the establishment of branches in other parts of the country, deposits could only be increased by expanding the region's overall level of economic activity or by winning customers away from competing institutions. Peter Brooke, a First National lending officer in the 1950s and a strong advocate of aiding local business, later explained the rationale for New England lending as follows. Money lent to a company in California will probably escape the bank's sphere of activity. But a loan to a firm in Lynn, Massachusetts, to take one example, will result in payments to suppliers in nearby Peabody and Somerville. Upon receiving this money, the Peabody and Somerville firms will deposit the funds with their banks. Sums lent locally thus tend to filter back into the regional banking system and, likely as not, back to the First National, the area's largest bank.[34]

Brooke might have added that the loan to the original customer in Lynn—to the extent that it helps that firm prosper and grow—increases the likelihood that this company will hold large future deposits with its principal bank. Statistics on commercial bank deposits demonstrate the impact on Massachusetts banks of the era's stagnant regional economy. Total deposits in Bay State institutions grew at a pace that was significantly less than the national rate.[35]

The health of the deposit base was never far from bank managers' minds. In a later speech the president of the First National urged officers to think of key banking services not solely as routes for making a profit but also as a means of increasing deposits:

> Deposits are our life blood. We are not just in the Personal Trust business, the Corporate Trust business, the Factoring business, or in foreign banking, solely to sell these useful services. We engage in these activities for another reason also . . . to attract deposits. . . . We usually think of ourselves as selling these services . . . but I would like also to have you think . . . that through these services we are *buying* deposits.[36]

In the years after World War II, the desire of the First National and other Boston institutions to build local deposits would lead to a policy of aggressive lending to a set of local companies with great growth potential: the electronics spinoffs.

Exactly when and how the Boston banks began catering to the spinoff firms is not clear. William H. Raye Jr. was a young lending officer with the First National during World War II. He later claimed that his bank began lending in 1943 to spinoff firms emerging from the massive research activity at the MIT-based Radiation Laboratory. In 1946, Raye said, he wrote a memo for his superiors arguing that continued decline in traditional New England industries was inevitable and could hurt the bank's future earnings. Intellectual capital was the area's strongest remaining asset, the memo held, and the First National should support its potential through strong financial backing to the fledgling spinoff sector. Raye claimed that the First National adopted this strategy, and that he directed a bank program of energetic lending to approximately 40 spinoff companies between 1946 and 1950.[37]

If this account is accurate, it would represent an early engagement of significant magnitude with the emerging Boston spinoff sector. Forty firms probably constituted the entire universe of spinoffs active in the area by 1950. Financing of the type described would have given firms near Boston an important boost in a highly competitive market. The account is plausible. Raye had personal knowledge of the electronics industry's potential, as his father was on the board of directors of Submarine Signal, an important Massachusetts producer of sonar and radar equipment that would later merge with Raytheon. The First National became acquainted with the possibilities of the sector as the bank extended large, government-guaranteed "V" loans to Raytheon during World War II. The credits financed Raytheon's defense electronics production. Raye was likely one of the First National officers managing these loans. In a 1948 speech on the First National's activities, the vice president of the bank named electronics as an industry in which the institution had an important presence.[38]

It seems clear that certain Boston-area banks acted in a supportive manner toward small science-based companies in this early period. A principal of the applied physics spinoff EG&G later told of being refused credit by one of the city's lenders soon after the war: the officers at this institution haughtily stated that they lent against collateral, not brains. The budding entrepreneurs then tried another of the city's banks, which proved amenable to brains-based lending. Similarly, officers at a bank interviewed by an MIT student for a 1949 research project reported that while their institution generally did not lend to businesses less than a year old, the bank had recently begun financing receivables on a government contract (a typical arrangement for spinoff lending) for a firm that was only three months old but had quality management known to the bank's personnel. An MIT undergraduate studying financing for Boston-area electronics spinoffs in the late 1950s stated that firms founded in 1945, 1946, and 1948 were among those he investigated that from an early point in their existence relied heavily on vigorous bank lending to finance growth.[39]

If the Boston-area banks indeed provided strong support to early spinoffs, it is likely that this activity did not arise solely from initiatives within the banking institutions. The efforts of the New England Council and of Federal Reserve Bank of Boston president Ralph Flanders probably helped persuade financiers to shed established practices and support the risky but potentially rewarding spinoff companies. The regional growth advocates pushing to increase financing for local industry almost certainly crossed paths with personnel of the First National Bank of Boston. As the largest and most influential bank in New England, the First National likely had a representative on the committee that Boston Fed president Flanders assembled to investigate commercial lending to small companies.[40] As a rising figure in the First National hierarchy, lending officer Raye was undoubtedly aware of Flanders's impassioned call at the 1945 regional banking conference for a greater volume of "marginal" loans to small local companies as a means of building up regional industry.[41]

Whatever early commitment to the spinoff sector may have existed among Boston bankers apparently did not last. William L. Brown became a lending officer at the First National in late 1953, where he worked under Raye's supervision. Brown reported that Raye at this point took a conservative approach to the electronics industry, lending only to the most established companies and insisting that the bank not deal with the spinoffs. Peter Brooke, who joined the First National several years later, similarly recalled that the bank did not have an active spinoff lending program in the mid-1950s.[42] The recollections of Arthur F. F. Snyder, who also began work in Boston banking at this time, offer a possible explanation. Snyder recalls that his first employer, the Shawmut Bank, pursued some level of electronics lending in the early 1950s. This is logical: Boston's premier venture capitalist, ARD president Georges Doriot, sat on the bank's board of directors. In 1953 or 1954, according to Snyder, a Shawmut loan to an important electronics company went spectacularly bad, leading the bank's officers to swear off lending to the entire sector. Snyder believes that the problems at the borrower were part of a general slump in the local electronics industry. The sector did see a serious, though short-lived, downturn in New England sales and employment due to a falloff in government demand at the end of the Korean War.[43] This slump, together with the misfortune that befell Shawmut's electronics lending, may have led all of the Boston banks to adopt a more cautious approach toward the industry and particularly toward the small, vulnerable spinoff firms.[44]

However these early events played out, a number of Boston banks moved decisively into spinoff lending in the mid- to late 1950s. First National Bank of Boston officer Brown stated that at the time he joined the lending staff in late 1953, the electronics spinoffs appeared to him to hold the promise of replacing the area's lost industry. Contravening the directions of his superiors, he covertly called on these companies to assess their needs and perhaps even extend loans. Peter Brooke similarly reported that the electronics spinoffs seemed to him to hold the potential to spur regional renewal at the time he joined the First National in 1956, but that the bank's officers were paying little attention to the possibilities. Brooke said he prepared a memo for superiors at the bank laying out his assessment.[45] At some point, probably in about 1957, a dispute broke out among the lending officers of the First National about whether to cultivate the business of the electronics spinoffs. The issue was adjudicated by a top executive of the bank. This manager laid down a new policy that was remarkable for commercial banking, an industry then notorious for its reluctance to lend to little-known small firms. The First National executive decreed that the bank would form a special team of officers with expertise in the technology industry. While any officer could make a loan (long the First's policy), *no one could turn down a loan request from a spinoff company before this group examined the application.* Included on the team were Raye, Brown, and Brooke. By 1960, as regional firms won numerous NASA contracts, the group had been dubbed the "space men."[46] Some of the smaller Boston institutions moved into (or returned to) spinoff lending during the same period. Arthur Snyder took a position at this time with the Merchants National Bank. He discovered the potential of the spinoff sector in 1956 or 1957, after lending to a firm manufacturing guided missiles. Snyder then acted to develop the electronics lending business at his new employer. The New England Trust Company also became active in the field.[47]

Having decisively committed to spinoff lending in the mid- to late 1950s, the Boston banks worked with extraordinary energy to develop the business.[48] To locate potential customers, loan officers leafed through telephone books and industrial directories, monitored the press for announcements of new firm formation, and prowled the warehouse districts where the companies maintained offices. Merchants National officer Snyder later described the situation by saying that he was driving up one side of Route 128 looking for new technology customers and Peter Brooke of the First National was driving down the other side doing the same. Having located a prospect, the bankers performed a careful analysis of its business outlook, investigating the company's financial condition, products, customers, and likely growth path. The examination was far more thorough than the treatment accorded normal loan applicants and resembled the way in which venture capitalists considered a potential investment. If everything checked out, the bankers would extend a loan. This credit would often take the form of accounts receivable financing, in which the borrowers pledged the proceeds of a contract, usually with the government, as collateral. Government-guaranteed "V" loans and unsecured credits were also used, depending on the situation. The initial amounts were generally small—$15,000 to $25,000—with short maturities of thirty to ninety days. The credits were renewed indefinitely as long as the borrower's condition remained sound and were increased to accommodate the needs of the business. The First National originally lent electronics entrepreneur An Wang $50,000 in the late 1950s. As the company prospered in the ensuing years, the amount of the loan ballooned to $1 million. A technology specialist at the First National also helped Wang bring in outside capital.

The "space men" of the First located additional investment capital for numerous other spinoff clients. The bank's officers established excellent connections with investors in New York, where much of the country's venture capital still concentrated. First National bankers had close ties to the Rockefeller venture capital organization and to the many investment banks and trust funds that were active in the field on a less formal basis. William Brown stated that he knew of a dozen or more sources of New York venture capital that would invest in spinoff firms essentially on his recommendation. Peter Brooke brought so many Boston-area spinoff investment opportunities to the attention of the Bessemer Trust, a family-controlled New York fund, that he was asked upon leaving commercial banking to take charge of the trust's venture capital operation, a position he held for several years. In addition to providing finance, the Boston banks gave invaluable management assistance to the area's spinoff companies. Lending officers referred entrepreneurs to auditors and legal counsel and assisted in finding skilled personnel in financial control, production, and marketing. They also helped set up partnerships with like-minded firms and aided companies with overseas sales. (A 1960 account of spinoff lending at the First National Bank of Boston appears in appendix 3.)

The First National became so enamored during this era with the promise of the electronics spinoffs that it moved to take complete control of the Boston-area market for financing these firms. Deploying its superior resources, the bank elbowed competing institutions out of the field. For instance, the First National won An Wang's business by giving the entrepreneur an unsecured credit line twice as large as the personally guaranteed loan granted to him by the Merchants National Bank. Pushed out of the mainstream market for spinoff loans, Arthur Snyder at Merchants National devised a new approach to the electronics industry.[49] Officers at the First National had little tolerance for badly managed spinoffs and cut off credit to such firms when serious trouble arose. As the companies teetered on the edge of insolvency, Snyder stepped in with a rescue program. He pressed for changes in personnel and worked to resolve difficulties in strategy, marketing, financial structure, internal controls, and other areas. All this was done gratis, simply for the privilege of taking over the troubled company's loan. Numerous firms were revived in this manner, as Snyder became something of an expert in high technology corporate turnarounds.

The short-term profits to be realized on loans to electronics spinoffs were not the primary motivation for the Boston bankers who so eagerly courted firms in this sector. The amounts involved were usually modest, at least initially. The goal instead was to secure the spinoffs as customers, in the belief that as much larger organizations in the future, the companies would likely maintain significant deposits and funds managed in trust with their principal bank. Behind these corporate aims stood the awareness that spinoff enterprise presented a promising avenue for reviving the regional economy as a whole. A 1960 account of spinoff lending at the First National described the officers of the bank as "thoroughly aware of the potential importance of these highly specialized businesses to the future of the region." The First later characterized the goal of the Small Business Investment Company (SBIC) it set up in 1959 to make equity investments in promising small businesses as "assist[ing] the New England region in attaining the technical and commercial innovations necessary to offset an economic decline of the area."[50]

The commitment of the Boston banks to the electronics spinoffs represented a dramatic shift from earlier attitudes about small business finance and the possibilities of technologically advanced industry. At the New England Council's 1943 panel on venture capital, First National president Charles Spencer claimed that there was nothing his institution could do to improve financing for the region's small companies. But in 1945, Spencer was described as eager to do everything possible for regional industry. At some point—beginning in the mid-1940s and then temporarily stopping, or beginning for the first time in the mid-1950s—Spencer's bank started energetically lending to small technology firms. It did so by extending endlessly renewed short-term loans that essentially substituted for venture capital: precisely the kind of financial support the bank president had earlier asserted his institution could never provide. A similar change of attitude toward the economic potential of technology took place at the Merchants National Bank. In 1940, the institution was a participant in the Research Advisory Service, a network of Northeast bankers that referred small manufacturers to researchers who could assist their companies. The executive who served as Merchants National's contact person for this service complained bitterly at the time of the "complete unawareness of the bank's [other] officers of the importance of research." But by 1947, the bank was publishing a bulletin entitled *Results from Research* that gave monthly updates on technological advances throughout industry. At some point after World War II, Merchants National as well became an important lender to the spinoff sector.[51]

It is unclear to what extent the development campaign of New England business spurred the Boston banks' 1950s commitment to financing local spinoffs. In the recollections of those involved, the banks' engagement with the spinoffs arose from the individual initiative of innovative lending officers. Larger forces may have been at work, however. The New England Council and likeminded persons endeavored during the 1940s to convince area bankers to take the supportive approach toward local industry that the lenders ended up pursuing with the spinoffs. Attempts to change financiers' behavior may have been even more far-ranging than is known. The development campaign of regional business certainly lasted well beyond World War II. The NEC continued to push for growth, although the organization's focus on small business finance questions waned after 1945. When the NEC's activities sputtered following an early 1950s change of leadership, the Boston Chamber of Commerce again became an active presence in the development field. Boston Chamber officials devoted significant attention to happenings in electronics. In 1955, the chamber's Business and Industrial Development Committee set up a special team to encourage the growth of the local electronics and atomic energy industries. In 1962, after Boston lost out to Houston in the competition for the NASA space center, the Boston Chamber rallied the heads of MIT, the First National Bank, and a leading utility behind plans for a regional corporation that would allow New England's small electronics producers to bid collectively on NASA contracts.[52] If nothing else, the activities of the NEC, the Boston Chamber of Commerce, and like organizations constantly drew the attention of area businessmen and financiers to the structural problems of the regional economy and the importance of developing new local industries.

Even if the 1950s commitment to spinoff lending arose completely within the Boston banks—with external pressures playing no role—the actions of these institutions were consistent with the logic of New England's recovery campaign. Service-sector firms such as banks, utilities, railroads, and retailers were the most energetic supporters of the development drive by regional business. This was so because companies in the service sector were tied to the region, and their future prosperity depended on an upturn in the area economy. The Boston banks provided strong financial support to local spinoffs for the same reasons that they backed the New England Council: doing so held the promise of revitalizing the New England economy and of rejuvenating the regional banking business in the process.

Finance for Spinoff Companies in Other Electronics Centers

The deep engagement of Boston bankers with the spinoff sector contrasted sharply with financiers' attitudes toward such companies in other centers of advanced electronics. In early 1957, as the aggressive spinoff lending effort of the Boston banks was getting under way, a trade journal reported difficult circumstances for small electronics firms in the country as a whole. Amid stringent conditions in the credit markets, banks were cutting back loans to small borrowers, leaving small electronics makers facing a financial squeeze. By the end of the year, tight money had become the "number one problem" in electronics. Small producers seeking relief reportedly turned to factors—financing organizations that had a dubious reputation in business circles and charged much higher interest rates than banks.[53]

The most detailed picture of the financing available to electronics spinoffs outside New England comes from an early 1960s study of companies in and around Los Angeles.[54] The report's authors conducted extensive interviews in 1959–60 with the managers of forty-five small firms. Finance emerges in the study as a significant problem area. Los Angeles commercial banks lent to many of these firms on the accounts receivable basis seen in Boston and often repeatedly renewed short-term credits. The bankers' approach to the companies was much less accommodating, however. The Los Angeles banks were clearly not promoting the growth of local spinoffs, unlike in Boston. Loan amounts were less sizable for small electronics firms in Los Angeles. The city's bankers were hesitant about extending loans exceeding a company's net worth, which happened quite routinely in Boston. The credit lines granted to Los Angeles firms were subject to yearly cleanup requirements, meaning the loans had to be fully paid off for a month or two each year. This crimped short-term company finances and forced some spinoff managers to obtain substitute credit from alternate sources. Several Los Angeles electronics executives complained that area bankers did not seem to understand the special needs of their industry, treating them like any other kind of company. Los Angeles bank managers recognized that small firms had an important place in the electronics sector and would continue to do so. But bankers were doing nothing to ease conditions for the spinoffs. Lenders "realized that small research-based electronics firms would have a permanent place in the industry, *possibly requiring* more specialized attention," the study's authors wrote. While the report devotes extensive attention to the question of equity financing for small electronics firms, there is no mention of the city's banks helping companies tap the formal and informal markets for venture capital, as occurred so dramatically in Boston. The study does include extensive discussion of the pros and cons of credit from nonbank lenders (essentially factors). Seeking finance from such organizations was obviously a serious possibility for small electronics firms in Los Angeles.[55] In addition, many of the firms in the Los Angeles study were much larger than the early-stage spinoffs that received significant financial support in Boston.

Less information is available on the circumstances facing electronics spinoffs in other locations outside New England. For the important New York City area, one item in the trade press is at least suggestive. A New York organization active by early 1960 was identified as a new source of finance for the area's small electronics firms. The Electronics Funding Corporation would work to improve companies' liquidity through the purchase and leaseback of their capital equipment.[56] Purchase and leaseback is a standard avenue of corporate finance, and the new organization would doubtless help New York's smaller firms. However, it could only assist companies that were well enough established to own significant amounts of equipment, a plateau not yet reached by many early-stage spinoffs. Several years later, a researcher with the Federal Reserve Bank of Philadelphia examined conditions for small science-based companies in that region. Executives at Philadelphia-area firms thought "local banks could be of much greater assistance." By contrast, according to the same investigator, spinoff managers in the Boston area believed the area's commercial banks to be understanding and highly supportive of their industry. "Financing a venture like ours is a lot easier here in Boston than in many other places," one said.[57]

The financial situation of Boston-area spinoffs differed dramatically from conditions for small electronics firms in other centers of the industry. Elsewhere, spinoff companies struggled with unsympathetic bankers who put yearly cleanup requirements on loans and provided scant assistance in securing additional equity. At times, these firms had to raise funds from factors or through the sale and leaseback of their equipment. In Boston, by contrast, the spinoff entrepreneur faced an embarrassment of riches in the financial field. Beginning in the mid-1950s and possibly earlier, the city's commercial banks competed for the spinoff business. The banks extended loans on easy terms, assisted in raising venture capital, and provided management advice. And if one's company got into trouble and bank credit was cut off, a seasoned financier might step in and direct a turnaround, simply to secure the firm's banking business.

The Impact of Financial Support on the Growth of Boston-Area Spinoffs

The superior financial assistance available to Boston-area spinoffs had a concrete impact, facilitating the companies' expansion. Strong financial backing was particularly important in the early stages of a firm's existence, when money was tight and outside funds were essential to capitalize fully on growth opportunities in highly competitive markets. The development path of individual Bay State spinoffs demonstrates these dynamics. The case of Wang Laboratories provides a vivid example of what occurred.

Brilliant Chinese immigrant An Wang founded this company in 1951. Wang earned a Harvard Ph.D. in applied physics in 1948 and worked for several years at the university's Computation Laboratory, then an important center of computer research. While at the Harvard lab, Wang invented the memory core, resolving a key difficulty in early computer design. (IBM later purchased the rights to the device for a sizable sum.) Wang Laboratories began as a one-man operation selling memory cores to military and industrial buyers. The company also did design work on a consulting basis for the Defense Department and other customers and made a well-selling instrument used in the burgeoning field of numerically controlled machine tools.[58] According to Peter Brooke, then a loan officer at the First National Bank of Boston, Wang Laboratories missed opportunities in the military procurement field during this early period due to a shortage of finance. Wang Laboratories repeatedly won the initial Pentagon contract to design a new electronic device. The company then lost out in the follow-up bidding to manufacture the instrument in quantity because it did not have sufficient funds to cover the costs of starting up production.[59] Despite these difficulties, Wang Laboratories by 1958 had ten employees and annual revenues in excess of $50,000. Expansion strained the firm's finances, even though Wang had secured a $25,000 loan from the Merchants National Bank, one of the smaller Boston lending institutions.[60]

At this juncture, Brooke of the First National Bank approached Wang. The First had by this time begun its aggressive pursuit of electronics spinoff business. In place of the Merchants National credit, Brooke arranged a $50,000 First National loan with more favorable terms. The added funds reduced the financial pressure on the small firm. But according to Wang, the bank loan "did not permit me to recruit the administrative, sales, and engineering people I needed to maintain the momentum of growth of the company." Wang and Brooke therefore discussed locating an outside investor with the necessary cash. Brooke eventually found a promising candidate in machine tool manufacturer Warner and Swasey. Wang had calculated that "we needed $150,000 over the next year and a half to cover our expansion needs." It was thus agreed that Warner and Swasey would pay $50,000 for a minority ownership stake in Wang Laboratories while lending the smaller company up to $100,000. Recounts Wang: "Peter Brooke basically acted as broker to this alliance, mediating between myself" and a Warner and Swasey executive.[61]

The resources brought in through the Warner and Swasey deal allowed Wang Laboratories to expand rapidly and become a serious player in the fast-growing office computer industry. According to Wang, the "capital and loans I obtained from [Warner and Swasey] enabled me to develop [a] photosetting device" that soon became the company's leading product. Sales of the instrument brought in nearly $1.5 million of revenue in the early 1960s. More important, the Warney and Swasey funds covered the costs of developing a desktop calculator for scientific and technical users. The machine, an early form of desktop computer, was a revolutionary innovation. Wang Laboratories soon brought out a user-friendly version of the same device for nontechnical corporate customers. Largely on the strength of its calculator sales, Wang's company mushroomed from 35 employees in 1964 to over 400 in 1967, with sales of $6.9 million in the latter year. Growing loans from the First National facilitated the firm's expansion during this period.[62]

By the late 1960s, Wang Laboratories was poised to break into the top rank of computer makers. With a series of pathbreaking minicomputer and word processing products, the company had by the early 1980s become a major international computer manufacturer with 25,000 employees. Like many high-flying technology firms, Wang Laboratories ultimately faltered. Brought low by mismanagement and a flawed transition from minicomputers to personal computing, the firm went into a nosedive in the mid-1980s.[63] These later events do not detract from the company's earlier successes and their impact on the regional economy. Wang's explosive growth created thousands of Bay State technology jobs; helped attract entrepreneurs, workers, and investors to the area; and provided a platform for the launch of additional electronics spinoffs.

Led by an engineering genius with sharp business instincts, Wang Laboratories was certain to succeed. The point here is that assistance from the First National brought in the resources the firm needed to realize its full potential. With this financial backing, the company during the 1960s made the jump from a viable small operation to a mid-sized one ready to challenge industry leaders in a core market. Without the financing provided and arranged for by the First National Bank, Wang Laboratories would necessarily have followed a slower growth path. Its contribution to the regional economy would accordingly have been less significant. The histories of other Boston-area technology spinoffs similarly demonstrate the key role of local financial support in company success.[64]

Conclusion: The Emergence of Route 128

By the early 1960s the Boston area had emerged as the country's leading hub for spinoff electronics. Boston outpaced the previously dominant spinoff centers of New York City and Los Angeles, where such activity withered away. Boston's Route 128 achieved this status as a rising, self-reinforcing spiral of entrepreneurial success took hold. Route 128 spinoffs grew more rapidly than similar firms elsewhere, creating broader platforms from which subsequent new companies could spring. The accumulating examples of successful firms encouraged ever greater numbers of local scientists and engineers to launch their own spinoffs. Boston's prominence in the field attracted to the region trained technical people who were interested in starting companies. The growing business opportunities drew increased investment money, as numerous venture capital firms were organized in the area beginning in the late 1950s.

This cycle of activity created important new employment in New England when the advanced electronics sector mostly produced military and space-related equipment for the government. The implications for the future were even greater. Markets broadened as advanced electronics evolved into the modern computer and software industries, turning out products that were increasingly directed at corporate and, later, consumer buyers. Having established itself as a leading center for electronics spinoffs, the Boston area was poised to claim a significant share of this much larger and more profitable market. It did so in spectacular fashion, led by highly successful local startups such as Digital Equipment, Wang Laboratories, and Lotus. Route 128's star has dimmed in recent years due to the even greater dynamism of the San Francisco area's Silicon Valley. Boston nonetheless remains one of the most important centers of technology industry in the country. Due in part to the sector's growth, New England in the 1980s again became one of the most prosperous regions of the United States.[65]

Boston was certain to emerge as an electronics spinoff center of considerable importance in the post–World War II era. The presence of MIT and affiliated laboratories ensured this outcome. These institutions provided a jumping-off point for a steady flow of entrepreneurs with knowledge of the latest techniques in a range of electronics and applied physics fields. But with a local academic research base as its only advantage, the Route 128 complex would probably have been substantially smaller than it in fact turned out to be. Numerous market niches won by Boston-area companies would likely have been claimed by producers elsewhere—especially firms in the older centers of New York and Los Angeles and in the growing technology hub near San Francisco. The greater financial support available in the Boston area gave enterprises there a key advantage, beyond the strengths in academic research. This financial backing enabled Massachusetts firms to surpass competitors elsewhere and secure leading positions in the electronics industry. These dynamics contributed significantly to the growth of the Route 128 complex, enabling it to reach the magnitude that was actually attained. The willingness of Boston-area financiers to provide strong backing to local spinoff entrepreneurs stemmed from the earlier decline of traditional manufacturing in the region. Downsizing created a need for replacement industries and the determination to do what was necessary to develop them.

Long-established New England industries saw continued plant closures in the post–World War II years, despite the growth of electronics production near Boston. Deindustrialization therefore remained an important regional concern. How New England leaders responded to industrial decline in the era after the war is explored next.

CHAPTER 7

Responses to Deindustrialization in New England during the Cold War Years

> You adjust yourself to the closings and layoffs as it comes along. . . .
> Mostly all the mills I worked in are all shut down today.
>
> FORMER MASSACHUSETTS TEXTILE WORKER ALBERT COTE,
> 1985, IN BLEWETT, *LAST GENERATION*

Electronics progressed impressively in New England during the decades after World War II. Other new sectors also emerged in the region during that era. The open-shop status of most of the area's developing industries contributed to their growth potential. A number of years passed, however, before the expansion of New England's newer sectors reached significant magnitude. The growing industries also proved susceptible to periodic downturns. Meanwhile, downsizing continued in textiles and other traditional sectors. For these reasons, deindustrialization was the principal economic reality in New England for substantial stretches of the Cold War era.

Two episodes of dramatic deindustrialization took place in New England during the Cold War years. The first occurred in the late 1940s and early 1950s and stemmed from widespread plant closures in textiles and other established sectors. The regional economy then experienced a dozen years of relatively strong growth. In the late 1960s a second sequence of significant downsizing took hold, continuing well into the ensuing decade. Job losses in the later period occurred in traditional industries, which were by then much diminished, and also in new, technologically advanced sectors such as electronics.

The initiatives carried out in response to New England's deindustrialization in the 1920s and 1930s were present once more in the Cold War–era cycles of downsizing. As New England leaders sought to counter the effects of industrial decline in the post–World War II period, they again pursued retrenchment, federal assistance, and economic development. In exploring this activity, the focus, as before, is on what occurred in Massachusetts.

The Cold War–era events discussed in this chapter, together with previously examined material on the 1920s and 1930s, provide an opportunity to survey responses to deindustrialization in New England over a sixty-year span. There was much consistency in the efforts to counter downsizing over this lengthy period. Changes took place as well. The continuities and discontinuities in deindustrialization policy are explored in the chapter's conclusion.

Deindustrialization in New England during the Years after World War II

Deindustrialization was a central economic reality in New England in the years following 1945, as it had been in the 1920s and 1930s. Downsizing occurred despite the significant defense-related production that took place in the area during the 1940s and 1950s. Massachusetts, the largest New England state, was hard hit by the trends sweeping the region. After dropping from 667,000 in 1923 to 461,000 in 1939, manufacturing employment soared in Massachusetts under the impetus of World War II demand. In 1947, as peacetime economic conditions returned, Bay State factory payrolls stood at 582,000. Industrial decline resumed at that point, to be briefly interrupted by the burst in output that accompanied early 1950s rearmament. Massachusetts manufacturing employment totaled 586,000 in 1951 and sank thereafter in a generally steady manner, hitting 531,000 in 1955 and 492,000 in 1960.[1] Over the period 1947–60, the number of manufacturing jobs in the commonwealth fell by 15.5 percent. This was a significant decline, although the drop-off in factory employment during the 1920s and 1930s had been twice as severe. Table 7.1 summarizes the relevant statistics. For the New England region as a whole, 16 percent of factory jobs were lost in the period 1947–58.[2]

The picture was more favorable in terms of overall employment. Due to growth in the service sector, the total number of jobs in Massachusetts rose from 1.73 million in 1947 to 1.82 million in 1955, an increase of 5.1 percent. Employment in the New England region increased by 6.4 percent over the same period. Although these changes were positive in absolute terms, area employment rose at a fraction of the national rate.[3] Indeed, as compared to the United States as a whole, Massachusetts employment growth in the immediate postwar years was as weak as it had been in the 1920s (see appendix 1).

Employment losses in New England manufacturing in the years after

Table 7.1. Manufacturing Employment in Massachusetts, Various Years, 1923–1960

	Workers (in thousands)
1923	667
1939	461
1943	712
1946	594
1947	582
1951	586
1955	531
1960	492
Percent change 1923–1939	-30.9%
Percent change 1947–1960	-15.5%

Sources: Commonwealth of Massachusetts, *Report of the Special Commission Relative to Establishment of a State Department of Commerce* (December 1945), 75; Massachusetts Department of Labor and Industries, *Census of Manufactures in Massachusetts*, 1953, 1960 (figures for "production and related workers").

World War II stemmed largely from declines in traditional industries, especially textiles, which again experienced widespread plant closures. In Massachusetts' core cotton and woolen-worsted sectors, the situation was catastrophic. Bay State cotton goods employment plummeted from 35,000 in 1946 to 19,000 in 1953 and 5,000 in 1960. The number of woolen and worsted jobs in the commonwealth similarly fell from 49,000 in 1946 to 25,000 in 1953 and 11,000 in 1960. Massachusetts saw significant although less drastic employment declines at this time in other lines of textiles, textile machinery, shoemaking, and leather.[4] The job losses were concentrated in the cities and towns where production centered. The impact in those locations was severe. Conditions were most dire in Lawrence, Massachusetts, long a hub of woolen and worsted manufacture. After several large wool-making operations closed in the early 1950s, manufacturing employment in the city plunged from 26,000 in 1946 to 14,000 in 1953. Joblessness in Lawrence hit 25 percent in July 1952, making the locale the "#1 Labor Surplus area in the country."[5]

New England's economic difficulties in the years following World War II gained national attention and inspired a significant amount of research, as had been the case before the war. In the early 1950s the president's Council of Economic Advisors and the National Planning Association each completed book-length studies of the regional economy.[6] The mass media devoted substantial space to the topic, with much of the coverage accentuating the negative. *Forbes* magazine's 1953 survey of the New England economy held that "depressive conditions, chronic for a half century, are still present."[7]

The Push for Retrenchment in Postwar Massachusetts

A push by business groups for retrenchment in social legislation and corporate taxes was one of the principal policy responses to deindustrialization in the Bay State during the years after World War II. In the early 1950s, business pressure for cutbacks concentrated on unemployment insurance. Examination of the retrenchment campaign focuses on that issue.[8] The business retrenchment drive of the postwar era had results resembling what had occurred in the 1920s. Employers secured a fraction of the cutbacks they sought in the unemployment insurance program. Meanwhile, efforts to reduce the state's corporate taxes were completely frustrated.

Labor's enhanced strength in post–World War II Massachusetts made retrenchment even harder to achieve than had been the case earlier. Union membership had greatly expanded in the Bay State in the 1930s and 1940s, as was true elsewhere. By one estimate, 33 percent of commonwealth workers were union members in 1951. The state's unions formed a strong alliance with the Democratic Party, providing the party with significant financing and campaign legwork. In turn, most Democratic officeholders in the Bay State strongly supported labor's goal of expanding social programs such as unemployment insurance.[9] Even moderate Republican politicians, eager for working-class votes, were wary of antagonizing the state's unions.

In Massachusetts, as in other parts of the country, jobless insurance was an important social program controlled by state government and financed by taxes on employers' payrolls. Capital and labor in the commonwealth had long contended over the scope of the system. Employers routinely pressed for reductions in unemployment benefits and taxes. Unionists, in the meantime, agitated for higher payments and steeper levies. Although the state branches of the AFL and CIO were determined rivals on many questions, the two organizations were in complete accord on the desirability of strengthening the state's unemployment insurance system. Massachusetts at this time provided relatively generous jobless benefits, far above the level of payments in the southern states then taking over the textile industry.

The Bay State's unemployment insurance system fell into grave financial difficulty in the late 1940s, as benefits disbursed greatly exceeded taxes. A deficit resulted, depleting the state fund from which jobless insurance payments were made. The problem stemmed largely from high unemployment in Massachusetts, which led to sizable payouts of jobless benefits. Plant closures in traditional industries such as textiles accounted for much of the joblessness in the state. In accordance with the regulations governing the Massachusetts unemployment system, the financial shortfall of the late 1940s led to increases in the taxes on employers. Payroll tax rates went up in 1950, and the maximum allowable levy was imposed on all employers in 1951.[10] It was widely expected that the peak across-the-board tax rate would remain in effect for years to come.

Corporate interests responded to the increase in payroll taxes with a campaign for significant retrenchment in unemployment insurance. Employers sponsored an omnibus measure in the 1951 session of the Massachusetts legislature that would curtail jobless insurance in ways that business representatives and conservatives had advocated for years. The recent rate increases precipitated employers' actions. But corporate interests were clearly trying to capitalize on the situation to secure long-desired cutbacks in the jobless insurance program. The employer-backed bill of 1951 altered existing unemployment law in fifty ways. So extensive were the proposed changes, a business lobbyist asserted, that the measure "rewrites . . . rather than amends" the regulations governing the system. Most important, the measure would undo the recent dramatic increase in jobless insurance tax rates. With the state fund that financed benefits at a low ebb, reintroducing the lower rates previously in effect would threaten the solvency of the unemployment system. The employers' measure would also alter eligibility rules and benefit levels in numerous ways harmful to those without work. In making the case for their proposal, employers repeatedly pointed to the difficulties of the commonwealth's declining industries and the lower unemployment taxes in competing jurisdictions.

Business interests achieved almost none of the desired changes in unemployment insurance during the 1951 legislative session. A watered-down bill did win approval in the Republican-controlled Senate. But the Democrats who had a majority in the House of Representatives opposed even that measure. The Democratic governor then intervened, putting forward his own plan for unemployment insurance reform. The governor's proposal would leave benefits at their present level and continue the current high tax rates until a substantial balance had accumulated in the state's jobless insurance fund. The measure also restructured unemployment insurance taxes. The new tax scheme lessened the likelihood that the system would confront another financial shortfall in the future. Lawmakers eventually approved a plan that was close to the governor's proposal. The final measure included virtually none of the drastic restrictions on eligibility for unemployment benefits that had appeared in the original employer-backed bill.

Sharp cutbacks in jobless insurance appeared more likely after Republicans won control of the governorship and both houses of the state legislature in the 1952 elections. Christian Herter, the new GOP governor, had repeatedly attacked the incumbent's halting response to industrial decline and had occasionally voiced the rhetoric of retrenchment. Soon after winning office, Herter declared that the state "must have a more favorable legislative climate in which to hold and expand industry." The Republican took few steps in that direction after assuming power, however. On unemployment insurance, Herter pressed only for action that would reintroduce lower tax rates more quickly than was provided for under the 1951 reforms. Lawmakers approved the proposal in modified form. Since the measure merely speeded up a tax reduction that would have occurred anyway, it had no lasting impact on the competitiveness of Massachusetts industry. The GOP-controlled legislature altered jobless insurance in several other ways. Most important, lawmakers eliminated benefits for employees who voluntarily left their jobs. Vigorously opposed by the unions, the step gave Massachusetts some of the country's most stringent regulations on so-called voluntary quits. In all of the legislative activity involving Bay State unemployment insurance in the early 1950s, this step was the only real defeat for labor. While a harsh blow to one group of workers, the change represented but a fraction of the cutbacks sought by business in an era of deindustrialization.

Business groups had even less success in reducing corporate taxes. Private-sector advocates persistently sought cuts in the commonwealth's high levies on enterprise during this period. They often argued that the steep rates were a key handicap in interstate competition. Despite this pressure, the legislature in 1950 actually increased state levies on business.[11] In 1952 lawmakers took no action on the recommendation of a legislative special commission that corporate taxes be eased. After taking over the governorship the following year, Republican Herter took few steps to bring about business tax cuts. Herter did seek to pare levies in 1954, as his bid for reelection loomed, but not in a way that directly aided business. The governor that year recommended, and legislature approved, a one-time 25 percent cut in *personal* income taxes.

Federal Assistance to Declining Industries and Areas in Postwar New England

The federal government took a variety of actions to assist locales and industries affected by deindustrialization in the years after World War II. The measures included strong trade protection for the textile industry; directing federal purchases into labor surplus areas; and a new program of federal assistance for redevelopment efforts in deindustrialized locales. These steps brought concrete, though limited, benefits to New England. Unionists and liberals from New England were at the forefront of the drive to secure federal aid. The range of federal initiatives for countering industrial decline during this period reflected the increased influence of unions and liberals in the political process following the New Deal. It exemplified as well the growing place of government in economic life during the post–World War II years.

Activist economist Seymour Harris was a key individual calling for a decisive federal response to New England's industrial decline. Harris earned an economics Ph.D. at Harvard and taught there for most of his career, eventually serving as department chair. A prolific author, he published more than forty books on a wide range of economic topics. Within his discipline, Harris was a stalwart liberal. Along with better-known colleagues Alvin Hansen and Paul Samuelson, Harris championed the new economics of Keynes in academic and policymaking circles. Harris spent much time seeking to shape public policy in ways consistent with his academic views. During World War II he worked for the Office of Price Administration, a locus of liberal thinking. After the war Harris was a public advocate for the liberal lobbying group Americans for Democratic Action. He advised Adlai Stevenson on economic questions during the 1956 presidential campaign and played the same role in John F. Kennedy's 1960 run for the presidency.[12] During the early 1950s Harris became deeply concerned about the decline of textile manufacturing in New England. In succeeding years he served as a leading advisor to regional officials on conditions in the cloth-making sector and related state and federal policies.

One means of federal assistance to the textile sector backed by Harris and others was trade protection. In the years after World War II, trade protection for textiles took the form of exemptions from the overall national policy of opening the country's market to the products of foreign industry. The U.S. government had long aided industries vulnerable to foreign competition through tariffs and other devices. These import barriers were steadily reduced in the postwar years, continuing the shift away from high tariffs that dated to the 1930s. Low-cost Japanese producers particularly benefited from the enhanced access to American markets made possible by the lessened trade restrictions.[13] U.S. textile imports grew dramatically in the postwar years, facilitated by the new openness to trade. Shipments of Japanese textiles saw especially marked increases. Imports accounted for a small fraction of total American cloth consumption, even at the increased levels. But surging shipments of certain fabrics posed a strong challenge to manufacturers in those product lines. For example, U.S. imports of cotton sheets and pillowcases from Japan increased by a factor of 15 between 1953 and 1955. The new foreign competition compounded the pressure on some firms in the downsizing New England textile sector and also jeopardized certain southern mills.[14]

New England interests pushed energetically for relief from the new foreign competition. The region's governors, acting through the Conference of New England Governors (CNEG), coordinated many of the lobbying efforts. In 1951 the CNEG formed a committee to examine ways of aiding the area's textile industry. Seymour Harris headed the textiles panel, which remained in operation until the end of the decade.[15] In 1955, as a round of trade negotiations loomed, Harris and the CNEG pressed to keep existing fabric tariffs in place. The region's governors also urged the imposition of quotas on cloth imports from Japan.[16]

Pressure from textile interests in New England and elsewhere had a considerable impact on federal policy. Responding to the call by New England governors for an end to reductions in cloth tariffs, Eisenhower administration officials noted that in the published enumeration of articles on which trade concessions were being considered, "the textile lists are short and avoid important items." To address the problem of rising imports of Japanese cotton goods, the administration negotiated an accord in which that country's manufacturers agreed to limit their shipments to the United States.[17]

Seymour Harris and other New England representatives put forward creative arguments about the regional impact of national economic policies as they lobbied for favorable action on trade. The New Englanders asserted that federal officials should take into account how existing national policies damaged the region before enacting trade measures that would further harm the area. Appearing before a congressional committee in 1955 to oppose further reductions in the protection for textiles, Harris asserted that "tariff policy is but one facet of national [economic] policy" and that "interference with the free market by the government has greatly injured New England's competitive position." He continued, "It would be the height of folly for the government now to revert to free market principles through tariff cuts with injury to New England when interference with the free market has hurt New England."[18] Harris identified "tax policies" as a prime example of federal action that damaged the New England economy. He claimed, apparently on the basis of published statistics, that "the operations of the Treasury tend to take money out of this region to build up its competitors. In one year, as much as $1 billion was taken out of New England ... about 7 per cent of its income."[19] Inquiring further into these issues, Harris found that in the period 1934–54, Massachusetts received from federal aid programs $86 per $1,000 of federal taxes borne, whereas ten poor states received from aid programs an average of $371 per $1,000 of taxes borne.[20] Harris's studies on the regional impact of federal spending prefigured the efforts of congressional representatives from the Northeast and Midwest during the Sunbelt-Snowbelt clash of the 1970s.

Steps to direct or "channel" federal purchasing and related investment into locales with high unemployment were another avenue of federal aid to deindustrializing regions in the postwar era. In New England and elsewhere, industrial downsizing was the leading cause of the geographically concentrated joblessness targeted by these programs.

Efforts to channel federal purchases and otherwise aid locales with high unemployment reflected the downsizing that was increasingly widespread in economically developed parts of the country during the decades after World War II. Outside New England, traditional industries saw permanent employment declines at this time in Pennsylvania and other mid-Atlantic states, West Virginia, and sections of the Midwest. Coal mining, textiles, railroad equipment manufacturing, steel, and autos were among the sectors affected. The job losses stemmed from overcapacity, falling demand, shifts of production to low-wage areas, automation, and other factors.[21]

Efforts to channel federal government orders into locales with elevated levels of joblessness began during the administration of Harry Truman. Attention focused on defense spending, which was the largest component of the national budget and rose dramatically with the rearmament that accompanied the outbreak of the Korean War. In New England, many felt that the area was not getting a fair share of the increased defense expenditures. New Englanders calculated that additional Pentagon orders placed with firms in their region would ease unemployment in localities hard-pressed by plant closures. By late 1951 New England unionists and politicians of both parties were agitating for action on the issue. At least partly as a result of New England demands, Truman administration officials moved to channel defense orders into areas of labor surplus. In February 1952 the Office of Defense Mobilization issued Manpower Policy No. 4, which called on procuring agencies to take steps in this direction. New England textile manufacturers stood to receive the greatest benefits from the program. Rules for textiles issued later in 1952 specified that parts of orders would be "set aside" for firms operating at less than full capacity in locales with extensive unemployment. Implementation of the policy was slowed by the reluctance of military procurement officers to depart from established purchasing procedures.[22]

The channeling effort carried on under the administration of Dwight Eisenhower, albeit with further hiccups. Southerners in Congress had opposed the venture from the outset, since orders directed to New England textile producers were lost to firms in their region. In late 1953 the southerners succeeded in watering down the regulations governing the channeling program. Eisenhower then stepped in to protect channeling, ordering procurement agencies to continue reserving portions of their orders for firms in locales with high joblessness.[23]

The federal effort to channel defense contracts into labor surplus areas did little to relieve the chronic unemployment in those locations. A fundamental difficulty, apart from obstruction by procurement officers and areas losing business, was that purchases could only be directed to firms able to manufacture what the military required. For many products, no such companies existed in areas of high unemployment. Overall, contracts worth $133 million were subject to channeling between March 1952 and December 1956, creating an estimated 7,000 man-years of employment in the targeted areas. Since this total was divided between numerous locales and spread over a period of almost five years, the impact on a given place at one point in time was necessarily limited.[24]

The Eisenhower administration devised its own program to direct military production into locales with elevated joblessness. The plan targeted investment instead of orders, granting tax benefits to companies building defense production plants in labor surplus areas. Future Massachusetts governor Christian Herter was an early advocate of the new approach. In 1952, while serving as a U.S representative from the Bay State, Herter called for this type of federal aid to deindustrializing regions. Eisenhower's investment initiative seems to have created more employment in depressed locales than the channeling of orders initiated by Truman. Under Ike's program, sixty-four plants qualifying for the extra tax write-off had been set up in areas of high unemployment by 1957, employing 16,000 workers on an ongoing basis.[25] This figure was still quite limited, given the extent of unemployment in labor surplus areas across the nation.

Federal measures to aid deindustrializing locales up through the mid-1950s served mainly to demonstrate how little U.S. officials could do for these locations, given existing policy tools. Unionists and liberals were aware of this reality and pushed for new forms of federal action in this field. Pressure from these groups eventually resulted in the creation of the Area Redevelopment program.

Union official Solomon Barkin had a key role in bringing the Area Redevelopment effort into being. The son of socialist Jewish immigrants, Barkin attended City College of New York in the mid-1920s while teaching courses at a Yiddish high school where Marxian and reform ideas dominated the curriculum. He then entered the Ph.D. program in economics at Columbia University. There he studied with adherents of the institutionalist school, which emphasized the shortcomings of the market and the need for government intervention in economic life. Barkin left Columbia without completing his dissertation. In 1933 he joined the National Recovery Administration (NRA), where he worked with Sidney Hillman, head of the Amalgamated Clothing Workers and a member of the NRA's Labor Advisory Board. In 1937 Hillman set up the Textile Workers Organizing Committee, later to become the TWUA. Barkin was hired as the new organization's research director. Like many CIO officials, Barkin entered the post–World War II period with a social democratic vision of activist government policies that would rectify a wide range of social and economic problems. He remained with the TWUA until 1963, at which point most unionized textile mills had closed. He then worked at the Organization for Economic Cooperation and Development (OECD) and as an economics professor at the University of Massachusetts.[26]

Barkin was the unionist most involved in designing and securing implementation of a federal program to aid areas hit by industrial downsizing.[27] As research director of the TWUA, the leading textile union, Barkin had long worried about the impact of declining New England cloth production on the region's displaced workers and on his own organization. In the years following World War II, he proposed a number of initiatives for addressing the problem, including comprehensive planning for industrial change and a state government program to aid troubled textile firms. None of these ideas made much progress toward implementation. His advocacy of federal assistance for deindustrialized locales had greater impact. As early as 1952 Barkin called within CIO circles for federal aid to what were known at the time as "depressed areas." Proposals for a comprehensive federal program to revitalize depressed areas received serious consideration in Congress from the mid-1950s onward. The measure that eventually became law was sponsored by Democratic Senator Paul Douglas of Illinois, a leading spokesman for liberal economic policies. Barkin claimed to have first drawn Senator Douglas's attention to the problem of deindustrialized locales. He served on the small task force that Douglas assembled to draft legislation on the subject.

The Douglas bill was initially introduced in 1955. The measure authorized a range of assistance, including aid for factory construction, accelerated tax amortization for privately built plants, money for the construction of community facilities, and preferences in government purchasing. Barkin testified before Congress on behalf of the legislation and helped assemble a union-backed national group that spent years lobbying for the bill's passage. (Economist Seymour Harris was one of those who helped mobilize support for the measure.) Backing for the legislation centered in a broad coalition of industrial states. Strong support was provided by the AFL-CIO and several of that organization's constituent unions, including textile workers (the TWUA), auto workers, steel workers, and mine workers.[28] Concerted resistance to the proposal came from right-leaning business organizations and southern conservatives. To win broader backing for the measure, Douglas included poverty-stricken rural counties, and eventually Indian reservations, among the areas that would qualify for assistance.

The Douglas bill won congressional approval in 1958 and again in 1960 but was vetoed on both occasions by President Eisenhower. Massachusetts Senator John F. Kennedy had favored the measure from the outset, and his election as president ensured enactment of the program. The Douglas bill became law in early 1961. It provided $390 million in funding, to be spread over four years, for an Area Redevelopment Administration (ARA) within the Department of Commerce.

Given the scale of the problem, the amounts appropriated were far from generous. Moreover, the available resources had to be shared with places that had not appeared in the original plan for aid to depressed industrial locales, such as poor rural zones and Indian reservations. These factors ensured strict limits on the assistance deindustrialized areas would receive from the ARA. As of March 1965, when nearly all the appropriated money had been spent, the agency had committed $25 million for fifty-one New England projects that had the potential to create 7,700 jobs. The area redevelopment effort was renewed through the Economic Development Act of 1965, which shifted the focus of the program to the provision of public works.[29]

In addition to sparse resources, a key weakness of the ARA and subsequent efforts was the nature of the assistance provided. The philosophy behind these programs was that areas in economic difficulty should be aided in becoming more attractive to potential employers. No consideration seems to have been given to the kind of coercion envisaged in the Ellenbogen textile bills of the mid-1930s and the original 1937 draft of the Fair Labor Standards Act.[30] Had they passed, the latter measures would have protected the remaining jobs in New England textiles by forcing wages at competing southern firms up to the levels prevailing in the North. The counterpart in the area redevelopment sphere would be to compel employers to locate new industrial facilities in zones with labor surpluses, rather than just encouraging them to do so. The regional development programs of some European countries in the post–World War II decades included such steps.[31] Regulations of this type detract from economic efficiency, but they are effective in creating new employment in locales that badly need it. Of course, given the more conservative political landscape of the United States, it would have been extremely difficult to secure legislative approval for coercive measures of this kind.

Economic Development Efforts in Postwar Massachusetts

A renewed regional push for economic development was a central response to the factory closures that spread through New England after World War II.[32] Particularly notable was the intensification of growth-promotion efforts by state government. In Massachusetts, public development activity reached a peak during the governorship of Christian Herter, who took office in early 1953. The Republican Herter made the promotion of growth his primary policy for countering industrial downsizing, although he periodically expressed rhetorical support for retrenchment.[33] Due largely to the governor's efforts, Massachusetts set up a new government economic development agency and established a publicly chartered, privately run entity to lend needed funds to small business. Private development efforts coordinated by business associations continued during the postwar era, paralleling the activity in the public sector.

Pivotal to Herter's growth-promotion program was a drive to establish a state Department of Commerce that would work for the development of the commonwealth economy. The new agency would replace the smaller Development and Industrial Commission that had been set up in the 1920s under a slightly different name to encourage growth.[34] By calling for the establishment of a Department of Commerce, Herter revived a troublesome question in Bay State politics. In the mid-1940s, a Democratic governor had pushed to replace the Development and Industrial Commission with just such an agency. Soon afterward a legislative special commission recommended with near unanimity that a large, very well funded Department of Commerce be set up. The plan ran into trouble when a leading conservative Republican lawmaker insisted that a smaller development agency be created instead. A legislative deadlock ensued, and the idea was not broached again in the years that followed. In his 1953 inaugural address, Herter called on Massachusetts lawmakers finally to set up a Department of Commerce. Soon afterward, the governor submitted a bill laying out a detailed blueprint for the agency. Local chambers of commerce enthusiastically backed the plan. The commonwealth was in "desperate need" of such a growth-promotion body, declared the president of the Greater Boston Chamber of Commerce. The governor's proposal passed the legislature with relative ease.[35]

The circumstances surrounding the Department of Commerce's creation demonstrated how the views of politicians and businessmen on the appropriate role of government had changed in the wake of the New Deal. During the 1920s, GOP officeholders and corporate managers had generally opposed plans to create significant new public programs in the economic domain. In 1953, by contrast, the Republican governor of Massachusetts pushed hard for the establishment of a new development agency, and key elements of the business community supported the proposal.[36]

Governor Herter advanced a second major growth initiative in 1953. He worked to establish a development credit corporation (DCC) in Massachusetts to complement the new Department of Commerce. DCCs were a recently devised type of private-sector organization that provided long-term financing to small and medium-sized companies in need of such support. DCCs pooled funds from financial institutions, using the money to extend loans that were too risky to be taken on by conventional lenders. The funds made available by DCCs created new jobs and preserved existing ones under threat. The organizations were attractive in areas of the country seeking to build up or revitalize their economic base. Maine set up the first DCC in 1950.[37] Proposals to create such an institution in Massachusetts had been before the legislature in preceding years, but nothing concrete had resulted. Herter took decisive action on the issue early in his term. He convened a committee of business leaders eager to set up a DCC. This group secured commitments to participate from those in business and financial circles. The governor then assembled a lengthy, impressive list of incorporators for the project. The bill providing the necessary public charter for the DCC sailed through the legislature. The new entity, called the Massachusetts Business Development Corporation (MBDC), began operations soon afterward. Other New England states, responding to the same pressures that affected Massachusetts, established government economic development agencies and development credit corporations during the 1950s.[38]

The economic development institutions created in Massachusetts at Governor Herter's behest energetically pursued pro-growth agendas. The commonwealth's new Department of Commerce carried on a wide range of endeavors, with a primary focus on strengthening the ailing manufacturing sector. The agency worked to bring in new employers from out of state and encouraged the formation of industrial development organizations at the community level. The department devoted considerable effort to strengthening the commonwealth's existing manufacturers, especially small ones. In addition, the Department of Commerce gathered and published vast quantities of information about development possibilities in individual cities and towns; conducted public relations campaigns touting the commonwealth's attractiveness as a place to do business; and advertised the Bay State as a tourist destination. The other new Massachusetts development institution, the MBDC, carried out an active lending program. Using funds borrowed from participating banks and insurance companies, the MBDC had by the end of 1957 approved 99 loans worth a total of $13.9 million. This lending supported the creation or preservation of 15,000 jobs. Virtually all the organization's loans went to manufacturers. Constructing or renovating additional factory space for companies with growth potential was a prime use of MBDC monies. As of late 1957, nearly a third of the organization's lending had gone to localities where plant closures had caused high levels of unemployment.

Development efforts carried out completely within the private sector continued in Massachusetts and New England during the postwar period, paralleling the high-profile initiatives undertaken by government. The New England Council remained a central player in the growth-promotion field. One of the organization's important initiatives in the years after World War

II was working to convince a major U.S. steelmaker to set up a New England plant. NEC leaders calculated that a local supply of raw steel would stimulate the growth of metal fabricating companies in the region. The project proved unfeasible in the end. The NEC also campaigned for a strong New England presence in the emerging atomic power industry. One of the country's first commercial atomic reactors operated in Massachusetts, and NEC efforts doubtless contributed to this outcome.[39]

The New England Economy into the 1960s

New England experienced substantial prosperity beginning in the mid-1950s. This was a significant change after decades in which economic difficulty was the peacetime norm. In the key manufacturing sector, employment stabilized as growth in emerging industries offset decline in older ones. Massachusetts accordingly saw a slight increase in the number of factory jobs, from 498,000 in 1958 to 508,000 in 1967. For New England as a whole, manufacturing employment between these years rose from 1.05 million to 1.14 million.[40] Meanwhile, the number of jobs in the service sector expanded impressively. As a result, total employment increased by 11.3 percent in Massachusetts and 13.0 percent in New England between 1955 and 1965. Although not as rapid as the 20.0 percent increase in total U.S. employment during the same period, the region's performance was much better in comparative terms than in the years immediately after the war.[41] The change in material conditions was such that even liberal economist Seymour Harris, who was deeply concerned about the decline of traditional New England industries, averred in 1958 that the region as a whole "enjoyed a suitable share of our flourishing national prosperity."[42]

Much of New England's industrial expansion of this period occurred in the kinds of sophisticated, high value-added industries upon which regional development advocates had long focused.[43] Advanced electronics and applied physics were important growth sectors in New England after World War II. In the nascent Route 128 high technology complex, employment increased at firms large and small. Department of Defense orders accounted for much of the growth in this sector. Skilled labor was essential to the region's success in the manufacture of aircraft engines, where extremely precise work was required. Located in the region were both of the industry's leading producers: Pratt and Whitney of Connecticut and General Electric's engine-building operation in Lynn, Massachusetts. Pentagon orders provided the bulk of the region's aircraft engine business at this time.

Electronics and aircraft were two of New England's most rapidly growing industries in the postwar period. Massachusetts was the regional center for electronics production. Commonwealth employment in the sector soared from 29,000 in 1949 to 87,000 in 1962.[44] In aircraft manufacture (mostly of engines), New England employment rose from 24,000 in 1950 to 73,000 in 1962.[45]

The region's relatively low industrial wages, caused by high unemployment in the declining mill towns, facilitated growth in other sectors. Cheap labor was key in static electronic components, a segment of the electronics industry in which technological innovation played little role. Output of static components such as capacitors, resistors, and transformers originally concentrated in New York, but by the 1950s producers were looking to reduce labor costs. Numerous firms moved to locales of declining industry in New England. Among the former textile-making cities that became centers of static electronic components production were New Bedford, Massachusetts; Nashua, New Hampshire; and Willimantic, Connecticut. Other manufacturing sectors expanding in New England at this time included metalworking, precision casting, precision tools, and plastics.

Significant employment gains also occurred in the service sector. New England's banks and insurance companies did a sizable volume of business with customers outside the region, and employment in these industries increased markedly between 1950 and 1960. Higher education brought in substantial income. In Massachusetts during the early 1960s, more than half the students and 60 percent of the income received by private universities and colleges originated outside the state. Advanced medical services were an increasingly important form of "exports" for New England. As many as a third of the patients at several elite Massachusetts hospitals came from beyond the state's borders. In business services, New England organizations did a growing amount of work for companies external to the region; management consulting and research and development were particularly important fields. Tourism continued as an important source of revenue from non–New England individuals vacationing in the area.[46]

Many of the expanding sectors in the New England economy were not unionized. This was the case for almost all of the growing service industries. It was also true for segments of manufacturing, where low-wage assembly positions and the smaller electronics spinoffs were generally open shop. The lack of union work rules facilitated the growth of non-union industries in New England.[47] Electronics and other industries expanded in the region at this time despite the higher taxes and increased regulation of investors enacted during the New Deal period. These restrictions tended to slow the emergence of new industries.

Many individuals in centers of traditional New England industry did not share in the overall prosperity seen in the region beginning in the mid-1950s. High unemployment prevailed in hard-hit mill cities, even as some local manufacturing jobs were created. In March 1955, during a rising business cycle, unemployment remained above 20 percent in Lawrence and stood at 10.3 percent in Lowell and 7.1 percent in Fall River. Joblessness persisted in these locales despite significant out-migration. Fall River lost 10 percent of its population between 1950 and 1960, as the number of city residents between the ages of fifteen and thirty-four declined by a fifth.[48]

Studies conducted during the period documented the difficulties confronting workers displaced by plant shutdowns. One researcher tracked operatives after the 1948 closure of a New Hampshire textile mill. Although most of the displaced workers found new jobs, doing so required an average search of twenty weeks. Only 40 percent of those who had held skilled jobs at the textile plant found another skilled post. Workers typically earned "considerably less" in their new positions than they had in the old ones. Many had to accept jobs outside the cloth-making industry, a change that took place "at the expense of the workers' accumulated skills and income[-earning potential]." Of the displaced New Hampshire operatives, 13 percent did not have a position and were not looking for new employment at the time research was conducted. Older individuals, especially women over age sixty, were particularly likely to meet this fate. A separate study of a New England textile mill closing of the same era produced similar findings.[49]

Interviews with former millworkers from Lowell, Massachusetts, show how the general patterns identified in these studies manifested themselves in individual lives. The New England economy was in better condition for most of the post–World War II period than it had been in the late 1920s and Depression years. Displaced millworkers thus had an easier time locating substitute employment after World War II than had been the case in the 1920s and 1930s. Numerous individuals found postwar work in the growing electronics sector. Accounts from the period after World War II nevertheless reveal multiple job displacements and significant downward mobility as workers accepted less desirable new employment. Operatives who continued to work in textiles experienced repeated plant closures as long-established employers shut down one by one.

Henry Dickenson's story exemplifies these themes. Dickenson worked in Lowell's Boott cotton mills from 1922 until the company closed in 1954. At that point, a series of job displacements began. The lower earnings in non-textile positions observed in postwar studies of former millworkers were clearly apparent in Dickenson's case:

> After I got out of the Boott in 1954 . . . I had a chance to work in the Merrimack [a textile manufacturer]. . . . I only worked there a little while, and then that mill folded up. . . . So I was out of work. Toward the last of it [at the Merrimack] I was getting around $1.75 an hour. The only thing I could get was working with a plumber for just over a dollar [an hour]. Then that blew up. Then I started to get a job in Symphonic, making radios and things like that. I started there for a dollar an hour. Then that went out, and I was sixty-nine, so I retired.[50]

Albert Cote's multifaceted employment history provides a particularly dramatic example of the disruptions seen by textile workers. Cote worked in the highly skilled position of loom fixer for a textile mill that closed in 1941, then as a loom fixer at the Boott mills. He left Boott around 1950, initiating what turned out to be an extended series of displacements. Cote experienced downward mobility during his last years in textiles, as he repeatedly accepted employment in the less prestigious and less well paid position of weaver. Having departed the Boott mills, he

> worked a year or two in the Wood mill in Lawrence as a weaver. Then from there, we got laid off. From there I got a job [as a loom fixer] in the Merrimack mill. . . . Then that closed down, and I worked in Uxbridge [Massachusetts] as a loom fixer and a weaver. I didn't stay there too long.

Cote worked numerous jobs outside the textile industry in the years that followed. He left one position due to low pay and was forced out of several others by external circumstances including a buyout, a layoff, and a bankruptcy. He finally landed solid employment at electronics producer Honeywell, where he stayed until retirement. Cote was stoical as he reflected on how starting out in a declining industry had resulted in a highly mobile work record: "You adjust yourself to the closings and layoffs as it comes along. . . . Mostly all the mills I worked in are all shut down today."[51]

Responses to Industrial Downsizing in Massachusetts during the 1970s and 1980s

After reviving in the mid-1950s, New England experienced generally good economic conditions for a dozen years. Prosperity of this kind had not been seen in the area during peacetime since just after World War I. In the late 1960s, the regional economy again turned sour.[52] Employment reductions took place in a range of manufacturing sectors. Downsizing continued into the following decade. Sustained job losses occurred due to a confluence of negative developments. Long-troubled older industries—such as textiles, apparel, leather, and footwear—were again battered by competition from elsewhere in the country and abroad. In Massachusetts between 1967 and 1977, employment in leather manufacturing plummeted from 44,000 to 23,000, while the number of textile jobs fell from 38,000 to 28,000. Job losses also occurred in New England's high technology sectors. Industries such as electronics and computers had seen strong growth in Massachusetts and elsewhere in the preceding decades. Heavily reliant on sales to the government, these sectors suffered as defense expenditures fell off with the Vietnam pullout and space-related purchases declined following the Apollo moon shots. With older and new industries all shedding jobs, employment in Massachusetts' manufacturing sector declined from 508,000 in 1967 to 408,000 in 1977, a drop of 20 percent. In New England as a whole, the number of manufacturing jobs fell by 17 percent during these years. Total employment grew at low rates in Massachusetts and New England in this period. (Appendix 1 shows the Bay State's very weak job growth at this time.) Industrial downsizing therefore resulted in high levels of joblessness. Unemployment in Massachusetts reached 8 percent during 1972. In 1975, amid a severe national recession, commonwealth joblessness hit 11 percent, several percentage points above the national average.

Structural economic decline produced serious fiscal difficulties for state government. Massachusetts had relatively generous public services in this era, with levels of per capita spending by state and local government among the highest in the country. Welfare expenditures accounted for a significant share of total state outlays by the early 1970s, the caseload having skyrocketed from 170,000 in 1960 to 750,000 in 1972. Soaring spending and a sputtering economy combined to produce budget deficits of alarming size. The budget shortfall for 1975 was so significant that the state could not find buyers for the notes issued to cover the gap, rendering it temporarily bankrupt.

As area leaders dealt with structural economic difficulties in the 1970s and 1980s, they pursued initiatives of all three of the types observed in earlier eras of industrial decline. Retrenchment, federal assistance, and economic development were once again in evidence as regional leaders grappled with the challenges of deindustrialization.

Loud calls for retrenchment emanated from representatives of business during this period. In Massachusetts attention focused on the high level of taxation in what critics derided as the commonwealth of "Taxachusetts." Spending for social programs was another prime target. The First National Bank of Boston—so central in the private-sector development push of an earlier era and still the region's largest lender—played a key role in these efforts. James Howell, an energetic economist with a flair for publicity, took charge of the bank's research department in 1970 and quickly moved to the fore of the debate about revitalizing the state economy. In 1971, the newsletter of the First National research department asserted that establishing a "rational business environment" was necessary to restore prosperity. The next year, a New Bedford manufacturer attracted widespread attention with an open letter to state legislators identifying high unemployment insurance taxes as a key factor inhibiting the commonwealth's competitiveness. The First National bolstered this claim, documenting a widespread belief among Massachusetts industrialists that the state's jobless insurance taxes were unduly heavy. The bank's research department also criticized government spending that was "too high for the sluggish economy to support"; a tendency to burden business with "antipollution measures and social benefits" more extensive than those elsewhere; and the "fantastic rate of increase" seen in "welfare spending" during the preceding years.[53] Rankings by the Fantus Company, an industrial location advisor, seemed to substantiate the corporate sector's charges. In 1975, Fantus rated the business climate in Massachusetts forty-sixth among the 48 continental states, a statistic frequently cited by critics.[54]

Pressure from Massachusetts business to cut taxes and social programs lasted into the early Reagan years, even though economic conditions in the state began to improve as early as 1976. In 1978, according to observers, "the lion's share of the rhetoric coming from businesses . . . was that [Massachusetts'] high tax burden and bad business climate were driving firms to expand out of state." The following year, executives of fifty of the largest private employers in the commonwealth formed the Massachusetts Business Roundtable to maintain the push for retrenchment.[55] Taxation emerged as a particular worry of the state's high technology companies during the later 1970s. The concern of these firms was not corporate levies but rather the high Massachusetts taxes on individuals (personal income and property taxes) that discouraged well-paid engineers and managers from accepting local jobs. In 1977, the companies organized their own lobby, the Massachusetts High Technology Council. The group threw its support behind tax-cutting proposals including Proposition 2½, an initiative on the 1980 ballot limiting levies on property to 2½ percent of the value of a home.[56]

The steady pressure from Massachusetts business for retrenchment produced significant results over a considerable span of years. Taxes and overall government spending saw sizable reductions. With the backing of liberal Republican governor Francis Sargent, the state legislature in 1973 approved a set of reductions and credits on corporate levies known as "Mass Incentives." The package temporarily increased the business tax credit for new investment, phased out a duty on inventories and machinery, and enabled firms to reduce their tax liability by carrying forward losses from prior years. In 1978, during the term of liberal Democratic governor Michael Dukakis, the state stopped counting export sales in calculating a corporate levy, producing a sizable break for the firms affected. Conservative Democrat Edward King took over as the state's chief executive in 1979 after upsetting Dukakis in the gubernatorial primary. King promised to limit spending, cut revenues, and keep an open ear to the concerns of business. Under his leadership, the state slashed the levy on capital gains, trimmed the duty on personal income, and reduced excise taxes. Massachusetts voters approved Proposition 2½ in 1980. Facing the threat of another initiative, the legislature then removed a 7.5 percent income tax surcharge instituted during the state's 1975 fiscal crisis. Repeated rounds of tax cutting resulted in substantial reductions in the size and cost of commonwealth government. From a peak of 372,000 in 1978, public employment at the state and local levels dropped to 319,000 in 1981. The Bay State tax burden, calculated as a percentage of personal income, fell from 9 percent above the national average during the first Dukakis administration to 10 percent below the national average in 1984.[57]

The retrenchment instituted during this period in Massachusetts included significant reductions in social programs for the working class and the poor. During the 1970s, the commonwealth tightened the rules governing unemployment insurance in a number of ways detrimental to workers. Benefits were reduced for unemployed individuals receiving pensions from previous employment and eliminated for those whose joblessness did not stem solely from the actions of the employer. In 1975, business groups won approval for an eagerly sought measure ending jobless benefits for persons who left their positions voluntarily. (Lawmakers had stopped benefits for such workers in 1953 and later reinstituted them.) The legislature took this step in the face of energetic opposition from the state AFL-CIO. Union leaders were unable to reverse any of these changes in succeeding years, despite repeated attempts to do so. In 1976, with the finances of the unemployment insurance system in parlous condition, Governor Dukakis proposed numerous additional changes sought by business groups. Lawmakers refused many of these steps but did tighten in several ways the requirements for receiving jobless benefits.[58] As part of the efforts to bridge the state's 1975 fiscal chasm, the commonwealth also sharply cut welfare payments.[59]

Many Massachusetts leaders looked to the national government for aid in dealing with the economic difficulties of the 1970s. Calls for federal assistance were thus a central element in the Bay State's response to the renewed industrial decline of this period. One manifestation of this dynamic was a concerted push for enhanced federal spending in the "Snowbelt" states of the Northeast and Midwest, which were hard hit by industrial downsizing at this time. Congressman Michael J. Harrington of Massachusetts was the central figure in mounting the Snowbelt campaign. (Although a fiery liberal, Representative Harrington is not to be confused with the similarly named Democratic Socialist poverty fighter active in the same era.)

Michael J. Harrington was born into a politically prominent family in Salem, Massachusetts. He graduated from Harvard in 1958, then earned a degree from Harvard Law School. Eager to enter politics and intensely ambitious, Harrington held a seat on the Salem City Council at age twenty-four, won the first of several terms in the Massachusetts legislature at twenty-eight, and was elected to the U.S. House of Representatives at thirty-three. Harrington's career embodied the sixties-era shift of liberalism toward sociocultural and foreign policy concerns. He maintained an arms-length relationship with the Massachusetts unions and won election to Congress in a "WASPy" Boston-area district largely through outspoken opposition to the Vietnam War. Described by one observer as possessing a "straightforward, aggressive personality that demands action," Harrington repeatedly challenged established procedures during his years in the House. In the mid-1970s, he disclosed secret information on CIA activities in strife-torn Chile, actions that led to his reprimand by the House Armed Services Committee. In assembling a caucus of rank-and-file congressional representatives to lobby for the interests of the industrial states, Harrington threatened the traditional, committee-oriented approach to policymaking cherished by senior lawmakers.[60]

Representative Harrington and other leaders of the Snowbelt drive had worried for years about the relative economic decline of the Northeast. Their campaign finally gained momentum in the mid-1970s, due to the hemorrhage of manufacturing jobs, the disproportionate increase in Northeast energy costs, and rising voter demands for action. In the early 1970s, Harrington organized the New England Congressional Caucus to address the region's economic concerns. First National Bank of Boston economist James Howell and an official of the still-extant New England Council helped create a research office to support the regional grouping's work. Frustrated by the organization's lack of dynamism, and envisioning the New England states as part of a larger economic area, Harrington in 1976 approached congressional leaders from the mid-Atlantic and Midwest. He proposed the establishment of a caucus of representatives from all parts of the nation's traditional manufacturing heartland. Smoothing the way for this effort were recent media reports demonstrating that these states received less in federal expenditures than they paid in taxes, while the South and West received more. The bipartisan Northeast-Midwest Congressional Coalition soon formed to lobby for an enhanced flow of federal dollars to the participating states. Nearly half the members of the House of Representatives belonged to the group. Outside Congress, Democratic New York governor Hugh Carey organized a similar organization, known as the Coalition of Northeastern Governors, to press for increased federal aid to his home region.[61]

The Northeast-Midwest Coalition carried out research on the geographic distribution of federal spending and advocated changes that would benefit the areas it represented. The coalition achieved a number of victories. It secured alterations to the formulas for the distribution of urban development and education aid that brought increased funding to the Northeast and Midwest. Underlining the link to previous efforts for economically assisting the Northeast, the coalition discovered and won a more forceful application of the largely forgotten Defense Manpower Policy No. 4. The Truman administration had issued this directive in 1952. It called for federal procurement dollars to be channeled into depressed areas and was originally instituted at least in part due to lobbying by New England representatives seeking assistance at a time when the regional economy was experiencing structural decline.[62]

In Massachusetts, state and local officials sought other types of U.S. government assistance for the ailing commonwealth economy. Federal grants helped finance the redevelopment of the old textile districts of Lowell into an acclaimed national historical park. Through innovative proposals for remaking older cities, the state won a level of federal Urban Development Action Grant (UDAG) funding in the late 1970s that was far out of proportion to its share of the national population. The Massachusetts Foreign Business Council, set up under Governor King, used UDAGs to attract foreign employers to locations in the commonwealth with high unemployment.[63]

Some business organizations also sought federal government assistance for the ailing economies of Massachusetts and other Snowbelt states, although public officials were the primary advocates of such measures. First National Bank of Boston economist James Howell set up a Massachusetts-based organization in the mid-1970s to work toward these goals. Like other entities agitating on behalf of the Snowbelt, the group, called the Council for Northeast Economic Action (CNEA), sought to prop up the regional economy through an increased haul of federal dollars. Fittingly enough, the body financed its work through grants from several U.S. government departments. A 1979 study by the CNEA attracted national attention by challenging the basis on which federal urban aid was distributed. Older industrial cities confronting structural economic problems tended to have the heaviest fiscal burden, the report claimed. Aid should therefore be distributed in a way that took difficulties in the economic base of a municipality into account. Such action would likely redirect federal funds to the cities of the Northeast and Midwest, including those in Massachusetts.[64] The CNEA also tried to quantify the "capital gap" faced by entrepreneurs in the region and elsewhere and studied the role banks could play in local growth efforts. (The CNEA's report on the latter subject, titled *How Banks Participate in Local Economic Development*, was essentially an updated version of the 1920s study carried out for the New England Council on the services banks offered to local industrial customers.)[65] The CNEA additionally provided technical expertise to the Snowbelt coalition, publishing in the late 1970s a quarterly report on economic conditions in the states of the Northeast and Midwest.[66]

Economic development efforts took place on a broad scale in Massachusetts beginning in the early 1970s. Commonwealth leaders encouraged the growth of new industries to offset structural problems in existing ones. The private sector had a part in these endeavors. But what stands out is the growing and increasingly innovative role of state government. While the commonwealth's public efforts in this domain had begun decades before, state leaders brought noteworthy energy and imagination to the growth-promoting task beginning in the mid-1970s. So diverse and significant were its efforts in the field that one set of scholars termed Massachusetts "a national leader in creating new roles for states to play" in economic development policy.[67]

Notable private-sector development activity took place in Massachusetts after structural difficulties struck the economy at the end of the 1960s, notwithstanding the increasing importance of state government. The First National Bank of Boston, led by the research department's irrepressible economist Howell, stood at the forefront of these efforts. In a 1972 report, the bank called for an "industrialization program" that would identify the manufacturing sectors with the greatest local growth potential and take steps to aid their expansion. The study listed a series of technically sophisticated industries in which job creation could take place, although it offered few particulars on how to facilitate their success.[68] Another development initiative with heavy involvement from outside the public sector was Jobs for Massachusetts. Launched in 1972 with private financing, this group of high-ranking officials from business, labor, and government mounted an intensive campaign to persuade out-of-state companies to locate in the commonwealth. A chief executive of the First National Bank of Boston played a key role in these activities. By 1975, those involved decided to downplay corporate recruitment and concentrate on nurturing the expansion of the state's existing economic base.[69]

Innovative state government-led efforts to encourage growth in Massachusetts began in the mid-1970s, during the first Dukakis administration. The high technology industries had by this point become a key motor of the regional economy. Numerous development efforts focused on untapped possibilities in this field. Improved financing for small technology companies was a particular area of interest. Studies conducted at the time by academics and regional financiers posited the existence of "capital gaps" that prevented local entrepreneurs from obtaining funding for worthwhile ventures. First National economist James Howell was one of the first to express concern about this issue. Key research on the subject was carried out by Peter Brooke, a leading area venture capitalist who had articulated in the 1950s the need to develop new local industry.[70]

State government efforts to strengthen the commonwealth economy led to the creation of numerous growth-promoting institutions.[71] To help bridge the shortfall in financial backing for high technology firms, the Bay State set up its own venture capital body, the Massachusetts Technology Development Corporation (MTDC). Like private organizations in the field, the MTDC assessed applications from early-stage companies and made equity investments in those with outstanding growth potential. The state government also acted at this time to leverage additional venture funding from the private sector. Massachusetts had begun taxing the investments of local life insurance companies several years before, and insurers wanted to escape this levy. In exchange for removing it, the companies agreed to set up a new financing vehicle, the Massachusetts Capital Resources Corporation (MCRC). The entity would lend money to firms that had the potential to generate new employment but could not secure support from other sources. Insurers viewed the establishment of MCRC as the necessary cost of tax relief and were taken aback when the operation proved financially successful. Fewer development initiatives were launched during the governorship of Edward King. The state did at this time create a new agency, the Massachusetts Foreign Business Council, to encourage foreign corporations to invest in the commonwealth. Under the Centers for Excellence program initiated during Dukakis's second term as governor, Massachusetts sought to encourage the growth of research-based industries. It did so by providing financial assistance to business-university partnerships set up to develop new products and production processes. In the mid-1980s Centers for Excellence were established in polymers, biotechnology, marine sciences, solar power, and a number of more traditional industries. Several scholars of economic development consider Centers for Excellence to be a frank example of "industrial policy" at the state level. In a sense, the effort brought to fruition the vague proposals for a Massachusetts "industrialization program" enunciated by First National economist Howell more than a decade before.[72]

Conclusion: Comparing Responses to Deindustrialization in New England over a Sixty-Year Period

This volume has surveyed responses to deindustrialization in the New England region, and especially the state of Massachusetts, from the 1920s through the 1980s. In comparing the actions taken over this substantial stretch of time, distinct continuities in the patterns of activity are evident. Continuities can be seen in two areas. First and most important, there were strong parallels in the initiatives pursued at different times in response to industrial decline in New England. Second, support for the various measures for countering deindustrialization generally came from the same kinds of interest groups. An important discontinuity is also apparent. The role of state and federal government in formulating responses to industrial decline changed dramatically, becoming more important as the years progressed.

The first and most critical continuity in responses to deindustrialization involves the strikingly similar initiatives for countering industrial decline in widely disparate periods. In Massachusetts, responses to downsizing in the early and mid-twentieth century strongly resembled what transpired in the state when the same issue arose during the 1970s. All these eras witnessed activities that can be categorized under the headings of retrenchment, federal assistance, and economic development. The similarities extended beyond the broad patterns of action undertaken. Specific steps for countering industrial decline in the earlier era closely resembled initiatives pursued more recently.

To take one example, as New England struggled with the effects of deindustrialization in the 1950s, regional economist Seymour Harris quantified the degree to which national policies aided the economy of the southern states. He used this data to bolster the case for federal programs that would benefit his beleaguered region. U.S. Representative Michael J. Harrington was doubtless unaware of Harris's earlier efforts when he organized the Northeast-Midwest Congressional Coalition in response to the economic difficulties of the 1970s. Nonetheless, in pushing for a redirection of federal resources from the Sunbelt to the Snowbelt states, the Massachusetts congressman pursued a very similar course of action. Underlining the resemblance between earlier and more recent endeavors, Snowbelt advocates of the 1970s discovered and won a more stringent application of a longstanding directive (Defense Manpower Policy No. 4) that channeled federal purchases into areas of labor surplus. This policy had originally been enacted in the 1950s, at least partly at the behest of New England representatives seeking federal assistance for deindustrializing locales in their region.

As another example of the detailed similarities between older and more recent events, New England businessmen seeking to revitalize the regional economy in the 1920s and 1930s studied how banks could promote local growth and set up institutions to increase the flow of finance to small area companies. In response to the economic troubles of the 1970s, financiers and public officials in Massachusetts took precisely the same steps.

The second area of continuity between earlier events and those of the recent era involves the supporters of the measures undertaken. Backing for the various initiatives to counter industrial decline generally came from the same interest groups. Thus business was consistently the prime advocate of retrenchment. This applied as much to 1920s Massachusetts battles over the working hours of women in manufacturing as to 1970s fights over social programs and taxes. Industrialists and others facing out-of-state competition tended to be particularly vocal in pushing for retrenchment.[73] These groups typically advocated reductions in social legislation and business taxes even in good times. When the economy slumped, they stepped up the pressure for cutbacks.[74]

Unions and liberals were the leading advocates of federal assistance to industries and areas hit by deindustrialization in the different eras under consideration. These groups were especially prominent in backing plans for far-reaching forms of federal aid. In the 1930s, liberals and unionists from textiles and other sectors affected by low-wage competition sought strict national regulation of labor standards as a means of protecting northern jobs. During the 1950s, these groups initiated proposals for federal redevelopment assistance to depressed locales. Liberal politicians from the Northeast also originated the 1970s Snowbelt drive to claim a larger share of federal spending.[75]

Businesses in service industries dependant on the overall prosperity of their home areas were consistently at the forefront of efforts to restore growth in regions hit by deindustrialization. New England service-sector companies led the 1920s drive to revitalize the area economy. Massachusetts chambers of commerce, with many such firms in their membership, enthusiastically supported post–World War II proposals to establish a state Department of Commerce with a development mission. During the 1970s, the largest Boston bank called for an "industrialization program" to strengthen the local economy, and a chief executive of the bank was a key figure in Jobs for Massachusetts, which worked to create additional employment in the state. Commonwealth financiers were also prominent in 1970s efforts to close the "capital gap" and increase the funds available to local entrepreneurs.

Additional economic development advocates emerged as government took a more expansive role in promoting growth. Public officials and activists were centrally important here, with those on the liberal end of the political spectrum notably more enthusiastic than their conservative fellows about government activity in this domain. The pattern was evident in the warmer attitude among Democrats than Republicans toward creating a Massachusetts Department of Commerce in the years following World War II. It can be seen more recently in the range of Bay State development programs introduced during the gubernatorial terms of the liberal Michael Dukakis.

Despite the general tendency of particular groups to support certain initiatives, actors in the political economy were not always tied to a single approach. Some institutions and individuals deeply involved in formulating responses to deindustrialization backed more than one type of activity. This pattern was visible in earlier years and also apparent more recently. In the period between the world wars, the New England Council supported to at least some degree all three of the initiatives for countering industrial decline. The group was established to press for economic development, lobbied at times for retrenchment, and pushed for moderate forms of federal assistance to the region's textile producers. Massachusetts politician Christian Herter behaved in like fashion in the early 1950s. As a U.S. representative for the Bay State, Herter urged federal aid for labor surplus areas in the form of accelerated tax amortization for new defense plants. As governor he pushed to establish new development institutions in the commonwealth and also called for mild retrenchment measures. During the 1970s, activist economist James Howell of the First National Bank of Boston similarly pursued multiple initiatives for countering industrial decline.[76]

The continuities in responses to deindustrialization over time did not arise by coincidence. Responses to industrial decline were similar because these efforts were essentially determined by the structure of the political economy. The interests of the various economic actors affected by deindustrialization changed little. These groups responded to downsizing in ways that accorded with their interests.

Business organizations typically seek to reduce taxes and regulatory restrictions even in good times. When core industries went into decline, it was logical for businesses to step up the pressure for retrenchment and assert that cutbacks were necessary to restore competitiveness. Unions exist to increase wages and improve conditions for their members. For much of the twentieth century, liberal activists sympathized with worker aspirations and agitated for their realization. Unions and liberals long looked to the federal government to rectify socioeconomic problems that could not be addressed locally. When industries with active unions began to downsize, it was natural for unionists, supported by their liberal allies, to seek federal action that would temper the competitive threats causing plant closures, provide aid to displaced workers, and assist in the rehabilitation of deindustrialized locales.[77] The business prospects of service-sector companies linked to a region's economy—in fields such as banking, transportation, utilities, and retail—depend on the overall level of local economic activity. The extent of general prosperity in a given location similarly determines residents' opportunities for employment and earnings. All regional economies are powered by area industries that sell to the outside world. When these sectors stalled, residents and managers of locally oriented service companies had enormous incentives to search for replacement industries and support government efforts to do likewise.

A key discontinuity was also present in New England's responses to deindustrialization, despite the significant continuities that existed. The discontinuity involved the changing role of state and federal government in formulating responses to industrial decline. Government activity in this domain became more centrally important as the years progressed. The place of the public sector in countering downsizing was initially quite limited. It reached a significant level by the mid-twentieth century and became increasingly vital thereafter—albeit with some tailing off in certain areas of activity in the period since the 1970s.

The enlarged role of the public sector in formulating responses to deindustrialization was consistent with broader changes in governance. Government in the United States expanded dramatically during the New Deal years and continued to grow for decades after the 1930s. The expansion in public-sector activities was most pronounced at the federal level, but state and local government increased in size as well. Then, beginning in the late 1970s, the prominence of the free-market approach to governance championed by laissez-faire conservatives led to some diminution in the scale of activities at all levels of government.[78]

The evolution in the extent of public sector involvement in formulating responses to deindustrialization is easiest to see with regard to measures for promoting development. The role of government in this field grew steadily more important over time, with no notable reduction of the public sector's place in the recent era. When New England first experienced industrial downsizing, the New England Council, a private business association, spearheaded the drive to revitalize the regional economy. Government did have a part in the era's attempts to stimulate growth: the state of Massachusetts in 1929 set up a development commission to promote local industry and had earlier helped establish textile schools to aid struggling fabric manufacturers. The recovery campaign organized by business nevertheless predominated in the initial period. The role of government became more prominent in the post–World War II era, as exemplified by the establishment of the Massachusetts Department of Commerce. But private-sector endeavors to encourage growth remained important after the war. Boston banks promoted the expansion of technologically advanced startup companies through a concerted lending push, and the New England Council continued its development work. By the 1970s, government had a central place in almost all Massachusetts measures to promote growth, from the Technology Development Corporation to the Foreign Business Council to the Centers for Excellence. The era's only growth-inducing step carried out wholly in the private sector—the establishment by commonwealth insurance companies of an industrial lending fund (the Massachusetts Capital Resources Corporation)—was a quid pro quo for the repeal of a state government tax on the insurers.

The expanding place of the public sector was also evident during much of the twentieth century in federal efforts to assist declining industries and areas. The growing public role in this domain can be seen in the proliferation of measures to ease the burdens of deindustrialization. In the 1930s and 1940s, strict national regulation of labor standards was the principal proposed avenue of federal aid to the troubled textile industry of the North. When the problem reemerged in the postwar era, a variety of approaches was pursued, including expanded import protections, channeling defense contracts to labor surplus areas, federal aid for area redevelopment, and preliminary efforts to compensate for industrial decline by tilting national programs in New England's favor. Additional steps taken by the 1970s included a major push to increase the Snowbelt's share of a much enlarged pot of federal disbursements. The scope of federal efforts for countering deindustrialization has lessened since that time. The federal area redevelopment program was significantly cut back in the early 1980s, reflecting the rising influence of laissez-faire conservatives who opposed a program that interfered in the free market.[79]

The reasons for discontinuity in the responses to New England's industrial decline become clearer when viewed in the context of America's changing political economy. Unlike much of the rest of the country, New England faced the challenges of industrial downsizing for a good part of the twentieth century. Since downsizing was a long-lasting regional reality, the responses to it were forged during dramatically different periods of national political economy. The shifting context shaped in important ways the measures for countering deindustrialization in New England. This was true in terms of the range of initiatives advanced to deal with industrial decline, the extent of government involvement in the actions taken, and the degree of political support that various endeavors received.

New England first confronted industrial downsizing in the 1920s, a relatively conservative era when corporate interests were strong and skepticism reigned about public-sector action to address economic problems. The initiatives put forward during the 1920s to counter New England's deindustrialization accorded with these larger political realities. The private sector dominated the period's efforts to develop new industries in New England to replace those in decline. State governments did take steps to encourage growth during that era, but these were dwarfed by the scale of private undertakings. Furthermore, at the federal level, virtually no measures were taken to assist New England's struggling textile industry. The federal role at this time was limited to backing the voluntary efforts of fabric manufacturers to stabilize competitive conditions.

In the succeeding period, when liberal political forces were ascendant, the picture was significantly different. The 1930s saw federal government attempts to provide forceful assistance to the embattled textile producers of the Northeast. After World War II, when liberalism remained potent, multiple federal initiatives were pursued to aid struggling industries and areas. The pressure for federal action was so significant after the war that even the Eisenhower administration, which generally sought to limit public undertakings, initiated a program of assistance to deindustrialized locales (through tax benefits for defense plants in labor-surplus areas). In 1961, under a new Democratic president, the most important postwar federal effort to address deindustrialization, the Area Redevelopment program, went into effect. State government activity to counter industrial decline also increased in the years after World War II. Massachusetts and other states set up new economic development agencies and spurred the formation of private-sector entities (the development credit corporations) to encourage growth.

Policies for countering deindustrialization shifted again in the more conservative political context of the 1970s. Efforts to secure retrenchment in social legislation and taxes, which had been present since the 1920s but had realized few victories, achieved striking successes in the 1970s and after. Cutbacks in the name of improving competitiveness were enacted in states such as Massachusetts and at the national level. Dramatic cuts also took place in the federal area redevelopment effort. The area redevelopment program was initially targeted for elimination by the Reagan administration, even though industrial downsizing was a serious problem in that era. In the late 1980s and 1990s, conservative officeholders determinedly opposed federal initiatives (described in the next chapter) to enhance industrial competitiveness, arguing that the programs violated laissez-faire.

The shifting responses to deindustrialization from the 1920s through the late twentieth century demonstrate that politics had great influence in shaping policy. The basic responses to industrial decline and the interest groups that backed these responses stayed relatively constant over time. But in determining the specific initiatives that were put forward and the level of support that particular policies received, the relative strength in a given period of liberal and conservative approaches to governance was decisive.

CHAPTER 8

Conclusions

The responses to deindustrialization in twentieth-century New England have significance well beyond what occurred in one small region. The broader importance of New England events is explored in this concluding chapter. A number of topics are addressed.

First, the three-part model of responses to deindustrialization seen in New England is applicable in other places. The same pattern was apparent in the United States on the national level when deindustrialization became a countrywide problem beginning in the 1970s. It was visible as well in other developed countries, which saw widespread downsizing during the same period. Indeed, there is every reason to expect to see the three types of activity examined here in any location experiencing the decline of established industries.

Second, the responses to deindustrialization in New England demonstrate important realities about the political economy of the modern United States. The initiatives for countering industrial decline afford insights on the growing power of corporations, the vulnerability of American unions, the existence of "industrial policy" in the United States, and the importance of private-sector endeavors to promote the growth of new industries.

Finally, an assessment of the effectiveness of responses to deindustrialization in New England and elsewhere makes clear the limited utility of much that was done. This appraisal spotlights as well the efficacy of economic development efforts that encourage the growth of new industries to replace those in decline.

U.S. Responses to Deindustrialization and Problems of International Competitiveness in Recent Decades

Numerous developed economies saw established industries go into decline in the last decades of the twentieth century. The initiatives for countering deindustrialization in these places closely resembled what occurred in New England in the period from the 1920s through the 1980s. The similarities are demonstrated by examining responses to the downsizing of the recent era in the United States on the national level, and in other developed countries, with a focus on Western Europe.

The United States confronted deindustrialization on a broad scale during the 1970s and early 1980s.[1] The period's job losses were most severe in the traditional industrial states of the Northeast and Midwest, although plant closures took place throughout the country.[2] Total U.S. manufacturing employment fell from 13.7 million in 1977 to 12.4 million in 1982 and 11.8 million in 1986, a decline of 14 percent over the period 1977–86.[3] Adding to the difficulties in the industrial sector, the national economy experienced a marked slowdown from the mid-1970s through the early 1980s. Growth in per capita GNP, which had been strong in the preceding years, was less than 1 percent annually in 1974–81. The post-1973 period also saw a sharp drop in productivity, a decline in real hourly wages, and sustained rates of high inflation without precedent in modern American history.[4]

Surging imports contributed to the downsizing of this era in established U.S. industries such as textiles, apparel, automobiles, steel, and consumer electronics and even occurred in cutting-edge sectors such as semiconductors. As a result, plant closings were accompanied by growing fears about the competitiveness of American industry. These concerns continued into the presidency of Bill Clinton, even though overall economic indicators improved in the mid-1980s.

The three responses to industrial decline seen in New England over the course of the twentieth century were all evident at the national level in the United States during the 1970s and 1980s.

Corporate demands for retrenchment were a prominent feature of national policy debates in that era. In 1974 *Business Week* recommended changes to the revenue codes that would substantially reduce the federal taxes paid by corporations. Calls for a national program of "reindustrialization" or "economic renewal" were increasingly heard in the ensuing years as the structural problems in manufacturing became more apparent. Among the components of the proposed program were allowances for accelerated depreciation on business investment and other reductions in corporate income taxes. Corporate interests also demanded easing of the vigorous consumer and environmental regulations put into place in the preceding years.[5]

With U.S. politics moving steadily to the right and policymakers increasingly influenced by free-market thinking, substantial reductions in corporate taxes and business regulation took place beginning in the mid-1970s. The federal government repeatedly loosened the revenue laws during the 1970s in ways that reduced the levies paid by business. The tax legislation that President Ronald Reagan pushed through in his first year in office gave breaks to numerous industries and further eased depreciation allowances, resulting in sharply reduced corporate levies.[6] Cutbacks also took place in consumer and environmental regulation. In the late 1970s, partly in response to business pressures, Congress and President Jimmy Carter reined in the aggressive regulation in these areas that they had earlier supported. The Reagan administration mounted a wide-ranging drive to roll back consumer, environmental, and other restrictions on corporate behavior.[7] When economic competitiveness emerged as a key political issue in the late 1980s, the George H. W. Bush administration responded by further weakening environmental, consumer, and workplace safety regulations in the name of enhancing the competitiveness of U.S. producers.[8]

Federal assistance to regions and industries hit by structural economic difficulty was another important field of activity in the United States during the 1970s and 1980s. The federal government pursued a broad range of endeavors to soften the impact of industrial downsizing. Some of the initiatives were new, while others continued longstanding national efforts.

Trade protection was a key avenue of federal assistance to declining sectors. Import competition was a major cause of the era's deindustrialization, and the federal government responded with new protective measures. Aid in most cases took the form of voluntary export restraints by which U.S. officials won commitments from foreign producers to limit their shipments to the United States. Repeated action along these lines occurred in steel. In 1969 the Lyndon Johnson administration negotiated accords with manufacturers in Europe and Japan that limited the rate at which steel imports could increase. President Richard Nixon oversaw the enactment of similar arrangements in 1971. The Carter administration adopted a more comprehensive program that established minimum prices for steel products and provided small manufacturers with funds to upgrade equipment. The Reagan administration returned to the previous approach, arranging voluntary restraints on steel imports in the early 1980s.[9] Import restrictions took effect in a number of other U.S. industries in this era. In textiles, longstanding pressures for protection led to a series of international agreements limiting imports, culminating in the Multifiber Arrangements of the 1970s. The Carter administration negotiated agreements restricting imports of footwear from Korea and Taiwan. President Reagan arranged restraints on shipments of Japanese automobiles and motorcycles.[10] All these measures served principally to slow rather than halt the decline of U.S. manufacturing.

In the case of the Chrysler Corporation, the government went beyond assistance to a troubled industry and became deeply involved in efforts to save a single producer. Long the weakest of the Big Three U.S. carmakers, Chrysler faced the prospect of bankruptcy during the American auto industry's late 1970s downturn. Hundreds of thousands of jobs at the corporation and its suppliers were at risk. Chrysler president Lee Iacocca approached the federal government seeking aid. Federal officials eventually agreed to provide $1.5 billion worth of loan guarantees. This assistance, together with the restrictions on automobile imports from Japan secured by the Reagan administration, enabled the company to execute a turnaround.[11]

Federal support for displaced workers was another innovative form of aid to those in industries facing import competition. Congress first provided in 1962 for what was called trade adjustment assistance. Rigorous eligibility rules limited participation, but the volume of assistance mushroomed after requirements were eased in 1974. The program had 49,000 beneficiaries and a budget of $70 million in 1976; 157,000 beneficiaries and a budget of $258 million in 1978; and a budget of $1.6 billion in fiscal 1980. Theoretically focused on retraining, adjustment assistance in practice mostly provided extended unemployment insurance benefits for workers displaced by imports.[12]

The 1970s push by congressional representatives from the Northeast and Midwest that secured a larger share of federal spending for the so-called Snowbelt states was another form of federal aid to areas experiencing deindustrialization and regional economic stagnation. The effort was described in detail in the previous chapter.

The federal program of redevelopment assistance to locales hit by deindustrialization continued in the 1970s and constituted an important form of government aid. Initiated in 1961 as Area Redevelopment, the program was reorganized in 1965 under the renamed Economic Development Administration (EDA). The revamped effort focused on providing infrastructure that would make qualifying areas attractive to new employers. EDA funds supported the construction of water and sewage systems, harbors, airports, and industrial facilities. EDA also extended subsidized loans to new employers and assisted with local redevelopment planning. Mid-1970s amendments to the program made areas adversely affected by imports eligible for assistance.

(The federal redevelopment effort, which never received rich resources, was drastically scaled back in the ensuing years. Reagan administration officials saw the entire undertaking as contrary to free-market principles and targeted EDA for elimination. The agency's funding dropped by 68 percent between 1981 and 1983 and remained at low levels through the year 2000.)[13]

Economic development was a principal response to the structural economic difficulties of the 1970s and after in the United States. Spurred by industrial downsizing, growing imports, and fears about U.S. competitiveness, Americans leaders from the 1970s through the 1990s looked for ways to strengthen the national economy. The result was a variety of measures to foster the emergence of new industries and fortify those already in existence. Receiving particular emphasis were steps to stimulate laboratory research with practical applications and to commercialize new technologies in a more effective manner.

One set of initiatives involved simply changing the law to permit methods of organizing and commercializing research that had previously been banned. Several statutes aimed to increase the direct contribution to economic development of laboratory research at universities and federal agencies. The Bayh-Dole Act, approved by Congress in 1980, allowed universities for the first time to patent the results of federally funded research. Measures passed in subsequent years granted tax breaks and other incentives to firms that set up collaborative research arrangements with universities. The Technology Transfer Act of 1986 made possible for-profit collaborations between companies and agencies of the federal government. The various legal changes had dramatic effects. Before 1980, universities received approximately 250 patents per year. By fiscal 1998 the number of university patent applications exceeded 4,800. Industry financing for academic research soared as well, increasing nearly eightfold between 1980 and 1998.[14]

The National Cooperative Research Act of 1984 was another important legal modification that encouraged economic development. Until this time, anti-trust regulations had prevented corporate competitors from carrying out joint research and development projects. R&D consortiums of this type were commonplace in Japan and had been pinpointed as a factor in the rapid advance of that country's industries. The 1984 law eased the anti-trust restrictions, allowing American firms to establish collaborative research arrangements if they faced foreign competition. Companies quickly took advantage of the opportunity, forming "well over 100" consortiums by 1989.[15] The best known was Sematech, a Pentagon-backed research cooperative of American semiconductor makers that helped win back a share of the market from the Japanese companies that had taken a leading position in the industry.[16]

The federal government also took active steps during this era to boost the technological competitiveness of American industry. These measures contrasted with the essentially passive changes just described, which in most cases simply expanded the range of permissible activity by nonfederal institutions such as corporations and universities. Most prominent among the new initiatives were two based in the U.S. Department of Commerce.

The starting point for these efforts was 1988 legislation that renamed the commerce department's National Bureau of Standards as the National Institute of Standards and Technology (NIST) and gave the agency the added mission of improving the technological capabilities of the nation's manufacturers. An important vehicle for achieving this goal was the new Advanced Technology Program (ATP), through which the government disbursed grants to support research and development at private companies. The allotments, which ranged into the millions of dollars, could only go to projects in the "generic, precompetitive" stage where the technology in question was not yet commercially viable. Recipients had to demonstrate that their advance, if successful, would provide concrete benefits to the national economy. They were also required to cover part of the cost of the research to be carried out. Competition for the money was vigorous. Of the 660 applications submitted for the first three rounds of ATP disbursements, only 60 received support. Much ATP funding went to high technology fields. But efforts in established industries received support as well, such as a project to improve the production and assembly of automobile components. ATP effectively made the federal government into a venture capitalist, with the payoff coming in the form of increased national economic competitiveness rather than financial gain.[17]

The Manufacturing Extension Partnership (MEP) was the second innovative effort run by NIST. Less heralded than ATP, MEP nonetheless provided important benefits to a key segment of the nation's industrial base. The program's premise was that in an era of rapid technological change, small and medium-sized manufacturers lacking a research and development capability could easily lose touch with the most up-to-date methods. MEP provided such companies with easy access to this information. "We're the staff person they can't afford," stated NIST's director. MEP functioned through a network of centers where company managers could consult with experts on the latest developments in manufacturing and management. Numerous MEP facilities operated as joint ventures between NIST and universities or technological institutes. Many received funding from state and local sources, in addition to federal dollars.[18]

Introduced in the last year of the Reagan administration, ATP and MEP stagnated under the presidency of George H. W. Bush. Incoming President Bill Clinton gave the programs a central place in his push for concerted federal action to enhance competitiveness. Clinton sought to raise the NIST budget from $58 million in fiscal 1994 to $805 million in fiscal 1998, with a corresponding increase in the funding for ATP. MEP grew exponentially during the Clinton years, expanding from seven centers in 1993 to seventy-eight in 1998, with a presence in all fifty states.[19] ATP and MEP operated despite harsh opposition from laissez-faire conservatives in Congress, who viewed the programs as unwarranted intrusions into the free market.

Responses to Deindustrialization and Concerns about Competitiveness in Other Developed Countries

Developed countries throughout the world experienced downsizing in established industries in the 1970s and after, as was the case in the United States. Due to shifts in demand, import competition, and the state-supported building of excess capacity in some industries, developed countries saw plant closures in textiles, shipbuilding, steel, coal, and other sectors.[20] Downsizing contributed to fears about the international competitiveness of some developed economies. Such concerns were particularly salient in European nations with generous welfare state provisions that significantly raised the cost of production. To counter these difficulties, developed countries implemented policies resembling all three of the initiatives pursued in response to deindustrialization in the United States.

National government assistance to declining industries initially dominated the response of advanced economies outside the United States to the structural changes of the 1970s and after. Trade protection was an important instrument of national government assistance, since import competition was a major cause of deindustrialization in other developed countries. New restrictions on trade provided significant aid to declining sectors. Growing shipments of textiles and apparel from lower-income countries pushed most advanced economies to restrict imports of these products. The limits culminated in the Multifiber Arrangements of the 1970s. To curb increasing imports of steel, European countries negotiated voluntary restraints on shipments of the metal from Japan and other producing nations. Most European countries also reached market-sharing agreements with Japanese auto manufacturers that were tantamount to import restraints.[21]

Expansion of subsidies to producers was another means by which national governments assisted downsizing industries. Payments of this type had long existed in developed countries, but their extent mushroomed in response to the economic difficulties of the late twentieth century. Between 1964 and 1982, industrial subsidies as a percentage of GDP rose from 1.2 percent to 3.7 percent in Italy and from 0.65 percent to 1.4 percent in Japan. An example of this activity involved the subsidies by which West Germany maintained employment in coal mining as demand for coal fell off. The national government paid mining companies for each underground shift worked and compensated utilities for burning coal instead of oil. By 1978 public aid amounted to an enormous 37 percent of value added in West German coal mining.[22]

Demands for retrenchment in social legislation and business taxes have been an increasingly prominent feature of European politics in recent years. Business leaders and conservative politicians called for action in these areas. Retrenchment advocates sought to improve competitiveness and to ease the fiscal burden of costly social welfare programs.[23] High-profile confrontations resulted in several places.

In France, proposals to ease broad-ranging social protections were put forward repeatedly over a years-long period. Some change took place, but determined resistance from unions and protesters killed a number of reform projects. In the mid-1990s, attempts to lower the minimum wage for youth jobs and to reduce the pensions of rail workers and other public employees were abandoned in the face of determined resistance. French lawmakers did tighten pension eligibility rules for public workers in 2003. The national legislature in 2005 made it easier for small employers to lay off recently hired workers. But a 2006 plan to expand the liberalized layoff rules for young workers provoked massive protests and was withdrawn.[24]

In Germany, concerns over competitiveness, together with the fiscal burdens of German reunification, led to wide-ranging proposals for retrenchment beginning in the mid-1990s. Cutbacks were sought by both Christian Democratic and Social Democratic governments. Amid considerable sociopolitical conflict, reductions occurred in sickness pay, pensions, health care, unemployment insurance, and the rules governing layoffs.[25] Retrenchment in welfare state protections took place in many other continental locations during this period. Corporate tax rates were also reduced in a number of European countries, including Germany.[26]

Measures to encourage economic development have attracted less attention than other responses to deindustrialization in developed countries abroad. Substantial activity nonetheless occurred as countries sought to foster the growth of new industries and enhance the competitiveness of existing ones.

A number of innovative development efforts occurred in Germany. To help break down the traditional arms-length relationship between the corporate world and academia, West Germany in 1978 established the Technical University of Hamburg-Harburg. Set up in a region hard hit by industrial downsizing, the institution encourages faculty members in science and engineering to collaborate with the private sector and start their own companies. The university has become a model within Europe for the economic benefits that can flow from closer ties between the academy and the corporate world. To overcome a lagging performance in the commercial exploitation of advances in biotechnology, the German government in the mid-1990s began providing matching investment funds to biotechnology companies in targeted regions. The effort doubtless contributed to the entrepreneurial surge that followed. By the year 2000 Germany had a flourishing biotech industry with six hundred firms.[27]

Other countries adopted similar measures to promote growth. In Italy, the public sector had long facilitated the success of industrial districts in the country's North where networks of small firms produced world-class specialty goods using flexible manufacturing techniques. City and regional governments in these locales stepped up their promotional activities when new competitive challenges emerged in the 1970s. A key measure was setting up public programs to diffuse information on shifting world markets and advances in production and management. The efforts decisively aided some manufacturers in adapting to a changed competitive environment. In Finland, public support for R&D in technologically advanced sectors began in the 1970s and shifted into high gear during a deep recession in the early 1990s. Seeking to diversify away from traditional, resource-based industries, the national government provided massive public support for private-sector R&D in information and communication technology and other fields. The government development strategy helped the Finnish firm Nokia emerge as a leading producer of cellular telephone handsets and related hardware. Between 1995 and 2001, the country's employment in electrical equipment manufacturing more than tripled.[28]

There are striking similarities between what occurred in the United States and events in these foreign locations. When textiles and other established industries went into decline in twentieth-century New England, area leaders pursued retrenchment, federal assistance, and economic development. The same policies were followed in the United States at the national level when deindustrialization became a countrywide problem. The pattern was evident as well in other developed countries where downsizing occurred.[29]

Since it applies so widely, the three-part model of responses to deindustrialization developed from the study of New England can serve as a general template. Each of the three types of activity examined here should be present in any economically mature area experiencing deindustrialization. All the responses to industrial decline seen in a given location should fit into one of the three categories of action described. Deindustrialization is virtually an inevitable occurrence in developed economies. Activities of the type considered here should thus be seen in a very broad range of places.

Deindustrialization and the Political Economy of the Modern United States

The responses to downsizing in textiles and other established New England sectors have significance beyond the immediate issue of industrial decline. The initiatives for countering deindustrialization in twentieth-century New England demonstrate important realities about economic policymaking and political economy in the modern United States. Insights are possible on a range of issues.

To begin with, the changing outcome through time of retrenchment battles in Massachusetts highlights the growth in corporate power since the 1970s. Deindustrialization almost inevitably produces a campaign by business groups and conservatives for cutbacks in social legislation and taxes. But these efforts do not necessarily achieve their aims. As textiles downsized in 1920s Massachusetts, corporate interests lobbied vigorously for the repeal of key items of social legislation. They failed to secure the desired changes, although they eventually won reductions in business taxes. Similar efforts undertaken as textile plants closed in the early 1950s produced a comparable outcome of limited cutbacks in assistance to the unemployed and no change in business taxes. A different reality prevailed in more recent times. Massachusetts business lobbies won substantial cutbacks in social programs (and taxes) as established industries downsized during the 1970s, a pattern that was also evident in national policymaking.

The reasons for the changed outcome in the more recent period are not entirely clear. Decline in the economic and political power of Massachusetts' unions surely contributed to the success of the state's retrenchment advocates in the 1970s.[30] This factor alone does not seem determinative, however. Massachusetts unions had impressive yet limited strength in the 1920s, when attempts at retrenchment fell short. During the 1970s, when significant cutbacks took place, organized labor retained considerable muscle in the commonwealth.[31] Changes in the influence exerted by business lobbies probably helped account for developments in the Bay State. Recent research highlights the increasing sway of corporate interests in national policymaking during the 1970s.[32] The political power of corporate groups likely increased in Massachusetts as well during those years, and this probably aids in explaining the greater degree of Bay State retrenchment in that period.

Whatever explains realities in 1970s Massachusetts, it is striking how the results of retrenchment battles differed through time. Particularly dramatic is the contrast between outcomes in the 1920s and more recently. These events point to the surprising conclusion that the political economy of Massachusetts—and perhaps of the United States as a whole—was further to the right in the 1970s than it had been in the supposedly conservative 1920s.

Federal efforts to counter deindustrialization in the 1930s also have implications for U.S. political economy. These events highlight the significance of New Deal proposals to lessen the geographic vulnerability of the U.S. labor movement. A grave weakness of the robust American unions that emerged in the 1930s was the concentration of their strength in certain regions—in the Northeast and Midwest and on the Pacific Coast. The geographic restrictions on labor's power meant that unionized employers could be undercut by competitors in the open-shop strongholds of the South and inland West, where wages remained low and workplace regulations were lax.[33] This scenario played out in the post–World War II period. New low-wage competitors emerged in parts of the country that were hostile to unions. Employers in heavily unionized regions shifted production to open-shop locales. And congressional representatives from areas with weak unions backed policies that sapped labor's strength throughout the nation.

It was apparent in the 1930s that events might transpire in this way. Realities in cotton textiles demonstrated what could occur. Beginning in the 1920s and continuing during the New Deal years, low-wage open-shop cotton manufacturers in the South undermined the high-wage fabric producers of New England, where there was a substantial union presence.

In grappling with the effects of deindustrialization, New Deal reformers worked to halt these processes through strong federal action. The Ellenbogen textile bills would have enacted stringent controls over labor standards in the cloth-making industry. The original 1937 draft of the Fair Labor Standards Act would have regulated tightly all sectors where wage differences were a key factor in interregional competition. While not forcing open-shop employers to unionize, the proposals would have raised wages decisively in non-union locales. The measures would have had an important impact, had they been enacted and vigorously enforced. With their cost advantage reduced or even eliminated, open-shop producers in less unionized parts of the country would have been less able to drive competitors in union-friendly regions out of business.[34] Unionized employers in regions where labor was strong would have had less incentive to shift output to open-shop areas. Such realities would have strengthened the country's unions. The plunge of union membership in recent decades—which stems in considerable part from the move of production to open-shop locales within the United States—would have been less pronounced as a result.[35]

New Deal–era proposals for dramatically raising labor standards in open-shop regions did not come close to winning approval. Had the acts passed, enforcing them would have been a major challenge. The point remains that in the reform-minded atmosphere of the mid-1930s, serious plans were put forward that would have helped alleviate what later emerged as a significant vulnerability of the national union movement.

The economic development activities undertaken in New England and in other parts of the country are important too for understanding U.S. economic policymaking. The widespread presence of these growth-promotion efforts demonstrates the true dimensions of industrial policy in the United States.

The plant closures and concerns about economic competitiveness experienced by the United States from the 1970s through the 1990s led numerous liberal thinkers and politicians to call for concerted national action to bolster the nation's industries. Under the heading of "industrial policy," advocates called for federal planning and financial support to strengthen existing sectors and foster the emergence of new ones. In arguing for a large-scale federal program, supporters pointed to the ambitious growth-promotion measures undertaken in countries of Western Europe and East Asia.[36] The sweeping federal initiative sought by industrial policy backers in this country was never implemented. But substantial activity, involving a range of actors, did take place.

The federal measures in this domain have been outlined in this chapter. These included legal changes that allowed companies to cooperate with each other and with universities and federal laboratories in carrying out research. Important as well were programs like ATP and MEP, through which the government sought to enhance the competitiveness of industrial producers.[37]

Development activity in individual states mirrored the growth-promoting steps taken by the federal government. During the 1970s and 1980s, Massachusetts launched a number of initiatives to encourage development, supplementing the longstanding promotional activities of the state Department of Commerce. The new measures included establishing a venture capital organization (the Massachusetts High Technology Development Corporation) and providing public support for research in targeted areas (the Centers for Excellence). Numerous states took similar steps.[38] As in Massachusetts, many state-level development efforts aimed to foster the expansion of locally based businesses, rather than attracting into the state existing firms located elsewhere.[39] In some areas, local government mounted meaningful efforts to develop new industries. Important growth-promotion work also took place in the private sector, such as the Jobs for Massachusetts initiative in the Bay State.

The United States has thus seen a diversity of development activities, occurring at different levels of government (federal, state, local), with substantial participation by private-sector actors. Taken together, these efforts amounted to an industrial policy of significant dimensions.

The multiple, uncoordinated development measures differed substantially from the unified federal effort sought by industrial policy backers. This was not necessarily negative, as there were distinct advantages to the decentralized approach for promoting growth. Structuring development initiatives in a decentralized way was consistent with established patterns of American political culture. State and local government and the private sector have long held important responsibilities in numerous areas of policymaking. This accorded with the desires of the electorate and reflected national traditions of limited central government.

The decentralized approach to growth promotion also avoided a major pitfall of centrally controlled development efforts: the tendency to pursue grandiose, ill-conceived projects that misallocate taxpayers' money.[40] With responsibility for government growth initiatives divided among multiple public entities, each pursuing different endeavors, there was little chance of significant resources being wasted on a limited number of ventures. Private-sector development efforts could not squander government monies since no public funds were used. Moreover, those financing growth-promotion activities in the private sector had strong incentives to ensure that resources were deployed wisely.

The industrial policy carried out in the United States during recent decades was, of course, not new. What occurred throughout the country in the contemporary era was simply an intensification of the development initiatives that had taken place for more than a century in areas affected by structural economic decline.

Growth-promotion efforts that occurred entirely in the private sector are a prominent feature of the economic development activity explored in this volume.[41] Endeavors of this type were particularly important at earlier points in time. The potential of completely private action to encourage growth receives little attention in the significant literature on development, which focuses almost exclusively on government programs.[42] The New England experience demonstrates that nonstate actors can play a critical role in promoting growth. The private New England Council conducted most of the important economic development activity carried out in the region through the mid-twentieth century, including the push to improve financial support for small technologically advanced firms. All the institutions that financed the area's technology spinoffs—whether commercial banks or venture capital funds—operated in the private sector. Moreover, the New England example has parallels elsewhere. The promotional efforts of area business leaders largely accounted for the location of much of the U.S. aircraft industry in Los Angeles during the period after World War I.[43] Local capitalists, together with academics, helped initiate the 1950s drive to diversify the North Carolina economy by attracting knowledge-based industries to Raleigh-Durham's Research Triangle Park.[44] Although private-sector development initiatives have received little systematic attention from scholars of the modern United States, endeavors of this type may have helped numerous regions transition to new forms of economic activity as older industries waned.

The place of private institutions in encouraging development has clearly diminished in recent years. Government agencies have dominated the growth-promotion efforts of the contemporary period in the United States and abroad. The public sector can of course mobilize greater resources for advancing development—a clear advantage of the government-led approach. A role nevertheless remains for private entities in the growth-promotion field. Private-sector institutions had some part in the mostly state-led Massachusetts development efforts of the 1970s and 1980s. Jobs for Massachusetts, a predominantly private organization, recruited new employers and helped existing ones expand. Commonwealth insurance companies set up a private-sector venture financing body (the Massachusetts Capital Resources Corporation). Similar dynamics occurred elsewhere. In Houston, Texas, the private sector dominated the development drive that was launched in the early 1980s. The effort, which sought to offset the decline of traditional local industries, strongly resembled the New England Council's promotional work in the pre–World War II era.[45]

Assessing Responses to Deindustrialization

The initiatives for countering deindustrialization seen in New England and other areas were characterized by strengths and weaknesses. An assessment of the various initiatives that were pursued demonstrates the limited utility of retrenchment, the inadequacy of federal assistance to deindustrializing locales, and the value of efforts to develop new sources of growth.

Calls for retrenchment have been a central response to downsizing in New England textiles and other established industries. Supporters of this approach assert that cutbacks in government regulations and business taxes are indispensable for preventing further plant closures in locales experiencing deindustrialization. Such steps have little utility in the U.S. context. Taxes and regulations in this country typically have a marginal impact on a firm's total costs and thus on its competitiveness. The viability of an industry in a particular location is instead principally determined by economic fundamentals such as comparative wage rates, levels of manager and worker skill, and proximity to inputs and customers.

Preventing further industrial decline is generally not even the real aim of retrenchment drives, as close inspection of retrenchment efforts in New England reveals. Typically, business groups had pressed for the same kinds of cutbacks in the prosperous periods preceding downsizing. The changed context of deindustrialization simply added plausibility to retrenchment advocates' claims that such action was necessary to remain competitive. The realities of corporate finance give company managers clear motives to press for cutbacks in taxes and regulations, even though changes in these areas have limited effects on competitiveness. Firms make money by bringing in revenues exceeding their costs. Monies paid in taxes and expended to comply with regulations add to costs and thereby reduce profits. Conversely, each dollar saved through lower taxes and reduced regulatory compliance goes "straight to the bottom line" as an extra dollar of aftertax profit.

To be sure, a point can be reached where the tax and regulatory burden on companies grows so heavy that it causes genuine difficulties for competitive viability and employment. Instances of this can be found in Western Europe, where the corporate sector has less influence on policymaking and the welfare state is more extensive. An outstanding example is the regulations, once common on the Continent, that impose heavy charges on companies laying off employees. The rules give executives strong disincentives against hiring additional workers whom they may wish to discharge during future business downturns.[46] There are few onerous constraints of this kind in the United States. The burden of government regulations and taxes is generally lighter here than in other developed countries, despite constant corporate rhetoric to the contrary.[47]

Demands for retrenchment are admittedly difficult to fend off in times of industrial decline when policymakers are under intense pressure to do *something* to improve the situation. Particularly tempting are reductions in corporate taxes, a step for which there is no clearly defined group of losers.[48] Such measures, however likely to take place, should be recognized as mostly political in inspiration, having little impact on the underlying problem of deindustrialization.

Federal assistance to economically declining locales is well worthwhile, in contrast to the largely futile nature of retrenchment. Deindustrialization has devastating consequences for the workers and communities directly affected. For the federal government to take steps easing the local impact of plant closings is an appropriate and desirable use of state power. Government action in this area is comparable to worker's compensation and unemployment insurance, programs that also soften the harsh effects on individuals of the modern economy's functioning. Although valuable, government intervention on behalf of deindustrializing areas should be recognized as the policy equivalent of a bandaid. Such programs generally cannot succeed in a permanent and meaningful sense. Even if success in this domain were achievable, it might not be desirable. The reason stems once more from the dynamics of industrial location in a market economy. In such a system, fundamentals such as labor cost and access to resources determine the site of particular productive activities. If an existing industry in a given locale becomes uncompetitive on the basis of these essential factors, definitively redressing the situation is typically beyond the scope of government power.

The proposed federal action of the 1930s to raise wages in southern textile mills to the level of competing factories in the North provides a good example. More decisive government intervention in the workings of the market economy is hard to imagine. Yet even if the forceful measures under consideration had been enacted, they would have delayed, not prevented, the disappearance of the New England textile industry. In the decades after World War II, textile manufacturers in poorer countries increasingly challenged established producers in the developed world.[49] By the 1950s, low-price imports, especially from Japan, were becoming a substantial factor in the U.S. industry, which by that time was located largely in the American Southeast. Trade restrictions held off the foreign threat for a time, but many American producers eventually succumbed to competition from countries such as South Korea, Taiwan, Turkey, and China.[50] U.S. textile mill employment fell dramatically as a result, from 860,000 in 1973 to 490,000 in 1996 and about 300,000 in 2003.[51] Most northern textile jobs saved by federal action in the 1930s would thus have disappeared beginning in the 1970s. Little could be done to halt the job-destroying surge of foreign fabric into this country, short of absolute limits on textile imports that would have contravened the longstanding U.S. international economic policy of lowering worldwide trade barriers.[52]

Nor would halting cloth imports necessarily have been desirable. Textile manufacturing was one of the first modern industries to appear in New England, the U.S. South, and previously underdeveloped economies such as Korea and China because factory production of cloth requires limited technology, capital, and worker skill. This makes the sector an ideal one for less developed locales beginning the industrialization process. Such places must industrialize if they are to achieve the gains in wealth that can lift the mass of their population out of poverty. To achieve industrial growth, these locations need access to the markets of rich countries, including the United States.

The inability of federal assistance to stave off deindustrialization permanently is more clearly apparent in cases where the decline of an existing sector stems from a falloff in demand, rather than a shift in the location of production. A number of important American industries suffered this fate in the twentieth century, including woolen textiles (consumers increasingly preferred other fabrics), anthracite coal (purchasers shifted to other sources of heat), and railroad equipment (a victim of the growing reliance on motor vehicle transportation). Federal action can do little to aid manufacturers and workers in industries where demand for the final product is disappearing.

Similarly limited is the potential of assistance efforts such as the U.S. Area Redevelopment program to spur growth in deindustrializing regions. In many locations, there are few possibilities for expansion in new industries to offset the decline of old ones. This applies particularly to outlying locales where remoteness would create disadvantages for new producers. In Britain, the national government initiated efforts to rehabilitate the deindustrializing North and West of the country before World War II, yet numerous local economies in these regions stagnate to this day.

Programs of national assistance can also grow to disproportionate size, so that enormous resources are expended to preserve existing employment. The case of German coal mining provides an example. As other energy sources became more attractive to post–World War II buyers, the German national government began subsidizing coal to protect underground jobs. The subsidies ballooned over time until the annual costs to the public sector per mining job saved approximated the yearly wages of a miner.[53] It would have been more beneficial to shut down the mines and spend a smaller amount on severance payments to the displaced workers, together with redevelopment assistance to the affected localities.

In the United States, of course, the problem is not that too much has been done for industries and locales hit by deindustrialization, but rather not enough. Despite the constraints on what can be achieved, the hard-hit mill towns of New England and other locales experiencing structural economic decline merited greater assistance. More could and should have been spent on aid to such places through the Area Redevelopment program and other efforts.

The limits to what retrenchment and federal assistance can accomplish for deindustrializing locales highlights the importance of economic development, the remaining response to downsizing. An area can only recover meaningfully from the dislocation caused by plant shutdowns through the expansion of new job-creating industries. In helping to generate additional employment, ably executed growth-promotion campaigns substantively aid this revitalization process. Mounting an effective development drive is difficult, however—again because of the dynamics of industrial location in a market system. Economic activity generally locates on the basis of fundamental competitive factors. Fostering the growth of an industry in an area where it has not flourished on a free-market basis thus necessitates overcoming the built-in advantages of established locales of production. The obstacles to doing so are such that many growth-promotion efforts fail completely, while successful initiatives often produce limited gains.[54]

Promotional efforts in newly emerging industries have greater potential for success. In established industries, production typically concentrates in a limited number of places. During the early stages of an industry's existence, by contrast, the locational pattern is often not fixed. Producers may exist in multiple places during the early phase, including in some locales that will later fade as centers of production. An effective development drive mounted in one location during the early period can give producers there vital advantages over competitors elsewhere. Firms in the growth-seeking area thrive as a result, and the locale eventually emerges as an important hub of the growing industry. This competitive success produces ongoing benefits, as the continuing expansion of the industry creates a steady stream of new jobs in the area.

Such a sequence occurred in New England. Efforts to stimulate the growth of Boston-area electronics companies facilitated the rise of the Route 128 technology complex. Local electronics employment grew dramatically in the ensuing decades, and the region long remained an important locus of electronics and computer production. The assistance provided to Boston-area firms in the crucial early stages yielded benefits that lasted for generations.[55]

The emergence of new industries benefits nearly everyone in regions hit by deindustrialization. Many of the gains admittedly accrue to those in the corporate sphere. Capitalists in service-sector industries—the strongest private backers of growth-promotion efforts—reap sizable returns from improved local economic conditions. Entrepreneurs in the new, expanding industries realize significant profits. But the rise of new industries benefits the broader community as well. Tax collections increase, providing resources to pay for badly needed social services. The morale of area residents improves. Most important, growing companies often provide numerous jobs for the working class, the group hardest hit by industrial decline. To be sure, not all workers laid off from declining industries find jobs in the new growing sectors. In the contemporary era, when expanding industries are frequently in services, rather than manufacturing, employees in the new positions may receive inadequate pay and benefits. Nevertheless, new industries that take hold in deindustrialized locales are likely to be a significant source of working-class employment.[56] Growth-promotion efforts can thus help in concrete, meaningful ways to rectify the social and economic devastation wrought by deindustrialization. For this reason, development efforts are potentially the most fruitful of the range of initiatives pursued in response to industrial decline.

Appendix 1

Rates of Job Creation in Massachusetts and the United States

Statistics on total employment give a more complete picture of a developed region's overall economic situation than figures on manufacturing employment alone. This is so because gains in service-sector employment can compensate to a degree for drops in the number of manufacturing jobs—a dynamic seen in New England from the 1920s onward. Government officials only began gathering statistics on total employment in the late 1930s. For the period up through 1940, figures on the number of "gainful workers" from the decennial U.S. census provide a rough indication of employment levels.

The table that follows gives Massachusetts and U.S. statistics on gainful workers (for 1880–1940) and employment (for 1939–88). Also shown are percentage changes in these numbers between different points in time. The ratio of percentage changes in Massachusetts to percentage changes in the United States, which appears in the last column, permits an easy comparison between rates of job growth in Massachusetts and in the country as a whole.

The impact of industrial decline is clearly apparent in the table. During the period 1880–1920, before the onset of deindustrialization in New England, the number of gainful workers in Massachusetts expanded at approximately the national rate, exceeding it in some decades and trailing close behind in others. By contrast, between 1920 and 1930, when significant factory closures began, the number of gainful workers in Massachusetts increased at less than a third of the national rate. The results for the 1930–40 period were also grim. Bay State job creation approached the national level with the World War II economic boom, then fell back to the comparative lows of 1920–30 amid a wave of plant closures in the late 1940s and early 1950s. Employment creation again neared the national rate in the relatively prosperous era from the mid-1950s through the late 1960s, then dropped during the downsizing of 1969–75 to the worst comparative level yet seen. After 1975, job creation was near or above national rates in a restructured Bay State economy based on high technology industry and business and financial services.

Table A.1. Gainful Workers and Employment in Massachusetts and the United States, 1880–1988

NUMBER OF GAINFUL WORKERS, 1880–1940 (IN THOUSANDS)

| | Massachusetts | | United States | | |
	Number of workers	% change since 10 years before	Number of workers	% change since 10 years before	Ratio of Mass. 10-year % change to U.S. 10-year % change
	(1)	(2)	(3)	(4)	(2) / (4)
1880	721		17,392		
1890	982	36.2%	22,735	30.7%	1.18
1900	1,208	23.0%	29,073	27.9%	0.83
1910	1,531	26.7%	38,167	31.3%	0.85
1920	1,728	12.9%	41,614	9.0%	1.42
1930	1,814	5.0%	48,829	17.3%	0.29
1940	1,703	-6.1%	49,625	1.6%	n.a.

NONAGRICULTURAL EMPLOYMENT, 1939–1988 (IN THOUSANDS)

| | Massachusetts | | United States | | |
	Number of workers	% change since previous date	Number of workers	% change since previous date	Ratio of Mass. % change to U.S. % change
	(1)	(2)	(3)	(4)	(2) / (4)
1939	1,367		30,603		
1947	1,727	26.3%	43,857	43.3%	0.61
1955	1,815	5.1%	50,641	15.5%	0.33
1960	1,901	4.7%	54,189	7.0%	0.68
1969	2,249	18.3%	70,384	29.9%	0.61
1975	2,273	1.1%	76,945	9.3%	0.11
1982	2,622	15.4%	89,566	16.4%	0.94
1988	3,131	19.4%	105,210	17.5%	1.11

Sources: U.S. Bureau of the Census, *Historical Statistics*, Part 1, 123 (on "gainful workers"), 129; U.S. Bureau of Labor Statistics, *Employment, Hours, and Earnings, States and Areas, 1939-82, 1988-94*; U.S. Bureau of Labor Statistics, *Employment, Hours, and Earnings, United States, 1909-84, 1988-96*.

Appendix 2

Cotton Textile Mill Wages

The table that follows shows wages for selected categories of workers in cotton textile plants of New England and the South in July 1933, just before the cotton textile code of the National Recovery Administration (NRA) went into effect. The statistics demonstrate that a significant pay gap between northern and southern mills existed at this time. (The differential had been even wider in previous decades.) The figures also reveal the wide dispersion in pay levels across the hierarchy of skill within cloth-fabricating plants in both regions. The highly skilled loom fixers earned at least twice what was received by the lowest-paid category of workers, trimmers or inspectors.

The seven groups of workers shown here were selected from a list of twenty categories of cotton textile mill labor given in the source. The first three occupations were generally all-male and the last two jobs typically female. Unskilled laborers in cotton textiles were not among the twenty occupations listed in the source; they received lower wages than any of the positions shown.

Table A.2. Wage Rates for Selected Occupations in New England and Southern Cotton Textile Mills, July 1933

	New England	South	Southern Wage as a Percentage of New England Wage
	Wage (cents per hour)		
Loom fixers	46	32	70%
Card grinders	34	27	79%
Slubber tenders	31	21	68%
Male weavers	30	24	80%
Female weavers	28	22	79%
Frame spinners	24	16	67%
Trimmers or Inspectors	21	16	76%

Source: Hinrichs, "Historical Review of Wage Rates," 1171.

Appendix 3

A Contemporary Account of Spinoff Banking at the First National Bank of Boston

The following article appeared in a Boston newspaper in 1960.

'Total Banking' Concept Created by First National for Research

Research-based businesses in the broad field of electronics, metals, chemicals, atomics, and nucleonics cannot be properly serviced with old-line banking concepts. This was the conclusion reached by the management of The First National Bank of Boston some years ago, when the infant industries started sprouting along Route 128.

Thoroughly aware of the potential importance of these highly specialized businesses to the future of the region, The First evolved a new concept to handle their needs, which it calls "to[t]al banking." To carry it out, the Bank established a separate group to concentrate on the particular needs of research-based businesses.

"The relative unfamiliarity of these concerns with the business problems of small companies . . . ," says Lloyd Brace, chairman of the bank's board, "was balanced by an equal degree of unfamiliarity on our part, not only with the type of help they would need but also with the complexities of their products and processes. We still have a long way to go on the latter," Brace adds with a wry smile, "but as a result of our early start and the concentration of our special service group, we feel we have today a working knowledge of the needs of such companies and a sound program for helping meet them."

Briefly, the bank stands ready to assist a research-based company almost from the moment of its conception. It is often asked to suggest legal and audit counsel. The scientific-minded management may also seek help in locating personnel trained in the functions of finance, production and marketing. As the situation develops, the bank may be able to arrange introductions to other concerns with similar interests, to the benefit of both parties. And the bank's extensive files and nationwide correspondent network provide a ready source of credit information.

"Our interest in new companies is well known," says William Raye, vice president in charge of the special group (known internally as the space men) handling the financing of research-based companies. "As a result we frequently open the door to sources of venture capital, and once the firm gets on its feet, the bank can assist in more direct ways.

"In a number of situations, unsecured loans, accounts receivable financing and V-loan financing have all been made available to the same company within a period of a very few years, as changing conditions and improving financial status have indicated. In other words, we try to bring our knowledge and experience to bear across the whole financing spectrum."

The technically oriented companies of the Boston area also show an unusual interest in international operations. . . . Here again, The First contributes to total financial service through its extensive International Division. Research-minded customers can be introduced to their counterparts overseas, making possible the exchange of business leads, as well as engineering, production and research information. Arranging suitable overseas banking connections is another important service of this division.

Assisting smaller businesses is nothing new to The First. "By starting with them early and working right along with them, we feel we have been able to play a real part in their growth over the years," says Roger Damon, since last October the bank's president. "What sets these technical growth outfits apart from other smaller businesses is that the almost insatiable demands of industry and defense on their services preclude normal deliberate growth."

Pointing up the bank's conviction that these research-based companies are the pace-setters of the future, Mr. Damon concludes: "Any officer of this bank is authorized to make a loan . . . but as far as research-based companies are concerned, no loan is refused until it has been carefully reviewed by the group specializing in this field."

Source: *Boston Sunday Herald*, June 5, 1960, "First Annual Electronics Review," 10.

Notes

Abbreviations

AIM GM	*Annual Report of . . . General Manager, Associated Industries of Massachusetts*
ARD Materials	American Research and Development Corporation Historical Materials
ARDC 1946	"American Research and Development Corp. 1946" folder in RF-FRBB
AWCR	*American Wool and Cotton Reporter*
BankBoston Off-Site	First National Bank of Boston Historical Materials, BankBoston off-site storage facility
BankBoston On-Site	First National Bank of Boston Historical Records, BankBoston headquarters Research Library
BCoC	Greater Boston Chamber of Commerce Records
BG	*Boston Globe*
CLM	Consumers League of Massachusetts Records
IRDD	U.S Department of Commerce Records (RG 40), Records of the Industrial Research and Development Division, Office of Technical Services
Labor and Industries	Commonwealth of Massachusetts, *Annual Report of the Department of Labor and Industries*
MA AFL	*Proceedings . . . Annual Convention, Massachusetts State Branch, A.F. of L.*
Mass Dept Comm	Commonwealth of Massachusetts, *Report of the Special Commission Relative to Establishment of a State Department of Commerce* (December 1945)
Mass Stats Manufrs 1920–1938	Massachusetts Department of Labor and Industries, *Statistics of Manufactures in Massachusetts, 1920–1938*

Mass Tax 1927	Commonwealth of Massachusetts, *Report of the Special Commission Appointed to Investigate the Entire Subject of State, County and Local Taxation* . . . (December 1927)
MIT-OP	Massachusetts Institute of Technology, Office of the President, 1930–59 Records
NACM	National Association of Cotton Manufacturers—Northern Textile Association Collection
NEC-SC	New England Council Steel Committee Records
NEGTC	New England Governors' Textile Committee
NENL	*New England News Letter*
NYT	*New York Times*
RF-FRBB	Ralph Flanders Materials, Federal Reserve Bank of Boston
RF-SU	Ralph E. Flanders Papers, Syracuse University
TW	*Textile World*

Complete citation information for these sources appears in the bibliography. For annual publications, the year of the relevant report is indicated in the citation (e.g., *MA AFL 1905* for the 1905 union convention). For the location of materials within a manuscript collection, 10/61 denotes a document in box 10, folder 61, and 10/"Legislation" indicates a document in box 10, "Legislation" folder.

Introduction

1. See Dublin and Licht, *Face of Decline*; most essays in Cowie and Heathcott, *Beyond the Ruins*; Cowie, *Capital Moves*; Hartford, *Where Is Our Responsibility?*; Sugrue, *Origins of the Urban Crisis*, chaps. 5, 6; Cumbler, *Social History of Economic Decline*; Friedman, "Communities in Competition." Hartford's work is particularly notable, as it, like this volume, probes the demise of textile manufacturing in twentieth-century New England. Examining the efforts of the CIO-affiliated Textile Workers Union of America to protect the interests of its New England members in the post–World War II decades as the region's textile firms downsized, Hartford probes the thoughts and actions of union officials, employers, and rank-and-file workers. Hartford's study makes an invaluable contribution to the literature on deindustrialization, but his concerns are almost entirely different than mine. While Hartford concentrates on developments at individual cloth-making firms and in the textile industry as a whole, my focus is solely on the impact of downsizing on the broader world of politics and public policy. Hartford also focuses on attempts to counter downsizing in the post–World War II era, whereas in matters directly related to textiles, my emphasis is on events in the 1920s and 1930s.

2. Galenson, *Migration of the Cotton Textile Industry*; Kane, *Textiles in Transition*; Scranton, *Figured Tapestry*, chaps. 6, 7; Gross, *Course of Industrial Decline*.

3. Locally based initiatives to generate new employment in locations experiencing plant

closures are examined in Gregory Wilson, "'Our Chronic and Desperate Situation'"; McKee, "Urban Deindustrialization"; Dublin and Licht, *Face of Decline*, chap. 5; Heathcott and Murphy, "Corridors of Flight"; O'Mara, *Cities of Knowledge*, chap. 4; and Gillette, *Camden after the Fall*.

4. On federal assistance to deindustrialized locales, see Gregory Wilson, *Communities Left Behind*. Proposals for plant closing legislation in the United States and Canada are discussed in High, *Industrial Sunset*, chaps. 5, 6. Business efforts to repeal labor legislation hampering competitiveness in declining industries are noted in English, *Common Thread*, 31–33, 117–19.

The impact of deindustrialization on the political economy—including government policy and the effects on the balance of power between regions—is also explored in the considerable social science literature on economic restructuring. This scholarship, for the most part now several decades old, also examines the extent of decline and renewal in industrial regions of the United States and the effects of downsizing on workers and communities. Representative works include Bensman, *Rusted Dreams*; Bluestone and Harrison, *Deindustrialization of America*; Eisinger, *Rise of the Entrepreneurial State*; Markusen, *Regions*; Rodwin and Sazanami, *Deindustrialization and Regional Economic Transformation*; Sawers and Tabb, *Sunbelt/Snowbelt*; Wallace and Rothschild, *Deindustrialization and the Restructuring of American Industry*; Zysman and Tyson, *American Industry in International Competition*.

5. "Political economy" is defined in the broadest possible terms for the purposes of this study. As used here, the term encompasses any kind of organized effort by economic actors to influence economic outcomes, while "the political economy" means the set of political and economic arrangements obtaining at a particular time as a result of these efforts.

Economic actors such as manufacturers, workers, and consumers typically seek to advance their interests through structured organizations such as trade associations or labor unions. The assertion of these interests usually involves pressing for some kind of government action—the enactment of new regulations or the repeal of existing ones; raising or lowering taxes. However, organized efforts to influence economic outcomes can take place entirely within the private sector, without government involvement. An example is the almost exclusively private-sector attempts of New England businessmen to regenerate the regional economy in the 1920s and 1930s.

6. The focus on events in Massachusetts simplifies consideration of a six-state region. Given its size (Massachusetts accounted for about half of New England's manufacturing employment in the post–World War I era), concentrating there does not distort the interpretive picture.

7. Events did not always transpire in as clear-cut a manner as the three-initiative paradigm of responses to deindustrialization (retrenchment, federal assistance, economic development) indicates. In some instances there was overlap between the initiatives. This was most obvious with regard to tax reductions. Cuts in the taxes on industry, advocated by manufacturers in the declining sectors, fell into what is defined here as the retrenchment response to deindustrialization. But tax exemptions, a similar policy instrument, were also an important tool used by localities seeking to attract new industry; these exemptions fell into what is described here as the economic development approach. Despite some fuzziness around the edges, the three-initiative model reflects what was done in response to deindustrialization in New England and is a useful tool for making sense of a complicated series of events.

8. Shermer, "Sunbelt Boosterism"; Shermer, "Origins of the Conservative Ascendancy"; Friedman, "Exploiting the North-South Differential"; Orejel, "Factories in the Fallows." An important older work on this topic is Cobb, *Selling of the South*.

Chapter 1. Deindustrialization in New England

1. Pusateri, *History of American Business*, 125–33; Winifred Barr Rothenberg, "The Invention of American Capitalism: The Economy of New England in the Federal Period," in Temin, *Engines of Enterprise*, 95–100.

2. Stanley L. Engerman and Kenneth L. Sokoloff, "Technology and Industrialization, 1790–1914," in Engerman and Gallman, *Cambridge Economic History of the United States*, 2:373; Peter Temin, "The Industrialization of New England, 1830–1880," in Temin, *Engines of Enterprise*, 116–20; Pusateri, *History of American Business*, 135–36.

3. Clark, *History of Manufactures*, 1:565–75; Temin, "Industrialization," 124–25, 142; Khan and Sokoloff, "'Schemes of Practical Utility,'" 291.

4. *Monthly Review* (Federal Reserve Bank of Boston), October 1948, 1–7; Grow, "'Boston-Type Open-End Fund,'" esp. 26–31; Brown, *Inventing New England*. Agriculture played a "small and passive role" in New England's nineteenth-century industrialization, mostly by providing labor for the growing industrial sector (Temin, "Industrialization," 109–10). Locales outside the industrial core of the region, particularly the less developed parts of northern New England, nevertheless continued to depend heavily on agriculture and natural resource sectors such as fishing, forestry, and quarrying. This reliance continued into the twentieth century.

5. Joshua Rosenbloom, "The Challenges of Economic Maturity: New England, 1880–1940," in Temin, *Engines of Enterprise*, 158.

6. Dublin, *Women at Work*; Juravich et al., *Commonwealth of Toil*, chaps. 1, 3, 5; Abrams, *Conservatism in a Progressive Era*, 11; Dawley, *Class and Community*.

7. Lazerow, "'Workingman's Hour,'" 200–20; Juravich et al., *Commonwealth of Toil*, chaps. 6, 7, 9; Abrams, *Conservatism in a Progressive Era*, 11; Asher, "Business and Workers' Welfare," 452–55; Beyer, "History of Labor Legislation," 55–60.

8. Wells and Perkins, *Trends in New England Industries*, 7.

9. All percentages and employment totals in this and the following paragraph were calculated from 1919 figures reported in U.S. Bureau of the Census, *Fourteenth Census of the United States*, vol. 8, tables 48 and 54. Cotton small wares were included with cotton textiles, and cut stock and findings with boots and shoes. The percentages for value added are lower than those for employment because of the low average wages paid in almost all of these industries.

10. After Massachusetts, the worst performers among the twenty-one leading industrial states in terms of change in manufacturing employment over the 1923–39 period were Pennsylvania (−21.6 percent), Rhode Island (−21.1 percent), Wisconsin (−18.9 percent), and New York (−16.7 percent). Vermont and New Hampshire were not among the twenty-one leading manufacturing states. Manufacturing employment in Vermont, which had a very small industrial sector, fell by 29.3 percent in the years 1923–39; the decline was 25.9 percent in New Hampshire. The drop-off was 11.3 percent in Connecticut and 9.2 percent in Maine over the same period. States in the South were the best performers, as measured by change in manu-

facturing employment in the years 1923–39, led by North Carolina (+55.6 percent) and South Carolina (+31.2 percent). All statistics from Commonwealth of Massachusetts, *Report of the Special Commission Relative to Establishment of a State Department of Commerce* (December 1945), 75–76 (hereafter cited as *Mass Dept Comm)*; New England totals are my calculations. Total U.S. manufacturing employment changed little between these two years, falling from 8.19 million in 1923 to 7.80 million in 1939, a drop of 4.8 percent (U.S. Bureau of the Census, *Historical Statistics of the United States*, part 2, p. 666).

11. *Mass Dept Comm*, 81–82. The figure for cotton goods employment includes cotton small wares.

12. The percentages are my calculations from figures appearing in Massachusetts Department of Labor and Industries, *Annual Report of the Statistics of Manufactures* (1921), 25–27.

13. Massachusetts Department of Labor and Industries, *Statistics of Manufactures in Massachusetts, 1920–1938*, 22 (hereafter cited as *Mass Stats Manufrs 1920–1938*); Wolfbein, *Decline of a Cotton Textile City*, 28, 38–43.

14. Adamic, "Tragic Towns of New England," 750–52.

15. Parker, *Lowell*, 5; percentages of population decline calculated from census figures in Massachusetts Department of Corporations and Taxation, *Seventeenth Annual Report on the Statistics* (1922) and *Twenty-Fifth Annual Report on the Statistics* (1930); Adamic, "Tragic Towns of New England," 749; Wolfbein, *Decline of a Cotton Textile City*, 142–43.

16. Ragan, "Organization, Management, and Significance," 106–8.

17. Robert J. Watt, "A Wage and Hour Program for the States," 34–35, in *Wage and Hour Legislation*; Commonwealth of Massachusetts, *Annual Report of the Department of Labor and Industries*, 1932, 6–7 (hereafter cited as *Labor and Industries*, with year).

18. Blewett, *Last Generation*, 182–83.

19. Blewett, *Last Generation*, 210, 211.

20. Hareven and Langenbach, *Amoskeag*, 354, 366, 367–68.

21. Palmer, *Another Tale of Two Cities*, 7; Adamic, "Tragic Towns of New England," 755.

22. Parker, *Lowell*, 5–6; "Up From Bankruptcy," *The Survey*, July 1, 1931, 344, 361–64.

23. Adamic, "Tragic Towns of New England," 749; Tinsley et al. to Fuller, Feburary 2, 1927, Greater Boston Chamber of Commerce Records (hereafter cited as BCoC), Case 79/710-1; Rogers, "Address before the Committee," 1.

24. *Forbes*, May 10, 1924, 148; *Nation's Business*, December 1925, 29; *Boston Herald*, January 14, 1924, 24; Frederick Steele Blackall Jr. address, November 16, 1944, Frederick Steele Blackall Jr. Papers, vol. II (2/13/36–12/4/45).

25. The following pages summarize my detailed examination of the decline of the New England cotton textile industry and its implications for modern political economy. For the full account, with complete citations, see Koistinen, "Causes of Deindustrialization." For a recent piece that offers a dramatically different account of the causes and meaning of the decline of northern textiles, see Friedman, "Exploiting the North-South Differential."

26. Blicksilver, *Cotton Manufacturing in the Southeast*, 12.

27. It was frequently asserted, at the time and more recently, that the competitiveness of New England cotton firms was fatally undermined by incompetent managers who failed to invest adequately in up-to-date equipment. These claims probably have some merit, but their

importance is overstated. On this issue, see Koistinen, "Causes of Deindustrialization," 498–500, 506–8.

28. *American Wool and Cotton Reporter* (hereafter cited as *AWCR*), January 19, 1928, 55.

Chapter 2. Retrenchment

1. Bluestone and Harrison, *Deindustrialization of America*, 180–82, 185–88; Vogel, *Fluctuating Fortunes*, 113–239. Similarly in Massachusetts, corporate interests during the 1970s won substantial cutbacks in the state unemployment insurance program. The changes are described in chapter 7.

2. This account of the push for legal limits on working times in Massachusetts is based on Juravich et al., *Commonwealth of Toil*, 9–11, 22–26; Blewett, *Constant Turmoil*, chap. 4; Beyer, "History of Labor Legislation"; Simon, "Textile Workers, Trade Unions, and Politics," 197–226; Abrams, *Conservatism in a Progressive Era*, 182–83, 231–32, 234; Dubofsky, *State and Labor*, 44–45. Most of the laws limiting working hours for women in manufacturing applied to child operatives as well. The latter provisions proved much less controversial in the 1920s, as business lobbyists made no attempt to repeal them.

3. Alice Kessler-Harris observes that in many U.S. industries, laws limiting the laboring hours of women were one of a number of tools used by male unionists attempting to keep lower-paid female workers out of the labor force. Kessler-Harris notes as well that a different pattern obtained in industries (such as textiles) where women had long constituted a significant part of the workforce. See Kessler-Harris, *Gendering Labor History*, 24–31, 61–62, and page 62 and after on the different dynamics in heavily female industries.

4. Beyer, "History of Labor Legislation," 24, 49–52; Lahne, "Labor in the Cotton Mill," 91; *Proceedings . . . Annual Convention, Massachusetts State Branch, A.F. of L 1902*, 22 (hereafter cited as *MA AFL*, with year).

5. *MA AFL 1902*, 22–23; *MA AFL 1904*, 30–31; *MA AFL 1905*, 33; *MA AFL 1906*, 28–29; *MA AFL 1907*, 21–22, 31–32, 34–35.

6. Beyer, "History of Labor Legislation." Unions led the drive to enact the Massachusetts hours of work laws central to the present discussion. Middle-class reformers initiated campaigns for other items of Bay State social legislation, including Progressive Era measures such as workmen's compensation and minimum wages for female workers. In New York State, middle-class reformers similarly headed Progressive Era efforts that secured numerous pieces of protective labor legislation. On New York, see Greenwald, *Triangle Fire*, chaps. 5–7.

7. Beyer, "History of Labor Legislation," 36, 38–40; Jacoby, "Women's Trade Union League," 19–22; lists of legislation supported by the Consumers League of Massachusetts, 1908–16 and 1917–26, Consumers League of Massachusetts Records (hereafter cited as CLM), 1/2; Consumers League of Massachusetts Executive Committee Minutes for December 5, 1917, and October 2, 1918, CLM 1/10.

8. Beyer, "History of Labor Legislation," 40–42; *Boston Globe* (hereafter cited as *BG*), April 1, 1919, 5, and April 10, 1919, 16.

9. For hours of work regulations in the textile-producing states as of 1923, see Massachusetts Department of Labor and Industries, *Report of a Special Investigation*, 16–17. For the regulations as of 1935, which had by that time changed in several states, see Cotton Textile

Institute, "Cotton Facts and Figures," prepared by the Cotton Textile Institute, October 1938, pages 89, 89A, in National Association of Cotton Manufacturers—Northern Textile Association Collection (hereafter cited as NACM), 10/117.

On efforts in Maine, New Hampshire, and Rhode Island to enact a 48-hour law during the 1920s, see *New York Times* (hereafter cited as *NYT*), October 16, 1923, 23; *NYT*, February 26, 1925, 23; *NYT*, December 17, 1928, 49. The shorter work week prevailed for a time at many companies in Rhode Island and New Hampshire following the UTW's 1918-19 campaign to institute 48 hours, but manufacturers restored the 54-hour week at most mills after a six-month strike in 1922. Massachusetts employers could not follow suit since state law enforced a 48-hour week. On the 1922 strike, see Tilden, "New England Textile Strike." On the prevalence of night work in the South after World War I, see Wright, *Old South, New South*, 209-10.

10. Union membership from Massachusetts Department of Labor and Industries, *Annual Report . . . Statistics of Labor Organizations*, 4. The census figure on the number of "gainful workers" in Massachusetts (1.73 million in 1920) was used as an estimate of the state's labor force. Statistic from U.S. Bureau of the Census, *Historical Statistics*, part 1, 129.

11. This sketch of early twentieth-century Massachusetts unionism is based on Hartford, *Where Is Our Responsibility?*, chaps. 1 and 2; Vecoli, "Anthony Capraro and the Lawrence Strike"; Juravich et al., *Commonwealth of Toil*; and *MA AFL 1925*, 14-15.

12. During a lengthy 1928 strike in New Bedford, according to one observer, the "the unorganized workers . . . followed the lead of the unions" throughout the conflict. See "Is Wage Reduction the Best Way to Lower Costs?," *Factory and Industrial Management*, January 1929, 51-53. Craft and ethnic exclusionism among skilled workers prevented more widespread union participation in New Bedford and Fall River.

13. On the origins and activities of the organization, see *History of the Massachusetts State Federation*, 1925 membership on 61-62.

14. Widespread factory closures in New England cotton textiles did not begin until about 1924, although the competitive problems of regional producers were apparent before that time. With a wide gap between the legal limit on working hours in Massachusetts and the caps in other textile-producing states, commonwealth manufacturers might well have mounted a sustained drive to ease the statutes even if the cotton industry had been in good condition in the 1920s. The context of industrial decline undoubtedly attracted more attention to the issue than would otherwise have been the case and increased cotton manufacturers' chances of success.

15. In addition to the publications cited in notes that follow, see Ashmun Brown, *Study of the Cotton Industry*; Robert M. Brown, "Cotton Manufacturing"; and Kenneth Moller, "What Can New England Do About Its Textile Problems," *Textile World* (hereafter cited as *TW*), January 12, 1924, 1.

16. The results of the climactic 1928 legislative fight were reported in front-page banner headlines in at least one Boston newspaper—see *BG*, March 29, 1928. An excellent source on the annual fights over the hours of work laws in the state legislature—by its formal, colonial-era title the Great and General Court of the Commonwealth of Massachusetts—is the newspaper clippings in CLM 29/499. The various annual publications of the legislature, most importantly Commonwealth of Massachusetts, *Bulletin of Committee Work*, were also very useful

254   Notes to Pages 34–38

in tracking the progress of the particular pieces of legislation discussed in this chapter. These legislative sources are not specifically cited in notes that follow.

17. Joseph Thoron obituary, *NYT*, March 30, 1901; Ward Thoron obituary, *Boston Evening Transcript*, March 1, 1938, 9; minutes of stockholders meeting of February 15, 1920, Merrimack Manufacturing Company Records, Volume 2A; "Senator Butler's Mills," February 17, 1926, clipping and February 24, 1927, clipping, both in CLM 29/499; *AWCR*, March 17, 1932, 52.

18. *BG*, January 23, 1924, 3.

19. *Before the Committee on Labor and Industry*; *TW*, February 16, 1924, 43.

20. *TW*, February 16, 1924, 43–44; *BG*, February 14, 1924, 22.

21. In the splendidly anachronistic language used by the General Court, the petitioner who had initiated the proposal was given "leave to withdraw."

22. Wilkie and Tager, *Historical Atlas of Massachusetts*, 68.

23. Huthmacher, *Massachusetts People and Politics*, chaps. 4, 5. Democrats also benefited from recent inroads by the party's candidates among Massachusetts African Americans, who had earlier voted solidly Republican. All these trends intensified in the decade that followed, allowing Democrats to contest state offices on an equal basis with the GOP from the 1930s onward.

24. "Senator Butler's Mills."

25. See Huthmacher, *Massachusetts People and Politics*, 16–17; William Butler entry, *National Cyclopaedia of American Biography*, 30:302–3. Walsh profited from the Republicans' Bull Moose schism to win one-year terms as governor in 1913 and 1914. Support for progressivism, foreign policy questions, and wartime prosperity facilitated his narrow 1918 Senate victory against the old-line Republican incumbent.

26. Huthmacher, *Massachusetts People and Politics*, 102–4, 107–11; David Walsh entry, *American National Biography*, 22:564–65.

27. "Senator Butler's Mills"; "The 48-Hour Bill," February 18, 1926 clipping, and "Butler Not," February 18, 1926, clipping, both in CLM 29/499; "Against 54-Hour Law," February 19, 1926, clipping, CLM 29/499; "Hearing, March 16th. Repeal of 48 Hour Law," 1922, section beginning with testimony of Mr. Newdick, page 5, CLM 29/500.

28. Walsh handily defeated Butler in the November 1926 election. The 48-hour law incident did Butler's election bid considerable harm, according to Huthmacher, *Massachusetts People and Politics*, 134–35. When the question of working hours came before the legislature again the following year, the Democrats sought further political mileage from the issue, with the party's House caucus deciding on a formal position against any attempt to water down the 48-hour law. See "Democrats Oppose . . . ," January 27, 1927 clipping in CLM 29/499.

29. Tinsley et al. to Fuller, February 2, 1927, BCoC, Case 79/710-"New England Council"-1; Stacy to Peters, March 7, 1928, BCoC, Case 12/311-210-19; *AWCR*, January 19, 1928, 52.

30. Hennessy, *Four Decades of Massachusetts Politics*, 241, 304, 341–42, 349–51, 356–57; *Industry*, January 7, 1928, front cover; *Mass Stats Manufrs 1920–1938*, 9.

31. In letting women work in textile factories until 10:00 p.m., the proposal would merely apply to cloth-making the standard that currently existed in the commonwealth's other manufacturing sectors. (Recall that the intent of the 6:00 p.m. limit was not to prevent women from laboring in textiles at night but rather to prevent any late work at all from taking place in Bay

State textile plants.) While Massachusetts's 48-hour law was a stricter version of the 54-hour cap found in neighboring jurisdictions, no other fabric-producing state had anything nearly as stringent as the commonwealth's ban on work after 6:00 p.m. by female textile operatives.

32. *MA AFL 1928*, 15; *Report of Hearing*.

33. *BG*, March 21, 1928, 9; *BG*, March 28, 1928, 16; *BG*, March 29, 1928, 1, 3; Joint Committee on Industrial Conditions for Women and Children in Massachusetts, program and minutes for meeting of March 26, 1928, CLM 25/418; Wiggin to members of the House of Representatives, undated, CLM 25/420; *Report of Hearing*, 20–22, 59.

34. The analysis of roll calls described in what follows was carried out by matching information on the voting records of House members on labor issues from Massachusetts State Federation of Labor, *Roll Calls of the Massachusetts Legislature, 1927–28*, with data on party affiliation and legislative district in *Public Officials of Massachusetts* (1927–28).

35. On the nine roll call votes on labor issues (other than the night work bill itself) that took place during the 1927 and 1928 legislative sessions, these representatives did not once oppose the position of the state AFL.

36. Wilkie and Tager, *Historical Atlas of Massachusetts*, 68; Abrams, *Conservatism in a Progressive Era*, 182.

37. The lawmakers strongly inclined toward reform registered one, or at most two, votes against the labor position during the 1927 and 1928 legislative sessions.

38. For example, Frank Eaton, who voted twice for and six times against the union-backed position on the other roll calls, came from the shoemaking town of Brockton. Charles Foote, who compiled an otherwise perfect anti-reform record, with no votes for labor and seven against, hailed from industrial Pittsfield. Thomas Crowther, who defended the night work law during the floor debate preceding the roll call (*BG*, March 29, 1928, 3) despite no votes for and three against the unions, represented Fall River.

39. In the 1928 elections that took place half a year after the House retained the night work law, Walsh won a full six-year term in the U.S. Senate by a considerable margin; Al Smith edged out Herbert Hoover in the commonwealth's presidential race; and the Democratic candidate nearly won the governorship after a campaign calling for expanded state social programs that would benefit the working class. See Huthmacher, *Massachusetts People and Politics*, 180, 185–87.

40. Bay State manufacturers mounted a major push to revoke the six o'clock law in textiles in early 1933. The effort was again frustrated by resistance from labor and reform groups. Shortly thereafter, the U.S. Congress approved the National Industrial Recovery Act (NIRA), which provided for codes of fair competition in each industry. The draft code for cotton textiles limited working times in all the industry's plants to two 40-hour shifts per week. This was a drastic cut for Dixie mills and promised to divert significant business to the depressed cloth factories of New England.

As matters stood, Massachusetts workers would not receive the full benefit of the new federal regulations. The state's ban on female labor in textiles after 6:00 p.m. would prevent commonwealth mills using women on both shifts from running all of the permitted 80 hours per week. To enable Massachusetts textile operatives to work all of the allowed 40 hours, Bay State unionists in conjunction with commonwealth labor officials crafted a proposal to suspend the

6:00 p.m. law temporarily. The measure would allow female operatives in textiles to work until 10:00 p.m.—the standard in the state's other industries. The Massachusetts legislature approved the measure as soon as the NIRA cotton code was finalized, despite some opposition from rank-and-file union members and certain labor-friendly lawmakers.

These events demonstrate that in the 1930s, as before, employer attempts to roll back labor legislation were likely to fail when unions and their reform allies defended the status quo. The same laws could be modified, however, when leaders of the labor camp supported change. Union officials were willing to make such concessions when workers would receive concrete benefits in return.

The Massachusetts legislature renewed its suspension of the six o'clock law in 1935 and did so again in 1936, when the NIRA was no longer operative, again with the backing of labor leaders. Additional suspensions of the six o'clock law took place on a regular basis into the post-war era. See chapter 3 on the NIRA cotton textile code. On the other events described here, see documents in CLM 28/479, 28/483, 29/493, 29/503; documents in NACM 5/44, 9/104; *MA AFL* for 1933, 1935, and 1936; Massachusetts Legislative Documents 1933 (Senate, No. 1) and (House, No. 1558).

41. Estimates prepared by a Massachusetts mill engineer of the period demonstrate the extent of these effects. According to the statistics, a mill running 48 hours per week could produce cotton cloth at a cost of 61.1 cents per pound. Increasing operating hours to 54 hours a week—possible if the 48-hour law was amended as employers sought—would reduce costs to 60.4 cents a pound. Raising weekly hours to 75—possible if mills ran a partial second shift in the evening, which repeal of the night-work law would facilitate—would lower costs to 58.9 cents a pound. The effect on profits would be greater than the impact on costs. If the cotton cloth in this example were sold at a hypothetical price of 61 cents a pound, the mill loses money running a 48-hour week; realizes a slight profit of 0.6 cents a pound with a 54-hour week; and has a much more substantial profit of 2.1 cents a pound with a 75-hour week. Cost figures, which were either stated in the source or read off a graph of production costs vs. working hours, are from Chas. T. Main, Engineer, "Status of the Cotton Textile Industry in the United States," February 24, 1926, pages 24–25, in BCoC, box 12A/311–210–19, "New England Industries—Surveys—Cotton (3)."

42. Federal statistics on operating rates in the industry demonstrate these realities. Spindles, the devices for spinning fibers into yarn, are the standard measure of capacity in cotton textiles. Each month, the U.S. Census Bureau collected figures, by state, on the number of cotton textile spindles in place and the total number of hours these spindles were active. Dividing the second number by the first allowed government statisticians to calculate active spindle hours per spindle in place. The latter figure provides a good index of the industry's overall operating rate, or rate of capacity utilization. With one 48-hour shift per week, a Massachusetts mill could run about 203 hours in an average month (allowing for somewhat more than four weeks in the average month and about ten holiday days off per year).

Bay State cotton factories last approached this level of activity in early 1923, hitting a high of 197 hours in March. This was the final period of reasonably prosperous conditions for commonwealth producers. Peak running hours were well below this level from that time forward: the highest point reached in the years that followed was 175 hours in March 1927. For most of the 1922–28 period during which the Massachusetts legislature considered easing the hours of work laws, the state's cotton mills ran between 110 and 160 hours per month. Statistics on overall operating times here and in the next note are from *Activity in the Cotton Spinning Industry* (U.S. Bureau of the Census), 1922–28.

43. Statistics compiled by the Massachusetts state government in late 1923 and early 1924 show significant numbers of the commonwealth's cotton firms running all of the legally permitted hours. Thus in December 1923, when the Massachusetts cotton industry as a whole operated 137 hours, 36 percent of the Bay State firms canvassed operated full-time in the week the survey was conducted. The latter percentage is from the Massachusetts survey as reported in various issues of *Monthly Review* (Federal Reserve Bank of Boston) for 1924.

44. *Report of Hearing*, 36.

45. See, for example, the testimony of one business representative in *Report of Hearing*, 36. This individual conceded at the same time that textile mills operating at night on a *permanent* basis could without difficulty find sufficient numbers of male workers to staff the late shift. For a similar comment on permanent night operations with male workers by another business witness, see *Report of Hearing*, 21.

46. As one union representative explained in 1928, "if there is a rush order comes into any of the mills in New Bedford, they put women on through the day, and then after the women are done men start on the machines. From the carding department to the spinning, the weaving, and all through every department the rush order is taken care of" (*Report of Hearing*, 76). In normal circumstances, a heavily female work force tended the carding and ring spinning machines.

47. *Report of Hearing*, 60, 69, 87.

48. The Federal Reserve Bank of Boston reported nighttime operations at textile firms in Lawrence and Fall River in late 1922 and early 1923. See *Monthly Review* (Federal Reserve Bank of Boston), January 1, 1923, 9, and February 1, 1923, 9; *Monthly Review*, March 1, 1923, 9. During a 1927 legislative debate over changes to the hours of work statutes, a proponent of the existing laws asserted that textile mills in Fall River were currently working overtime. See "Only Five Votes . . . ," March 18, 1927 clipping, CLM 29/499. These were both periods of high operation in the industry, suggesting that the late work taking place was not of lengthy duration.

49. Newspaper clippings in CLM 29/499 (for appearances before the legislature); *Before the Committee on Labor and Industry*; Thoron, "Handicaps of Northern Textile Mills"; *Problems of Eastern Cotton Manufacturers*.

50. See documents in Case 12/311-210-19, "New England Industries—Surveys—Cotton (1)" and box 12A/311-210-19, "New England Industries—Surveys—Cotton (3)," both in BCoC.

51. Merrimack was one of the oldest cotton manufacturers in Massachusetts. In the post–World War I era, its Lowell facility had a strong position in lucrative markets for several quality grades of fabric produced by a small number of U.S. companies, most located in the North. Information is not available on operating rates at the Lowell fabricating plant, but these rates can be inferred from reported data on levels of operation at the Merrimack finishing mill, which processed the cloth manufactured at the Lowell plant. After reaching or approaching full capacity several times during flush periods in the early 1920s, the finishing mill operated at around 50 percent of capacity for the rest of the decade, hitting a peak of at most 70 percent

of capacity during a boom in 1928. Capacity utilization at Merrimack's Lowell fabricating plant would have been at approximately these levels.

Consultants reported in the early 1930s that Merrimack's Lowell plant was much too large for current or probable future requirements. They also criticized the longstanding company policy of maintaining large inventories. Due to this practice, Merrimack had on hand at the end of 1928 an 8- to 10-month month supply of almost all lines of cloth despite an unprecedented volume of sales that year.

Taken together, this information demonstrates that the Bay State's hours of work laws did not constrain Merrimack's Lowell operations in the 1920s. Since it was operating far below capacity, the company could meet any surges in demand by hiring additional operatives for the existing 48-hour day shift. If even this step was not sufficient to accommodate requirements, the company could at any moment dip into the large inventories of fabric that were always on hand.

On all these points, see documents in Merrimack Manufacturing Company Records, box 45 and volumes 13, 47, 48, 61. In addition to manufacturing high quality cloth at the Lowell plant, Merrimack had since the 1890s produced coarser grades of cotton textiles at a facility in Alabama.

52. *Problems of Eastern Cotton Manufacturers*, 8–12, 15.

53. The question of hours of operations, fixed costs, and the effect on profits is discussed for the Massachusetts cotton industry as a whole at the beginning of this section of the chapter. In more prosperous times, Merrimack could theoretically try to make up the shortfall in running hours by hiring men only for part-time work on the late shift. It would be unwieldy to pursue such a system on an ongoing basis, however, and in a tighter labor market the necessary male employees might not be available.

54. A 1925 comment by Thoron to an official of the Boston Chamber of Commerce during the dispute over publication of the chamber's cotton textiles study provides additional evidence that the long run was the key factor in the mill manager's thinking. Explaining his determination to see Massachusetts amend the 48-hour law, Thoron asserted that "so long as our competitors are not restricted to a 48 hour week we feel this restriction in this State must *eventually* be fatal to us." See Thoron to Coonley, July 2, 1925, BCoC, Case 12/311-210-19, "New England Industries—Surveys—Cotton (1)," emphasis added. For a similar remark by another Bay State cotton manufacturer of this era, see *Report of Hearing*, 28.

55. The walkouts threatened by the UTW in 1919 as part of its push for the 48-hour week have been mentioned already. Workers at cotton mills in northeastern Massachusetts went on strike in 1922 to contest a pay cut (Tilden, "New England Textile Strike"). New Bedford operatives struck for six months in 1928 to oppose a wage reduction in that city (see "Is Wage Reduction the Best Way to Lower Costs?," *Factory and Industrial Management*, January 1929).

56. "Short Hours . . ." October 15, 1925 clipping, CLM 29/499; *AWCR*, October 27, 1927, 50.

57. *TW*, January 12, 1924, 31; June 2, 1926 letter to stockholders, page 2 in *Everett Mills*; *AWCR*, December 10, 1931, 37; Fisher letter to NACM members, February 20, 1934, NACM 6/68.

Even out-of-state industrialists got into the act. In a pamphlet issued in the 1930s, the Pennsylvania Manufacturers Association contended that heavy taxes and unreasonable labor laws had ruined the manufacturing sector of Massachusetts and needed to be avoided in Pennsylvania lest a similar fate befall the latter state. See Warren F. Doane, *The Flight of Capital and Industry from Massachusetts: Authoritative Facts and Official Figures Showing the Consequences of Unsound Taxation and Uneconomic Labor Legislation—In Decreased Employment, Diminished Wages and Increased Taxes* . . . (Philadelphia: Pennsylvania Manufacturers' Association, 1935).

58. Capacity calculated from statistics in June 2, 1926 letter to stockholders, page 1 in *Everett Mills*.

59. These assertions by industrialists had a counterpart in the repeated claims by labor that lack of investment and mismanagement were the key reasons for the downsizing of the industry in New England. For instance, one union witness at the 1928 hearing asserted that conditions in cotton would improve "when they get some proper management into the mills and modernize their mills," while a second attacked the companies' "watered capital" (*Report of Hearing*, 59–60, 65). Although certainly present among New England producers, underinvestment and mismanagement were secondary factors in the industry's decline. Numerous well-managed regional cotton firms with up-to-date equipment were forced out of business during the 1920s. (For more on this issue, see Koistinen, "Causes of Deindustrialization.") A key difference between the distortions of labor and those of capital regarding the demise of cotton manufacturing in Massachusetts is that the former had no direct implications for public policy, while the latter—in highlighting the supposed need to ease existing labor laws—emphatically did.

60. *Report of Hearing*, 75–76.

61. *Report of Hearing*, 62.

62. *Report of Hearing*, 72; on the Fall River wage cut, see "Is Wage Reduction the Best Way to Lower Costs?," *Factory and Industrial Management*, January 1929, 51–53.

63. *Report of Hearing*, 88, 90. As Massachusetts unionists probably recognized, the existing hours of work laws might *already* be having this effect. Due to current law, certain Bay State firms may have been losing some business by running a single shift of 48 hours rather than the 54 hours they would otherwise have operated. To the extent that the lost orders went to other, less competitive Massachusetts firms, the 48-hour law was serving to spread the available work around among a larger number of Bay State workers.

64. *Report of Hearing*, 87, 90.

65. "Only Five Votes . . . ," March 18, 1927 clipping in CLM 29/499, emphasis added on "organization of manufacturers"; *Report of Hearing*, 59.

66. *Report of Hearing*, 87, emphasis added.

67. Wiesman to Anderson, February 15, 1933, CLM 29/493.

68. "Bennett Weaves Gloom . . . ," Febuary 15, 1923 clipping, and "Says Mills May . . . ," February 6, 1924 clipping, both in CLM 29/499. In both cases the quotations are from journalists' summaries of the testimony.

69. *Report of Hearing*, 70–71.

70. *Report of Hearing*, 66–68.

71. *Report of Hearing*, 73–75.

72. *Report of Hearing*, 78–80.

73. *Industry*, November 25, 1933, 1, and December 8, 1934, 5–6, 8; *History of the Massa-*

chusetts State Federation, 91–92. Key changes in the early years of the program increased the level of payments from 50 percent to 66⅔ percent of the average weekly wage, extended the maximum duration of benefits from 300 to 500 weeks, and reduced the waiting time before the start of benefits from fifteen days to ten.

74. *Industry*, November 7, 1925, front cover; *Annual Report of . . . General Manager, Associated Industries of Massachusetts, 1930*, 75–76 (hereafter cited as *AIM GM*, with year).

75. Massachusetts Department of Labor and Industries, *Report of an Investigation as to the Causes of Existing Unemployment . . .* (January 1931); *Industry*, December 19, 1931, 1, and November 19, 1932, 1–4; *Industry*, December 2, 1933, 1–3, and December 8, 1934, 1–4.

76. See, for example, the booklet issued by employers groups in the industrial city of Taunton, in Sinclair Weeks Papers, 3/"Unemployment Reserves." Arguing against proposals for state unemployment insurance, the author of the pamphlet cited the experience of textiles and asserted that overly strict social legislation rendered commonwealth manufacturers uncompetitive, resulting in their liquidation.

77. *AIM GM 1927*, 156–58.

78. See Bernstein, *Lean Years*, especially chap. 2; Brody, *Workers in Industrial America*, chap. 2; Dubofsky, *State and Labor*, chap. 4.

79. Lichtenstein, *State of the Union*, chap. 1; Dubofsky, *State and Labor*, chap. 5; Brody, *Workers in Industrial America*, chap. 3.

80. Commonwealth of Massachusetts, *Report of the Special Commission Appointed to Investigate the Entire Subject of State, County and Local Taxation . . .* (December 1927), 13–17 (hereafter cited as *Mass Tax 1927*); *Industry*, November 26, 1927, 1; statement of the legislature's committee on taxation, April 28, 1930, page 3, Massachusetts Legislative Documents 1930 (House, No. 1324); National Industrial Conference Board, *Fiscal Problem*, 68–69. Tax and spending amounts for 1916 and 1926 are directly comparable since the purchasing power of the dollar was nearly identical in these two years.

81. *Mass Tax 1927*, 14–17; *Taxation and Public Expenditure*, 6.

82. National Association of Cotton Manufacturers, "An Analysis of Taxes Paid by Cotton Mills," *Transactions of the National Association of Cotton Manufacturers*, nos. 122 and 123 (meetings of May and October 1927), 313–14, 325.

83. Fall River figures in the text and this note calculated from statistics in Donahue, *Causes of the Financial Breakdown*, 32.

Fall River cotton mill assessments rose 134 percent between 1917 and 1921. Over the same period, assessments on nontextile corporate property rose from $17.8 million to $32.4 million (an increase of 82 percent) while assessments on individually owned property rose from $49.5 million to $59.1 million (a gain of 19 percent). City assessors were clearly milking corporations, especially the large textile firms, to shield the city's small property owners from tax increases.

84. Donahue, *Causes of the Financial Breakdown*, 6, 17–18, 25–28; U.S. House, Committee on Labor, *To Rehabilitate and Stabilize*, 148. It is likely that one reason Fall River officials raised mill assessments so dramatically at this time is that they believed the companies could afford to pay. World War I and the years just afterward were a highly profitable time in the cotton industry due to enormous demand during and just after the conflict and rising prices for raw cotton in the early 1920s that produced dramatic, if unsustainable, profits (see Koistinen, "Causes of

Deindustrialization," 495, 502). By inflating assessments on the textile mills, Fall River leaders were able to finance expansions in government services while limiting increases in the taxes on individually owned, primarily residential property.

Fall River had to borrow the $1 million to finance the tax refunds ordered by the courts in 1925. The burden of this debt, together with questionable fiscal practices and the shrinkage of the city's tax base due to widespread cotton mill closures in the ensuing years, precipitated the city into bankruptcy in 1930. The result was harsh cuts in spending and state supervision of city finances for years to come. See Donahue, *Causes of the Financial Breakdown*, especially 3–13.

85. National Association of Cotton Manufacturers, "An Analysis of Taxes Paid," 319.

86. *AIM GM 1923*, 29–31; Hennessey, *Four Decades of Massachusetts Politics*, 309, 356.

87. *Industry*, January 22, 1927, 1, and November 12, 1927, 1; *Industry*, November 26, 1927, 1.

88. *Taxation and Public Expenditure*; *Report of Mr. John F. Tinsley*.

89. The state government's excise tax on corporations included a levy on corporate income that was straightforward and uncontroversial and a tax on companies' capital stock, or "corporate excess," that was fiendishly complex and produced constant disputes between firms and the state tax commissioner over the amount due. The state tax on personal incomes had a wide range of rates that varied according to the source, rather than the amount, of income and took no account of the ability to pay. Sources on the Massachusetts tax system of the 1920s include National Industrial Conference Board, *Fiscal Problem,* and the reports of the special legislative commissions on taxation cited later.

90. Inequities in the tax system remained a prominent political issue in Massachusetts for decades after World War II and eventually fed support for the tax-slashing Proposition 2½ of 1980.

91. *Transactions of the National Association of Cotton Manufacturers*, nos. 122 and 123, 296–98, 312; National Association of Cotton Manufacturers, "An Analysis of Taxes Paid," 313–15, 318.

92. "To The Special Commission to Revise the Laws of the Commonwealth Relative to Taxation . . . Suggestions of the Merrimack Manufacturing Company . . . ," undated, NACM 184/2280; *Mass Tax 1927*, 34; Thomas Smith, *Cotton Textile Industry*, 156–58.

93. *AIM GM 1927*, 96.

94. *Mass Tax 1927*, 34–35.

95. This paragraph is based on *Mass Tax 1927*, 10–11, 16–17; *Industry*, November 19, 1927, 1, and November 26, 1927, 2; *AWCR*, January 19, 1928, 52.

96. The public school systems in Massachusetts and other New England states during this period were patronage-controlled jobs machines that drove up municipal budgets.

97. Commonwealth of Massachusetts, *Final Report of the Special Commission Established to Investigate Municipal Expenditures and Undertakings* . . . (1929), 14–22.

98. Commonwealth of Massachusetts, *Report of the Special Commission . . . State, County and Local Taxation* . . . (December 1929); April 28, 1930 statement of the legislature's committee on taxation, Massachusetts Legislative Documents 1930 (House, No. 1324); Commonwealth of Massachusetts, *Report of the Special Commission . . . State, County, and Local Taxation* . . . (December 1930), 3.

99. *AWCR*, December 11, 1930, 51; Freeland, Bates & Lawrence, *Brief Study of Industrial*

Massachusetts, 6; *New England News Letter* (hereafter cited as *NENL*), second January issue, 1932, 3; Commonwealth of Massachusetts, *Report of the Special Commission . . . State, County, and Local Taxation . . .* (December 1930), 4–6; *NENL*, second January issue, 1932, 1; *NENL*, first March issue, 1932, 6; *NENL*, August 1932, 2–3; *Policy of the Massachusetts Division*, 5, 14; Commonwealth of Massachusetts, *Report of the Special Commission . . . Changes in the Tax Laws . . .* (January 1932), 7, 9.

100. Commonwealth of Massachusetts, *Report of the Special Commission . . . Changes in the Tax Laws . . .* (January 1932), 9–10, 13, 16–17; *Public Officials of Massachusetts* (1931–32), 147.

101. *BG*, March 1, 1932, 17.

102. I estimate that the 1.95 million Fall River spindles still in place in 1932 had an assessed value in 1926 of at least $44.9 million. By contrast, the assessment on these spindles in 1932 was $17.0 million. A later study of Fall River finances reported the individual assessments on seven city mills for the years 1926 and 1932. Of the seven, the company receiving the smallest proportional reduction between the two years saw its valuation fall by 59 percent. See Donahue, *Causes of the Financial Breakdown*, 33; percentage drop is my calculation.

103. *AIM GM 1927*, 97; Wolfbein, *Decline of a Cotton Textile City*, 137–40; *Industry*, January 22, 1927, 6, and February 11, 1928, 5.

104. The reduction in tax revenue from textile firms produced fiscal stress even as municipalities cut expenditures and sharply increased taxes on other mill town property owners. At some point during the 1920s and 1930s, Lowell, Fall River, and New Bedford all had to borrow against future revenue to keep up with current expenses. The finances of each city ended up under some form of state supervision. See Parker, *Lowell*, 5–6; Municipal Securities Service, "Special Report: The Financial Condition of the City of Lowell, Mass. . . . ," February 24, 1932, and statement of Arthur T. Safford, September 10, 1932, both in Flather/Boott Mills Collection, "Emphemera" boxes, "General Financial Condition/Statistics, etc." folder; Thomas Smith, *Cotton Textile Industry*, 159; Donahue, *Causes of the Financial Breakdown*, especially 3–13; Wolfbein, *Decline of a Cotton Textile City*, 138.

105. Fisher to all Massachusetts Mills, March 2, 1936, NACM 9/107; Commonwealth of Massachusetts, *Report of the Special Commission Relative to Taxation of Tangible and Intangible Property . . .* (January 1936), 5–6.

106. *BG*, January 15, 1936, 8; Fisher to all Massachusetts Mills, March 2, 1936, NACM 9/107.

107. The tax rate figures (which are rounded) are for American Thread plants in both cities. They appear in the table "Machinery Tax on Massachusetts Cotton Mills, 1935 Valuations," June 12, 1936, NACM 9/107.

108. *Business Week*, June 27, 1936, 18. Higher local rates would also increase the levies paid by manufacturers on their real estate, which remained subject to local taxation. This would negate a portion of the tax relief that had just been granted. Manufacturers would nevertheless come out far ahead under the revised system.

109. *Business Week*, June 27, 1936, 18; *MA AFL 1936*, 44; Steele to all Massachusetts mills, supplement to bulletins of March 2nd and 4th, March 19, 1936, NACM 9/107; *BG*, March 25, 1936, 21. For Long's previous advocacy of local tax reduction, see *Industry*, November 19, 1927, 3, and *TW*, October 10, 1931, 42.

110. Figures from *Mass Stats Manufrs 1920–1938*; Commonwealth of Massachusetts, *Report*

of the Special Commission Relative to Taxation of Tangible and Intangible Property . . . (January 1936), 5.

111. Vogel, *Fluctuating Fortunes*, 8.

112. Wolfbein, *Decline of a Cotton Textile City*, 140–41. In Massachusetts as a whole, despite reduced local textile mill assessments and the 1936 exemption of textile and other manufacturing machinery from local property taxes, cotton goods employment fell from 98,900 in 1925 to 44,700 in 1936 and 38,900 in 1939. Figures for the earlier years include cotton small wares and are calculated from numbers in *Mass Stats Manufrs 1920-1938*, 9. The 1939 figure is from *Mass Dept Comm*, 81.

113. The mill engineer cited earlier in this chapter estimated in 1926 that production costs of a northern mill producing medium-grade goods would be $24.00 per spindle per year, excluding the cost of buying and transporting materials. Of this amount, taxes were estimated at $0.75 per spindle per year, 3.1 percent of the total. See Chas. T. Main, Engineer, "Status of the Cotton Textile Industry in the United States," February 24, 1926, pages 22–23, in BCoC, box 12A/311-210-19, "New England Industries—Surveys—Cotton (3)." Computations by an official of the Pacific Mills of Lawrence, Massachusetts in 1938 showed taxes accounting for 2.8 percent of total costs. See Pacific Mills controller to Fisher, October 20, 1938, NACM 11/125. The tax figure in both cases presumably included federal levies on corporate income as well as state and local taxes.

Production costs at Dixie plants were generally about 15 percent lower than at northern mills, with most of the advantage stemming from the South's cheaper labor. For comparative statistics on manufacturing costs in New England and the South, see Koistinen, "Causes of Deindustrialization," 501.

Chapter 3. Federal Assistance

1. Galambos, *Competition and Cooperation*, 40–42, 89–92, 133–37; Kennedy, *Profits and Losses in Textiles*, 126–28, 252.
2. Galambos, *Competition and Cooperation*, 11–112.
3. Galambos, *Competition and Cooperation*, 106–7, 119–38.
4. On associationalism, see Joan Hoff Wilson, *Herbert Hoover,* and Hawley, *Great War.*
5. Galambos, *Competition and Cooperation*, 102–3, 114–15, 125–26, 128–30.
6. Galambos, *Competition and Cooperation*, 139–75.
7. Galambos, *Competition and Cooperation*, 157–61.
8. Galambos, *Competition and Cooperation*, 161–62.
9. Galambos, *Competition and Cooperation*, 105, 115, 151. Statistics from the early 1920s cited in the previous chapter demonstrate that certain Massachusetts cotton producers operated full schedules even when the Bay State textile industry as a whole fared poorly. Such firms may have accounted for much of the nonconformer element of the North.
10. Galambos, *Competition and Cooperation*, 177, including footnote.
11. Galambos, *Competition and Cooperation*, 178–88; Colin Gordon, *New Deals*, 167–70; Vittoz, *New Deal Labor Policy*, 78–92; Himmelberg, *Origins of the National Recovery Administration*, 181–212.
12. Hawley, *New Deal and the Problem of Monopoly*, 31–32.

13. Galambos, *Competition and Cooperation*, 179–98; *Labor and Industries 1933*, 6; Himmelberg, *Origins of the National Recovery Administration*, 189.

14. This and the following paragraph are based on Galambos, *Competition and Cooperation*, 204–26, and Hodges, *New Deal Labor Policy*, 50–55.

15. Hodges, *New Deal Labor Policy*, 55–57; *Labor and Industries 1933*, 5.

16. Hodges, *New Deal Labor Policy*, 56; Vittoz, *New Deal Labor Policy*, 122.

17. Increases in average wages are in nominal terms and are calculated from data sheets, both dated March 6, 1935, in NACM 3/30 and 6/58. Differentials from Hinrichs, "Historical Review," 1173.

18. On machine hours, see Hodges, *New Deal Labor Policy*, 57, and Vittoz, *New Deal Labor Policy*, 123.

19. Hodges, *New Deal Labor Policy*, 56–58, 89; Galambos, *Competition and Cooperation*, 248–50, 284, 286; Vittoz, *New Deal Labor Policy*, 125–26. A shortfall in demand necessitated these steps. In the midst of a deep depression, national markets could not absorb the quantity of goods the country's cotton mills could turn out operating 80 hours per week.

20. *NYT*, March 3, 1935, sect. 4, 6; Hodges, *New Deal Labor Policy*, 133–34.

21. On the lackadaisical response of the Bruere Board to code violations involving workloads and union organizing (discussed later in the chapter), see Hodges, *New Deal Labor Policy*, 62–72.

22. *NYT*, July 10, 1933, 3; *NYT*, July 17, 1933, 1, and July 18, 1933, 13; U.S. House, Committee on Labor, *To Rehabilitate and Stabilize*, 66, 73; "Suggested Basis for Establishing Minimum Wages by Groups," undated, NACM 3/31. Union leaders charged that one method by which management evaded the rule on wage differentials was to reclassify workers into skill categories slated to receive lower increases in pay, although there was no change in the actual work performed.

23. See, for example, the July 25, 1933, agreement between these parties in NACM 3/31.

24. When the New England industry was heavily unionized after World War II, varying wage formulas applied to companies in different parts of the region. A Fall River–New Bedford wage formula covered firms in southeastern New England while the North-Textron formula applied to companies in the northern Massachusetts–New Hampshire–Maine area. See documents in Edith Nourse Rogers Papers, 14/181.

25. Hall et al., *Like a Family*, 186–96, 212–19; English, *Common Thread*, chaps. 5, 6.

26. Hall et al., *Like a Family*, 289–304; Hodges, *New Deal Labor Policy*, 61.

27. Hall et al., *Like a Family*, 304–9; Hodges, *New Deal Labor Policy*, 54–55, 61–62, 72.

28. Hodges, *New Deal Labor Policy*, 96–118; Hall et al., *Like a Family*, 328–52.

The early to mid-1930s saw one other initiative that, if successful, might have helped stabilize conditions in cotton textiles. This was an attempt to get various states to harmonize their labor laws at a uniformly high level of protection. Efforts focused on concluding interstate compacts guaranteeing that strong existing labor regulations would remain in place. Massachusetts spearheaded the drive for interstate labor law compacts. The campaign drew considerable support in the Northeast and in some other parts of the country, and advocates hoped to draw in southern states as well. The initiative encountered significant technical and political difficulties and eventually fizzled out. See Koistinen, "Dealing with Deindustrialization," 158–65.

29. On the dramatic growth in union power during the 1930s, see Lichtenstein, *Most Dangerous Man in Detroit*, chaps. 4–7; Dubofsky, *State and Labor*, chaps. 5–6; Stebenne, *Arthur J. Goldberg*, 11–19, 25–29; Stebenne, "IBM's 'New Deal,'" 55.

30. Galambos, *Competition and Cooperation*, 288–89.

31. Francis Gorman entry in Fink, *Biographical Dictionary*, 259–60; Hodges, *New Deal Labor Policy*, 98–106.

32. Henry Ellenbogen entry in Stone, *Congressional Minyan*, 96–98.

33. The account of the drafting of the Ellenbogen legislation in this and the following paragraph is based on UTW Executive Council minutes, June 12, 1935 meeting, page 1028, July 25, 1935 meeting, page 1030, September 13, 1935 meeting, pages 33–34, in Textile Workers Union of America Papers, Third Installment, 674/"UTW Executive Council, 1935–1936"; "Proceedings of the Twenty-Fourth Annual Convention, American Federation of Hosiery Workers" (July 1935), 52–54, box 6, folder 1, and "Proceedings of the Twenty-Fifth Annual Convention" (April 1936), 54–55, box 7, folder 2, both in American Federation of Hosiery Workers Records, Part II; *NYT*, July 20, 1935, 24, and July 27, 1935, 24; *NYT*, November 22, 1936, sect. 2, 4; Vittoz, *New Deal Labor Policy*, 130.

34. Despite its conservatism, the UTW was an industrial union that sought to organize all of the country's textile workers, whatever their ethnicity or level of skill.

35. The text of the bill appears in U.S. House, Committee on Labor, *To Rehabilitate and Stabilize*, 1–15; the emphasis in the quotation is added.

36. U.S. House, Committee on Labor, *To Rehabilitate and Stabilize*, quotation on 15; *NYT*, December 8, 1935, sect. 2, 4, and March 1, 1936, 32.

37. U.S. House, Committee on Labor, *To Rehabilitate and Stabilize*, 89–161, 295–308, 535–40.

38. U.S. House, Committee on Labor, *To Rehabilitate and Stabilize*, 160.

39. U.S. House, Committee on Labor, *To Rehabilitate and Stabilize*, 239–42.

40. U.S. House, Committee on Labor, *To Rehabilitate and Stabilize*, 218–19, 224–26, 232, 582–85, 588–89.

41. U.S. House, Committee on Labor, *To Rehabilitate and Stabilize*, 244–48.

42. Its leaders tried to portray this organization as including all types of southern manufacturers, but it seems clear that the group actually represented the sort of marginal, semi-rural firms that made up much of the "chiseler" element in textiles. See, for example, U.S. Senate, Committee on Education and Labor, *Fair Labor Standards Act of 1937*, 781.

43. U.S. House, Committee on Labor, *To Rehabilitate and Stabilize*, 32–33, 488, 398, 528.

44. U.S. House, Committee on Labor, *To Rehabilitate and Stabilize*, 406, 408–9, 422.

45. This paragraph is based on U.S. House, Committee on Labor, *To Rehabilitate and Stabilize*, 95–97, 106–7, 453–63, 750–54; Paulsen, *Living Wage for the Forgotten Man*, 98.

46. The manager of the (unionized) New Bedford cotton mill who represented the NACM at the hearing critiqued the Ellenbogen proposal on numerous points. He charged that the government commission that would enforce the law would be overly bureaucratic and might disrupt established relations between management and the New Bedford unions. He claimed that by raising wages, the measure would expose American textile producers to new competition from low-wage manufacturers in Japan and other countries. He also complained about a host of secondary issues, including regulations on the use of aged workers, a ban on employee fines,

provisions that discouraged layoffs, and charges on manufacturers for the expense of policing the new rules. See U.S. House, Committee on Labor, *To Rehabilitate and Stabilize*, 453–63.

The following year, New England cotton manufacturers opposed with equal determination the original 1937 version of the Fair Labor Standards Act (FLSA). The proposal, which is discussed later in the chapter, would have affected the cotton industry in the same way as the Ellenbogen bill. The president of the NACM feared that the commission administering the FLSA regulations would "be appointed for political reasons" and "subject to political pressure" and that this body would have "very broad powers," including authority "to set all wages." See "Memorandum: Fair Labor Standards Act," May 28, 1937, NACM 9/112; Fisher to All Members, May 26, 1937, NACM 9/113; Fisher to All Northern Mills, June 1, 1937, NACM 9/113.

47. U.S. House, Committee on Labor, *To Rehabilitate and Stabilize*, various pages.

48. *NYT*, March 12, 1936, 8; U.S. House, *National Textile Bill*, 2, 5, 9. Among employers, only silk and rayon manufacturers endorsed the rewritten proposal. Particularly brutal competition had emerged in this industry as tiny family-run operations challenged established producers. Those realities probably accounted for the support from that sector's industrialists, which was in any case half-hearted. See *Business Week*, April 25, 1936, 16–17.

49. U.S. House, *National Textile Bill*, 12.

50. *NYT*, November 10, 1936, 13, and November 22, 1936, sect. 2, 4; *NYT*, May 21, 1937, 14, and May 22, 1937, 1.

51. See, for example, the exultant tone of the speeches in *Wage and Hour Legislation in Action*.

52. Paulsen, *Living Wage for the Forgotten Man*, 30–33, 54–55; Vittoz, *New Deal Labor Policy*, 82–87.

53. Paulsen, *Living Wage for the Forgotten Man*, 53–62, 64–65, 68; Schulman, *From Cotton Belt to Sunbelt*, 255, note 44; *Public Papers and Addresses of Franklin D. Roosevelt* (1936), 5:505, 624–26, and (1937), 6:118.

54. Stories by Arthur Krock in *NYT*, June 4, 1937, 22, and June 13, 1937, 3.

55. Paulsen, *Living Wage for the Forgotten Man*, 65–75.

56. This and the following paragraph are based on *American National Biography*, 5:159–60, 502–4; Kennedy, *Freedom from Fear*, 353–54; Paulsen, *Living Wage for the Forgotten Man*, 39–40.

57. Paulsen, *Living Wage for the Forgotten Man*, 39, 71, 75–79. On Justice Department support for regulation of the labor standards of some workers above the legally fixed minimums, see "Report on Legislative Drafting Project," undated memo from Walter Pope to Solicitor General Reed, pages 10–11, in Paulsen Justice Department Materials.

58. U.S. Senate, Committee on Education and Labor, *Fair Labor Standards Act of 1937*, 47.

59. Cummings diary, entries for April 15 and April 20, 1937, Homer Cummings Papers, box 235; "Report on Legislative Drafting," 11, Paulsen Justice Department Materials; Paulsen, *Living Wage for the Forgotten Man*, 74–75.

60. Paulsen, *Living Wage for the Forgotten Man*, 76–78.

61. "Proposed Fair Labor Standards Act of 1937," undated memo with notation "Ben Cohen's explanation of May 20 draft of Labor Bill," in Paulsen Justice Department Materials; *NYT*, June 13, 1937, 3.

62. U.S. Senate, Committee on Education and Labor, *Fair Labor Standards Act of 1937*, 155–72, 943–48; Paulsen, *Living Wage for the Forgotten Man*, 87, 89.

Sidney Hillman saw the Fair Labor Standards Act as a key element of a multi-pronged political and organizing effort that would transform the South; see Fraser, *Labor Will Rule*, chap. 14, especially 377–78. The bill's provisions for regulating wages above the minimum make Hillman's enthusiasm for the measure fully understandable.

63. Paulsen, *Living Wage for the Forgotten Man*, 70–71, 75–77, 79–80, 83, 85–87, 91; *NYT*, May 27, 1937, 4.

64. Paulsen, *Living Wage for the Forgotten Man*, 83.

65. U.S. Senate, Committee on Education and Labor, *Fair Labor Standards Act of 1937*, Edgerton and Murchison testimony; documents in NACM, 9/112 and 9/113. Quotations are from NACM bulletin, June 1, 1937, NACM 9/113, and statement of resolutions approved at meeting of northern mills, June 7, 1937, NACM 9/112.

66. Paulsen, *Living Wage for the Forgotten Man*, 88; U.S. Senate, Committee on Education and Labor, *Fair Labor Standards Act of 1937*, 751–80, 807–15.

67. Paulsen, *Living Wage for the Forgotten Man*, 72–74, 83, 90–91; Leuchtenburg, *Franklin D. Roosevelt*, 231–39.

68. *NYT*, June 9, 1937, 4; Paulsen, *Living Wage for the Forgotten Man*, 91–130; Leuchtenburg, *Franklin D. Roosevelt*, 261–62.

69. Hodges, *New Deal Labor Policy*, 180–88; documents in NACM 11/126; Hartford, *Where Is Our Responsibility?*, 83–84; Schulman, *From Cotton Belt to Sunbelt*, 68–72.

70. On the successful CIO-led organizing push in northern textiles that began in 1937, see Hartford, *Where Is Our Responsibility?*, 59–86, and Fraser, *Labor Will Rule*, 380–87.

71. For a fuller account, including citations, of TWUA efforts to raise southern wages through government action during and just after World War II, see Koistinen, "Dealing with Deindustrialization," 194–200. The National War Labor Board case is also described in Hartford, *Where Is Our Responsibility?*, 84–86.

72. Zelizer, *On Capitol Hill*, chap. 2.

73. This and the following paragraphs on organizing efforts in the post–World War II South are based on Minchin, *Fighting against the Odds*, 38–71, 127–33. See also Minchin, *What Do We Need*.

74. The North-South wage differential in textiles narrowed markedly over time, although it continued to exist. In cotton textiles, the differential was 39 percent in mid-1933, before the imposition of the NIRA cotton code; 18 percent in 1934, with the cotton code in place; 12 percent during World War II; and less than 10 percent in the late 1940s. See Hinrichs, "Historical Review," 1173; Hartford, *Where Is Our Responsibility?*, 95, 114. Adding to the labor-cost gap between employers in the two regions were employer-financed social welfare programs controlled at the state level, such as unemployment insurance. Benefits and employer taxes in these programs were generally higher in the North than in the South. See Koistinen, "Public Policies for Countering Deindustrialization," 331–32.

75. Hartford, *Where Is Our Responsibility?*, chaps. 5, 6; Morris, *Woolen and Worsted Manufacturing*. Woolen producers had long been plagued by stagnant demand and likely feared that low-cost southern textile manufacturers would enter their industry. These factors may have contributed to the postwar exodus from the North of established woolen producers.

76. Fixing prices for final cotton goods would not work because these constantly fluctuated

with the cost of raw cotton, which accounts for a significant share of the expense of the finished product. Allocating market shares would be difficult in an industry with so many producers.

77. The United Mine Workers (UMW) had since the late nineteenth century been an important presence in the bituminous coal mines of the North. The union made significant inroads in the newer coal areas that arose in the Appalachian South. Fierce employer opposition devastated most southern and many northern locals in the 1920s, but the UMW engineered a dramatic rebound in 1933. With many southern and almost all northern operators facing strong union representation, unionized firms in both regions sought to control the threat of low-price coal from the industry's marginal, non-union mines, located principally in the South. After the demise of the NIRA, associations of large employers in the two regions cooperated with the UMW to push through a "little NRA" for coal, the Guffey Act of 1935. The bill permitted price fixing, contained protections for collective bargaining, and made it possible to impose union wage scales on non-union producers. The Supreme Court ruled the act unconstitutional the following year because of the taxation system by which it was enforced. Department of Justice officials and Senator Guffey then huddled in Washington with representatives of the principal operators and the UMW and had equally effective replacement legislation before Congress within 48 hours. That measure won congressional approval in early 1937. Neither the revised Guffey Act nor the later unionization of virtually all northern and southern producers was sufficient to stabilize fully conditions in bituminous coal. This was largely due to declining demand for the industry's product. See Vittoz, *New Deal Labor Policy*, 112–18; *NYT*, May 21, 1936, 1.

78. *NYT*, March 3, 1935, sect. IV, 6, and April 13, 1935, 6; *NENL*, April 1935, 4–5. The threat of Japanese imports was only resolved in 1937 when, after lengthy negotiations, a voluntary export restraint agreement was concluded with Japanese manufacturers. See *NYT*, January 10, 1937, 41, and January 22, 1937, 36; *NYT*, December 20, 1938, 46. The accord was the first in what would be a decades-long string of such agreements with low-cost Asian producers in textiles and other industries.

Chapter 4. Economic Development

1. On the distinction between the old and new approaches to economic development, see Eisinger, *Rise of the Entrepreneurial State*, and also Fosler, *New Economic Role*, Graham, *Losing Time*, 191–201, Fosler, "Does Economic Theory Capture." Scholars of economic development have more recently discerned a "third wave" of state growth-promotion policies, succeeding the first wave of smokestack chasing and the second-wave entrepreneurial approach. The third wave emphasizes encouraging the expansion of entire industrial sectors, rather than individual firms, and on using the ensemble of state economic policies to accomplish this goal. (See, for example, Bradshaw and Blakely, "What Are.") The third wave has much in common with the second and is a logical extension of the development strategy pursued in New England decades before.

2. Gregory Wilson, "'Our Chronic and Desperate Situation'"; McKee, "Urban Deindustrialization"; Friedman, "Communities in Competition," chap. 4; Gillette, *Camden after the Fall*; Dublin and Licht, *Face of Decline*, chap. 5; O'Mara, *Cities of Knowledge*, chap. 4; Heathcott and Murphy, "Corridors of Flight." O'Mara and Heathcott and Murphy explore attempts in

Philadelphia and Saint Louis to develop technology-intensive new industries to replace jobs lost in traditional manufacturing. Those endeavors most closely resemble the New England growth-promotion efforts examined here.

3. Dublin and Licht highlight the role of private-sector actors, including local chambers of commerce and a utility provider, in redevelopment efforts in the Pennsylvania anthracite region; see *Face of Decline*, chap. 5.

4. Leavitt, "Textile Manufacturers"; Richter, "Philadelphia College of Textiles and Science"; Copeland, *Cotton Manufacturing Industry*, 135.

5. This and the following paragraph are based on Blewett, *To Enrich and to Serve*, 31–34, and James Smith, "Our Textile School."

6. Bennett to Crawford, August 8, 1939, Lowell Technological Institute Collection, 64/"Bennett, Howard."

7. Copeland, *Cotton Manufacturing Industry*, 136–37; Blewett, *To Enrich and To Serve*, 33, 36; Merrill, "History of the Lowell Technological Institute," 83, 85–87, 92; MIT press release, October 4, 1949, Massachusetts Institute of Technology, Office of the President, 1930–59 Records (hereafter cited as MIT-OP), 140/6. A 1918 amendment to the Massachusetts constitution banned all government funding of private educational institutions, jeopardizing the state subsidies the textile schools received. (The amendment aimed at ending public support for parochial education; its effect on the textile schools was inadvertent.) Keeping the textile schools operating in these circumstances necessitated a public takeover, with the state providing all subsequent funding.

8. Merrill, "History of the Lowell Technological Institute," 90–91; Blewett, *To Enrich and to Serve*, 71. The use of specialized education to strengthen the textile industry of the Northeast was soon copied by competing states in the South. Between 1898 and 1905, colleges in the Carolinas, Georgia, Mississippi, and Texas opened departments of textile studies. These programs developed more slowly than their equivalents to the North, however, and southern manufacturers seem initially to have been less supportive than their northern counterparts (Copeland, *Cotton Manufacturing Industry*, 138–39). Higher education was thus another area in which the regional divergence in the industry manifested itself, as southern textile manufacturers focused on low labor costs while northerners emphasized training, research, and quality.

9. Although the New England Council was the region's key private-sector growth-promotion organization during the interwar period, other private groups were active as well. The Boston Chamber of Commerce remained concerned with development issues, especially increasing New England's foreign trade and improving the Port of Boston. Local chambers of commerce spearheaded efforts to bring new manufacturing into cities hit by plant closures. State manufacturers' associations also had a role. A principal goal of the Associated Industries of Massachusetts (AIM) was limiting the cost of production by seeking cutbacks in social legislation and business taxes. But AIM also took active programmatic steps that promoted the growth of the industrial economy (while advancing the interests of its members). The organization worked to increase the use of research by industrial firms; organized a conference on the use of style in marketing industrial products; hosted exhibits of quality Massachusetts manufactures; and coordinated with area colleges and universities to improve the training of future corporate managers. On AIM's activities, see *Industry*, February 9, 1924, 1–3, and Febru-

ary 16, 1924, 1–4; *NENL*, March 25, 1927; *AIM GM 1927*, 161–62; *AIM GM 1930*, 40–41. AIM, the Boston Chamber of Commerce, and many other New England business organizations had institutional memberships in the New England Council.

10. On business associations in general, an important study is Galambos, *Competition and Cooperation*.

11. On the broad scope of this group's activities, see Boston Chamber of Commerce, *The Boston Chamber*.

12. Boston's industrial sector saw a drop-off in output in the years preceding World War I, even as manufacturing flourished in the broader metropolitan area and in the state as a whole. In response, the Boston Chamber set up an Industrial Development Corporation to invest in promising but cash-strapped small companies in the city and an Industrial Development Board to aid manufacturers confronting logistical and regulatory difficulties and to publicize Boston's economic advantages. The organizations operated for only a few years. See documents in BCoC, Case 51/335-1 and 335-4; Boston Industrial Development Board, *Boston: The Place*.

13. Chamber President to members of the Massachusetts legislature, February 20, 1915, BCoC, Case 51/334-19; French, *New England*; All New England Week, Boston City Committee statement, March 3, 1925, BCoC, Case 72/364-100-1.

14. On the frivolous activities of the Massachusetts State Chamber of Commerce in mid-1924, as the region first experienced sharp employment losses in textiles and shoes, see Stacy to Cox, June 5, 1924, in Governor Channing Cox Correspondence. The general secretary of the Massachusetts Chamber was a member of the New England Council, but the Bay State organization and its officers played an insignificant role in virtually all the economic development activities described in this chapter.

15. "New England's Industries," June 1923 draft memorandum, BCoC, Case 12/311-210-1.

16. "Rousing New England Interest in New England Industry," Coonley speech excerpt and statement of Chamber's directors and past officers attached to November 17, 1923 letter, BCoC, Case 12/311-210-1.

17. "Committee on New England Industries," April 12, 1926, BCoC, Case 12/311-210-2.

18. Titles include Boston Chamber of Commerce, *Shoe Manufacturing Industry*, *Cotton Manufacturing Industry*, and *Foundry and Machining Industries*.

19. "Report of the Special Committee of the Committee on Commercial and Industrial Affairs," May 19, 1924, and Vice President's letter, May 26, 1924, both in BCoC, Case 72/364-100-1.

20. Fragmentary biographical information on Lawrence appears in *Who Was Who in America*, 6:241; *BG* obituary, December 17, 1973, 32; *AWCR*, March 13, 1924, 16; and *Who's Who in the New England Council*, 3. A Boston Chamber of Commerce official described Lawrence as "one of the leading businessmen of Boston" (McKibben to Mead, June 29, 1924, BCoC Case 72/364-100-2). His role in regional development efforts brought Lawrence considerable prominence. In the late 1920s he served on President Hoover's Committee on Recent Economic Changes and wrote articles for national publications.

21. On the Brahmins, see Amory, *Proper Bostonians*, and the Boston chapter in Jaher, *Urban Establishment*.

22. Kennedy, *Profits and Losses in Textiles*, 20–26, 30–39; November 9, 1929 *Daily News*

Record clipping filed with the finding aid to the Lawrence and Company collection (MSS 761), Baker Library Historical Collections, Harvard Business School, Boston, Mass.

23. Undated letter from J. S. Lawrence, and letter "To the All New England Week Committee," June 23, 1924, Governor Channing Cox Correspondence; Cox to Proctor, June 23, 1924, and Watson to Cox, August 5, 1924, Governor Channing Cox Correspondence; *Addresses before the Stockholders of Federal Reserve Bank*, 9; *TW*, September 27, 1924, 31–35.

24. Watson to McKibben, October 4, 1924, and Lawrence memorandum, January 27, 1925, both in BCoC, Case 72/364-100-1.

25. On the fears of organizations in outlying areas, see Wheeler, *New England Council*, 8–9, 11, 14.

26. The sources consulted do not conclusively establish—but do very strongly suggest—that individuals in the corporate sector arranged *beforehand* for the New England governors to call at their 1925 conference for the area's business leaders to establish an organization that would address the region's economic problems. See All New England Week, Boston City Committee statement, March 3, 1925, BCoC, Case 72/364-100-1; *Opening Remarks of President James W. Hook*, 1; New England Council, *New England Today*, 4–5; Wheeler, *New England Council*, 9.

27. "The New England Conference," September 12, 1925, address by George B. Chandler, BCoC Case 79/710-"New England Council"-1.

28. *New England Council: Objectives*, 5, emphasis added. The creation in 1922 of the Joint New England Railroad Committee (Storrow Committee) provided a model of cooperative regional action and may have helped lay the groundwork for the New England Council. Each New England governor appointed members to this body, which examined railroad policy and recommended action to deal with the weak finances of the area's leading rail carriers. See *Report of the Joint New England Railroad Committee*.

29. On associationalism, see Joan Hoff Wilson, *Herbert Hoover*, and Hawley, *Great War*.

30. "The New England Conference." There are several possible explanations for the radically decentralized structure New England business leaders originally envisaged for the new body. Such an arrangement could be useful in persuading less powerful groups that the organization would not be dominated by leading industries and Boston-based interests. The longstanding antipathy of New Englanders to centralized authority of any kind may have been a factor. The political aspirations of business associationalists might also have come into play. Private-sector leaders such as Lawrence may have believed that the privileged position of the era's business groups in formulating social and economic policy could be consolidated by making the centralized decision making of the corporate world somewhat more open and representative.

31. "The New England Conference," 3.

32. This and the next paragraph are based on *NYT*, November 12, 1925, 10; *BG*, November 13, 1925, 32; *BG*, November 14, 1925, 12.

33. New England Council, *1930 Blue Book*, 14–15.

34. Wheeler, *New England Council*, 13–14; Frederick Steele Blackall III interview, February 26, 1996; Hook to Hudson, December 2, 1936, James William Hook Papers, 39/"Letters NEC," section "H" (on the budget).

35. New England Council, *1930 Blue Book*, 16–17.

36. *National Cyclopaedia of American Biography*, vol. G, 306–7; "Biographical Sketch of Karl Taylor Compton," MIT-OP 59/5.

37. New England Council, *1930 Blue Book*, 23–24. Of the other sixteen members of the Massachusetts and Rhode Island state councils at this time, three came from the metalworking industries, as described in the next paragraph of the text. Among the remaining thirteen state council members, ten came from a miscellany of sectors. Included were individuals active in the manufacture of textiles, bank notes, paint, and ranges and furniture; executives at United Fruit, a printing company, and a granite quarry; an attorney on the Massachusetts Industrial Accident Board; and the commissioners of agriculture for the two states. The other three state council members headed companies for which the line of business could not be determined.

38. Vice president of National Shawmut Bank to Liming, December 1, 1926, BCoC, Case 79/710-"New England Council"-1; Cross memorandum, December 26, 1941, MIT-OP 158/17.

39. On the strong trade organization in machine tools, see Wagoner, *U.S. Machine Tool Industry*.

40. Synopsis of Lawrence address in *Addresses before the Stockholders of Federal Reserve Bank*, 7, 10.

41. New England Council, *Day in New England*; Hook to Sharpe, November 4, 1936, James William Hook Papers, 39/"Letters NEC," section "S."; Compton to Flanders, July 2, 1937, and attached pamphlet entitled *A New Project in Industrial Relations*, in Ralph E. Flanders Papers, Syracuse University (hereafter cited as RF-SU), 33/"Mass. Inst. of Technology—1937"; November 24, 1939 press releases, in *News about New England*.

42. Flanders address, August 12, 1945, page 8, in RF-SU 130/"Prospects for New England."

43. An earlier account of NEC efforts in research and technology, including the work of the New Products Committee (which is discussed later in the text), appears in Etzkowitz, "Enterprises from Science."

44. Chandler, *Visible Hand*; Galambos, "Technology, Political Economy."

45. Joan Hoff Wilson, *Herbert Hoover;* Hawley, *Great War*.

46. On the Filene brothers, see *National Cyclopaedia of American Biography*, 45:421; *NYT*, August 28, 1957, 27 (Lincoln Filene obituary); *American National Biography*, 7:906–8.

47. Metropolitan Life Insurance Company, *Better Business*, 3.

48. Metropolitan Life Insurance Company, *Better Business*, 10, 17–18.

49. New England Council Research Committee, *Directory*, 4, 6, 7.

50. New England Council Research Committee, *Directory*, 2, 3, 14. The NEC had a role in producing updated versions of the directory, which were published under somewhat different titles in 1939 and 1947.

51. *New England Council Announces*; New England Council, *Year of Progress*, 19–20; *Research and New England*, 20; *NENL*, second November 1930 issue, 18.

52. Creange, *3-Phase System*.

53. Thompson and Lichtner Company, *Merchandising New England Products: Shoes*, and companion reports on cotton dress goods and knitted underwear and hosiery, at Baker Library, Harvard Business School, Boston, Mass.; *TW*, November 20, 1926, 36, and November 27, 1926, 1; *Research and New England*, 21.

54. Boston Chamber of Commerce, *Shoe Manufacturing Industry,* and *Cotton Manufacturing Industry.*

55. *TW,* November 20, 1926, 36. Both Filene, chair of the committee supervising the reports, and Thompson, head of the firm that authored them, held liberal political views—one more reason they would not support a recovery strategy based on retrenchment. Thompson was an officer of the Taylor Society, which had been conservative but moved to the left after World War I. In the early Depression years, Thompson backed what amounted to Keynesian policies for reflating the economy. See documents in RF-SU 76/"Sanford E. Thompson."

56. New England Council, *New England Today,* 9.

57. On the latter corporate labs, see insert in *NENL,* first September 1931 issue.

58. As late as the 1940s one national directory of commercial laboratories showed a strong concentration in the industrial states. A regional breakdown of the principal laboratories listed in the directory is as follows: New England, 2; mid-Atlantic, 8; five states of the industrial Midwest, 5; Pacific Coast, 7; all other states, 10. See American Council of Commercial Laboratories, *Directory.*

59. April 8, 1940 press release, page 1, in *News about New England*; Cross to Compton, October 17, 1940, pages 1–2, MIT-OP 158/7.

60. *NENL,* second November 1930 issue, 16; Norton to Compton, November 28, 1930, and Holland to Hudson, December 1, 1930, both in MIT-OP 118/1; "Proposal of an Industrial Research Institute," MIT-OP 117/2. MIT wanted the NEC to guarantee the new center a minimum level of income for ten years, a commitment the latter organization was understandably reluctant to make. With the deepening Depression reducing the willingness of small firms to pay for industrial research, the project was scrapped.

61. "The New in New England," reprint from May 1932 issue of *Industrial Bulletin* (Arthur D. Little, Inc.), in New England Council Steel Committee Records (hereafter cited as NEC-SC), 2/17c; "Meeting of Executive Committee," November 19, 1936, James William Hook Papers, 39/"Letters NEC," section "N"; *NENL,* May 1938, 1.

62. Committee of New England Research Consultants, *Opportunities.*

63. Weed to Baxter, August 19, 1939, MIT-OP 158/2.

64. Compton address in eleventh *New England Bank Management Conference* (1940), 12.

65. *American National Biography,* 5:300–3; *National Cyclopaedia of American Biography,* 42:3–5.

66. Documents in MIT-OP 58/5 and 58/8.

67. Compton to Proctor, January 14, 1939, MIT-OP 174/16.

68. Summaries of the committee's work appear in Compton's June 1940 report to the NEC in MIT-OP 158/5; his November 1940 address in eleventh *New England Bank Management Conference* (1940); and his June 1941 address in the "New England Industrial Research Foundation, Inc." pamphlet, MIT-OP 158/10. See also Etzkowitz, "Enterprise from Science."

69. Compton address in "New England Industrial Research Foundation, Inc.," 5.

70. Cross to Flanders, October 16, 1940, MIT-OP 158/7.

71. "New England Industrial Research Foundation, Inc."; "Preliminary Prospectus, New England Industrial Research Foundation, Inc.," MIT-OP 158/9; New England Industrial Research Foundation, Report of the Director for 1942–44, page 1, MIT-OP 158/15.

72. Cross memorandum, December 26, 1941, MIT-OP 158/17.

73. Cross to Compton et al., December 26, 1941, MIT-OP 158/17; Compton to Cabot, July 3, 1941, and Cabot to Compton, July 17, 1941, MIT-OP 158/10; Stevenson to Harmon, November 24, 1941, MIT-OP 158/17; Stevenson to Compton, September 26, 1942, MIT-OP 158/11.

74. New England Council, *United New England*, 3–11.

For a full account of the NEC's publicity effort and the economic development concerns motivating it, see Koistinen, "Public Relations as Redevelopment Tool."

75. On industrial development efforts of the 1920s and 1930s in a range of deindustrializing New England cities, see Palmer, *Another Tale of Two Cities*; *Industry*, December 29, 1934; Ragan, "Organization, Management, and Significance"; Wolfbein, *Decline of a Cotton Textile City*, 107–25; and undated Lowell Industrial Development Co. flier, Flather/Boott Mills Collection, "Ephemera" boxes, "Commercial Establishments" folder. For criticism of the inducements used to attract industry, see *Labor and Industries 1930*, 116–20, and New England Council, *Year of Progess*, 23.

Attempts to bring new industries into towns hit by deindustrialization at times encountered resistance from manufacturers who still operated in those locations and benefited from the downward pressure on wages created by elevated levels of unemployment. Thus, managers of Lowell textile firms resisted the establishment of new manufacturing ventures in the city during World War II (Miller, *Irony of Victory*, 116–18), and Lawrence industrialists acted in the same manner during the postwar period (Hartford, *Where Is Our Responsibility?*, 190–91). In these instances the interests of existing manufacturers were pitted against those of businessmen in locally oriented sectors such as banking, retail, and real estate as well as the general population. All of the latter groups would benefit from the creation of additional employment in locales hit by plant closings.

A similar dynamic transpired in state-level policymaking in Massachusetts after World War II. Commonwealth manufacturers opposed efforts to set up new economic development institutions in the state, while more broad-based groups, such as chambers of commerce, enthusiastically supported the initiatives. On the post-1945 events, see Koistinen, "Public Policies for Countering Deindustrialization," 339–41, and Koistinen, "Political Economy of Regional Redevelopment," 8–13.

76. This paragraph is based on *Report of the Committee on Public Relations*, 3, 6–9; New England Council, *Year of Progress*, 25–26; *NENL*, second January issue 1932, 1; *NENL*, first March issue, 1932, 6; *NENL*, August 1932, 2–3, and March 14, 1936, 1.

77. Here the NEC's economic development effort overlapped with the policy of retrenchment, examined in chapter 2, that many in the business world pursued in response to industrial decline.

78. *New England Today*, 15; November 29, 1939 press release, in *News about New England*; *NENL*, October 19, 1936, 1, 4, 5; Wells and Perkins, *New England Community Statistical Abstracts*.

79. New England Council, *Year of Progress*, 58–59; New England Council, *United New England*, 43; *NENL*, July 14, 1927; *Industry*, September 10, 1927, 6.

80. *Report of the Agricultural Committee*, 3–7; New England Council, *New England Farm Marketing*.

81. *Report of the Committee on Recreational Resources.*

82. Wheeler, *New England Council*, 21; Frederick Steele Blackall III interview, February 26, 1996; New England Council, *New England and the New England Council*, 1–2.

83. *Report of the Agricultural Committee*, 7.

84. The property tax and NIRA episodes are discussed in chapters 2 and 3, respectively.

85. In one sense the establishment of state economic development bodies did not represent a departure. Massachusetts and all other states had long pursued policies intended to facilitate growth by building transportation links, publishing economic statistics, and the like. Still, in establishing agencies that promoted the expansion of particular industries, state government was returning to a level of sectoral intervention in the economy not seen in the Northeast since the manufacturing subsidies of the late eighteenth century. The high tariffs in place throughout this period of course constituted a national policy on behalf of growth in certain industrial sectors.

86. Allen inaugural address, January 3, 1929, Massachusetts Legislative Documents 1929 (Senate, No. 1), 20–21.

Although the structural problems of Massachusetts manufacturers motivated Allen to call for the creation of a development agency, in putting forward his proposal the governor actually downplayed the commonwealth's economic difficulties, citing figures from a recent study indicating that industrial conditions had stabilized. The tendency of New England leaders to emphasize the positive relentlessly in discussing the beleaguered area economy, and their reasons for doing so, are examined in Koistinen, "Public Relations as Redevelopment Tool."

87. *Magazine of Wall Street*, March 22, 1930, 876. The fact that Allen headed a Boston leather house that had undoubtedly been hurt by the downturn in the shoe industry may have made him more willing to see the strictest formulations of laissez-faire contravened.

The political imperatives driving state government development efforts, which were evident in the events of the 1920s, are examined in detail for the post-1945 period in Koistinen, "Public Policies for Countering Deindustrialization."

88. Successive drafts of the measure appear in Massachusetts Legislative Documents 1929 as House, No. 1172, House, No. 1229, and Senate, No. 393. Although labor had a seat on the commission, the body's strong business orientation quickly became apparent. As their first chair, commission members selected Frederick Payne, head of a Massachusetts tap and die firm, who had recently been elected president of AIM, the state manufacturers association.

89. *BG*, April 2, 1929, evening edition, 8.

90. *Labor and Industries 1930*, 103–4, 106–7; *Labor and Industries 1931*, 127–28; *Labor and Industries 1932*, 154–55. By 1932 the body had been renamed the Industrial and Development Commission (*Labor and Industries 1932*, 154). It was disbanded in 1933, apparently as a result of a state fiscal crisis (*Labor and Industries 1933*, 159). Later reconstituted, it operated in the late 1930s as the Development and Industrial Commission.

91. *Labor and Industries 1930*, 107–9; *Labor and Industries 1931*, 126, 129.

92. The authors of one commission publication from the late 1930s went to such lengths to portray the Bay State in a favorable light that they unintentionally voiced an ironic humor about local conditions. Issued to promote Massachusetts as a site for industrial investment, this seventy-five-page brochure was distributed to manufacturers around the country

and overseas. The booklet touted oft-cited advantages of a commonwealth location, including skilled labor, proximity to major markets, and a lifestyle and scenery attractive to executives. It went beyond this, however, to consider how the "ebb and flow of economic factors have again placed striking advantages in the Bay State." Thus the numerous plant closures in traditional industries meant that the commonwealth had available "plenty of industrial sites and factories that can be purchased or leased at modest prices . . . [i]n communities that have always been manufacturing centers." See Massachusetts Development and Industrial Commission, *In Black and White*, 1, 2, 17, with enclosed letter to Harvard librarian, December 27, 1937, in Widener/Pusey Library, Harvard University.

93. *Labor and Industries 1930*, 106, 115; *Labor and Industries 1931*, 127–28.

94. *Labor and Industries 1930*, 104, 109–10; *Labor and Industries 1931*, 123.

95. Undated, untitled statement regarding Remington arms plant, Edith Nourse Rogers Papers, 13/170.

96. See the survey results in unidentified January 20, 1952 clipping and October 26, 1952 *Lowell Sun* clipping, both in Lowell Technological Institute Collection, 76/"Clippings." Similar information from the 1920s for the three Massachusetts textile schools appears in the "National Association of Manufacturers Dinneny" statement attached to Eames to Walsh, November 21, 1928, in BCoC, Case 12/311-210-19 (1).

97. Board of Trustees minutes, March 2, 1942, page 2, MIT-OP 158/13; Stevenson to Compton, September 26, 1942, MIT-OP 158/11; New England Industrial Research Foundation, Report of the Director for 1942–44, page 2, MIT-OP 158/15; Compton to Bird, March 10, 1943, MIT-OP 158/14; minutes of meeting of founders and trustees, May 26, 1944, MIT-OP 158/15.

98. Committee of New England Research Consultants, *Opportunities*, 12. The report's recommendations were off base in other respects. The study noted production opportunities for regional manufacturers in a range of aircraft sectors—from complete planes to airframe components to upholstery for the seats—but did not emphasize engines and instrumentation. New England producers in the latter two industries had natural advantages and achieved great success in future years.

99. New England Council, *Progress Report*, 2.

Chapter 5. Small Business Financing in Mid-Twentieth-Century New England

1. Ralph Flanders address, *Commercial and Financial Chronicle*, November 29, 1945, 2608; U.S. Joint Committee, *Volume and Stability of Private Investment*, 465; *Second Report of New England Council's Special Committee*, 12; Freeland & Warren, *Report of a Study*, 28–29. The latter study cited contemporary instances of bankers and chambers of commerce maintaining lists of local investors, a persistence of the traditional practice.

2. Paper by Philip W. Moore of Schroder, Rockefeller and Company, *Commercial and Financial Chronicle*, May 25, 1950, 2163; *Second Report of New England Council's Special Committee*, 12–13; Lincoln and Therese Filene Foundation, *Memorandum*, 10–11. For a similar account of traditional venture capital markets and their decline in the 1920s see Reiner, "Transformation of Venture Capital," 5–6, 10–13.

3. U.S. House, Select Committee, *Study and Investigation*, part 1, 218–19; Dubofsky, *State and Labor*, 68 (on Disque).

4. Lincoln and Therese Filene Foundation, *Memorandum*, 20; U.S. House, Select Committee, *Study and Investigation*, Part 1, 875–76; Reiner, "Transformation of Venture Capital," 10–11, 13–15. For a comprehesive account of studies of the 1930s and 1940s on the difficulties of small business in obtaining finance, see Weissman, *Small Business and Venture Capital*, especially 34–52.

5. See Bean, *Beyond the Broker State*, and material in Records of the Industrial Research and Development Division, Office of Technical Services (hereafter cited as IRDD), box 64, and General Correspondence File, boxes 920–26, U.S. Department of Commerce Records (RG 40). On Western support for development and small business, see Nash, *World War II and the West*, especially 180–88.

6. Stoddard, "Small Business Wants Capital," 265; "Report by Subcommittee of Committee on Legislation of Conference of Presidents of the Federal Reserve System on Financial Aid to Small Business," June 11, 1945, Ralph Flanders Materials, Federal Reserve Bank of Boston (hereafter cited as RF-FRBB), "Venture Capital" folder; Weissman, *Small Business and Venture Capital*.

7. Frederick S. Blackall Jr. address, sixteenth *New England Bank Management Conference* (1946), 23.

8. Hook address, ninth *New England Bank Management Conference* (1938), 22. Similarly, William Stoddard, assistant to the liberal Lincoln Filene, described the Mead bills as "a sign, a portent, and a challenge to privately controlled capital: unless it does the job, social controlled capital will do the job" (Stoddard, "Small Business Wants Capital," 265). The objectives of a Chicago organization set up during this period to promote industrial growth were described as including "Preservation of America's Private Enterprise System" and "Cooperation for Full Production and Employment." See the brochure in IRDD 61/"National Foundation for Science and Industry."

9. *Commercial and Financial Chronicle,* March 29, 1945, 1406; *New England War Bulletin*, September 1944, 8; testimony of Lloyd Brace and Edward J. Stewart, in U.S. House, Select Committee, *Study and Investigation*, part 1, 826–32, 947–49.

10. *Credit and Financial Management*, November 1950, 11–13.

11. Joseph Powell, "Report on Trip to Ten Cities," September 9, 1946, RF-FRBB, "American Research and Development Corp. 1946" folder.

12. Reiner, "Transformation of Venture Capital," 135–61. The Bing Crosby Foundation set up in Los Angeles by the entertainer was another example of action by a wealthy individual. The Manufacturers Capital Corporation in New York, which was formally sponsored by the Lee, Higginson investment bank, was probably yet another. Both are mentioned in Powell, "Report on Trip."

13. Unsigned, undated "Plan for the Formation of a Company to Encourage and Facilitate the Development of New Inventions, Products, Processes, and Industries," Lee DuBridge Papers 121/8. Another notable early organization was the fund set up in Detroit to aid conventional small manufacturers by investment banker H. R. P. Lyttle. See *Investment Dealers Digest* clipping, August 26, 1946, American Research and Development Corporation Historical

Materials (hereafter cited as ARD Materials). In a separate but related field were several early leveraged buyout organizations set up in Chicago, such as the Atlas Corporation and the Chicago Corporation. See Reiner, "Transformation of Venture Capital," 163–66.

14. On the latter two organizations, see *San Francisco News*, October 6, 1947, 18; *Barron's*, March 29, 1954, 3.

15. *NENL*, May 1946, 6; brochure in IRDD 61/"National Foundation for Science and Industry."

16. On the Whitneys and Hodges, see February 21, 1949 *Barron's* clipping in ARD Materials. The Whitneys may have participated in the Hodges organization from its inception, as Whitney investment advisor Benno C. Schmidt was an original member of the Hodges board; see *San Francisco News*, October 6, 1947, 18.

17. For the Mellons, see Reiner, "Transformation of Venture Capital," 158–59. In addition to Hodges, two venture capital firms were established in the San Francisco area immediately after World War II: the Industrial Capital Corporation, and Pacific Coast Enterprises, which at first apparently went by the name of Fisher & Heller. See Reiner, "Transformation of Venture Capital," 205–16, and Powell, "Report on Trip."

Developmental motives were probably also at work in the founding of the Stanford Research Institute, an important industrial research center set up at this time near San Francisco. Plans originally called for the center to be located in Los Angeles under the name Pacific Research Foundation, but the necessary funding could not be secured. The institute was then set up at Stanford University, with Bay Area businessmen providing most of the necessary support. See Judge and MacLean to Hutchison, February 6, 1947, and Hutchison to Bowers, February 21, 1947, IRDD 62/"Stanford Research Institute."

New Deal veteran Thomas Corcoran had connections to venture capital and worked with the Pacific Industries Development Corporation, which was active by 1951. This may have been another early Bay Area promotional organization. Consult the relevant file, when it opens to researchers, in box 508, Thomas Corcoran Papers, Manuscript Division, Library of Congress.

18. Freeland & Warren, *Report of a Study*, especially 5–8, 12, 17, 18.

19. Freeland & Warren, *Report of a Study*, 8, 12.

20. Freeland & Warren, *Report of a Study*, 6.

21. Filene statement in U.S. Senate, Special Committee, *Small Business Problems*, 1–2; Lincoln and Therese Filene Foundation, *Memorandum*, 38.

22. *NENL*, May 1936 supplement, 7–9; Lincoln and Therese Filene Foundation, *Memorandum*, 13–14, 17–18, and citation on 39; Cross to Flanders, October 16, 1940, and Cross to Compton, December 28, 1940, page 4, in MIT-OP 158/7; Compton address, June 24, 1941, MIT-OP 158/10.

23. U.S. Senate, Special Committee, *Small Business Problems*, 2–8; Flanders to Compton, December 18, 1939, RF-SU 57/"MIT 1939"; Cox to Haussermann, May 31, 1940, and Cross to Richmond, June 3, 1940, both in MIT-OP 158/5; Compton to Cross, October 14, 1940, MIT-OP 158/7.

24. Available evidence does not conclusively demonstrate that the organizers of Enterprise Associates sought to bolster regional development, but this was very likely the case. Several principals of Enterprise Associates tried to set up a similar organization in Rhode Island—an

area even harder hit by industrial downsizing than Massachusetts—and after World War II one leading participant publicly avowed his determination to create more New England jobs.

25. Compton to Cross, October 19, 1939, MIT-OP 158/3; Cross to Compton, July 10, 1940, memorandum re Enterprise Associates, July 15, 1940, and Livingstone to Cross, July 15, 1940—all in MIT-OP 158/5; *Fortune*, March 1950, 80; Charles F. Adams, Jr. interview, August 29, 1996.

26. Compton to Cross, October 19, 1939, MIT-OP 158/3; Russell Adams, *Boston Money Tree*, 277–78; *Moody's Manual* (1950), 590; *Industry*, March 1946, 42. For another account of Enterprise Associates, see Ante, *Creative Capital*, 75–78.

27. Livingstone to Compton, January 20, 1942, MIT-OP 137/6; U.S. House, Select Committee on Small Business, *Availability of Long-Term Credit*, 38; *Fortune*, August 1945, 135.

28. This and the following paragraph are based on Minot, *Theta of Delta Kappa Epsilon*, 214; Hodgkins, *Brief Biographies, Maine*, 52; *Biographical Sketches of the Members of the 96th Maine Legislature*, 4; *NYT*, November 24, 1935, F1, and October 14, 1936, 42, and October 26, 1936, 27; *NYT*, December 21, 1937, 35, and October 16, 1940, 39; *BG*, 3 Aug. 1953, 2; *Portland Press-Herald* (Portland, Me.), August 5, 1948, 24 (Maine Securities Co. advertisement), and August 3, 1953, 1–2; "State House Report," *Biddeford Daily Journal* (Biddeford, Me.), August 15, 1953, 8; Peters, *Maine Central Railroad Company*.

29. Transcripts of Chase's speeches and the panel on venture capital appear in *New England War Bulletin*, October 1943 supplement, 1–10.

30. Charles C. Abbott, professor of business economics at the Harvard Business School, chaired the panel. For a list of committee members, see *New England War Bulletin*, January 1944, 9.

31. *New England War Bulletin,* February 1944, 6–7.

32. Blackall speech to New England Conference, November 16, 1944, page 4, in Frederick Steele Blackall Jr. Papers, "Vol. II—2/13/36–12/4/45."

33. *New England War Bulletin,* October 1944; *Proceedings of the Twentieth Annual Meeting of the Stockholders* (1944), 9; Mezerik, *Revolt of the South and West*, xii.

34. *New England War Bulletin,* September 1942, 9; various items published by the Massachusetts Committee on Post-War Readjustment; February 21, 1945 memo, BCoC Case 79/710-4; *Boston Herald*, September 29, 1944; *Christian Science Monitor*, November 28, 1945; *Mass Dept Comm*; Joseph Kennedy speech, in *Proceedings of the Twenty-First Annual Meeting of the Stockholders* (1945); Ralph Flanders speech, July 30, 1945, RF-SU 130/"What Can a Dept. of Commerce Do for Mass."; Griswold and Hammond to Doriot, October 25, 1945, MIT-OP 103/4.

35. *American National Biography*, 8:87–88; *Who Was Who in America*, 5:237; *Fortune*, August 1945, 135–36, 264–72.

36. *Proceedings of the Twentieth Annual Meeting of the Stockholders* (1944), 17–18; *Proceedings of the Twenty-First Annual Meeting of the Stockholders* (1945), 17–18.

On the Boston Fed's ambitious program to increase bank support of the area's farmers, see *United States Investor*, August 11, 1945, 1473–78, and the Zehner presentation in *Proceedings of the Twenty-First Annual Meeting of the Stockholders* (1945).

37. *First Report of New England Council's Special Committee*, 4.

38. Flanders address, fifteenth *New England Bank Management Conference* (1945), 26. Flan-

ders went on to discuss the possibility of encouraging more such lending through Federal Reserve guarantees of repayment.

39. Fifteenth *New England Bank Management Conference* (1945), 28–31.

40. Griswold and Hammond to Doriot, October 25, 1945, MIT-OP 103/4. The letter was discussed earlier.

41. For accounts that underemphasize regional concerns in the establishment of ARD, see Reiner, "Transformation of Venture Capital," 166–78; Liles, *Sustaining the Venture Capital Firm*, 21–22, 24–38; Adams, *Boston Money Tree*, 279–81. These works did not draw on the range of sources used here. Etzkowitz, "Enterprises from Science," properly credits the developmental motives of ARD's founders but overstates the role of MIT officials in bringing ARD into existence. For a recent account that draws on some of the materials used here, see Ante, *Creative Capital*, 107–12.

42. *First Report of New England Council's Special Committee*, 10.

43. "Report on the American Research and Development Corporation," October 21, 1946, page 1, RF-SU 132/"Am. Res. & Dev. Corp. 1946." The author of this detailed report is not identified, but the document states that in September 1946 he conducted a week-long "field inquiry" in Boston, including interviews with many of ARD's principals.

44. Flanders to Sproul, June 30, 1945, RF-FRBB, "Venture Capital" folder.

45. "Report on the American Research and Development Corporation," 3–4.

46. See Henriques, *Fidelity's World*, 87–97, for an account of Griswold's role in lobbying for the Investment Company Act of 1940 and other legislation of this era of crucial importance to the investment trust industry. The clause of the Investment Company Act, Section 12(e), had the backing of the investment trust industry, which was eager to ward off charges that its activities were depriving small firms of needed equity capital, and of the SEC, which in the Roosevelt years was an enthusiastic advocate of venture capital. See "Report on the American Research and Development Corporation," 4, and the testimony of SEC official David Schenker excerpted in U.S. Joint Committee, *Volume and Stability of Private Investment*, 461–62. One of the few bright spots at the New England Council's 1943 panel on venture capital was a suggestion by Griswold that 12(e) corporations be formed to channel money managed by fiduciaries to small business. As of 1945 no venture capital companies had been formed under 12(e). ARD was one of the few that ever was.

47. "Report on the American Research and Development Corporation," 4; note clipped to Claflin to Flanders, August 27, 1945, RF-FRBB, "Venture Capital" folder.

48. *American Research and Development Corporation: Registration Statement*, 3.

49. In public statements on the aims of ARD, Flanders and others always emphasized national goals of bolstering innovation and expanding production and employment. But the "Report on the American Research and Development Corporation," and the other initiatives on behalf of the region mounted at this time by Flanders, Griswold, and David demonstrate that their primary motive in organizing ARD was to support industrial recovery in New England. Twenty years later, ARD president Georges Doriot described the motivations of the organization's founders in the following terms: "With textiles and other industry flowing out of New England after World War II, [Karl Compton, Merrill Griswold and Ralph Flanders] saw the

need for new investment in new technologies to compensate for the losses" (*Electronic News* clipping, November 8, 1965, ARD Materials).

50. Jackson to Flanders, April 26, 1946, RF-FRBB, "American Research and Development Corp. 1946" folder (folder hereafter cited as ARDC 1946); Flanders address to the National Association of Securities Commissioners, *Commercial and Financial Chronicle*, November 29, 1945, 2576; Griswold to Flanders, April 4, 1946, and Wisconsin-related correspondence, April 9–May 16, 1946, RF-FRBB, ARDC 1946.

51. Griswold to Flanders, April 4, 1946, RF-FRBB, ARDC 1946; U.S. Securities and Exchange Commission, *In the Matter of American Research and Development Corporation*.

52. Maclaurin to Flanders, February 15, 1946, RF-FRBB, "Venture Capital" folder; "Progress Report re. Proposed Development Capital Corporation," January 26, 1946, and undated sheet of "Luncheon Acceptances," Vannevar Bush Papers, 26/"Compton (1943–46)"; Griswold to Flanders, April 4, 1946, and Ford to Flanders, May 31, 1946, both in RF-FRBB, ARDC 1946; U.S. Joint Committee, *Volume and Stability of Private Investment*, 451–52.

53. *Fortune*, February 1949, 84; "Conservatives Join in Revitalizing Economy," undated *Finance* clipping, ARD Materials. On MIT, see Ford to Flanders, May 31, 1946, RF-FRBB, ARDC 1946; on Rosenwald, see Reiner, "Transformation of Venture Capital," 176. Institutional investors in ARD are listed in American Research and Development Corporation, *Annual Report, 1949*. Of the $3.2 million in paid-up shares outstanding soon after the company began operations, investment trusts held $1.2 million, insurance companies $300,000 (undoubtedly almost all from John Hancock), educational institutions $225,000, and individuals $1.5 million.

54. On possible chief executives for the corporation and Doriot's eventual selection, see Compton-Doriot correspondence, April 24, May 8, and May 10, 1946, MIT-OP 74/6, and Powell to Flanders, November 8, 1946, RF-FRBB, ARDC 1946.

55. U.S. Senate, Committee on Finance, *Revenue Revisions of 1950*, 599.

Chapter 6. Small Business Finance and Electronics Spinoff Companies along Route 128

1. On the electronics industry and the role in it of spinoff companies, see Lécuyer, *Making Silicon Valley*; Barrett, *To the Digital Age*; Saxenian, *Regional Advantage*; Noble, *Forces of Production*; David Mowery and Nathan Rosenberg, "Twentieth-Century Technological Change," in Engerman and Gallman, *Cambridge Economic History*, 3:876–904; Estall, *New England*, 79–109; Hund, "Electronics Industry"; Parrott, "Technological and Institutional Innovation"; New York State Department of Commerce, *Electronics Industry*; and surveys of Massachusetts electronics in *Industry*, November 1944, 9–16, 47–48, and September 1952, 7–16, 37–42.

2. The industry always had nebulous boundaries. According to one technical definition, a product that depended on a variable and controlled flow of electrons was "electronic." A more accessible rule of thumb held that a device containing a vacuum or radio tube, or later a transistor or semiconductor, was electronic.

3. Two-thirds of the R&D costs of the electrical equipment industry were paid by the U.S. government as late as 1964 (Noble, *Forces of Production*, 8).

4. The term "spinoff" seems to be of 1960s vintage. The firms were also described as science-

based companies, new research-based enterprises, and companies "exploding away" from larger organizations.

5. See New Products Committee report, June 28, 1940, MIT-OP 158/5; Cross to Brown, August 30, 1940, MIT-OP 158/6. Patent attorney from Cross to Stevenson, September 21, 1940, MIT-OP 158/6. On technological innovation in nineteenth-century industry, see Khan and Sokoloff, "'Schemes of Practical Utility.'" A key study of the rise of corporate R&D labs is Reich, *Making of American Industrial Research*.

6. Scott, *Creative Ordeal*, chaps. 2–3.

7. Packard, *HP Way*, chaps. 2–4.

8. The "industry news" section of *Electronics*, the field's leading trade journal, featured short announcements during this era of the establishment of new firms. Some examples: "Mr. Emil R. Capita, designer of high frequency bombarders has announced the formation of his own company, the Ecco High Frequency Corporation, 120 West 20th St., New York City . . . [to] manufacture high frequency bombarding and associated equipment" (April 1937, 62); "The Electrodyne Co., Boston, was formed recently to provide research and development service in electro-mechanics, vacuum-tube applications, and optics, as well as manufacture of electronic equipment" (April 1946, 340); "Radar Engineers, 1319 Second Ave., Seattle, Wash., has been established by W. L. Flock, W. T. Harrold, and W. D. Hayes, all former members of Radiation Laboratory, MIT, to provide consulting and manufacturing services in the field of microwave electronics" (May 1946, 308).

9. *AIM Directory of Massachusetts Companies*.

10. In its initial years Wang Laboratories, started in 1951, consulted on Pentagon projects, sold computer components to military buyers, and made a device used with the numerically controlled machine tools employed in defense production. Ken Olsen gained extensive experience on military computing projects at MIT's Lincoln Laboratory before founding Digital Equipment Corporation in 1957.

11. Contractually guaranteed union work rules that hindered investment in cost-saving technology could be a significant constraint on competitiveness in post–World War II American industry. This was a major concern in steelmaking; see Stebenne, *Arthur J. Goldberg*, 131–32, 197–215, 280–84. In New England textiles, resistance by unionized workers to the workload changes that accompanied equipment upgrades probably hindered to a degree new investment. This was true even though union officials encouraged workers to be flexible, so as to facilitate investment that was essential to northern firms' viability (Hartford, *Where Is Our Responsibility?*, 103–15, 123–30, 132–33, 139–40, 166–67). On how the absence of unions at one important manufacturer facilitated flexibility in the production process, see Stebenne, "IBM's 'New Deal,'" 60–62.

12. On the high level of federal taxes after 1950, and the acceptance by major corporate interests of this reality, see Stebenne, "Thomas J. Watson," 64–65.

13. Note, however, that the structure of federal taxes during this period encouraged investment in small companies with high growth potential, such as the electronics spinoffs. The returns on monies invested in small companies that grew rapidly came largely through increases in the stock price. These returns were taxed at the low capital gains rate of 25 percent. For money placed in the equities of large firms, by contrast, a substantial segment of the return

came in the form of dividends—which for wealthy shareholders would be taxed at the very high marginal rates then prevailing. The differential between the tax rates on dividends and capital gains also affected corporate acquisition patterns in 1940s textiles; see Hartford, *Where Is Our Responsibility?*, 91–92.

14. One investigator in the late 1950s found that the government was as bad as any corporate purchaser in making late payments to small producers. See Gibson, "Financing Small Electronics Firms."

15. See Roberts, *Entrepreneurs in High Technology*; Rosegrant and Lampe, *Route 128*; Lampe, *Massachusetts Miracle*; Parrott, "Technological and Institutional Innovation."

16. During the 1940s and 1950s MIT laboratories received more than a third of the $330 million in contracts administered by the Pentagon's Office of Scientific Research and Development (Saxenian, *Regional Advantage*, 13–14, and related footnote).

17. "Station and Studio Equipment Directory," *Tele-Tech*, October 1952, 129, 134, 151–52, 154, 182. The simple count of producers used here dramatically biases the tally toward the smaller firms that are of interest. Major producers like General Electric appear in the listings but receive the same weight as the smallest spinoffs.

The geographic distribution of companies in advanced sectors was similar in a directory published a decade earlier; see "1943 Electronic Engineering Directory Section," *Electronic Industries*, March 1943, 81–114. See also the discussion of the location of advanced electronics firms in the late 1950s, including the results of tallies similar to my own, in Hund, "Electronics Industry," 294–98. Another useful source for identifying company locations at this time is the Department of Defense publication *500 Military Prime Contractors Listed According to Net Value of Military Prime Contract Awards for Research, Development, Test, and Evaluation Work*, available annually beginning in the mid-1950s.

18. Hund, "Electronics Industry," 294; Dr. Louis Ridenour, "The Electronic West Coast—A New Way of Life," *Tele-Tech*, September 1952, 74–75.

19. These arrangements were discussed in chapter 4. On the intense cooperative research links between Caltech and aircraft and other manufacturers in the Los Angeles area, see Libby, "To Build Wings for the Angels." Research ties between Boeing and the University of Washington are noted in Markusen et al., *Rise of the Gunbelt*, 165–66.

20. *Electronics*, May 1946.

21. Compton to Bell, May 14, 1946, MIT-OP 158/1.

22. *Christian Science Monitor* clipping, August 15, 1946, ARD Materials.

23. Enterprise Associates head William Coolidge was also in charge of New Enterprises. The board of directors for the later organization also had familiar faces, including in 1946 Georges Doriot and investment bankers Charles F. Adams Jr. and James J. Minot. As before, a large number of investors—more than twenty—put money into the New Enterprises pool, which had $300,000 at its disposal. (The total capital available to Enterprise Associates is unknown, but their sole investment was for $50,000.) New Enterprises planned to maximize the use of this money by acting as a revolving fund, quickly selling off stakes in the companies in which it invested to participants in the pool, thereby freeing up the original capital for reinvestment. New Enterprises also had a more formal organizational structure, with a full-time staffer hired to get the fund into operation and screen investment proposals. As was the case with ARD, an

284 Notes to Pages 169–174

intensive round of consultation and recruitment, in this case mostly undocumented, preceded the establishment of New Enterprises. Staff member Eugene Hotchkiss reported talking to more than a hundred people before the company opened for business, including MIT's new president James Killian, the U.S. commissioner of patents, and officers at the First National Bank of Boston. See *Investment Dealers Digest* clipping, August 26, 1946, ARD Materials; *Fortune*, February 1949, 84; New Enterprises, Inc. brochure, March 1946, Vannevar Bush Papers, 52/"Hotchkiss"; New Enterprises, Inc. brochure, March 1947, MIT-OP 114/2; memorandum re New Enterprises, Inc., March 14, 1946, MIT-OP 159/1.

24. New Enterprises, Inc. brochure, March 1946.

25. *NENL*, May 1946, 6. ARD set up a similar organization, the Product Development Corporation, in 1953. Product Development presented proposals that ARD found promising but unsuitable for investment to established manufacturers looking to diversify their product line, receiving a commission when deals were consummated. See *Business Week*, September 25, 1954, 144.

26. "Report on the American Research and Development Corporation," October 21, 1946, pages 1, 10, RF-SU 132/"Am. Res. & Dev. Corp. 1946"; "Memorandum re. American Research and Development Corporation . . . ," page 6, RF-FRBB, "American Research and Development Corp. 1946" folder.

27. Undated Maclaurin speech, RF-FRBB, "Venture Capital" folder. That ARD would consider investments in these kinds of firms was the obvious conclusion to be drawn from Maclaurin's talk. Investors could of course profit from these opportunities by putting their money into ARD.

28. *Nation's Business*, November 1949, 37, 39, 78; *NYT*, February 17, 1952, 115; *Fortune*, April 1950; *Boston Sunday Globe*, December 29, 1968; American Research and Development Corporation, *Annual Report, 1951*.

29. Figures from Boston Evening Transcript, *Boston National Banks*.

30. "Southeastern Territory with Particular Reference to Textiles," undated memorandum from Vice President H. F. de C. Pereira, BankBoston On-Site, unlabeled folder with notation "[material] may be . . . of some historical importance, RCD."

31. Beal, *Second National Bank*, 53–69. Securing the institution's reputation seems to have been the prime motive for publishing this history of the bank. The tradition of "conservative" management that Beal proudly recounts may have impeded efforts to develop new types of customers.

32. *Boston Sunday Post*, December 21, 1947, A3; *American Banker*, January 28, 1964, 1, 13; Semenenko obituary, *BG*, April 27, 1980; "Boston's First Bank . . . ," *Christian Science Monitor*, March 21, 1958; "Final Chapter in Storied Saga . . ." *BG*, March 15, 1999; *America's Textile Reporter*, November 20, 1952, 35, 107–8.

33. New Business Committee memorandum, May 3, 1939, BankBoston On-Site, unlabeled folder with notation "[material] may be . . . of some historical importance, RCD."

34. Peter Brooke interview, June 27, 1996.

35. Commercial bank deposits increased as follows during this era: between 1929 and 1939, up 4.2 percent in Massachusetts, and up 16.1 percent nationwide; from 1939 to 1949 (a period of substantial inflation), up 101 percent in Massachusetts and up 155 percent nation-

wide; between 1949 and 1959, up 27 percent in Massachusetts and up 51 percent nationwide. Percentages calculated from statistics in Federal Reserve Bank of Boston, *New England Economic Almanac*, 43.

36. Roger Damon speech, January 17, 1961, BankBoston On-Site, "Annual Dinner (Officers and Directors)" folder, emphasis in the original.

37. Raye was deceased at the time of the research for this project. He told this story to a trade journal reporter and later to a British researcher. See *Electronic News*, June 24, 1968, 4–5, and Bullock, *Academic Enterprise*, 3, 26, 32–33, 36–38. The consistency of the two accounts, given fifteen years apart, and the insistence with which they were told gives them considerable credibility. What most likely occurred is that Raye did as he said in the mid-1940s, then at a critical point in the early 1950s came to believe that spinoff lending was too risky (see later in the text). Having been proved wrong on the latter point by subsequent events, he nonetheless felt that he deserved credit for his original prescience and initiative.

38. Notecards for Spring 1948 Dedham speech, BankBoston On-Site, "Speeches" folder.

39. Roberts, *Entrepreneurs in High Technology*, 191–92; Turnburke, "Aspects of New Enterprises—Finance," 43; Gibson, "Financing Small Electronics Firms," 29, 36–37.

40. The names of panel members were not made public.

41. The proceedings of the meeting were published. Raye was a member of the First National delegation to the New England banking conference two years later; see seventeenth *New England Bank Management Conference* (1947), 33.

42. William L. Brown interview, June 13, 1996, and Peter Brooke interviews.

43. Arthur F. F. Snyder interview, May 26, 1997; *New England Business Review*, April 1956, 1.

44. If the industry's post–Korean War downturn did lead to a retreat in spinoff lending by the Boston banks, this was the first instance of a pattern that apparently recurred. During the recession of 1969–70, many Route 128 companies went belly up. In the wake of this experience, the Boston banks seemingly became markedly cooler about lending to startup companies. See Proctor, "Attitude of Lending Officers," 15–17.

45. William L. Brown and Peter Brooke interviews.

46. William L. Brown interview; *Boston Sunday Herald*, June 5, 1960, "First Annual Electronics Review," 10. In 1959, a First National official discussed with a reporter the bank's establishment of a "special department" to handle lending to research-based companies. In 1958 or 1959, the bank hosted a three-day seminar with the presidents of fifty such firms to discuss the problems the companies faced. See *BG*, June 28, 1959, A-67; "Banking in a Dynamic Economy," undated clipping from *Commercial Bulletin* (Boston, Mass.), BankBoston Off-Site, packet #470 954.

47. Arthur F. F. Snyder interview.

48. This and the following paragraphs on spinoff lending by the Boston banks are based on the interviews with William L. Brown, Peter Brooke, and Arthur F. F. Snyder; *Boston Sunday Herald*, June 5, 1960, "First Annual Electronics Review," 10; Gibson, "Financing Small Electronics Firms," especially 36–39, 54–56; Griner, "Financing the Growing Electronics Enterprise," 3, 8, 35, 40–42; Wang, *Lessons*; Kenney, *Riding the Runaway Horse*.

49. The Merchants National Bank eventually merged with the New England Trust Company to form the New England Merchants Bank.

50. *Boston Sunday Herald*, June 5, 1960, "First Annual Electronics Review," 10; Kelley et al., *Venture Capital*, 74.

51. Cross memorandum, May 6, 1940, MIT-OP 158/5. Several issues of *Results from Research* can be found in IRDD 60/"Research Facilities and Laboratories (General)."

52. *Greater Boston Business*, November 1955, 14; *Boston Evening Post* clipping, November 15, 1962, in BankBoston Off-Site, packet #470 932/31-1; multiple clippings in BankBoston Off-Site, packet #470 953/31-1.

53. *Electronics*, January 10, 1957, 5, and December 20, 1957, 5, and January 24, 1958, 7.

54. Lamden and Pemberton, *Study of the Problems*.

55. Lamden and Pemberton, *Study of the Problems*, 8, 57, 99–103, 109–11, 128–29, emphasis added to quotation.

In selecting firms to investigate, the authors of the report used an expansive definition of "small." Only about 30 percent of the companies examined in the study had annual revenue of less than $300,000; probably 15 percent or fewer had yearly revenues approximating $100,000 (see 45–46, 57). Thus quite a few of the Los Angeles area companies reporting difficulties in financing were probably significantly larger than the several-person teams that typically constituted the entire personnel of early-stage spinoffs. In Boston, such tiny, recently launched outfits often received significant bank financing.

56. *Electronics*, February 19, 1960, 31.

57. Deutermann, "Seeding Science-Based Industry," 3, 5.

58. Wang, *Lessons*, chaps. 2–7.

59. Peter Brooke interview. For Wang's implausible account of his frustrations in military work, see *Lessons*, 110.

60. Wang, *Lessons*, 113; Kenney, *Riding the Runaway Horse*, 206. Annual revenue is estimated based on Wang's comments in *Lessons*, 103 and 112.

61. Wang, *Lessons*, 113–16; Kenney, *Riding the Runaway Horse*, 37, 206. An announcement of the Warner & Swasey deal appeared in *Wall Street Journal*, January 12, 1960, 9.

62. Wang, *Lessons*, 118–33, 142–43; Kenney, *Riding the Runaway Horse*, 196.

63. Kenney, *Riding the Runaway Horse*.

64. On the role of extensive lending from Merchants National Bank and the smaller Harvard Trust Company in the swift growth of 1950s Boston-area spinoffs Dunn Engineering and General Electronic Laboratories, see Gibson, "Financing Small Electronics Firms," and Kenneth Gordon, "Examination of Some Problems." On the role of equity investments by venture capital firm American Research and Development Corporation in the growth during this era of Boston-area spinoffs Tracerlab and Baird Laboratories, see "Their Money Seeks Adventure," *Nation's Business*, November 1949; Butters and Lintner, *Effect of Federal Taxes*, 16–18; "One Local Small Business . . ." *Christian Science Monitor* clipping, March 21, 1947, in ARD Materials.

65. Contributing as well to New England's economic success of the 1980s was job growth in other sectors, including business and financial services and higher education (especially at private universities and colleges). Lower taxes, weaker unions, and reduced regulation facilitated the return of regional prosperity.

Chapter 7. Responses to Deindustrialization in New England during the Cold War Years

1. Figures for 1923 and 1939 from *Mass Dept Comm*, 75. Post-1939 figures are for "production and related workers" as reported in Massachusetts Department of Labor and Industries, *Census of Manufactures in Massachusetts*, 1953 and 1960.

2. New England manufacturing employment fell from 1.25 million in 1947 to 1.16 million in 1954 and 1.05 million in 1958. Regional totals calculated from statistics on "production workers, total" for each of the region's states from the periodic U.S. Census of Manufactures, as reported in Dodd, *Historical Statistics*.

3. New England employment increased from 3.33 million in 1947 to 3.55 million in 1955. Over the same period, U.S. employment rose from 43.9 million to 50.7 million, an increase of 15.5 percent. Employment statistics from U.S. Bureau of Labor Statistics, *Employment and Earnings, States and Areas, 1939–72*, xiii–xiv. New England totals and percentage changes are my calculations.

4. Bay State industries saw employment levels decline as follows between the years 1946 and 1960: textile finishing, 8,400 to 6,200; silk and rayon goods, 7,900 to 5,100; textile machinery, 12,700 to 8,700; boots and shoes, 45,000 to 35,000; leather, 10,500 to 5,800. All employment statistics from Massachusetts Department of Labor and Industries, *Census of Manufactures in Massachusetts*, 1946, 1953, and 1960.

5. First page of "Recommendations for Federal Assistance . . . ," undated memo attached to Buckley to Eisenhower, February 26, 1953, Sinclair Weeks Papers, 44/"New England Textile Situation."

6. U.S. Council of Economic Advisers, *New England Economy*; Bright and Ellis, *Economic State of New England*. Harvard economist Seymour Harris participated in both these studies and published his own volume on the subject; see Harris, *Economics of New England*.

7. *Forbes*, July 15, 1953, 14. On negative media portrayals of the New England economy in the post–World War I era and the efforts of regional growth advocates to counteract this through a publicity campaign, see Koistinen, "Public Relations as Redevelopment Tool."

8. The following pages on the business retrenchment campaign of the 1950s and the section later in the chapter on the development efforts of Massachusetts state government during the same period summarize principal points from a much more detailed, previously published examination of these topics. For the full account, with complete citations and in-depth information on the political factors shaping commonwealth policies on industrial decline, see Koistinen, "Public Policies for Countering Deindustrialization."

9. On labor's significant influence in the Democratic Party at the national level during this era, see Stebenne, *Arthur J. Goldberg*, 61, 69–71, 179–84, 230–31; DiSalvo, "Politics of a Party Faction."

10. The top across-the-board rate imposed in 1951 was 2.7 percent of payroll. In 1949, before the increases took effect, the lowest rate was 0.5 percent and the average rate 1.5 percent.

11. On the 1950 tax increase, see Commonwealth of Massachusetts, *Report of the Special Commission on Taxation, Part V* (February 1952), 14–15, 17–18.

12. *NYT*, October 29, 1974, 40 (Harris obituary); Galbraith, "Seymour Edwin Harris"; Samuelson, "Seymour Harris"; Harris entry in *Who Was Who in America with World Notables*, 6:183.

13. Eckes, *Opening America's Market*, 140–41, 157–76.

14. New England Governors' Textile Committee (hereafter cited as NEGTC), *New England Textiles* (1957), II-141, II-143; NEGTC, *New England Textiles* (1958–59), II-31, II-32.

15. NEGTC, *Report on the New England Textile Industry*, 274; CNEG minutes, February 20, 1953, page 4, Office of the Governor of Connecticut Records, box 589 (Lodge).

16. NEGTC, *New England Textiles* (1956), ix, 1, 77–81; CNEG minutes, November 17, 1955, page 3, Office of the Governor of Connecticut Records, box 666 (Ribicoff).

17. NEGTC, *New England Textiles* (1956), 194–95; NEGTC, *New England Textiles* (1957), II-142; NEGTC, *New England Textiles* (1958–59), II-34; Eckes, *Opening America's Market*, 175. New England representatives continued to press in the late 1950s against easing trade protections for textiles.

18. NEGTC, *New England Textiles* (1956), 79.

19. NEGTC, *New England Textiles* (1956), 79, 82. See also Harris, *Economics of New England*, 105–6.

20. NEGTC, *New England Textiles* (1956), 118–19. According to Harris's analysis, similar findings resulted from looking at all federal expenditures, not just aid programs.

21. On industrial downsizing outside New England in the decades after World War II, see Gregory Wilson, "Before the Great Society" and *Communities Left Behind*; Dublin and Licht, *Face of Decline*; Friedman, "Communities in Competition"; Hartford, *Where Is Our Responsibility?*, 189; and "The Most Depressed Areas . . . Where They Are and Why—What to Do?," *Newsweek*, December 19, 1960, 78–81.

22. *NYT*, July 12, 1949, 14, and July 15, 1949, 1, 14; *NYT*, August 10, 1949, 1, and August 14, 1949, 33; Benti to Adams, October 15, 1951, and CNEG, January 4, 1952 minutes, pages 3–4, both in Office of the Governor of Connecticut Records, box 589; NEGTC, *Report on the New England Textile Industry*, 274; documents attached to March 11, 1953 memorandum by UTWA president Anthony Valente, Sinclair Weeks Papers, 44/"New England Textile Situation"; CNEG minutes, February 20, 1953, pages 4–5; Dillon, "Channeling Government Contracts," 279–80; *Depressed Industrial Areas*, 38–39; U.S. House, Committee on Banking and Currency, *Federal Assistance to Labor Surplus Areas*, 50. On early steps toward a national distressed areas policy, including channeling of federal contracts to labor surplus areas and other measures, see also Gregory Wilson, "Before the Great Society," 34–49.

23. Eisenhower to Lodge, March 21, 1953, and "U.S. Jobs for N.E. Textiles Sought" clipping, March 21, 1952, both in Office of the Governor of Connecticut Records, box 589; *Depressed Industrial Areas*, 39; U.S. House, Committee on Banking and Currency, *Federal Assistance to Labor Surplus Areas*, 50–51; NEGTC, *New England Textiles* (1958–59), II-21; *NYT*, December 30, 1953, 1, 8.

24. U.S. House, Committee on Banking and Currency, *Federal Assistance to Labor Surplus Areas*, 51–52; NEGTC, *New England Textiles* (1958–59), II-21.

25. U.S. House, Committee on Banking and Currency, *Federal Assistance to Labor Surplus Areas*, 52–53; NEGTC, *New England Textiles* (1958–59), II-21; *Washington Post*, May 28, 1954,

14; "Herter for Governor Headquarters (gordon campbell)," undated "speech material" from 1952 campaign, page 4, folder 893a, and March 11, 1953 Herter address in Fall River, page 2, folder 930—both in Christian A. Herter Papers.

26. Stabile, *Activist Unionism*, 8–14; Gregory Wilson, *Communities Left Behind*, 39–40; *NYT*, April 6, 2000, C25 (Barkin obituary).

27. This and the following two paragraphs are based on Hartford, *Where Is Our Responsibility?*, 183, 188; Gregory Wilson, *Communities Left Behind*, chaps. 1–2; Gregory Wilson, "Before the Great Society," 111–14, 117, 120–26, 128–44, 154–55; National Association of Manufacturers president Lightner to Weeks, August 25, 1958, and U.S. Chamber of Commerce brochure "Opposition to Federal Aid to Depressed Areas," both in Sinclair Weeks Papers, 26/"Commerce Dept., Area Development"; NEGTC, *New England Textiles* (1956), 9–15; NEGTC, *New England Textiles* (1958), I-44, I-45; NEGTC, *New England Textiles* (1958–59), II-19 through II-22; *Depressed Industrial Areas*.

28. Plant closures and automation had created geographic concentrations of unemployment in coal, autos, and steel as well as textiles.

29. U.S. Senate, Committee on Public Works, *Public Works and Economic Development*, 88, 93 (the statistics on New England ARA spending in this publication are "interim and informal"); Eisinger, *Rise of the Entrepreneurial State*, 100–5.

30. These proposals were discussed in chapter 3.

31. See, for example, Institute for Industrial Relations, *Area Redevelopment Policies*, 122–23, 136–38, 334, 338, 340–41.

32. As noted, this account of state government promotional efforts in 1950s Massachusetts summarizes principal points from an earlier more detailed examination of the topic. For that account, including full citations to sources, see Koistinen, "Public Policies for Countering Deindustrialization."

33. For a Republican governor of a liberal, labor-oriented state, Herter's policy choices were astute. Economic development initiatives would only encounter resistance—which could be managed—from factions within Herter's own party. Seeking cuts in social programs such as unemployment insurance would antagonize the state's powerful unions. For more on these points, see Koistinen, "Public Policies for Countering Deindustrialization."

34. As described in chapter 4, the agency was known at its inception as the Industrial Commission.

35. Massachusetts manufacturers and the conservative politicians they backed opposed the establishment of state development institutions since the commonwealth's economic weakness enhanced the competitiveness of existing industrial firms, holding down wages and discouraging obstreperous worker behavior on the shop floor. By contrast, chambers of commerce had numerous service-sector companies in their membership that would benefit from economic recovery. For more on these points, see Koistinen, "Public Policies for Countering Deindustrialization," and Koistinen, "Political Economy of Regional Redevelopment."

36. Proposed government programs of the 1920s resisted by leading Republicans and corporate interests would typically have been implemented at the federal level. (Examples include farm aid and public power.) Massachusetts's new Department of Commerce was, by contrast, an agency of state government. The growing acceptance by Republicans and businessmen of

enlarged public sector endeavors at all levels of government was nonetheless clear in the years after 1945. On how corporate leaders of this era became reconciled to "big government," see Stebenne, "Thomas J. Watson"; Collins, *Business Response to Keynes*.

37. For more on the establishment and operation of these innovative institutions, see Koistinen, "Development Credit Corporations."

38. See Koistinen, "Public Policies for Countering Deindustrialization," 348–49; Koistinen, "Development Credit Corporations."

39. On these NEC initiatives, see coverage for the years 1946–53 in *NENL* and *New Englander*; documents in NEC-SC; and *Atomic Energy and New England*.

40. Manufacturing employment in 1954 stood at 537,000 in Massachusetts and 1.16 million for the New England region. All statistics are for "production workers, total," from the U.S. Census of Manufactures, as reported in Dodd, *Historical Statistics*. New England totals are my calculation.

41. The percentages are my calculations, from figures reported in U.S. Bureau of Labor Statistics, *Employment and Earnings, States and Areas, 1939–72*. Comparative employment statistics for the immediate postwar period appear at the beginning of this chapter.

42. NEGTC, *New England Textiles* (1958), I-1.

43. The discussion that follows is based primarily on Estall, *New England*, and Eisenmenger, *Dynamics of Growth*.

44. Parrott, "Technological and Institutional Innovation," 216. Using a more restricted definition of "electronics," Estall put 1962 New England employment in this sector at 96,000, with about 65,000 of these jobs in Massachusetts. See Estall, *New England*, 81, 93 (map).

45. Estall, *New England*, 161, 164.

46. Estall, *New England*, 249–51; Eisenmenger, *Dynamics of Growth*, 102–3; "Changing Specialization and Bay State Growth," *New England Business Review*, April 1965, 2–8.

47. On the ways in which union work rules hindered competitiveness in post–World War II American manufacturing, see Stebenne, *Arthur J. Goldberg*, 131–32, 197–215, 280–84.

48. *Depressed Industrial Areas*, 10–11; Saxon, "Fall River," 73.

49. Bright and Ellis, *Economic State of New England*, 316–18.

50. Blewett, *Last Generation*, 164.

51. Blewett, *Last Generation*, 190–92.

52. This and the next paragraph are based primarily on Lampe, *Massachusetts Miracle*, 6–10. Statistics on employment are from U.S. Bureau of Labor Statistics, *Employment, Hours, and Earning, States and Areas, 1939–82*, vols. 1 and 2, and Dodd, *Historical Statistics*. Regional employment figures are my calculation.

53. Peirce, *New England States*, 37; Lampe, *Massachusetts Miracle*, 23, 40, 52; New England Regional Commission, *Labor Markets*. On the consumer and environmental regulations Massachusetts enacted in the early 1970s, which were some of the most stringent in the country, see Ronald F. Ferguson and Helen F. Ladd, "Massachusetts" chapters, in Fosler, *New Economic Role*, 35.

54. Lampe, *Massachusetts Miracle*, 59–73; Ferguson and Ladd, "Massachusetts," 35.

55. Lampe, *Massachusetts Miracle*, 11; Ferguson and Ladd, "Massachusetts," 42, 50; *BG*, October 17, 1979, 31.

56. Lampe, *Massachusetts Miracle*, 14–15; Ferguson and Ladd, "Massachusetts," 44, 53–56.

57. Lampe, *Massachusetts Miracle*, 9–10, 16; Kanter, "Theory of the 'Little' State," 118; Ferguson and Ladd, "Massachusetts," 35, 50, 54–56; *Christian Science Monitor*, January 3, 1983, 7; *Wall Street Journal*, February 5, 1980, 22.

58. Ferguson and Ladd, "Massachusetts," 34–35; Kanter, "Theory of the 'Little' State," 155–56; *BG*, March 28, 1975, 12, and November 5, 1975, 13; *BG*, November 7, 1975, 12, and November 8, 1975, 1, 5; *BG*, April 2, 1976, 1, 16, and April 21, 1976, 3; *Massachusetts State Labor Council, AFL-CIO Newsletter*, January 1975–Spring 1977; documents in Massachusetts AFL-CIO Records, boxes 3 and 6; Massachusetts Legislative Documents 1976 (House, No. 4624); Commonwealth of Massachusetts, *Acts and Resolves* (1976), Chap. 473.

59. Lampe, *Massachusetts Miracle*, 10; Ferguson and Ladd, "Massachusetts," 34–35.

60. Greene, *Nixon-Ford Years*, 242–43; Barone et al., *Almanac of American Politics 1978*, 384–86; Dilger, *Sunbelt/Snowbelt Controversy*, 8–10; Massachusetts State Labor Council, AFL-CIO, *Official Labor Record of the Massachusetts House and Senate*, 1965–66, 1967–68, in Massachusetts AFL-CIO Records, 25/1057; *Massachusetts State Labor Council AFL-CIO Newsletter*, August 1969, 1, and September 1969, 3; *NYT*, January 14, 1973, 72.

61. Dilger, *Sunbelt/Snowbelt Controversy*, 1, 8–11, 15–21; Cobb, *Selling of the South*, 197–98.

62. On the coalition's achievements, see Dilger, *Sunbelt/Snowbelt Controversy*, especially chaps. 2, 4, and 5. The genesis of Defense Manpower Policy No. 4 was discussed earlier in this chapter.

The successes of Snowbelt representatives almost inevitably provoked a response in the southern states that had much to lose. To counter the northern offensive and protect their existing share of federal dollars, representatives of Dixie made the Southern Growth Policies Board into an influential research and lobbying organization for the South. By the end of the decade, something of a stalemate had arisen between the two regional groupings. See Dilger, *Sunbelt/Snowbelt Controversy*, chap. 3; Cobb, *Selling of the South*, 200–2; Schulman, *Seventies*, 107.

63. Ferguson and Ladd, "Massachusetts," 48–49; "Sell Massachusetts," *BG*, August 26, 1980.

64. *NYT*, March 21, 1979, A1, D15, especially accompanying chart; *Wall Street Journal*, April 13, 1979, 6; *BG*, May 2, 1979, 33.

65. Council for Northeast Economic Action, *Empirical Analysis*; Council for Northeast Economic Action, *How Banks*. The 1920s New England Council study, Freeland & Warren, *A Report of a Study of Current Banking Services*, was discussed in chapter 5.

66. *Regional Data Quarterly* (Council for Northeast Economic Action), issues for 3rd and 4th quarters, 1978, especially the letters of transmittal.

67. Ferguson and Ladd, "Massachusetts," 33.

68. First National Bank of Boston, *Manufacturing Structure of New England*, 1–3, 14.

69. Ferguson and Ladd, "Massachusetts," 40–41; William L. Brown interview.

70. Ferguson and Ladd, "Massachusetts," 39–41, 43; Hill and Shelley, "Overview of Economic Development Finance," 25. One of the era's crucial reports on the subject is New England Regional Commission, *Capital Markets in New England*. The fact that the venture capital market of the mid-1970s was in the midst of one of its periodic slumps doubtless exacerbated the era's capital gap.

71. One reason for creating new public development institutions was stagnation at the existing one. The Massachusetts Department of Commerce was created in 1953 amid significant industrial downsizing and spearheaded the commonwealth's promotional efforts in the period that followed. The agency was a hive of activity in its first years of operation. This vitality later slackened, with the department's programs displaying little imagination and legislators perceiving it as a dumping ground for political appointees. This state of affairs was tolerable from the late 1950s through the late 1960s, when economic conditions in Massachusetts were relatively good. It became problematic when economic difficulties returned in the late 1960s. Governors took steps during the later period to revitalize the department, while at the same time seeking new avenues by which state government could encourage growth. See Kanter, "Theory of the 'Little' State," 149–58, and also Ferguson and Ladd, "Massachusetts," 40.

72. Ferguson and Ladd, "Massachusetts," 41, 44–45, 77; Eisinger, *Rise of the Entrepreneurial State*, 258–59; Kanter, "Theory of the 'Little' State," 95; "Sell Massachusetts," *BG*, August 26, 1980.

73. Locally oriented service-sector companies at times joined the push for retrenchment. In the 1970s, for example, the First National Bank of Boston was a prominent supporter of cutbacks in government programs. But the bank typically framed its arguments during this period in terms of the well-being of manufacturing and other area companies that competed in national markets.

74. Pressure for retrenchment from Massachusetts employers predated the onset of deindustrialization in the case of the 1920s fights over restrictions on the working hours of women and the 1950s battle about unemployment insurance. Similarly, in the early and mid-1960s, when the commonwealth economy was in relatively good condition, "damning the state's economic 'climate' [was] the business of big business" in Massachusetts. See "Massachusetts in '80 . . ." *BG*, February 10, 1980.

75. Support for less interventionist forms of federal assistance to troubled industries and areas was generally more broad-based. As early as the 1930s, cotton textile makers facing surging shipments of low-cost fabric from Japan called for new trade protections. In the 1950s, certain New England Republicans were among the advocates of channeling defense purchases and investment into labor surplus areas. In recent decades, manufacturers facing new import competition strongly backed additional trade protection. Unionists and liberals also supported government action in each of these cases, although other groups typically led the calls for federal assistance. On union support since the 1950s for trade protection in various industries, see Stein, *Running Steel*, 226, 235–37, and Vinod K. Aggarwal, with Stephan Haggard, "The Politics of Protection in the U.S. Textile and Apparel Industries," including 268, 293, in Zysman and Tyson, *American Industry*.

76. Howell campaigned for reductions in taxes and regulations on Bay State business; aided the Snowbelt campaign to win more federal aid for the region; and worked to spur the growth of new local industry.

77. It is also easy to see how federal assistance of this kind appealed to other groups, including companies that stood to receive aid; businesses tied to the area; centrist politicians; and the general public.

78. As David Harvey explains, the increasing prominence of free-market views among

U.S. policymakers of this era was part of a worldwide shift towards what is called "neoliberalism." Advocates of neoliberalism seek to "liberat[e] individual entrepreneurial freedoms and skills within an institutional framework characterized by strong private property rights, free markets, and free trade," while limiting state intervention in markets "to a bare minimum." Friedrich von Hayek and Milton Friedman were leading champions of these concepts. See Harvey, *Brief History of Neoliberalism*, 2–4, 19–22.

79. Reagan-era cuts in the area redevelopment program are discussed in the following chapter. The greater role over time of government in formulating responses to deindustrialization was even visible with respect to retrenchment. The expanded place of the public sector can be seen there in the scope and expense of the government programs that retrenchment advocates sought to cut back. As the years progressed, supporters of retrenchment contested public programs that were more expansive and costly—reflecting the growth in government that took place through time. In the 1920s, Massachusetts employers seeking cutbacks targeted the state's hours of work laws. The restrictions were minimal in form, although significant in impact. The statutes simply dictated at what times and for what periods managers could employ female workers. By contrast, Bay State firms seeking cutbacks in the 1950s focused their attention on unemployment insurance. This was an extensive program in which the state collected sizable sums in employer taxes and distributed benefits to jobless workers at levels determined by complex formulas. In the 1970s, employers seeking retrenchment again sought cutbacks in unemployment insurance and also pushed for cuts in welfare payments to poor families—another large, complicated, and expensive public program.

Chapter 8. Conclusions

1. Stein, *Running Steel*, 235, 253; Bluestone and Harrison, *Deindustrialization of America*, 36–37.

2. Manufacturing employment fell by 29 percent in Michigan and 25 percent in Ohio in the years 1977–82. The decline was 22 percent in New York State in the longer 1972–82 period. Figures are for manufacturing production workers and are calculated from statistics in Dodd, *Historical Statistics*.

3. U.S. Bureau of the Census, *Statistical Abstract*, 1991.

4. Vogel, *Fluctuating Fortunes*, 113.

5. *Business Week*, October 12, 1974, 123, and June 30, 1980, 127–31; *Boston Herald*, September 22, 1980, A15; Vogel, *Fluctuating Fortunes*, 145, 174–76, 193–227, 242–46.

6. Michael I. Luger, "Federal Tax Incentives as Industrial and Urban Policy," in Sawers and Tabb, *Sunbelt/Snowbelt*, 204–13; Stockman, *Triumph of Politics*, 57, 229–68. Legislation in 1982 undid a portion of the business tax reduction enacted in 1981, and the 1986 tax reform raised the levies on certain types of businesses, including large manufacturers (Vogel, *Fluctuating Fortunes*, 252–55, 279–82). Dramatic retrenchment in business taxes, stemming at least in part from fears about competitiveness, was nevertheless in effect at least temporarily in the early 1980s. Moreover, some of the era's business tax cuts were permanent.

7. Vogel, *Fluctuating Fortunes*, 148–50, 163–68, 172–73, 181–90, 246–51, 260–69. The regulatory easing of this period stemmed in part from a reaction against restrictions that were overly

burdensome. Concerns about hampering business in an era of economic stagnation also contributed. See Vogel, *Fluctuating Fortunes*, 228–37.

8. *Nation's Business*, May 1989, 32; *NYT*, June 30, 1992, A19, and July 2, 1992, A16; *NYT*, July 15, 1992, A14, and October 1, 1993, A16.

9. Stein, *Running Steel*, 219–23, 235–39, 281–82; Graham, *Losing Time*, 28–29; Vogel, *Fluctuating Fortunes*, 258.

10. Vinod K. Aggarwal, with Stephan Haggard, "The Politics of Protection in the U.S. Textile and Apparel Industries," 267–307, and David B. Yoffie, "Adjustment in the Footwear Industry: The Consequences of Orderly Marketing Agreements," 314, 338–41, both in Zysman and Tyson, *American Industry*; Vogel, *Fluctuating Fortunes*, 258; Graham, *Losing Time*, 35. Federal action to restrict imports in troubled industries was a long-established pattern. The first use of voluntary restraints to hold down imports and head off formal trade restrictions occurred in the 1930s, when Japanese manufacturers agreed to curtail rapidly growing shipments of certain cotton textile products (see text and notes at the end of chapter 3). U.S. textile producers again won restrictions on imports, especially from Japan, in the 1950s.

11. Graham, *Losing Time*, 13, 33–35, 125.

12. Weir, *Politics and Jobs*, 142–43; Stein, *Running Steel*, 224–25, 240, 267.

13. Eisinger, *Rise of the Entrepreneurial State*, 100–6; Gregory Wilson, *Communities Left Behind*, 150.

14. *Atlantic Monthly*, March 2000, 41; *Washington Post*, December 7, 1998, A15.

15. *Business Week*, April 7, 1986, 94–96; *Fortune*, June 5, 1989, 245–54; *Far Eastern Economic Review*, May 24, 1990, 68–70; Irwin and Klenow, "High-Tech R&D Subsidies," 325.

16. *Wall Street Journal*, February 17, 1987, 1; *Washington Post*, September 27, 1987, 1; *Fortune*, June 5, 1989, 245–54; *Far Eastern Economic Review*, May 24, 1990, 68–70; Irwin and Klenow, "High-Tech R&D Subsidies." The Pentagon helped finance Sematech because semiconductors were deemed to be a strategic industry.

17. *Wall Street Journal*, October 8, 1990, B7E; *Washington Post*, March 3, 1993, A15, and September 2, 1993, A25; *Chemical & Engineering News*, September 6, 1993, 19; *Industry Week*, May 2, 1994, 64.

18. *Washington Post*, September 2, 1993, A25; *Quality*, November 1996, 18.

19. *Washington Post*, March 3, 1993, A15; *Quality*, November 1996, 18, and May 1998, 12–14; *Industry Week*, May 2, 1994, 64.

20. Trebilcock et al., *Trade and Transitions*, 65, 116–17.

21. Trebilcock et al., *Trade and Transitions*, 51–53, 63–64, 66–67.

22. Trebilcock et al., *Trade and Transitions*, 88, 91–92; Storchmann, "Rise and Fall."

23. The shift toward a free-market approach to policymaking, although less pronounced in Europe than elsewhere, bolstered the Continent's push for retrenchment.

24. *Guardian*, March 15, 1994, 13; *Irish Times*, March 23, 1994, 6; *Financial Times*, August 28, 2003, 18; "A New Contract in France," *International Herald Tribune*, February 17, 2006; "Labor Law's Defeat," *International Herald Tribune*, April 12, 2006.

25. *NYT*, April 27, 1996, 1, and June 29, 1996, 33; *NYT*, April 7, 2002, 8; *NYT*, "Election Defeat May," February 4, 2003; *Washington Post*, June 16, 1996, A24; *Wall Street Journal*, July 1, 1996, B7; *International Herald Tribune*, July 2, 2002, 3; *Irish Times*, May 7, 2003, 10; *Christian*

Science Monitor, July 29, 2003, 1; "A Long, Hard Climb," *Economist*, October 18, 2003; "Will Hartz . . . ," *Business & Finance*, March 24, 2005.

26. Van Waarden and Lehmbruch, *Renegotiating the Welfare State*; *Economist*, May 2, 1998, 49; Swank and Steinmo, "New Political Economy," 643.

27. *Chronicle of Higher Education*, March 19, 1999, A49–50; *Los Angeles Times*, March 13, 2000, C1, C8.

28. Alaimo, "Villes et systèmes productifs locaux," 128–32; Werner, "Finland."

29. The three-initiative model of responses to deindustrialization is a powerful tool for making sense of a dense web of activity. Like most generalizations, however, it cannot completely encompass the full complexity of events. Thus some fuzziness, or overlap, continued to exist along the boundaries between the different initiatives for countering industrial decline identified in this study. For example, industrial subsidies are a policy tool frequently employed in recent times by countries experiencing economic distress. Under the analytical scheme set out here, these are categorized differently depending on the circumstances. German subsidies to the downsizing coal mining industry are considered to be an example of federal/national assistance, while the matching investment funds Germany provided to biotechnology companies—a form of subsidy—are classified as economic development.

30. On the declining political power of U.S. unions after the early 1960s, see Stebenne, *Arthur J. Goldberg*.

31. Union membership as a share of the Massachusetts workforce was about 15 percent in 1922 (see chapter 2) and about 25 percent in the mid-1970s (Hirsch et al., *State Union Membership*).

32. Phillips-Fein, *Invisible Hands*; Waterhouse, *Lobbying America*.

33. On the expansion of non-union manufacturing in the South during the post–World War II years and the threat this posed to organized labor, see Stebenne, *Arthur J. Goldberg*, 54, 118, 336–37; Friedman, "Exploiting the North-South Differential," 338–48.

34. Although they would have equalized wages, the New Deal legislative proposals discussed here would have left open-shop producers unconstrained by the union work rules that can significantly hamper productivity and raise costs at unionized employers. Producers in open-shop states would also have continued to benefit from state labor laws that were less strict and from lower levels of state and local taxes.

35. The New Deal legislative proposals would not have affected directly other causes of union decline, such as automation, import competition, union busting, and obstacles to organizing non-union workers.

36. The efforts are described in Graham, *Losing Time,* and Vogel, *Fluctuating Fortunes*, 258–60. Among the works backing an industrial policy approach are Graham, *Losing Time*; Zysman and Tyson, *American Industry*; Stein, *Running Steel*; and more recently Stein, *Pivotal Decade*.

37. A contemporary media account of ATP's activities was titled "Industrial Policy? It's Here." See *Industry Week*, May 2, 1994, 64.

38. Fosler, *New Economic Role*; Eisinger, *Rise of the Entrepreneurial State*; Graham, *Losing Time*, 193–203.

39. Encouraging the growth of locally based firms generally expands the total size of the na-

tion's economic pie, while recruiting out-of-state companies mostly moves existing economic activity from one place to another, which does little to increase the overall level of output.

40. See the discussion of this issue in Graham, *Losing Time*, chap. 7.

41. By growth-promotion efforts that occurred entirely in the private sector, I mean cases in which private interests conceived, organized, and *carried out* steps to encourage development. I do not mean instances in which private groups lobbied government for growth-promoting measures that were then implemented in the public sector.

42. Thus volumes such as Graham, *Losing Time,* and Zysman and Tyson, *American Industry,* call for enhanced growth-promotion efforts by the U.S. government, while works such as Johnson, *MITI and the Japanese Miracle,* and Amsden, *Asia's Next Giant,* highlight the development role of governments abroad.

43. Libby, "To Build Wings for the Angels." See also Markusen et al., *Rise of the Gunbelt*, chap. 5.

44. Luger and Goldstein, *Technology in the Garden*, chap. 5; Hamilton, "Research Triangle"; Louis Wilson, *Research Triangle*. The drive to set up Research Triangle Park did receive key public-sector support from North Carolina governor Luther Hodges and other state officials.

45. Joe R. Feagin and Robert E. Parker, "Economic Troubles and Local State Action: Some Texas Examples," in Wallace and Rothschild, *Deindustrialization and the Restructuring*, 127–53. The Houston effort put strong emphasis—as much contemporary growth-promotion activity does—on encouraging the development of technology-intensive industries. Houston promoters achieved a major success in 1988, beating out at least seven competing locales to become the new headquarters of Grumman's space systems group, which company officials had decided to move out of an increasingly crowded and expensive Long Island location. See Markusen et al., *Rise of the Gunbelt*, 126.

46. Under French law a company laying off a veteran employee can become involved in lengthy, costly litigation and may have to pay the discharged worker as much as two years of salary. See "A New Contract in France," *International Herald Tribune*, February 17, 2006. The regulations are clearly counterproductive in a country that has seen elevated levels of unemployment for decades.

47. The U.S. judicial system does impose a level of expense on companies not seen abroad, due to the very large awards that can be granted in corporate liability cases. Generally speaking, however, the burden of taxation and government regulations on business has been lighter in the United States than elsewhere. Data from the OECD and other sources show that this was the case in the 1970s and more recently for social security contributions as a percentage of GDP; public spending on assistance to the unemployed as a percentage of GDP; number of mandated vacation days; and ease of employee dismissal. See OECD, "Revenue Statistics: Comparative Tables," and "Labour Market Programmes"; Weinberg and Dukcevich, "World's Freest Labor Markets."

48. The burden of the resulting revenue shortfall is borne by society as a whole, in the form of countervailing increases in other levies and/or cuts in government services.

49. These post–World War II events of course recapitulated the way in which newer firms in the post–Civil War American South captured much of the U.S. cotton textile market from older Yankee producers.

50. Aggarwal, "Politics of Protection"; *NYT*, September 20, 1985, A1, and December 20, 1987, sect. 1, 12; *Washington Post*, October 13, 1985, D1, and July 10, 1986, E1; *Christian Science Monitor*, January 29, 1990, 9.

51. Carter et al., *Historical Statistics of the United States*, 4–586 (1973 and 1996 employment levels). The 2003 employment figure is my estimate, based on data in U.S. Bureau of the Census, *Statistical Abstract* (2006), 647. On the new definition of textiles adopted by government statisticians in 1997, see Carter et al., *Historical Statistics of the United States*, 4–586, 4–612; U.S. Bureau of the Census, *Statistical Abstract* (2004–5), 482, 630.

52. Had action been taken in the mid-twentieth century to protect producers in the northeastern United States by pushing up wage rates in the South, a higher-wage U.S. textile industry would have declined at an even more rapid pace in recent decades.

53. Subsidies in 2002, when there were 50,000 German coal miners, totaled €3.5 billion, or approximately €70,000 per job. Figures from Storchmann, "Rise and Fall," 1470, 1491; subsidy total in year 2000 euros.

54. As an example of the latter, the MBDC, the development credit corporation set up in Massachusetts in 1953, had by year-end 1957 made $14 million in loans, which supported the creation or preservation of 15,000 industrial jobs. Since the organization only extended financing to companies that did not qualify for conventional bank lending, many of these positions would not have existed in the state without the MBDC. While the MBDC's efforts were certainly worthwhile in an area that badly needed additional employment, the jobs created were a small fraction of total Bay State factory employment, which stood at 521,000 in 1957. See Koistinen, "Public Policies for Countering Deindustrialization," 343–44.

55. As earlier noted, a similar sequence seems to have occurred with regard to the aircraft industry in Los Angeles. Post–World War I efforts by Los Angeles businessmen to promote the growth of aircraft manufacturing helped make the city a major center of airframe production. Having rooted itself in that location, the aerospace industry prospered and grew in Los Angeles for decades to come.

56. Both of the displaced Lowell textile workers whose accounts are excerpted in the previous chapter found jobs in the growing electronics industry of Route 128. One of the men ended up in a desirable post with a major producer. Other veterans of Lowell's clothmaking industry had similar experiences; see, for example, the Arthur Morrissette interview in Blewett, *Last Generation*, 206–7. Lowell's proximity to Route 128 doubtless helped former textile operatives from that city secure employment in electronics.

Bibliography

Some of the published works used in this study are exceptionally rare. In these cases, the repository where the work was found is identified in the references. Manuscript collections and interviews are listed at the end of the bibliography.

Books, Articles, Reports, Proceedings, Government Documents, and Other Works

Abrams, Richard. *Conservatism in a Progressive Era: Massachusetts Politics, 1900–1912.* Cambridge: Harvard University Press, 1964.

Adamic, Louis. "Tragic Towns of New England." *Harper's Monthly* (May 1931): 748–60.

Adams, Russell B. Jr. *The Boston Money Tree.* New York: Crowell, 1977.

Addresses before the Stockholders of Federal Reserve Bank of New England by Frederic H. Curtis . . . and John S. Lawrence . . . [properly Frederick H. Curtiss, Federal Reserve Bank of Boston]. Delivered at stockholders meeting, November 1924. N.p., n.d. Available at Baker Library, Harvard Business School.

AIM Directory of Massachusetts Companies Serving the Electronics and Nucleonics Industry, rev. ed. N.p. [Boston?: Associated Industries of Massachusetts], 1957. Available at Baker Library, Harvard Business School.

Alaimo, Aurelio. "Villes et systèmes productifs locaux dans l'Italie contemporaine (1950–2000)." In *Villes et districts industriels en Europe occidentale, XVIIe–XXe siècles*, edited by Michel Lescure and Jean-François Eck, 119–36. Tours, France: Université François Rabelais, 2002.

American Council of Commercial Laboratories. *Directory of American Council of Commercial Laboratories.* N.p., n.d. [American Council of Commercial Laboratories, 1948?].

American National Biography, 24 vols. New York: Oxford University Press, 1999.

American Research and Development Corporation. *Annual Report* (1949, 1951). Historic Corporate Reports Collection, Baker Library, Harvard Business School.

American Research and Development Corporation: Registration Statement: As Amended and Effective August 8, 1946. Statement filed with the Securities and Exchange Commission. Historic Corporate Reports Collection, Baker Library, Harvard Business School.

Amory, Cleveland. *The Proper Bostonians.* New York: Dutton, 1947.

Amsden, Alice H. *Asia's Next Giant: South Korea and Late Industrialization.* New York: Oxford University Press, 1989.

Annual Report of . . . General Manager, Associated Industries of Massachusetts (1923–1930). Available at Baker Library, Harvard Business School.

Ante, Spencer E. *Creative Capital: Georges Doriot and the Birth of Venture Capital.* Boston: Harvard Business Press, 2008.

Asher, Robert. "Business and Workers' Welfare in the Progressive Era: Workmen's Compensation Reform in Massachusetts." *Business History Review* 43 (Winter 1969): 452–75.

Atomic Energy and New England: The Report of the New England Committee on Atomic Energy to the New England Governors' Conference. N.p., 1955.

Barone, Michael, Grant Ujifusa, and Douglas Matthews. *The Almanac of American Politics 1978.* New York: E. P. Dutton, 1978.

Barrett, Ross Knox. *To the Digital Age: Research Labs, Start-up Companies, and the Rise of MOS Technology.* Baltimore: Johns Hopkins University Press, 2002.

Beal, Thomas P. *The Second National Bank of Boston.* Boston: Second National Bank of Boston, 1958.

Bean, Jonathan J. *Beyond the Broker State: Federal Policies toward Small Business, 1936–1961.* Chapel Hill: University of North Carolina Press, 1996.

Before the Committee on Labor and Industry: Hearings on Senate 93 . . . 94 . . . and . . . 95 . . . : Statement of Ward Thoron . . . February 13, 1924. N.p., n.d. [Boston?, 1924?]. Available at Widener-Pusey Library, Harvard University.

Bensman, David. *Rusted Dreams: Hard Times in a Steel Community.* New York: McGraw-Hill, 1987.

Bernstein, Irving. *The Lean Years: A History of the American Worker, 1920–1933.* Baltimore: Penguin, 1960.

Beyer, Clara. "History of Labor Legislation for Women in Three States." *Bulletin of the Women's Bureau* (U.S. Department of Labor), no. 66. Washington, D.C.: GPO, 1929.

Biographical Sketches of the Members of the 96th Maine Legislature. Augusta, Me.: Daily Kennebec Journal, 1953.

Blewett, Mary H. *Constant Turmoil: The Politics of Industrial Life in Nineteenth-Century New England.* Amherst: University of Massachusetts Press, 2000.

———. *The Last Generation: Work and Life in the Textile Mills of Lowell, Massachusetts, 1910–1960.* Amherst: University of Massachusetts Press, 1990.

———. *To Enrich and to Serve: The Centennial History of the University of Massachusetts, Lowell.* Virginia Beach, Va.: Donning Company, 1995.

Blicksilver, Jack. *Cotton Manufacturing in the Southeast: An Historical Analysis.* Atlanta: Georgia State College of Business Administration, 1959.

Bluestone, Barry, and Bennett Harrison. *The Deindustrialization of America: Plant Closings, Community Abandonment, and the Dismantling of Basic Industry.* New York: Basic Books, 1982.

Boston Chamber of Commerce. *The Boston Chamber of Commerce: A Brief Statement of Its Committees, Their Personnel and Their Plan of Work for the Chamber Year 1917–1918.* Boston: Boston Chamber of Commerce, 1917. Available at Baker Library, Harvard Business School.

———. *The Cotton Manufacturing Industry of New England.* Boston: Boston Chamber of Commerce, 1926.

———. *The Foundry and Machining Industries of New England*. Boston: Boston Chamber of Commerce, 1926.

———. *The Shoe Manufacturing Industry of New England*. Boston: Boston Chamber of Commerce, 1925.

Boston Evening Transcript. *The Boston National Banks and Trust Companies: Reports of Condition at December 31, 1940*. Boston: Evening Transcript, n.d. [1941].

Boston Industrial Development Board. *Boston: The Place in Which to Manufacture, to Live, to Trade, to Visit*. Boston: Boston Industrial Development Board, 1915. Available at Mudd Library, Yale University.

Bradshaw, Ted K., and Edward J. Blakely. "What Are 'Third Wave' State Economic Development Efforts? From Incentives to Industrial Policy." *Economic Development Quarterly* 13 (August 1999): 229–44.

Bright, Arthur A. Jr., and George H. Ellis, eds. *The Economic State of New England: Report of the Committee of New England of the National Planning Association*. New Haven: Yale University Press, 1954.

Brody, David. *Workers in Industrial America: Essays on the Twentieth Century Struggle*. New York: Oxford University Press, 1993.

Brown, Ashmun. *A Study of the Cotton Industry North and South*. Providence: Remington Press, n.d. [1924?].

Brown, Dona. *Inventing New England: Regional Tourism in the Nineteenth Century*. Washington, D.C.: Smithsonian Institution Press, 1995.

Brown, Robert M. "Cotton Manufacturing: North and South." *Economic Geography* 4 (January 1928): 74–87.

Bullock, Matthew. *Academic Enterprise, Industrial Innovation, and the Development of High Technology Financing in the United States*. London: Brand Brothers and Company, 1983.

Butters, J. Keith, and John Lintner. *Effect of Federal Taxes on Growing Enterprises*. Boston: Harvard Graduate School of Business Administration, 1945.

Carter, Susan B., Scott Sigmund Gartner, Michael R. Haines, Alan L. Olmstead, Richard Sutch, and Gavin Wright, eds. *Historical Statistics of the United States: Earliest Times to the Present*, Millennial ed., 5 vols. New York: Cambridge University Press, 2006.

Chandler, Alfred D. *The Visible Hand: The Managerial Revolution in American Business*. Cambridge: Harvard University Press, 1977.

Clark, Victor S. *History of Manufactures in the United States, 1607–1860*, 2 vols. Washington, D.C.: Carnegie Institution, 1916.

Cobb, James C. *The Selling of the South: The Southern Crusade for Industrial Development, 1936–1980*. Baton Rouge: Louisiana State University Press, 1982.

Collins, Robert. *The Business Response to Keynes, 1929–1964*. New York: Columbia University Press, 1981.

Committee of New England Research Consultants, in cooperation with the New England Council. *Opportunities Available to New England Business in the Aeronautical Trades*. N.p., n.d. Available at Baker Library, Harvard Business School.

Commonwealth of Massachusetts. *Acts and Resolves Passed by the General Court of Massachusetts*. 1976.

---. *Annual Report of the Department of Labor and Industries.* Public Document No. 104. 1930–33.

---. *Final Report of the Special Commission Established to Investigate Municipal Expenditures and Undertakings and the Appropriation of Money under Municipal Authority.* 1929. Massachusetts Legislative Documents 1929: House, No. 1150.

---. *Report of the Special Commission Appointed to Continue the Work of Investigating Changes in the Tax Laws of the Commonwealth or Other Matters Relative Thereto.* January 1932. Massachusetts Legislative Documents 1932: House, No. 1160.

---. *Report of the Special Commission Appointed to Investigate the Entire Subject of State, County and Local Taxation, and Revenues from Fees and Other Sources.* December 1927. Massachusetts Legislative Documents 1928: House, No. 490.

---. *Report of the Special Commission Directed to Continue the Investigation of the Entire Subject of State, County and Local Taxation and Revenues From Fees and Other Sources.* December 1929. Massachusetts Legislative Documents 1930: House, No. 900.

---. *Report of the Special Commission Directed to Study the General Subject of State, County, and Local Taxation and the Taxation of Personal Income and of Corporations.* December 1930. Massachusetts Legislative Documents 1931: House, No. 200.

---. *Report of the Special Commission on Taxation, Part V: The Taxation of Business and Manufacturing Corporations.* February 1952. Massachusetts Legislative Documents 1952: House, No. 2114.

---. *Report of the Special Commission Relative to Establishment of a State Department of Commerce.* December 1945. Massachusetts Legislative Documents 1946: House, No. 300.

---. *Report of the Special Commission Relative to Taxation of Tangible and Intangible Property and Certain Related Matters.* January 1936. Massachusetts Legislative Documents 1936: House, No. 143.

Copeland, Melvin. *The Cotton Manufacturing Industry of the United States.* Cambridge: Harvard University Press, 1912.

Council for Northeast Economic Action. *An Empirical Analysis of the Unmet Demand in Domestic Capital Markets in Five U.S. Regions.* Washington, D.C.: U.S. Department of Commerce, 1981.

---. *How Banks Participate in Local Economic Development: Five Models.* N.p., 1982.

Cowie, Jefferson R. *Capital Moves: RCA's Seventy-Year Quest for Cheap Labor.* Ithaca: Cornell University Press, 1999.

Cowie, Jefferson, and Joseph Heathcott, eds. *Beyond the Ruins: The Meanings of Deindustrialization.* Ithaca, N.Y.: ILR Press, 2003.

Creange, Henry. *The 3-Phase System for the Mass Production of Style Goods: A Plan for Lifting New England Manufactures Out of Price Competition.* Address to the New England Council, Bretton Woods, N.H., September 1926. N.p., n.d.

Cumbler, John T. *A Social History of Economic Decline: Business, Politics and Work in Trenton.* New Brunswick: Rutgers University Press, 1989.

Dawley, Alan. *Class and Community: The Industrial Revolution in Lynn.* Cambridge: Harvard University Press, 1976.

Depressed Industrial Areas—A National Problem. Planning Document No. 98. Washington, D.C.: National Planning Association, 1957.

Deutermann, Elizabeth P. "Seeding Science-Based Industry." *Business Review* (Federal Reserve Bank of Philadelphia), May 1966, 3–10.

Dictionary of American Biography, 20 vols. plus supplements. New York: C. Scribner's Sons, 1928–58.

Dilger, Robert Jay. *The Sunbelt/Snowbelt Controversy: The War over Federal Funds.* New York: New York University Press, 1982.

Dillon, Conley H. "Channeling Government Contracts into Depressed Areas." *Western Political Quarterly* 16 (June 1963): 279–93.

DiSalvo, Daniel. "The Politics of a Party Faction: The Labor-Liberal Alliance in the Democratic Party, 1948–1972." *Journal of Policy History* 22, no. 3 (2010): 269–99.

Dodd, Donald B. *Historical Statistics of the States of the United States: Two Centuries of the Census, 1790–1990.* Westport, Conn.: Greenwood Press, 1993.

Donahue, John R. *Causes of the Financial Breakdown of the Local Government of Fall River, Mass., and Means Taken by Massachusetts to Re-establish the Finances of That City.* State of Connecticut Taxation Document No. 255. [Hartford?]: Tax Commissioner of Connecticut, 1933.

Dublin, Thomas. *Women at Work: The Transformation of Work and Community in Lowell, Massachusetts, 1826–1860.* New York: Columbia University Press, 1979.

Dublin, Thomas, and Walter Licht. *The Face of Decline: The Pennsylvania Anthracite Region in the Twentieth Century.* Ithaca: Cornell University Press, 2005.

Dubofsky, Melvyn. *The State and Labor in Modern America.* Chapel Hill: University of North Carolina Press, 1994.

Eckes, Alfred E. *Opening America's Market: U.S. Foreign Trade Policy Since 1776.* Chapel Hill: University of North Carolina Press, 1995.

Eisenmenger, Robert. *The Dynamics of Growth in New England's Economy.* Middletown, Conn.: Wesleyan University Press, 1967.

Eisinger, Peter K. *The Rise of the Entrepreneurial State: State and Local Economic Development Policy in the United States.* Madison: University of Wisconsin Press, 1988.

Ellenbogen, Henry. "Address to Hosiery Workers." In "Proceedings, American Federation of Hosiery Workers," (Jan. 1937), vol. I. American Federation of Hosiery Workers Records, Part II, box 9, folder 1.

Engerman, Stanley, and Robert E. Gallman, eds. *The Cambridge Economic History of the United States*, 3 vols. Cambridge: Cambridge University Press, 2000.

English, Beth. *A Common Thread: Labor, Politics, and Capital Mobility in the Textile Industry.* Athens: University of Georgia Press, 2006.

Estall, R. C. *New England: A Study in Industrial Adjustment.* London: G. Bell and Sons, 1966.

Etzkowitz, Henry. "Enterprises from Science: The Origins of Science-Based Regional Economic Development." *Minerva* 31 (Autumn 1993): 326–60.

Everett Mills. (Pamphlets. Financial History.) Letters to stockholders from management of Everett Mills, Lawrence, Mass. Available at Mudd Library, Yale University.

Federal Reserve Bank of Boston. *New England Economic Almanac*, 3rd rev. ed. Boston: Federal Reserve Bank of Boston, 1966.

Fink, Gary M. *Biographical Dictionary of American Labor*. Westport, Conn.: Greenwood Press, 1984.

First National Bank of Boston. *The Manufacturing Structure of New England: The Alternatives before Us*. Boston: First National Bank of Boston, 1972.

First Report of New England Council's Special Committee on Ownership and Finance. N.p., n.d. [Boston: New England Council, 1945].

Fosler, R. Scott. "Does Economic Theory Capture the Effects of New and Traditional State Policies on Economic Development?" In *Competition among States and Local Governments: Efficiency and Equity in American Federalism*, edited by Daphne A. Kenyon and John Kincaid, 247–50. Washington, D.C.: Urban Institute Press, 1991.

Fosler, R. Scott, ed. *The New Economic Role of American States: Strategies in a Competitive World Economy*. New York: Oxford University Press, 1988.

Fraser, Steven. *Labor Will Rule: Sidney Hillman and the Rise of American Labor*. New York: Free Press, 1991.

Freeland, Bates & Lawrence. *A Brief Study of Industrial Massachusetts*. N.p., n.d. [Boston: Massachusetts Industrial Commission, 1931?].

Freeland & Warren, Inc. *A Report of a Study of Current Banking Services*. Boston, n.d. [1929].

French, George, ed. *New England: What It Is, What It Is to Be*. Boston: Boston Chamber of Commerce, 1911.

Friedman, Tami J. "Communities in Competition: Capital Migration and Plant Relocation in the U.S. Carpet Industry, 1929–1975." Ph.D. diss., Columbia University, 2001.

———. "Exploiting the North-South Differential: Corporate Power, Southern Politics, and the Decline of Organized Labor after World War II." *Journal of American History* 95, no. 2 (September 2008): 323–48.

Galambos, Louis. *Competition and Cooperation: The Emergence of a National Trade Association*. Baltimore: Johns Hopkins University Press, 1966.

———. "Technology, Political Economy, and Professionalization: Central Themes of the Organizational Synthesis." *Business History Review* 57 (Winter 1983): 471–93.

Galbraith, John Kenneth. "Seymour Edwin Harris." *Review of Economics and Statistics* 57, no. 1 (February 1975): vi–vii.

Galenson, Alice. *The Migration of the Cotton Textile Industry from New England to the South, 1880–1930*. New York: Garland Publishing, 1985.

Gibson, Gary Lee. "Financing Small Electronics Firms in New England." B.S. thesis, MIT, 1960.

Gillette, Howard, Jr. *Camden after the Fall: Decline and Renewal in a Post-Industrial City*. Philadelphia: University of Pennsylvania Press, 2005.

Gordon, Colin. *New Deals: Business, Labor, and Politics in America, 1920–1935*. Cambridge: Cambridge University Press, 1994.

Gordon, Kenneth Frederick. "An Examination of Some Problems of Financing and Managing a New-Research-Based-Enterprise." M.S. thesis, MIT, 1960.

Graham, Otis. *Losing Time: The Industrial Policy Debate*. Cambridge: Harvard University Press, 1992.

Greene, John Robert. *The Nixon-Ford Years*. New York: Facts on File, 2006.

Greenwald, Richard A. *The Triangle Fire, The Protocols of Peace, and Industrial Democracy in Progressive Era New York*. Philadelphia: Temple University Press, 2005.

Griner, John A. "Financing the Growing Electronics Enterprise in New England." Report submitted for a course at Harvard Business School, January 12, 1959. Available at Research Library, Federal Reserve Bank of Boston.

Gross, Lawrence F. *The Course of Industrial Decline: The Boott Cotton Mills of Lowell, Massachusetts, 1835–1955*. Baltimore: Johns Hopkins University Press, 1993.

Grow, Natalie R. "The 'Boston-Type Open-End Fund'—Development of a National Financial Institution: 1924–1940." Ph.D. diss., Harvard University, 1977.

Hall, Jacquelyn Dowd, James Leloudis, Robert Korstad, Mary Murphy, LuAnn Jones, and Christopher B. Daly. *Like a Family: The Making of a Southern Cotton Mill World*. Chapel Hill: University of North Carolina Press, 1987.

Hamilton, W. B. "The Research Triangle of North Carolina: A Study in Leadership for the Common Weal." *South Atlantic Quarterly* 65 (Spring 1966): 254–78.

Harevan, Tamara K., and Randolph Langenbach. *Amoskeag: Life and Work in an American Factory-City*. New York: Pantheon, 1978.

Harris, Seymour. *The Economics of New England: Case Study of an Older Area*. Cambridge: Harvard University Press, 1952.

Hartford, William F. *Where Is Our Responsibility? Unions and Economic Change in the New England Textile Industry, 1870–1960*. Amherst: University of Massachusetts Press, 1996.

Harvey, David. *A Brief History of Neoliberalism*. New York: Oxford University Press, 2007.

Hawley, Ellis. *The Great War and the Search for a Modern Order: A History of the American People and Their Institutions, 1917–1933*. New York: St. Martin's Press, 1979.

———. *The New Deal and the Problem of Monopoly: A Study in Economic Ambivalence*. Princeton: Princeton University Press, 1966.

Heathcott, Joseph, and Maire Agnes Murphy. "Corridors of Flight, Zones of Renewal: Industry, Planning, and Policy in the Making of Metropolitan St. Louis, 1940–1980." *Journal of Urban History* 31 (January 2005): 151–89.

Hennessy, Michael E. *Four Decades of Massachusetts Politics, 1890–1935*. Norwood, Mass.: Norwood Press, 1935.

Henriques, Diana B. *Fidelity's World: The Secret Life and Public Power of the Mutual Fund Giant*. New York: Scribner, 1995.

High, Steven. *Industrial Sunset: The Making of North America's Rust Belt, 1969–1984*. Toronto: University of Toronto Press, 2003.

Hill, Edward W., and Nell Ann Shelley. "An Overview of Economic Development Finance." In *Financing Economic Development: An Institutional Response*, edited by Richard W. Bingham, Edward W. Hill, and Sammis B. White, 13–28. Newbury Park, Calif.: Sage Publications, 1990.

Himmelberg, Robert F. *The Origins of the National Recovery Administration: Business, Government, and the Trade Association Issue, 1921–1933*. New York: Fordham University Press, 1975.

Hinrichs, A. F. "Historical Review of Wage Rates and Wage Differentials in the Cotton-Textile Industry." *Monthly Labor Review* 40 (May 1935): 1170–80.

———. *Wages in Cotton-Goods Manufacturing.* U.S. Department of Labor Bulletin 663. Washington, D.C.: GPO, 1938.

Hirsch, Barry T., David A. Macpherson, and Wayne G. Vroman. *State Union Membership Density, 1964–2010* (database). http://www.unionstats.com, accessed January 9, 2012.

History of the Massachusetts State Federation of Labor, 1887–1935. N.p., n.d.

Hodges, James A. *New Deal Labor Policy and the Southern Cotton Textile Industry, 1933–1941.* Knoxville: University of Tennessee Press, 1986.

Hodgkins, Theodore Roosevelt, ed. *Brief Biographies, Maine: A Biographical Dictionary of Who's Who in Maine*, vol. 1, 1926–27. Lewiston, Me.: Lewiston Journal Company, n.d. [1926?].

Hund, James M. "The Electronics Industry." In *Made in New York: Case Studies in Metropolitan Manufacturing*, edited by Max Hall. Cambridge: Harvard University Press, 1959.

Huthmacher, J. Joseph. *Massachusetts People and Politics, 1919–1933.* Cambridge, Mass.: Belknap Press, 1959.

Industry (1924–52). Periodical published by the Associated Industries of Massachusetts.

Institute for Industrial Relations, UCLA. *Area Redevelopment Policies in Britain and the Countries of the Common Market.* Washington, D.C.: U.S. Area Redevelopment Administration, 1965.

Irwin, Douglas A., and Peter Klenow. "High-Tech R&D Subsidies: Estimating the Effects of Sematech." *Journal of International Economics* 40 (1996): 323–44.

Jacoby, Robin Miller. "The Women's Trade Union League." In *Papers of the Women's Trade Union League and Its Principal Leaders: Guide to the Microform Edition*, edited by Edward T. James. Woodbridge, Conn.: Research Publications, 1981.

Jaher, Frederic. *The Urban Establishment: Upper Strata in Boston, New York, Charleston, Chicago, and Los Angeles.* Urbana: University of Illinois Press, 1982.

Johnson, Chalmers A. *MITI and the Japanese Miracle: The Growth of Industrial Policy, 1925–1975.* Stanford: Stanford University Press, 1982.

Juravich, Tom, William F. Hartford, and James R. Green. *Commonwealth of Toil: Chapters in the History of Massachusetts Workers and Their Unions.* Amherst: University of Massachusetts Press, 1996.

Kane, Nancy Frances. *Textiles in Transition: Technology, Wages, and Industry Relocation in the U.S. Textile Industry, 1880–1930.* New York: Greenwood Press, 1988.

Kanter, Sandra. "Theory of the 'Little' State: Business-Government Relations in the Commonwealth of Massachusetts." Ph.D. diss., MIT, 1981.

Kelley, Albert J., Frank B. Campanella, and John McKiernan. *Venture Capital: A Guidebook for New Enterprises.* Boston: School of Management, Boston College, 1971.

Kennedy, Stephen Jay. *Profits and Losses in Textiles: Cotton Textile Financing Since the War.* New York: Harper and Brothers, 1936.

Kenney, Charles C. *Riding the Runaway Horse: The Rise and Decline of Wang Laboratories.* Boston: Little, Brown and Company, 1992.

Kessler-Harris, Alice. *Gendering Labor History.* Urbana: University of Illinois Press, 2007.

Khan, Zorina, and Kenneth Sokoloff. "'Schemes of Practical Utility': Entrepreneurship and Innovation among 'Great Inventors' in the United States, 1790–1865." *Journal of Economic History* 53 (June 1993): 289–307.

Koistinen, David. "The Causes of Deindustrialization: The Migration of the Cotton Textile Industry from New England to the South." *Enterprise and Society* 3 (September 2002): 482–520.

———. "Dealing with Deindustrialization: Economics, Politics, and Policy during the Decline of the New England Textile Industry, 1920–1960." Ph.D. diss., Yale University, 1999.

———. "Development Credit Corporations: Not-for-Profit Development Finance Institutions in the Postwar United States," *Business History* 54, no. 3 (June 2012): 424–40.

———. "The Political Economy of Regional Redevelopment: Business and Area Government in the Regeneration of the New England Economy." *Business and Economic History On-Line*, vol. 4: *The 2006 Annual Meeting*, 13 pp.

———. "Public Policies for Countering Deindustrialization in Postwar Massachusetts." *Journal of Policy History* 18 (2006): 326–61.

———. "Public Relations as Redevelopment Tool: Accentuating the Positive in Deindustrializing New England." *Business and Economic History On-Line*, Vol. 3: *The 2005 Annual Meeting*, 19 pp.

Lahne, Herbert J. "Labor in the Cotton Mill (1865–1900)." Ph.D. diss., Columbia University, 1937.

Lamden, C. W., and LeRoy A. Pemberton. *A Study of the Problems of Small Electronics Manufacturing Companies in Southern California*. San Diego: San Diego State College Foundation, 1962.

Lampe, David, ed. *The Massachusetts Miracle: High Technology and Economic Revitalization*. Cambridge: MIT Press, 1988.

Lazerow, Jama. "'The Workingman's Hour': The 1886 Labor Uprising in Boston." *Labor History* 21 (Spring 1980): 200–20.

Leavitt, Thomas W. "Textile Manufacturers and the Expansion of Technical Education in Massachusetts, 1869–1904." *Essex Institute Historical Collections* 108 (April 1972): 244–51.

Lécuyer, Christophe. *Making Silicon Valley: Innovation and the Growth of High Tech, 1930–1970*. Cambridge: MIT Press, 2006.

Leuchtenburg, William E. *Franklin D. Roosevelt and the New Deal*. New York: Harper and Row, 1963.

Libby, Joseph Edward. "To Build Wings for the Angels: Los Angeles and Its Aircraft Industry, 1890–1936." Ph.D. diss., University of California, Riverside, 1990.

Lichtenstein, Nelson. *The Most Dangerous Man in Detroit: Walter Reuther and the Fate of American Labor*. New York: Basic Books, 1995.

———. *State of the Union: A Century of American Labor*. Princeton: Princeton University Press, 2002.

Liles, Patrick R. *Sustaining the Venture Capital Firm*. Cambridge, Mass.: Management Analysis Center, 1977.

Lincoln and Therese Filene Foundation. *A Memorandum on Semi-Fixed and Permanent Capital for Small Business*. N.p. [Boston: Lincoln and Therese Filene Foundation], 1939.

Luger, Michael I, and Harvey A. Goldstein. *Technology in the Garden: Research Parks and Regional Economic Development*. Chapel Hill: University of North Carolina Press, 1991.

Markusen, Ann Roell. *Regions: The Politics and Economics of Territory*. Totowa, N.J.: Rowman and Littlefield, 1987.

Markusen, Ann, Peter Hall, Scott Campbell, and Sabina Deitrick. *The Rise of the Gunbelt: The Military Remapping of Industrial America*. New York: Oxford University Press, 1991.

Massachusetts Department of Corporations and Taxation. *Annual Report on the Statistics of Municipal Finances*. Public Document No. 79. 1922, 1930.

Massachusetts Department of Labor and Industries. *Annual Report on the Statistics of Labor for 1923*, Part III. *Statistics of Labor Organizations in Massachusetts, 1921 and 1922*. Labor Bulletin no. 140. 1923.

———. *Annual Report of the Statistics of Manufactures*. Public Document No. 36. 1921.

———. *Census of Manufactures in Massachusetts*, 1946, 1953, 1960 (mimeograph). Available at Massachusetts State Library, Boston.

———. *Report of a Special Investigation into Conditions in the Textile Industry in Massachusetts and the Southern States*. Boston: Arkwright Club, n.d. [1923?].

———. *Report of an Investigation as to the Causes of Existing Unemployment and to Remedies Therefor* . . . January 1931. Massachusetts Legislative Documents 1931: House, No. 1298.

———. *Statistics of Manufactures in Massachusetts, 1920–1938*. n.d.

Massachusetts Development and Industrial Commission, in cooperation with the Associated Industries of Massachusetts. *In Black and White: The Facts Concerning Industrial Advantages in Massachusetts*. Boston: Massachusetts Development and Industrial Commission, 1937.

Massachusetts State Federation of Labor. *Roll Calls of the Massachusetts Legislature, 1927–28, on Labor Measures*. Boston: Massachusetts State Federation of Labor, n.d. Massachusetts AFL-CIO Records, box 24.

McKee, Guian. "Urban Deindustrialization and Local Public Policy: Industrial Renewal in Philadelphia, 1953–1976." *Journal of Policy History* 16 (2004): 66–98.

Merrill, Gilbert R. "History of the Lowell Technological Institute." *Textile History Review* 3 (April 1962): 82–96.

Metropolitan Life Insurance Company, Policyholders Service Bureau. *Better Business through Research in New England Industry: Introduction and Summary of Findings*. Report prepared for the Research Committee of the New England Council. N.p, n.d.

Mezerik, A. G. *The Revolt of the South and West*. New York: Duell, Sloan, and Pearce, 1946.

Miller, Marc Scott. *The Irony of Victory: World War II and Lowell, Massachusetts*. Urbana: University of Illinois Press, 1988.

Minchin, Timothy J. *Fighting against the Odds: A History of Southern Labor Since World War II*. Gainesville: University Press of Florida, 2005.

———. *What Do We Need a Union For? The TWUA in the South, 1945–1955*. Chapel Hill: University of North Carolina Press, 1997.

Minot, John Clair. *Theta of Delta Kappa Epsilon: The Story of Sixty Years . . . the DKE Fraternity at Bowdoin College and Brief Biographies of Its Members*. Augusta, Me.: Kennebec Journal, 1904.

Moody's Manual of Investments, American and Foreign: Industrial Securities. New York: Moody's Investor Service, 1928–53.

Morris, James A. *Woolen and Worsted Manufacturing in the Southern Piedmont*. Columbia: University of South Carolina Press, 1952.

Nash, Gerald D. *World War II and the West: Reshaping the Economy*. Lincoln: University of Nebraska Press, 1990.

National Cyclopaedia of American Biography, 63 vols. New York: J. T. White, 1893–1984.

National Industrial Conference Board. *The Fiscal Problem in Massachusetts*. New York: National Industrial Conference Board, 1931.

New England Bank Management Conference (1938–47). Proceedings of the annual meeting. Available at Baker Library, Harvard Business School.

New England Council. *1930 Blue Book of Members and Committees*. N.p., n.d. New England Council Steel Committee Records, box 2.

———. *A Day in New England with Herbert Hoover* N.p., n.d. [Boston: New England Council, 1927?].

———. *New England and the New England Council*. Boston: New England Council, 1941. New England Council Steel Committee Records, box 2.

———. *New England Farm Marketing Conference . . . Boston . . . May 16 and 17, 1934* (mimeographed conference announcement). New England Council Steel Committee Records, box 2.

———. *New England Today and the New England Council*. Boston: New England Council, n.d. [1935?].

———. *Progress Report, November 1, 1926*. N.p. [Boston?: New England Council], 1926. New England Council Steel Committee Records, box 2.

———. *A United New England: Four Years of Progress: 1926, 1927, 1928, 1929*. N.p., n.d.

———. *A Year of Progress*. Publication prepared for November 1928 annual meeting. N.p., n.d. New England Council Steel Committee Records, box 2.

———. Research Committee. *A Directory of the College and University Research Facilities of New England*. Boston: New England Council, n.d. [1928]. Available at Baker Library, Harvard Business School.

The New England Council Announces the Third New England Conference. Flier for November 1927 annual meeting. N.p., n.d. Available at Baker Library, Harvard Business School.

The New England Council: Objectives and Accomplishments, 1933–1934. N.p., n.d. New England Council Steel Committee Records, box 2.

New England Governors' Textile Committee. *New England Textiles and the New England Economy*. Reports to the Conference of New England Governors. N.p., 1956–59.

———. *Report on the New England Textile Industry by Committee Appointed by the Conference of New England Governors*. N.p., 1952.

New England News Letter (1927–38, 1946–53). Periodical published by the New England Council.

New England Regional Commission. *Capital Markets in New England*. Boston: New England Regional Commission, 1975. Available in vertical file, Loeb Design Library, Harvard University.

———. *Labor Markets in New England*. Boston: New England Regional Commission, 1975. Available in vertical file, Loeb Design Library, Harvard University.

New England War Bulletin (1942–44). Periodical published by the New England Council.

New Englander (1953, 1957). Periodical published by the New England Council.

News about New England from the New England Council. Collection of press releases and related material issued by the New England Council. Boston: New England Council, 1939–40. Available at Widener-Pusey Library, Harvard University.

New York State Department of Commerce. *The Electronics Industry in New York State*. N.p., n.d. [Albany?: New York State Department of Commerce, 1957?].

Noble, David F. *Forces of Production: A Social History of Industrial Automation*. New York: Oxford University Press, 1984.

O'Mara, Margaret Pugh. *Cities of Knowledge: Cold War Science and the Search for the Next Silicon Valley*. Princeton: Princeton University Press, 2005.

Opening Remarks of President James W. Hook to the Governors' Session of the Thirteenth New England Conference, November 18, 1937 (mimeograph). New England Council Steel Committee Records, box 2.

Orejel, Keith. "Factories in the Fallows: Deindustrialization and the Making of Modern Rural Politics, 1945–1965." Paper delivered at the annual meeting of the Business History Conference, Philadelphia, Penn., March 2012.

Organization for Economic Cooperation and Development (OECD). "Labour Market Programmes: Expenditure and Participants." *OECD Employment and Labour Market Statistics* (database). doi: 10.1787/data-00312-en. http://www.oecd.org, accessed April 2, 2011.

———. "Revenue Statistics: Comparative Tables," 2010. *OECD Tax Statistics* (database). doi: 10.1787/data-00262-en. http://www.oecd.org, accessed April 2, 2011.

Packard, David. *The HP Way: How Bill Hewlett and I Built Our Company*. New York: HarperBusiness, 1995.

Palmer, Dwight. *Another Tale of Two Cities*. Region 1, Publication no. 67. Boston: National Resources Planning Board, 1942.

Parker, Margaret Terrell. *Lowell: A Study of Industrial Development*. Macmillan, 1940; repr. Port Washington, N.Y.: Kennikat Press, 1970.

Parrott, James A. "Technological and Institutional Innovation in Massachusetts Electronics." Ph.D. diss., University of Massachusetts, 1985.

Paulsen, George E. *A Living Wage for the Forgotten Man: The Quest for Fair Labor Standards, 1933–1941*. Selinsgrove, Penn.: Susquehanna University Press, 1996.

Peirce, Neal R. *The New England States: People, Politics and Power in the Six New England States*. New York: Norton, 1976.

Peters, Bradley L. *The Maine Central Railroad Company: A Story of Success and Independence*. N.p. [Maine Central Railroad Company], 1976.

Phillips-Fein, Kim. *Invisible Hands: The Making of the Conservative Movement from the New Deal to Reagan*. New York: W. W. Norton, 2009.

Policy of the Massachusetts Division, New England Council, presented at the Massachusetts State Dinner at the Ninth New England Conference. N.p., n.d. [1933?]. New England Council Steel Committee Records, box 2.

Problems of Eastern Cotton Manufacturers, Address by Ward Thoron . . . at a Joint Meeting of the Lions Club, the Rotary Club, the Kiwanis Club and the Lowell Chamber of Commerce, at Lowell Massachusetts, April 21, 1925. N.p., n.d. Available at U.S. Department of Labor Library, Washington, D.C.

Proceedings . . . Annual Convention, Massachusetts State Branch, A.F. of L. (1902–7, 1925–36; organization and publication names variable). Massachusetts AFL-CIO Records, box 1.

Proceedings of the . . . Annual Meeting of the Stockholders of the Federal Reserve Bank of Boston (1944–45).

Proctor, John. "The Attitude of Lending Officers in Boston, Cleveland, and Pittsburgh towards Financing New Businesses." M.S. thesis, MIT, 1973.

Public Officials of Massachusetts. Boston: Boston Review Publicity Service, 1927–28, 1931–32.

The Public Papers and Addresses of Franklin D. Roosevelt, 13 vols. New York: Random House, 1938–50.

Pusateri, C. Joseph. *A History of American Business.* Arlington Heights, Ill.: Harlan Davidson, 1984.

Ragan, Philip H. "The Organization, Management, and Significance of Industrial Foundations in New England." Ph.D. diss., Harvard Business School, 1951.

Reich, Leonard S. *The Making of American Industrial Research: Science and Business at GE and Bell, 1876–1926.* New York: Cambridge University Press, 1985.

Reiner, Martha Louise. "The Transformation of Venture Capital: A History of Venture Capital Organizations in the United States." Ph.D. diss., University of California, Berkeley, 1989.

Report of Hearing before the Committee on Labor and Industry of the Massachusetts Legislature, Senate Bill 149 . . . , Senate Bill 191 . . . From the Stenographic Record and Exhibits Submitted to the Committee. Boston: Associated Industries of Massachusetts, 1928.

Report of Mr. John F. Tinsley . . . to the Eighth Quarterly Meeting of the New England Council, Poland Spring, Maine, September 1927. N.p., n.d. Greater Boston Chamber of Commerce Records, case 79, file 710.

Report of the Agricultural Committee of the New England Council, 1926–1927. Report at annual meeting, New England Council, November 1927. N.p., n.d. New England Council Steel Committee Records, box 2.

Report of the Committee on Public Relations and Community Organization of the New England Council. Report at annual meeting, New England Council, November 1927. N.p., n.d. New England Council Steel Committee Records, box 2.

Report of the Committee on Recreational Resources of the New England Council. Report at annual meeting, New England Council, November 1927. N.p., n.d. New England Council Steel Committee Records, box 2.

Report of the Joint New England Railroad Committee to the Governors of the New England States, 2 vols. Cambridge, Mass.: University Press, 1923.

Research and New England Prosperity: Report of the Research Committee of the New England Council. Report at annual meeting, New England Council, November 1927. N.p., n.d. Available at Widener-Pusey Library, Harvard University.

Richter, Alan M. "Philadelphia College of Textiles and Science." *Textile History Review* 3 (January 1962): 47–53.

Roberts, Edward B. *Entrepreneurs in High Technology: Lessons from MIT and Beyond.* New York: Oxford University Press, 1991.

Rodwin, Lloyd, and Hidehiko Sazanami, eds. *Deindustrialization and Regional Economic Transformation: The Experience of the United States.* Boston: Unwin Hyman, 1989.

Rogers, Edith Nourse. "Address before the Committee Textiles." Edith Nourse Rogers Papers, box 9, folder 145.

Rosegrant, Susan, and David Lampe. *Route 128: Lessons from Boston's High-Tech Community.* New York: Basic Books, 1992.

Samuelson, Paul A. "Seymour Harris as Political Economist." *Review of Economics and Statistics* 57, no. 1 (February 1975), ii–v.

Sawers, Larry, and William K. Tabb, eds. *Sunbelt/Snowbelt: Urban Development and Regional Restructuring.* New York: Oxford University Press, 1984.

Saxenian, Annalee. *Regional Advantage: Culture and Competition in Silicon Valley and Route 128.* Cambridge: Harvard University Press, 1994.

Saxon, Bruce. "Fall River and the Decline of the New England Textile Industry, 1949–1954." *Historical Journal of Massachusetts* 16 (1988): 54–74.

Schulman, Bruce. *From Cotton Belt to Sunbelt: Federal Policy, Economic Development, and the Transformation of the South, 1938–1980.* New York: Oxford University Press, 1991.

———. *The Seventies: The Great Shift in American Culture, Society, and Politics.* New York: Free Press, 2001.

Scott, Otto, J. *The Creative Ordeal: The Story of Raytheon.* New York: Atheneum, 1974.

Scranton, Philip. *Figured Tapestry: Production, Markets, and Power in Philadelphia Textiles, 1885–1941.* Cambridge, U.K.: Cambridge University Press, 1989.

Second Report of New England Council's Special Committee on Ownership and Finance. N.p., n.d. [Boston: New England Council, 1945].

Shermer, Elizabeth Tandy. "Origins of the Conservative Ascendancy: Barry Goldwater's Early Senate Career and the De-Legitimization of Organized Labor." *Journal of American History* 95, no. 3 (December 2008): 678–709.

———. "Sunbelt Boosterism: Industrial Recruitment, Economic Development, and Growth Politics in the Developing Sunbelt." In *Sunbelt Rising: The Politics of Space, Place, and Region*, edited by Michelle Nickerson and Darren Dochuck, 31–57. Philadephia: University of Pennsylvania Press, 2011.

Simon, Jean-Claude G. "Textile Workers, Trade Unions, and Politics: Comparative Case Studies, France and the United States." Ph.D. diss., Tufts University, 1980.

Smith, James T. "Our Textile School—Its Origin and Development." In Trades and Labor Council of Lowell, Mass., *Lowell: A City of Spindles*, 225–43. Lowell: Trades and Labor Council, 1900.

Smith, Thomas R. *The Cotton Textile Industry of Fall River, Massachusetts: A Study of Industrial Localization.* New York: King's Crown Press, 1944.

Stabile, Donald R. *Activist Unionism: The Institutional Economics of Solomon Barkin.* Armonk, N.Y.: M. E. Sharpe, 1993.

Stebenne, David L. *Arthur J. Goldberg: New Deal Liberal.* New York: Oxford University Press, 1996.

———. "IBM's 'New Deal': Employment Policies of the International Business Machines Corporation, 1933–1956." *Journal of the Historical Society* 5, no. 1 (Winter 2005): 47–77.

———. "Thomas J. Watson and the Business-Government Relationship, 1933–1956." *Enterprise and Society* 6, no. 1 (March 2005), 45–75.

Stein, Judith. *Pivotal Decade: How the United States Traded Factories for Finance in the Seventies*. New Haven: Yale University Press, 2012.

———. *Running Steel, Running America: Race, Economic Policy, and the Decline of Liberalism*. Chapel Hill: University of North Carolina Press, 1998.

Stockman, David. *The Triumph of Politics: How the Reagan Revolution Failed*. New York: Harper and Row, 1986.

Stoddard, William. "Small Business Wants Capital." *Harvard Business Review* 18 (Spring 1940): 265–74.

Stone, Kurt F. *The Congressional Minyan: The Jews of Capitol Hill*. Hoboken, N.J.: Ktav Publishing, 2000.

Storchmann, Karl. "The Rise and Fall of German Hard Coal Subsidies." *Energy Policy* 33 (2005): 1469–92.

Sugrue, Thomas. *The Origins of the Urban Crisis: Race and Inequality in Postwar Detroit*. Princeton: Princeton University Press, 1996.

Swank, Duane, and Sven Steinmo. "The New Political Economy of Taxation in Advanced Capitalist Democracies." *American Journal of Political Science* 46 (July 2002): 642–55.

Taxation and Public Expenditure in New England. Panel proceedings, quarterly meeting, New England Council, June 1927. N.p., n.d. New England Council Steel Committee Records, box 2.

Temin, Peter, ed. *Engines of Enterprise: An Economic History of New England*. Cambridge: Harvard University Press, 2000.

Thompson and Lichtner Company. *Merchandising New England Products: Shoes*. Report at annual meeting, New England Council, November 1926. N.p., n.d.

Thoron, Ward. "Handicaps of Northern Textile Mills Competing with Those of the South." Extract from *The Manufacturer* (April 1924): 11–22. Available at Wilson Library, University of North Carolina, Chapel Hill.

Tilden, Leonard. "New England Textile Strike." *Monthly Labor Review* 16 (May 1923): 13–36.

Transactions of the National Association of Cotton Manufacturers (1927). Proceedings of semi-annual meeting.

Trebilcock, Michael J., Marsha A. Chandler, and Robert Howse. *Trade and Transitions: A Comparative Analysis of Adjustment Policies*. London: Routledge, 1990.

Turnburke, Vernon P., Jr. "Aspects of New Enterprises—Finance." B.S. thesis, MIT, 1949.

U.S. Bureau of Labor Statistics. *Employment and Earnings, States and Areas, 1939–72*. Bulletin 1370-10. Washington, D.C.: U.S. Bureau of Labor Statistics, n.d.

———. *Employment, Hours, and Earnings, States and Areas*, 2 vols., *1939–82*, (Bulletin 1370-17), *1988–94* (Bulletin 2454). Washington, D.C.: U.S. Bureau of Labor Statistics, 1984, 1994.

———. *Employment, Hours, and Earnings, United States, 1909–84*, 2 vols. (Bulletin 1312–12), *1988–96* (Bulletin 2481). Washington, D.C.: U.S. Bureau of Labor Statistics, 1985, 1996.

U.S. Bureau of the Census. *Fourteenth Census of the United States Taken in the Year 1920*, vol. 8: *Manufactures 1919*. Washington, D.C.: GPO, 1923.

———. *Historical Statistics of the United States: Colonial Times to 1970*, 2 parts. Washington, D.C.: U.S. Bureau of Labor Statistics, 1975.

---. *Statistical Abstract of the United States*. Washington, D.C.: U.S. Bureau of Labor Statistics, 1991, 1999–2006.

U.S. Council of Economic Advisers. Committee on the New England Economy. *The New England Economy: A Report to the President Transmitting a Study Initiated by the Council of Economic Advisers*. Washington, D.C.: GPO, 1951.

U.S. Department of Commerce. *Cotton Production and Distribution, Season of 1939–1940*. Bulletin 177. Washington, D.C.: GPO, 1940.

U.S. House. *National Textile Bill*. Report to accompany H.R. 12285. 74th Cong., 2nd sess., 1936. H. Rept. 2590.

---. Committee on Banking and Currency. *Federal Assistance to Labor Surplus Areas*. Report prepared by Sar A. Levitan. 85th Cong., 1st sess., 1957.

---. Committee on Labor. *To Rehabilitate and Stabilize Labor Conditions in the Textile Industry of the United States: Hearings before a Subcommittee of the Committee on Labor, House of Representatives, on H.R. 9072*. 74th Cong., 2nd sess. January 27–February 6, 1936.

---. Select Committee to Conduct a Study and Investigation of the National Defense Program in Its Relation to Small Business in the United States. *A Study and Investigation of the National Defense Program in Its Relation to Small Business: Hearings before the House Select Committee to Conduct a Study . . .* , Part 1: *Financial Problems of Small Business*. 79th Cong., 1st sess., March 20–May 17, 1945.

---. Select Committee on Small Business. *Availability of Long-Term Credit for Small Business: Hearings before the House Select Committee on Small Business*. 80th Cong., 2nd sess., March 15–June 20, 1948.

U.S. Joint Committee on the Economic Report. *Volume and Stability of Private Investment: Hearings before the Joint Committee on the Economic Report*, part 2. 81st Cong., 1st sess., December 6–16, 1949.

U.S. Securities and Exchange Commission. *In the Matter of American Research and Development Corporation*. File No. 812–440, promulgated August 7, 1946. Reprinted in Securities and Exchange Commission, *Decisions and Reports*, vol. 23, 481–90. Washington, D.C.: GPO, 1953.

U.S. Senate. Committee on Education and Labor and the House Committee on Labor. *Fair Labor Standards Act of 1937: Joint Hearings before the Committee on Education and Labor, United States Senate, and the Committee on Labor, House of Representatives, on S. 2475 and H.R. 7200*, part 2. 75th Cong., 1st sess., June 7–15, 1937.

---. Committee on Finance. *Revenue Revisions of 1950: Hearings before the Committee on Finance*. 81st Cong., 2nd sess., July 5–13, 1950.

---. Committee on Public Works. *Public Works and Economic Development Act of 1965: Hearings before the Committee on Public Works*. 89th Cong., 1st sess., April 26–May 3, 1965.

---. Special Committee to Study the Problems of American Small Business. *Small Business Problems: Small Business: Access to Capital*. 78th Cong., 1st sess., 1943. Committee Print 15.

Van Waarden, Frans, and Gerhard Lehmbruch, eds. *Renegotiating the Welfare State: Flexible Adjustment through Corporatist Concertation*. London: Routledge, 2003.

Vecoli, Rudoph J. "Anthony Capraro and the Lawrence Strike of 1919." In *Labor Divided: Race and Ethnicity in United States Labor Struggles, 1835–1960*, edited by Robert Asher and Charles Stephenson, 267–82. Albany: State University of New York Press, 1990.

Vittoz, Stanley. *New Deal Labor Policy and the American Industrial Economy.* Chapel Hill: University of North Carolina Press, 1987.

Vogel, David. *Fluctuating Fortunes: The Political Power of Business in America.* New York: Basic Books, 1989.

Wage and Hour Legislation in Action: Addresses Made at the Thirty-Eighth Annual Meeting of the National Consumers' League, New York City, December 9, 1938. N.p., n.d. [New York: National Consumers' League].

Wagoner, Harless. *The U.S. Machine Tool Industry from 1900 to 1950.* Cambridge: MIT Press, 1966.

Wallace, Michael, and Joyce Rothschild, eds. *Deindustrialization and the Restructuring of American Industry.* Greenwich, Conn.: JAI Press, 1988.

Wang, An, with Eugene Linden. *Lessons: An Autobiography.* Reading, Mass.: Addison-Wesley, 1986.

Waterhouse, Benjamin. *Lobbying America: The Politics of Business in an Age of Conservatism, 1968–1994.* Princeton: Princeton University Press, forthcoming.

Weinberg, Ari, and Davide Dukcevich. "The World's Freest Labor Markets." January 30, 2003. *Forbes.com*, accessed March 31, 2011.

Weir, Margaret. *Politics and Jobs: The Boundaries of Employment Policy in the United States.* Princeton: Princeton University Press, 1992.

Weissman, Rudolph. *Small Business and Venture Capital: An Economic Program.* New York: Harper and Brothers, 1945.

Wells, Ralph G., and John S. Perkins. *New England Community Statistical Abstracts.* Prepared for the Industrial Development Committee of the New England Council. Boston: Boston University College of Business Administration, 1st ed., 1937; 2nd ed., 1939; 3rd ed., 1942.

———. *Trends in New England Industries: A Statistical Study Based on the U.S. Census of Manufactures, 1919–1929–1931.* Boston: Boston University College of Business Administration, 1935.

Werner, Robert. "Finland: A European Model of Successful Innovation." *Chazen Web Journal of International Business,* Fall 2003, 19 pp. http://www.gsb.columbia.edu/chazenjournal, accessed December 5, 2007.

Wheeler, Walter. *New England Council: Its Beginnings, Its Work, and Its Future, 1925–1952.* New York: Newcomen Society in North America, 1952.

Who Was Who in America, 12 vols. Chicago: Marquis, 1896–1998.

Who's Who in the New England Council 1931. N.p., n.d. New England Council Steel Committee Records, box 2.

Wilkie, Richard W., and Jack Tager, eds. *Historical Atlas of Massachusetts.* Amherst: University of Massachusetts Press, 1991.

Wilson, Gregory S. "Before the Great Society: Liberalism, Deindustrialization and Area Redevelopment in the United States, 1933–1965." Ph.D. diss., Ohio State University, 2001.

———. *Communities Left Behind: The Area Redevelopment Administration, 1945–1965.* Knoxville: University of Tennessee Press, 2009.

———. "'Our Chronic and Desperate Situation': Anthracite Communities and the Emergence of Redevelopment Policy in Pennsylvania and the United States, 1945–1965." *International Review of Social History* 47 (2002): 137–58.

Wilson, Joan Hoff. *Herbert Hoover: Forgotten Progressive*. Boston: Little, Brown, 1975.

Wilson, Louis R. *The Research Triangle of North Carolina: A Notable Achievement in University, Governmental, and Industrial Cooperative Development*. Chapel Hill, N.C.: Colonial Press, 1967.

Wolfbein, Seymour Louis. *The Decline of a Cotton Textile City: A Study of New Bedford*. New York: Columbia University Press, 1944.

Wright, Gavin. *Old South, New South: Revolutions in the Southern Economy since the Civil War*. New York: Basic Books, 1986.

Zelizer, Julian E. *On Capitol Hill: The Struggle to Reform Congress and Its Consequences, 1948–2000*. New York: Cambridge University Press, 2004.

Zysman, John, and Laura Tyson, eds. *American Industry in International Competition: Government Policies and Corporate Strategies*. Ithaca: Cornell University Press, 1983.

Collections

American Federation of Hosiery Workers Records, Part II (Mss. 410). Archives Division, Wisconsin Historical Society, Madison, Wis.

American Research and Development Corporation Historical Materials. Held at the offices of American Research and Development Corporation, Boston, Mass.

Christian A. Herter Papers. Houghton Library, Harvard University, Cambridge, Mass.

Consumers League of Massachusetts Records. Schlesinger Library, Radcliffe Institute, Harvard University, Cambridge, Mass.

Edith Nourse Rogers Papers. Schlesinger Library, Radcliffe Institute, Harvard University, Cambridge, Mass.

First National Bank of Boston Historical Materials. Held at the off-site storage facility of what was at the time BankBoston, Boston, Mass.

First National Bank of Boston Historical Records. Held in the Research Library archives at the headquarters of what was at the time BankBoston, Boston, Mass.

Flather/Boott Mills Collection. Center for Lowell History, University of Massachusetts, Lowell.

Frederick Steele Blackall Jr. Papers. In possession of Frederick Steele Blackall III, Providence, R.I.

Governor Channing Cox Correspondence, Record Group Governor (GO5), Subgroup Correspondence Office, Series 972. Massachusetts Archives, Boston.

Greater Boston Chamber of Commerce Records. Baker Library Historical Collections, Harvard Business School, Boston, Mass.

Historic Corporate Reports Collection. Baker Library Historical Collections, Harvard Business School, Boston, Mass.

Homer Cummings Papers. Alderman Library Special Collections, University of Virginia, Charlottesville.

James William Hook Papers. Sterling Library Manuscripts and Archives, Yale University, New Haven, Conn.

Lee DuBridge Papers. Institute Archives, California Institute of Technology, Pasadena, Calif.

Lowell Technological Institute Collection. Center for Lowell History, University of Massachusetts, Lowell.
Massachusetts AFL-CIO Records. Du Bois Library Special Collections and Archives, University of Massachusetts, Amherst.
Massachusetts Institute of Technology, Office of the President, 1930–59 Records (AC004). Institute Archives and Special Collections, Massachusetts Institute of Technology, Cambridge.
Merrimack Manufacturing Company Records. Baker Library Historical Collections, Harvard Business School, Boston, Mass.
National Association of Cotton Manufacturers--Northern Textile Association Collection. Osborne Library, American Textile History Museum, Lowell, Mass.
New England Council Steel Committee Records. Sterling Library Manuscripts and Archives, Yale University, New Haven, Conn.
Office of the Governor of Connecticut Records (RG 5). State Archives, Connecticut State Library, Hartford.
Paulsen Justice Department Materials. Copies of documents in the U.S. Department of Justice Archives, Washington, D.C., relating to drafting of Fair Labor Standards Act of 1937. In possession of George E. Paulsen, professor emeritus, Arizona State University.
Ralph E. Flanders Papers. Bird Library Special Collections, Syracuse University, Syracuse, N.Y.
Ralph Flanders Materials. In records of former bank presidents held at Federal Reserve Bank of Boston, Boston, Mass.
Sinclair Weeks Papers. Rauner Special Collections Library, Dartmouth College, Hanover, N.H.
Textile Workers Union of America Papers, Third Installment (Mss. 396). Wisconsin Historical Society, Madison, Wis.
U.S. Department of Commerce Records (RG 40). National Archives, College Park, Md.
Vannevar Bush Papers. Manuscript Division, Library of Congress, Washington, D.C.

Interviews Conducted by the Author

Adams, Charles F. Jr., Lexington, Mass., August 29, 1996.
Baty, Gordon, Cambridge, Mass., November 19, 1996.
Blackall, Frederick Steele III, Providence, R.I., February 26, 1996.
Brooke, Peter, Boston, Mass., June 27, 1996.
Brown, William L., Boston, Mass., June 13, 1996.
Snyder, Arthur F. F., Boston, Mass., May 26, 1997.

Index

ACMA. *See* American Cotton Manufacturers Association
Adamic, Louis, 17, 20
Adams, Charles F., Jr., 148, 155, 283n23
Advanced electronics: applied physics sector, 162, 163, 202; Cold War–era and, 162, 164, 166; geographic distribution of, 166–67; government purchase of, 162, 281n3. *See also* Science-based spinoffs; Spinoffs
Advanced Technology Program (ATP), 226–27, 233
AFL. *See* American Federation of Labor
AFL-CIO, 198, 209
African Americans, 254n23
Agriculture, 250n4; New England Council committee on, 130–31
AIM. *See* Associated Industries of Massachusetts
Allen, Frank, 132–33, 275nn86–87
American Bankers Association, 143
American Cotton Manufacturers Association (ACMA), 69, 72
American Federation of Labor (AFL), 13, 28–30; CIO merger with, 95, 97; tax exemptions for manufacturing support from, 55; unionist break from, 53; in work hours issue, 32–33, 35. *See also* AFL-CIO
American Research and Development Corporation (ARD), 155–59, 280n43, 280n49, 281n53; product development, 284n25; spinoff financing by, 169–71, 284n27
American System of Manufactures, 11
Amory, Robert, 34, 109
Amoskeag Company, 19
Anti-trust laws, 72, 73
Applied physics sector, 162, 163, 202. *See also* Science-based spinoffs
ARA. *See* Area Redevelopment Administration
ARD. *See* American Research and Development Corporation

Area Redevelopment Administration (ARA), 198–99, 224
Area Redevelopment program, 197
Arkwright Club, 34, 36, 37, 48
Arthur D. Little, Inc., 123
Associated Industries of Massachusetts (AIM), 37, 44, 53, 260n76; economic development role of, 269n9; tax and government spending reduction campaign of, 57, 59, 61
Associationalism, 70, 102, 271n30; New England Council, 118
Atomic power industry, 202
ATP. *See* Advanced Technology Program
Aviation and aircraft manufacturing, 125, 135, 137, 276n98; benefits of assisting new field, 239, 297n55; electronics research concentrated in, 162, 166, 167; postwar (World War II) expansion, 202–3

Banks, Boston-based: attitude change in, 174, 179, 285n37; conference of 1945, 154–55, 172, 175–76, 279n38; deposit base, 173–74, 284n35; motivations for financing electronics spinoffs, 179; NASA contracts and, 177, 180; Snyder's approach, 178, 285n49; special department of First National Bank, 177, 178, 246, 285n46; spinoffs financed by, 170–80, 245–46, 285n37, 285n44, 285n46; studies of, 146–47, 211, 214. *See also specific banks*
Banks, outside New England, 181–82, 284n35, 286n55
Barkin, Solomon, 197–98
Batty, William, 49–50
Bayh-Dole Act, 225
Better Business through Research in New England Industry, 120
Binns, Abraham, 35, 46
Bituminous coal, 99, 268n77

320 Index

Black, Hugo, 92
Blackall, Frederick, Jr., 114, 115, 151, 157
Black-Connery Act, 92
Board of Municipal Finance, 60–61
Boot and shoe industry, 36, 102, 109, 122, 206, 287n4; decline of New England, 15, 21; Great Strike of 1860, 12–13; growth of, 11; New England share of U.S., 11; reliance on, 16; total employment 1927 and 1936, 64
Boston. *See* Banks, Boston-based; Business associations; *specific industries*; *specific topics*
Boston Brahmins, 109
Boston Chamber of Commerce, 107–10, 269n9, 270n12; industry studies conducted by, 108–9; Massachusetts Department of Commerce endorsed by, 200, 291n35; regional fair organized by, 109–10
Brooke, Peter, 173–74, 176–78, 183–84, 212
Brooklyn Polytechnic Institute, 167–68
Brown, William L., 176, 177, 178
Bruere Board, 76–79
Burge, Joseph, 84–86
Bush, George H. W., 223, 227
Bush, Vannevar, 163
Business associations: associationalism of, 70, 102, 271n30; in Boston 1939–1946, *145*; burden of government regulations on, 236, 296n47; continuities of initiatives over time, 216–17, 292n77; economic development key, 269n9; initiative role of local leaders, 5–6; machine tools, 115–16, 153; policymaking influence of, 64–65, 230, 231; regulation cutbacks sought by, 223, 293n7; retrenchment motivations of, 235–36; stabilization efforts by, 69–72, 79, 263n9, 264n28; tax reduction demands of, 54–64. *See also* New England Council; Private sector; Small business financing
Business Week, 222
Butler, William, 36–37, 254n28

Cabot, Godfrey, 128
Capacity, 74; utilization, 256n42, 257n51
Capital gaps, of 1970s, 212, 291n70
Capitalism, 20–21, 117, 139, 140
Capital-labor antagonism, 44–45, 258n55, 259n59; postwar (World War II), 190
Carey, Hugh, 210
Carter, Jimmy, 223–24
Centers for Excellence, 213, 218
Central Intelligence Agency (CIA), 209
Chase, Edward E., 149–51, 279n30

Chiselers, 71, 265n42
Chrysler Corporation, 224
CIA. *See* Central Intelligence Agency
CIO. *See* Congress of Industrial Organizations
Clinton, Bill, 222, 227
CLM. *See* Consumers League of Massachusetts
CNEA. *See* Council for Northeast Economic Action
CNEG. *See* Conference of New England Governors
Coalition of Northeastern Governors, 210
Coal mining industry, 99, 268n77; German, 228, 238
Code Authority, 74, 76, 86, 264n19. *See also* Cotton textile code, NRA; Hosiery industry and hosiery NRA code
Cohen, Benjamin, 89–92
Cold War era: advanced electronics industry and, 162, 164, 166; anti-union forces and, 96; deindustrialization overview, 187–88; spinoffs as flourishing during, 162, 164
Collective bargaining, 78, 92–93
Colson, Charles, 114
Committee on Ownership and Finance, New England Council, 145, 151, 154, 155, 279n30, 279n38; initial report of, 156; 1945 report, 172
Competition: cotton code and, 77; cotton industry, 14, 21, 40, 251n27, 253n14, 255n40; developed countries' deindustrialization and, 227–30; Ellenbogen textile bills and, 266n48; European trade protection and, 227–28; fair competition legislation, 255n40; labor standards and, 47; managerial expertise for improved New England competitiveness, 105; operating rates and, 41, 256n42, 257n43; postwar (World War II), 152; silk and rayon industry, 266n48; social legislation and, 49; spinoffs and, 164, 182; Thoron's concerns over, 258n54; unemployment insurance and, 260n76; union power and, 231. *See also* Economic development; Foreign import competition; North-South competition; Wage differentials
Compton, Arthur, 125
Compton, Karl, 114, 115, 125–27, 157, 168
Computer devices, Wang Laboratory, 184
Conference of New England Governors (CNEG), 110–11, 131, 194
Congress of Industrial Organizations (CIO), 53, 92; AFL merger with, 95, 97; Operation Dixie, 96. *See also* AFL-CIO
Connery, William, 92

Consumers League of Massachusetts (CLM), 31, 48, 49
Continuities, of initiatives to counter deindustrialization, 213, 214–17, 292nn74–77
Coolidge, Calvin, 31, 36
Coolidge, William A., 148, 155, 283n23
Coonley, Howard, 108–9, 110
Corcoran, Thomas, 89–92
Corporate excess, taxation on, 62–63, 261n89
Corporate power, 230
Cost-reduction and profit analysis: cotton industry, 40–41, 256n41; per spindle production cost and taxation, 263n113
Costs: interregional gap in, 97; labor, 23, 203; taxation share of total production, 65, 263n113
Cote, Albert, 205
Cotton textile code, NRA, 131; Bruere Board's disregard of, 76–77; Code Authority, 74, 76, 86, 264n19; competition and, 77; enforcement absence, 76; on minimum wage, 73–74; Piedmont evasion of, 76, 99–100; *Schecter* decision, 79; on work hours, 73–74
Cotton textile industry: active spindles in New England and Southern states, *22*; assessments on, 56, *56*, 260n83; automated mill invention, 10–11; capacity utilization, 256n42, 257n51; capital-labor antagonism, 44–45, 190, 258n55, 259n59; causes of decline, 21–25, 45, 259n59; competitiveness, 14, 21, 40, 251n27, 253n14, 255n40; cost-reduction and profit analysis, 40–41, 256n41; deindustrialization overview of, ix, 14–21, *15*, *16*; factory jobs percentage of, 16; female worker personal accounts, 50–52; interregional equilibrium, 23–24; labor accusations of mismanagement in, 259n59; liquidation, 24–25; market share loss, 14, *15*; mill shutdowns in 1950s, 97; night shift advantages and claims, 41, 257n45, 257n47; 1950s shutdowns, *22*; operating rates, 40–41, 256n42, 257n43; rush orders, 34, 41, 257n46; surplus output, 69; voluntary efforts to stabilize, 69–72, 79–80, 263n9, 264n28; wage rates for New England and Southern, *243*; widespread factory closures, 253n14. *See also* Competition; Night work; North-South competition; Southern states; Taxation; Wage differentials; Work hours
Cotton Textile Institute (CTI), 69–72, 98; as Code Authority, 74; Ellenbogen textile bill opposed by, 86; NIRA and, 73; surveys on cotton code adherence, 79

Council for Northeast Economic Action (CNEA), 211
Council of Economic Advisors, 189
Creange, Henry, 121
Cross, Wilbur, 83
CTI. *See* Cotton Textile Institute
Cummings, Homer, 91
Curley, James, 63
Curtiss, Frederick, 102, 103

Daust, Harold, 84
DCC. *See* Development Credit Corporation
Debt financing, 140
DEC. *See* Digital Equipment Corporation
Decentralized approach, to economic development, 233–34
Decline. *See* Deindustrialization; Initiatives to counter deindustrialization
Defense spending, 206; advanced electronics industry and, 162, 164, 166; labor surplus channeling program, 195–96, 210; postwar (World War II) expansion of orders, 202; spinoffs benefiting from, 163, 282n10
Deindustrialization: assessing responses to, 235–40; capitalists impacted by, 20–21; causes of cotton industry decline, 21–25, 45, 259n59; Cold War years, 187–88; cotton mill shutdowns in 1950s, 97; cotton textile industry overview of, ix, 14–21, *15*, *16*; date of start, 1; decline of traditional industries after World War I, 13–21, *15*, *16*; discontinuities in responses to, 6–7; historical scholarship on, 1, 104, 248n1, 248n3, 249n4; industries affected by, 289n28; initiative comparison over sixty years, 213–20, 292nn74–78, 293n79; mass media on, 189–90; New England case study relevance, 2; 1923–1939 employment decline in Massachusetts, *16*; in other developed countries, 227–30; overview of initiatives to counter, 2–9; political economy and, 2, 230–35, 249n4; political opposition to remedies for, 3–4; postwar (World War II), 188–90, 287n2, 287n4; principal responses to, ix–x; retrenchment link with, 64–66; study overview, ix–x; three-part model of initiatives to counter, 7, 9, 230, 249n7, 295n29; wool sector closing, 97, 267n75; work hour laws blamed for causing, 44–46, 259n59. *See also* Employment; Employment decline; Initiatives to counter deindustrialization
Deindustrialization, U.S., responses to recent era, 221–27

322 Index

Deindustrialization of America, The, 28
Democrats: African Americans, 254n23; conservative southern, 96; in elections of 1928, 255n39; Ellenbogen textile bills, 80–88, 255n39, 265n34, 265n42, 265n46, 266n48; night work bill of 1928 voting by, 39; reform-minded, 67, 190, 197; small business financing backed by, 158; union alliances of 1950s, 190; work hour reduction backed by, 29, 37, 39, 254n23
Depression: employment losses and, 64; small business financing and, 141, 147
Developed countries, deindustrialization initiatives, 227–30
Development. *See* Economic development
Development Credit Corporation (DCC), 200–201
Dewey and Almy, 140, 157
Dickenson, Henry, 205
Digital Equipment Corporation (DEC), 155–56, 164, 185, 282n10
Discontinuities, in initiatives to counter deindustrialization, 213–14, 217–20, 292nn78–79
Disque, Brice, 141
Dixie cotton mills. *See* Southern states
Doriot, Georges, 126, 148, 176, 280n49, 283n23
Douglas, Paul, 198
Douglas bill, 198–99
Downsizing. *See* Deindustrialization
Dukakis, Michael, 208–9, 212, 213, 215
Durant, Flora, 51–52

Earle, George, 83
Earnings. *See* Wages
Economic development, 102–38; aim and advocates of, 3, 249n7; AIM role in, 269n9; assessing efforts of, 135–38, 276n98; decentralized approach to, 233–34; electronics industry as key factor in, 160–61; entrepreneurial approach to, 104; federal legislation for U.S., 225–27, 294n16; government role in locally-based, 103, 193, 233, 295n39; growth-promotion of 1920s and 1930s, 5; importance of, 238–40; 1930s and 1940s, 5; 1970s research-based industry and, 213; overview of initiative, 102–4; postwar (World War II) efforts for, 168, 199–203, 289n33; Route 128 success, 185–86, 286n65; scholarship on, 104, 268n2; spinoffs potential for, 168–70, 180, 284n27; state agencies and role in, 103, 132–35, 275n88, 275n90, 275nn85–86; technology focus for, 168; textile schools for, 105–7, 136, 269n7; venture capital motivated by, 145, 278n17; in West Germany, 229. *See also* Industrialization; New England Council; Private sector; Small business financing; Venture capital; *specific industries*
Economic Development Act of 1965, 199
Economic Development Administration (EDA), 224–25
Economy, New England: structural vulnerabilities of, 14. *See also* Political economy
EDA. *See* Economic Development Administration
Education: postwar (World War II) income from higher, 203; textile research and, 106–7, 269n8
Eisenhower, Dwight, 196–97, 198
Electronics Funding Corporation, 182
Electronics industry: applied physics sector, 162, 163, 202; aviation-related focus of research in, 167; Cold War era as conducive to, 162, 164, 166; economic development and, 160–61; electronics defined, 281n2; outside of New England, 181–82, 286n55; post–Korean War slump in, 176, 285n44; postwar (World War II) growth, 187, 202, 203; Route 128 success, 185–86, 286n65; venture capital involvement in Boston, 5, 170–71, 177. *See also* Advanced electronics; Science-based spinoffs; Spinoffs
Ellenbogen, Henry, 67, 68; Gorman and, 80–83
Ellenbogen textile bills, 80–88, 255n39, 265n34; hearings on, 83–86, 265n42, 265n46; redrafting, 87–88, 266n48
Employment: defense channeling to areas of surplus labor, 195–96, 210; job creation rates in Massachusetts and U.S., 241; job increase between 1955 and 1965, 202, 290n40; Massachusetts and U.S. gainful workers and, *242*; multifaceted histories of displaced workers, 204–5; 1923–1960, *189*; 1927 compared to 1936, 64, 250n10; 1939–1988, *242*; 1946 Southern, 96; 1954, 290n40; 1958–1967 rise in, 202; 1960s rise in, 202; 1970s, 206; number of jobs preserved by MBDC, 201; temporary surge after NIRA enactment, 74; total rise between 1955 and 1965, 202; U.S. and New England rise in overall, 287n3
Employment decline: 1923–1939 Massachusetts, *15*, *16*, 250n10; 1925, 1936, and 1939 figures, 263n112; postwar (World War II), 188–89, *189*, 195, 204–5, 287n2; U.S. manufacturing total, 222, 293n2. *See also* Unemployment
Enterprise Associates, 149, 155, 168, 278n24; successor to, 169, 170, 283n23; technological orientation of, 148

Index   323

Entrepreneurial approach (to economic development), 104
Equity, traditional start-up, 140
Erskine, Virginia, 19–20
Europe: R&D, 229; retrenchment in, 228, 294n23; trade protection and competition concerns in, 227–28

Fair Labor Standards Act (FLSA), 68, 88–95, 265n46; amendments to, 96; drafters of, 89–92; modifications to, 91–92
Falante, John, 18
Fall River, 16, 17, 23–24, 38, 253n12; assessments on textile industry and taxpayers in, 56, 56, 61, 260n83; overassessment, 57, 61, 260nn83–84, 262n102; postwar (World War II) unemployment, 204
Federal assistance: advantages and limits of, 236–38; aim of, 3; Area Redevelopment Administration, 198–99, 224; assessing 1930s failure to gain, 237–38, 297n52; context for, 67–68; defense mobilization of labor surplus, 195–96, 210; in early and recent eras, 214, 215, 292n74; grants, 210–11; 1970s and 1980s U.S., 223–25; NIRA, 72–80, 255n40; political economy and, 231; in postwar (World War II) New England, 193–99; to small businesses, 141–42, 283n14; Snowbelt campaign of 1970s, 209–10, 211, 214, 291n62; trade protection as, 193–95, 223–24, 288n20, 294n10
Federal legislation: fair competition, 255n40; finance and investment, 156–57; unionism and, 255n40; for U.S. economic development, 225–27, 294n16. See also Federal assistance; Government; New Deal reform; Retrenchment; Social legislation; specific laws
Federal Reserve Act, 142
Federal Reserve Bank of Boston, 102, 109, 152, 153, 154, 175, 257n48
Federation of Women's Clubs, 31
Female workers: cotton worker on treatment of, 50–51; first minimum wage regulations for, 13, 90; night work proposal of 1928, 38–40, 46, 254n31, 255nn34–35, 255nn37–38; personal accounts of cotton workers, 50–52; six o'clock law, 28, 30–33, 41–42, 254n31, 255n40; work hour extension viewed by, 47–48, 50–52; work hour restrictions, 28–32, 252n2
54-hour work week proposals, 33, 252n9
Filene, A. Lincoln, 119–20, 122–23, 273n55, 277n8; bank study headed by, 146–47, 211

Financing: debt, 140; federal legislation, 156–57; government financing of science-based spinoffs, 166, 283n16; labor standards and textile, 6. See also Banks, Boston-based; Small business financing; Venture capital
Finland, 229
"First Class Bastard" individualism, 71–72
First National Bank of Boston, 128, 146, 150, 155, 171, 173–78, 210; Boston newspaper article of 1960, 245–46; industrialization programs of 1970s, 212; special department of, 177, 178, 246, 285n46; tax reduction campaign, 207; Wang Laboratories financed by, 183–85
Flanders, Ralph, 114, 115, 117, 147, 149, 152–53; as ARD prime mover, 156–59; bank conference address by, 154–55, 175–76, 279n38; spinoff financing promoted by, 175–76
FLSA. See Fair Labor Standards Act
Forbes, 189–90
Foreclosures, 20
Foreign import competition, 226; Japanese, 100, 194, 225, 227–28, 268n78; postwar (World War II), 237, 296n49; trade protection to counter, 223–24, 294n10
40-40 plan, 73, 76
48-hour law, 36–37, 252n9, 254n28, 254n31
France, 228, 296n47
Frankfurter, Felix, 90
Fuller, Alvin T., 37–38

Galambos, Louis, 71, 72, 263n9
General Strike of 1934, 79, 80–81
Germany, 228, 238
GNP. See Gross National Product
Golas, Joseph, 19
GOP. See Grand Old Party
Gorman, Francis, 46–47, 80–83
Government: advanced electronics purchased by, 162, 281n3; economic development role of, 103, 193, 233, 295n39; expansion and reduction over time, 217–20; financing role debate, 142–43, 277n8; political influence on public policy, 219–20; regulatory burden on businesses, 236, 296n47; science-based spinoffs financed by, 166, 283n16; V-loans of, 175, 177. See also State government, Massachusetts
Governors' conference, of New England states in 1925, 110–11
Grand Old Party (GOP): unemployment insurance cutbacks by, 192; work hours issue of Republicans and, 35–40. See also Republican Party

Great Strike of 1860, 12–13
Greene, Theodore, 83
Griswold, Merrill, 156, 157, 158, 159
Gross National Product (GNP), per capita, 222
Guffey Act of 1935, 268n77

Halliwell, John, 48, 49
Harding, W. P. G., 109
Harmon, Dudley, 114
Harrington, Michael J., 209–10, 214
Harris, Seymour, 193–95, 198, 202, 288n20
Hartford, William F., 248n1
Hartley, Fred, Jr., 88
Henderson, Leon, 92
Herter, Christian, 192, 199–201, 216, 289n33, 291n35
Hewlett, Bill, 163
Hewlett-Packard, 164
Higher education: postwar (World War II) income from, 203; textile industry and, 269n8
Hodges Research and Development, 144, 278n16
Hodsdon, Charles, 35
Holmes, Oliver Wendell, 90
Hook, James, 114, 115, 116, 143
Hoover, Herbert, 81, 116, 255n39; associationalism of, 70, 118; CTI backed by, 70, 71
Hosiery industry and hosiery NRA code, 67, 83, 84–86, 87
Hours of work. *See* Work hours
Houston, Texas, 235, 296n45
Howell, James, 207, 210, 211, 212, 213; multiple initiatives pursued by, 292n76
Hudson, Ray, 114

Iacocca, Lee, 224
IBM, 183
Individualism, "First Class Bastard," 71–72
Industrial decline. *See* Deindustrialization
Industrial Development Committee, New England Council, 129, 147, 274n75
Industrialization: agriculture role in, 250n4; assessing aid to new industries, 239–40, 297n56; First National Bank and 1970s, 212; growth and social reform in nineteenth-century New England, 10–13; legislation, 13; New England 1960s, 202–5; Piedmont post-reconstruction, 21–25; postwar (World War II) growth, 202–3; service sector, 12, 203, 215, 292n73; social problems arising with, 12
Industrial surveys, Boston Chamber of Commerce, 108–9

Inhibited capital, 151, 156
Initiatives to counter deindustrialization: assessing, 235–40; comparison over sixty years, 213–20, 292nn74–78, 293n79; continuities over time in, 213, 214–17, 292nn74–77; discontinuities over time in, 213–14, 217–20, 292nn78–79; interstate compact campaign, 264n28; New England context, 8–9; 1970s and 1980s, 206–13, 291n62; overlapping of three, 248n7; overview, 2–9, 249n7; political opposition to, 3–4; pursuit of multiple, 215–16, 292n76; regional leaders' role in, 5–6; unions and, 8–9. *See also* Economic development; Federal assistance; Retrenchment; Tax reduction initiatives
Insurance companies, 158
Investment Company Act of 1940, 156–58
Italy, 229

Japanese imports, 100, 194, 225, 268n78; restraints on, 227–28
Jennings, Harry, 84
Job losses. *See* Unemployment
Joyce, Martin, 48

Kennedy, John F., 198
King, Edward, 213
Knights of Labor, 13, 28–29
Korean War, 176, 195, 285n44
Ku Klux Klan, 35

Labor: capital-labor antagonism, 44–45, 190, 258n55, 259n59; reform, 12–13; work hours change motivations of, 46–52, 259n63. *See also* Social legislation; Unions and unionism; *specific unions*
Labor activists, Ellenbogen textile bill hearings testimonies by, 84–86
Laboratories, 170; commercial, 123–24, 183–85, 273n58; research-based industry and, 123–24, 170, 183–85, 225, 273n58; Wang, 183–85
Labor costs: postwar (World War II) electronics industry, 203; Southern cotton industry advantage of, 23
Labor force, new immigrants in, 32
Labor standards: absence of comprehensive, 68; competition and, 47; focus of federal assistance as, 67–68; interstate compact campaign to harmonize, 264n28; motivations for opposing change to work hour laws, 46–52, 259n63; postwar (World War II) efforts to equalize and

regulate, 95–99; southern state opposition to, 71; textile finance and, 6. *See also* Fair Labor Standards Act; National Industrial Recovery Act; Social legislation; Wages

Labor surplus, defense channeling to alleviate, 195–96, 210

Laissez-faire, 67, 99, 117, 133, 275n87

Lawrence, John S., 73, 109, 110–13, 270n20; New England Council presence of, 114, 115; state agency supported by, 133

Lawrence, Massachusetts, 13, 16, 20, 106, 109, 189, 204, 205, 263n113, 274n75

Leather manufacturing, 14, 189, 206

Legislation. *See* Federal legislation; New Deal reform; Social legislation; Work hours; *specific acts*

Liability law, 13

Liquidation: cotton textile industry, 24–25; scientific, 25

Lochner decision, 29

Lodge, Henry Cabot, 36

Los Angeles electronics industry, 166, 167, 181–82, 286n55

Lowell, 11, 16, 17, 19, 20, 274n75; postwar (World War II) unemployment, 204; senator defeated through union efforts, 30

Lowell School for Practical Design, 105

Lowell Textile School, 106, 136

Lubin, Isador, 92

Machine tools, 11, 115–16, 153, 183, 282n10

Maclaurin, Rupert, 158, 170

Male workers: double shift enforced on, 30; night shift staffing issue, 41, 247nn45–46

Manchester, New Hampshire, 16, 19–20

Manufacturing employment. *See* Employment

Manufacturing Extension Partnership (MEP), 226–27

Marketing practices, 136; New England Council studies and programs, 121–22, 127, 130

Massachusetts: expansion of welfare state, 52–53, 259n73; reason for focus on, 2, 249n6. *See also* State government, Massachusetts; *specific centers of manufacturing*; *specific topics*

Massachusetts Business Development Corporation (MBDC), 201

Massachusetts Business Roundtable, 207

Massachusetts Department of Commerce, 199–201, 291nn35–36, 292n71

Massachusetts Foreign Business Council, 211, 213, 218

Massachusetts High Technology Council, 208

Massachusetts Industrial Commission, 132–35, 275nn85–86, 275n88; disbanding and reforming of, 275n90; unintentionally ironic publication distributed by, 134, 275n92

Massachusetts Institute of Technology (MIT), 106, 117, 120, 160–61, 282n10; Compton, K., as president of, 125–26, 168; Division of Humanities, 126; Maclaurin and, 170, 284n27; Pentagon contracts, 166, 283n16; post-WW II era and, 168; Technology Plan, 123

Massachusetts State Chamber of Commerce, 108, 270n14

Massachusetts Tax Association (MTA), 60–61

Massachusetts Technology Development Corporation (MTDC), 212–13

Massachusetts Textile Council, 84

Mass Incentives, 208

Mass media, 189–90

Mass production, 124

MBDC. *See* Massachusetts Business Development Corporation

McMahon, Thomas, 80, 83

Mead, James, 142, 277n8

Medical services, 203

Mellon family, 145

MEP. *See* Manufacturing Extension Partnership

Merchants National Bank, 171, 177, 178, 179, 285n49

Merrimack Manufacturing Company, 33, 34, 58, 258n54; capacity utilization, 257n51; work hour laws impact on, 42–43, 257n51, 258n53

Metalworking, 11, 115–16, 203

Migration, 17, 204

Millworkers, personal accounts by, 18–20, 204–5

Mineral resources, 126–27

Minimum wage regulations: first female worker, 13, 90; FLSA, 95, 96; NRA cotton code, 73–74; pay levels below, 18

MIT. *See* Massachusetts Institute of Technology

Monsanto, 148

Morse, Richard, 148, 163

MTA. *See* Massachusetts Tax Association

MTDC. *See* Massachusetts Technology Development Corporation

Multifiber Arrangements, 223, 227

Murchison, Claude, 86, 93–94

NACM. *See* National Association of Cotton Manufacturers

NASA contracts, 177, 180

National Association of Cotton Manufacturers (NACM), 33–34, 44; CTI established by, 69–72; Ellenbogen textile bills opposed by, 86–87, 265n46; FLSA opposed by, 94, 266n46; tax reform lobbying by, 58

National Bureau of Standards, renaming, 226

National Consumers League, 31

National Industrial Recovery Act (NIRA), 72–80, 255n40; 40-40 plan, 73, 76; New England Council code writing for, 131; New England Council support for, 131, 132; voiding of, 68, 79, 89

National Institute of Standards and Technology (NIST), 226–27

National Labor Relations Act (Wagner Act), 87

National Planning Association, 189

National Recovery Administration (NRA), 82; coal industry's "little," 268n77; cotton textile code, 73–74, 76–77, 79, 99–100; earnings distribution before and after imposition of, 75; hosiery code, 84; successor agency to, 89; 30-30 plan, 76, 264n19; work hours and, 73, 74, 79–80; workload increase response to, 76–77. *See also* Cotton textile code, NRA

National Research Corporation (NRC), 148, 163

National Shawmut Bank, 115, 128, 171, 176

National Textile Act. *See* Ellenbogen textile bills

National War Labor Board, 95

NEC. *See* New England Council

NEIDC. *See* New England Industrial Development Corporation

Neoliberalism, 292n78

New Bedford, 16, 17, 257n46; strikes in, 253n12, 258n55; unionism in Fall River and, 38, 253n12

New Bedford Textile Council, 32, 33, 35, 38, 39, 49–50, 78

New Deal reform, 74, 80, 88; government expansion during, 217; key authors of legislation, 90; small business financing in, 142; union decline and, 232, 295n35

New England: case study relevance, 2; industrial growth and social reform in nineteenth-century, 10–13; initiatives context, 8–9; unique situation in, 7, 8. *See also* Massachusetts; *specific topics*

New England Conference, 111–12, 113, 271n30

New England Congressional Caucus, 210

New England Council (NEC): Agriculture Committee, 130–31; decentralized structure, 271n30; economic development role of, 102–3; formation of, 107–13, 271n28; Industrial Development Committee, 129, 147, 274n75; laboratories promoted by, 123–24, 273n58; leadership, 114, 115; legitimization concerns, 111, 271n28; mediation activities, 131; membership, 113, 114–16; New Products Committee, 125, 126–28, 147, 168; NIRA supported by, 131, 132; operations, 113–17; other economic development efforts, 128–32; philosophy and strategy, 116–17, 118; postwar (World War II) campaigns for new industries, 202; private sector growth-promotion and, 234; public relations department, 128–29; Recreation Committee, 131; research and technology initiatives, 117–28, 272n50, 273n55, 273n58; Research Committee, 119, 120–23, *145*, 146–47, 211, 272n50; retrenchment not endorsed by, 122, 273n55; Roosevelt, FDR, reelection and, 116–17; tax reduction efforts, 57, 129–30, 274n77; venture capital role of, 127, *145*, 147, 150. *See also* Committee on Ownership and Finance, New England Council

New England Industrial Development Corporation (NEIDC), 147–48

New England Industrial Research Foundation, 128, 136–37

New Enterprises, Inc., 169, 170, 283n23

New immigrant operatives, 32

New Products Committee, New England Council, 125, 126–28, *145*, 147, 168

New Products Day, 124

New Products Research Corporation, 169

New York City area electronics industry, 166–67, 182

Nickerson, John, 83, 86–87

Night work: advantages for cotton manufacturing, 41; as crucial to textile industry, 34; double shift enforced on male workers, 30; duration of need for, 42, 257n48; male workers for, 41, 247nn45–46; proposal of 1928, 38–40, 46, 254n31, 255nn34–35, 255nn37–38; restrictions, 29–30, 38–39, 70–71; six o'clock law, 28, 30–33, 41–42, 50, 254n31, 255n40; southern states, 47

NIRA. *See* National Industrial Recovery Act

NIST. *See* National Institute of Standards and Technology

Nixon, Richard, 223

Northeast-Midwest Congressional Coalition, 210, 214

North-South competition: cost gap, 97; implications of enforced wage equity, 100–101; interregional equilibrium and, 23–24; key factor in, 98; postwar (World War II) foreign competition mirroring, 237, 296n49. *See also* Wage differentials

Index   327

NRA. *See* National Recovery Administration
NRC. *See* National Research Corporation
Nucleonics. *See* Applied physics sector

Odd goods, 23
$1,000,000 Small Issues Corporation, 141
Operating rates, 40–41, 256n42, 257n43
Operation Dixie, 96
Opposition: CTI nonconformers, 71–72; Ellenbogen textile bill, 68, 86–87, 265n42, 265n46; FLSA, 68, 88–95, 265n46; political, 3–4; welfare program, 53, 260n76
Otis Company, 17
Overcapacity, 47, 69, 195, 259n63; 30–30 plan to address, 76, 264n19
Overtime bill, 30

Packard, David, 163
Payne, Frederick, 275n88
Payroll tax, 187n10, 191
Pennsylvania Manufacturers Association, 258n57
Pensions, 27, 52
Pentagon, Wang Laboratories contract with, 183
Perkins, Frances, 89
Personal accounts: displaced worker, 205; female cotton worker, 50–52; millworker, 18–20
Philadelphia, 182
Philadelphia Textile School, 105
Piedmont mills (in southern states): cotton code evasion by, 76, 99–100; fabric production shift to, 100–101; General Strike of 1934, 79, 80–81; market share growth of, 69; post-reconstruction era, 21–25; postwar (World War II) investment in, 97; postwar (World War II) shift to, 100–101; stretchout complaints, 76–77
Political economy: definition of, 249n5; deindustrialization and, 2, 230–35, 249n4; federal assistance implications for, 231; industrial policy and, 232; scholarship on, 1, 249n4; shifting context of, 7
Political opposition, to initiatives, 3–4
Polytechnic Research and Development, 167–68
Post–Korean War period, 176, 285n44
Post-Reconstruction (Civil War) industrialization, 21–25
Postwar era (World War II): competition, 152; deindustrialization trends in, 188–90, 287n2, 287n4; economic development efforts in, 168, 199–203, 289n33; electronics industry expansion, 187, 203; employment decline, 188–89, *189*, 195, 204–5, 287n2; federal assistance during, 193–99; foreign import competition, 237, 296n49; industrial growth, 202–3; investment in Piedmont mills, 97; private sector development efforts, 201–2; retrenchment push in Massachusetts, 190–93, 287n10; shift to Piedmont states, 100–101; state government programs, 199–201; technological focus for economic development, 168; unionism in, 190, 193, 203–4; wage equalization efforts, 95–100. *See also* World War I, decline of traditional industries after
Price fixing, 267n76, 268n77
Private sector: banks and venture capital development in, 234–35; economic development role of, 7, 103–4, 107–13, 201–2, 269n9, 270n12; Houston economic development efforts of 1980s, 235, 296n45; late 1960s and 1970s development activity, 212; 1920s and 1930s, 249n5; postwar (World War II) development support from, 201–2; scholarship gap on development and, 7, 234, 296n42; science-based spinoffs supported by, 167–68. *See also* Business associations
Product development, 125, 126–28, 147, 168. *See also specific corporations*
Product Development Corporation, 284n25
Property tax, 58–59, 61–64, 261n89, 262n108
Proposition 2{1/2}, 208, 261n90
Providence Central Labor Union, 80
Public relations, 128–29, 134, 275n86, 275n92
Public schools, 59, 261n96
Purchase and leaseback, 182

Radiation Laboratory, 166, 170, 174
Rand Development Corporation, 144
Raye, William H., Jr., 174–76, 177, 246, 285n37
Raytheon Corporation, 163, 168–69, 175
R&D. *See* Research and Development
Reagan, Ronald, 223, 227, 293nn6–7
Reconstruction Finance Corporation, 142
Recreation Committee, New England Council, 131
Reed-Prentice, 124
Reform. *See* New Deal reform; Social legislation; Tax reform; *specific issues*
Regional credit pools, 143
Reisroff, Bertha, 50–51
Republican Party, 70; dominance as GOP, 35; laissez-faire stance, 67; Massachusetts Department of Commerce acceptance by, 289n36; unemployment insurance cutbacks by GOP, 192; work hours stance of GOP and, 35–40

Research and Development (R&D), 225–26, 294n16; European, 229
Research-based industry: economic development of 1970s, 213; laboratories and, 123–24, 170, 183–85, 225, 273n58; New England Council initiatives for technology and, 117–28, 272n50, 273n55, 273n58; textile industry as, 106–7, 269n8
Research Committee, New England Council, 119, 120–23, 272n50; bank study by, 145, 146–47, 211
Research Week, 124, 126
Responses, to deindustrialization. See Initiatives to counter deindustrialization
Retrenchment: advocates of, 2–3, 235; aim of, 235–36; business association motivations for, 235–36; corporate power and, 230; definition, 2–3; deindustrialization link with, 64–66; European, 228, 294n23; key factor in success of, 64–65; local service sector efforts, 215, 292n73; New England Council not endorsing, 122, 273n55; 1970s, 207–9; overview by different eras, 214–17; postwar (World War II) Massachusetts push for, 190–93, 287n10; recent era efforts, 28, 223, 293n7. See also Economic development; Federal assistance; Social legislation; Tax reduction initiatives
Rhode Island School of Design, 105
Rogers, Edith Nourse, 10, 135
Roosevelt, Franklin: FLSA passed under, 88–95, 265n46; New England Council and, 116–17; popularity decline in 1937, 94, 95, 99
Rosenwald, Lessing, 159
Route 128, 9, 161, 185–86, 286n65

San Francisco, 278n17
Sargent, Francis, 208
SBIC. See Small Business Investment Company
Schechter decision, 79
Scholarship: on economic development, 104, 268n2; historical, 1, 104, 248n1, 248n3, 249n4; political economy, 1, 249n4; postwar (World War II), 189–90; on private sector development promotion, 7, 234, 296n42; on union power of 1920s, 53
Schools: public spending on, 59, 261n96; textile, 105–7, 136, 269n7
Science-based spinoffs, 162–63, 281n4; government financing for, 166, 283n16; outside New England, 181–82, 286n55; private-sector support for, 167–68. See also Electronics industry; Spinoffs

Scientific liquidation, 25
Second National Bank of Boston, 171, 172–73, 284n31
Securities, 141
Sematech, 225–26, 294n16
Service sector, 12, 115, 203, 215, 292n73
Sherman Anti-Trust law, 73
Shoes. See Boot and shoe industry
Six o'clock law, 28, 30–33, 41–42, 50, 254n31, 255n40
Slater, Samuel, 10
Small business financing, 139–59, 170–80; ARD establishment, 155–59, 280n43, 280n49, 281n53, 284n25, 284n27; assessing importance of new industries and, 239–40, 297n55; bank conference of 1945, 154–55, 172, 175–76, 279n38; Boston-area spinoffs helped by, 183–85; Depression era and, 141, 147; development entities 1939–1946, 145; federal assistance and, 141–42, 283n14; government role debate, 142–43, 277n8; inhibited capital problem, 151, 156; initial efforts to improve, 146–55, 278n24, 279n30; nationwide shortfall in, 140–46; organizations types, 143; technological focus of, 168–70, 283n28, 284n25; traditional routes of, 140–41. See also Banks, Boston-based; Enterprise Associates; First National Bank of Boston; Spinoffs
Small Business Investment Company (SBIC), 179
Smith, Al, 255n39
Smith, James T., 105–6
Snowbelt campaign, 209–10, 211, 214, 291n62
Snyder, Arthur F. F., 176, 177, 178, 285n49
Social legislation: competition issue and, 49; Ellenbogen textile bill proposal, 80–88, 265n34, 265n42, 265n46, 266n48; expansion of welfare state, 52–53, 259n73; frustrated efforts to roll back, 4, 26–27; national implications of 1920s battles over, 53–54; 1970s retrenchment efforts, 208–9; opposition to social protection programs, 53, 260n76; recent era retrenchment in, 28; in Southern states, 31–32; vanguard dynamic in, 48–49. See also Night work; Welfare; Work hours; specific acts; specific legislation
Social problems, industrialization and, 12
Social Security Act of 1935, 52–53
Southern states: active cotton spindles in New England and, 22; business associations in, 69; cloth quality, 23; CTI nonconformers in, 71; labor cost advantage, 23; labor standardization opposition in, 71; night shift in, 47; Operation

Dixie, 96; post-Reconstruction growth in, 21–25; shift to Piedmont advantages to, 100–101; Snowbelt campaign response of, 291n62; social legislation in, 31–32; union drives in, 78–79, 95–97; work hours issue based on, 31–32, 47; workload increase in, 76–77. *See also* North-South competition; Piedmont mills; Wage differentials

Southern States Industrial Council, 86, 93

Space men (First National Bank of Boston special department), 177, 178, 246, 285n46

Spencer, Charles, 150, 155

Spending, state and local government: business demands for reduction of taxes and, 54–64; MTA proposal to regulate, 60–61; 1916–1926 increased taxation and, 55–56, 260n80; 1970s, 207; public school, 59, 261n96; special commission on municipal, 59–60, 260n80; tax increase and, 55–56

Spinoffs: advanced electronics industry conducive to, 164; applied physics sector and, 162, 163; ARD venture capital financing of, 169–71, 284n27; Boston-area success of, 183–85; Boston banks' financing of, 170–80, 245–46, 285n37, 285n44, 285n46; competition and, 164, 182; defense spending facilitating, 163, 282n10; economic development potential from, 168–70, 180, 284n27; emergence of, 161–65, 281n4, 282n8; federal tax structure and, 282n13; finance obstacles for start-up, 165, 283n14; location of early, 165–68; outside of New England, 181–82; reason for existence of, 167; Route 128 success from financing, 185–86, 286n65; science-based, 162–63, 166–68, 281n4, 283n16; Snyder's approach to financing, 178, 285n49; success levels of, 164; taxation, 164–65, 282n13; union restrictions absence, 164, 282n11. *See also* Science-based spinoffs

Springs, Elliot, 71

Stanford Research Institute, 278n17

State government, Massachusetts: budget shortfall of 1970s, 206; business demands for reduced spending and taxation, 54–64; economic development role of, 103, 132–35, 275n88, 275n90, 275nn85–86; growth-promoting institutions, 213, 292n71; industrial policy, 213; innovative growth-promotion efforts of 1970s, 212; MBDC, 201; 1970s critiques of spending by, 207; postwar (World War II) programs, 199–201; retrenchment advocacy and, 2–3; taxation discrepancies, 261n89

State legislation: 48-hour law, 36–37, 252n9, 254n28, 254n31; during industrialization era, 13; push to enact worker protection, 28–32. *See also* Six o'clock law; Social legislation; Work hours

State Street Trust, 171, 172, 173

Steel industry, 223, 282n11

Stevens, J. P., 97

Stoddard, William, 277n8

Stratton, Samuel, 125

Stretchout, 76–77, 82

Strikes, 96, 253n12; General Strike of 1934, 79, 80–81; Great Strike of 1860, 12–13; over work hours, 258n55

Suicides, 19–20

Surveys, industrial, 109

Tariff policy, 194–95, 288n20

Taxation: assessments on Fall River corporations and taxpayers, 56, 56, 61, 260n83; on corporate excess, 62–63, 261n89; discrepancies and complexities in state, 261n89; Fall River overassessment, 57, 61, 260nn83–84, 262n102; 1916–1926 increased local, 55–56, 260n80; overassessments on Fall River, 57, 61, 260nn83–84, 262n102; payroll, 187n10, 191; as political issue, 261n90; production cost total share of, 65, 263n113; property and machinery, 58–59, 61–64, 261n89, 262n108; Proposition 2{1/2}, 261n90; spinoff financing and, 164–65, 282n13; state government spending driving increased, 55–56; textile industry and other taxpayers 1917–1932, 56

Tax reduction initiatives, 27–28, 56, 61–62, 249n7; AIM, 57, 61; business demands for, 54–64; Eisenhower plan, 196–97; fiscal stress caused by textile industry, 262n104; New England Council, 57, 129–30, 274n77; 1950s, 192; 1970s and 1980s, 207–8; 1980s, 223, 293n6; Proposition 2{1/2}, 208, 261n90; textile industry summary of achieved, 62, 262n104

Tax reform, 57–58, 63–64, 261n90; 1927 special commission on, 59; 1935 special commission on, 54, 63–64; proposal success in 1935, 63–64

Taylor Society, 122, 273n55

Technology: small business finance focus on, 168–70, 283n28, 284n25; start-ups, 162, 281n4; venture capital and, 148. *See also* Science-based spinoffs

Technology Plan, MIT, 123

Technology Transfer Act, 225

330 Index

Textile industry: bank financing of, 172; decentralized nature of, 87; decline of, 15, 16, 16–20; early, 11; employment decrease in 1925, 1936, and 1939, 263n112; General Strike of 1934, 79, 80–81; higher education and, 269n8; increased taxation on, 56, 56, 260n83; labor force, 32; labor standards and financing for, 6; night work as crucial to, 34; overcapacity, 47, 69, 76, 195, 259n63, 264n19; postwar (World War II) unemployment, 204–5; property and machinery taxation on, 58–59, 61–64, 261n89, 262n108; reduced tax revenue from, 262n104; research-based, 106–7, 269n8; silk and rayon competition, 266n48; structural unemployment, 20; tax assessments on Fall River, 56, 56, 260n83; tax reduction on, 62, 262n104; unionism, 29, 32. *See also* Cotton textile industry; Southern states; *specific topics*
Textile schools, 105–7, 136, 269n7
Textile Workers Union of America (TWUA), 95–96, 197, 198
30-30 plan, 76, 264n19
Thompson, Sanford, 121–22, 273n55
Thoron, Ward, 33–34, 36, 42; motives and concerns over work hour laws, 258n54; as NACM taxation committee head, 44; tax reduction lobbied by, 58; work hour concerns and actual impact on, 42–43, 257n51
Tinsley, John, 57
Tourism, 203
Trade protection, 193–95, 288n20; in Europe, 227–28; U.S. 1970s and 1980s, 223–24, 294n10
Tragic towns, 17
Truman, Harry, 195–96
TWUA. *See* Textile Workers Union of America

UDAG. *See* Urban Development Action Grant
UMW. *See* United Mine Workers
Unemployment: displaced workers, 17, 204–5, 224, 297n56; industries experiencing, 289n28; 1930s textile industry, 17; 1939, 16–17; 1955, 204; 1970s, 206; 1970s textile industry, 206; postwar (World War II) textile industry, 204–5; structural, 20. *See also* Deindustrialization; Employment; Employment decline
Unemployment insurance, 3, 52–53; competition issues and, 260n76; cutbacks in, 191; 1940s, 190–91; 1970s, 208–9; union defeat, 192; voluntary quits, 192, 208–9
Unions and unionism: AFL break with, 53; capital-labor antagonism, 44–45, 190, 258n55,
259n59; Cold War era anti-, 96; collective bargaining, 78, 92–93; cotton industry North-South comparison, 23, 78; cotton worker, 44; geographic restrictions on, 231; goals of, 53–54; manufacturer claims compared to, 259n59; Massachusetts, 32, 253n12; membership of 1920s and 1970s, 295n31; motivations for opposing work hours change, 46–52, 259n63; New Deal reform and, 232, 295n35; New England's mid-twentieth-century context of, 8–9; 1930s federal legislation and, 255n40; overcapacity problem cited by, 47, 259n63; postwar (World War II), 190, 193, 203–4; reform strategy of, 59; on rush order issue, 257n46; scholarship on 1920s, 53; in southern states, 78–79, 95–97, 99; spinoffs and, 164, 282n11; tax reduction endorsed by, 27; textile industry, 29; unemployment insurance defeat for, 192; vitality of 1920s, 53; wartime, 95; weakness in growth-seeking areas, 8; work hours issue and, 28–32, 35, 252n6, 255n40, 259n59; workload issue and, 97, 282n11. *See also specific unions*
United Mine Workers (UMW), 268n77
United States (U.S.): boot and shoe industry New England share of, 11; deindustrialization responses in recent decades, 221–27; employment decline statistics, 222, 293n2; federal assistance of 1970s and 1980s, 223–25; federal legislation for economic development in, 225–27, 294n16; gainful workers and employment in Massachusetts and, 242; job creation rates in Massachusetts and, 241; New England employment rise compared to, 202, 287n3; trade protection of 1970s and 1980s, 223–24, 294n10
United Textile Workers of America (UTW), 31, 32, 33; Ellenbogen textile bills sponsored by, 81–82, 83, 265n34; General Strike, 79, 80–81; work hours law defended by, 38, 46–47
Urban Development Action Grant (UDAG), 211
U.S. Department of Commerce, 226
UTW. *See* United Textile Workers of America

Venture capital: in Boston electronics industry, 5, 170–71, 177; Boston entities of 1939–1946, 145; capital gaps of 1970s, 212, 291n70; economic development motives behind, 145, 278n17; first organizations, 143–44, 145, 277n12, 278n16; inhibited capital problem, 151, 156; insurance company resistance, 158; New England Council role in, 127, 145, 147, 150, 168; New Products

Committee research into, 127, 147, 168; private sector role and, 234; regulatory obstacles, 156–58; San Francisco area, 278n17; shortage of, 140; spinoff funding by ARD, 169–71, 284n27; Stanford Research Institute funded by, 278n17; technology and, 148. *See also* Small business financing
V-loans, 175, 177
Vogel, David, 28, 64

Wage differentials: Ellenbogen textile bills to eliminate, 82; FLSA and, 95; North-South, *22*, 74–78, *75*, 243, *243*, 264n22, 264n24; post-WWII efforts to eliminate, 95–100
Wages: displaced worker, 204; earnings distribution before and after NRA, *75*; implications of enforced North-South equity, 100–101; postwar (World War II) equalization efforts, 95–100; wage rates for selected occupations in New England and Southern cotton mills, *243*; Walsh-Healey Act, 89; work hours law and, 46–47; workman's compensation payment percentage of, 259n73. *See also* Minimum wage regulations
Walsh, David, 36–37, 254n25, 254n28; 1928 election won by, 255n39
Walsh-Healey Act, 89
Wang, An, 177–78
Wang Laboratories, 183–85, 282n10
Warner and Swasey, 184
Wartime, unionism in, 95
Watered capital, 259n59
Weed, Charles F., 109, 114, 125
Weissman, Rudolph, 142
Welfare: caseload increase of 1970s, 206; expansion of Massachusetts programs, 52–53, 259n73; opposition to social protection programs, 53, 260n76
West Germany, 228, 229
Whitney, J. H., 144, 278n16
Women's Suffrage Association, 31
Women's Trade Union League (WTUL), 30–31, 38
Wool textile (woolen and worsted) industry, 11, 14, 15, 16, 69, 84, 87, 189; postwar (World War II) crash of, 97, 267n75
Workers: displaced, 17, 204–5, 224, 297n56; double shift enforced on male, 30; Massachusetts and U.S. 1880–1940, *242*; personal accounts of, 18–20, 50–51; push to legislate protections for, 28–32; skill classification, 77–78; union membership of highly skilled, 32. *See also* Female workers; Male workers
Work hours: AFL involvement in issue of, 32–33, 35; battles over, 32–40, 48, 253n16, 254n21; cost-reduction and profit analysis, 40–41, 256n41; cotton code on, 73–74; deindustrialization blamed on work hour laws, 44–46, 259n59; Democratic backing for reducing, 29, 37, 39, 254n23; female worker views on, 47–48, 50; 54-hour work week proposals, 33, 252n9; 40–40 plan, 73, 76; 48-hour law, 36–37, 252n9, 254n28, 254n31; GOP protectionism, 35–36, 39–40; labor motivations for opposing changes to laws on, 46–52, 259n63; manufacturer motivations for changing, 40–46, 259n59; 1924 hearing on, 34, 254n21; 1926 hearing on, 36–37, 254n28; 1928 hearing on, 38–40, 46, 254n31, 255nn34–35, 255nn37–38; NRA and, 73–74, 79–80; out-of-state manufacturer involvement in debate, 258n57; push to legislate Massachusetts, 28–32; Republican Party stance, 35–40; restrictions on women's, 28–32, 252n2; in Southern states, 31–32; stabilization efforts including limitations on, 72, 263n9, 264n28; strikes over, 258n55; 30–30 plan, 76, 264n19; unions and, 28–32, 35, 252n6, 255n40, 259n59. *See also* Night work
Workloads, 86, 97, 282n11; stretchout problem, 76–77, 82
Workman's Compensation Act, 50
Workmen's compensation, 27, 52, 259n73; AIM achieving limits to increase in, 53
Works Progress Administration, 16
World War I, decline of traditional industries after, 13–21, *15*, *16*
WTUL. *See* Women's Trade Union League

DAVID KOISTINEN is associate professor of history at William Paterson University of New Jersey.

THE UNIVERSITY PRESS OF FLORIDA is the scholarly publishing agency for the State University System of Florida, comprising Florida A&M University, Florida Atlantic University, Florida Gulf Coast University, Florida International University, Florida State University, New College of Florida, University of Central Florida, University of Florida, University of North Florida, University of South Florida, and University of West Florida.

WORKING IN THE AMERICAS
Edited by Richard Greenwald, Drew University, and Timothy J. Minchin, LaTrobe University

Working in the Americas is devoted to publishing important works in labor history and working-class studies in the Americas. This series seeks work that uses traditional as well as innovative, interdisciplinary, or transnational approaches. Its focus is the Americas and the lives of its workers.

Florida's Working-Class Past: Current Perspectives on Labor, Race, and Gender from Spanish Florida to the New Immigration, edited by Robert Cassanello and Melanie Shell-Weiss (2009; first paperback edition, 2011)

The New Economy and the Modern South, by Michael Dennis (2009)

Film Noir, American Workers, and Postwar Hollywood, by Dennis Broe (2009)

Americanization in the States: Immigrant Social Welfare Policy, Citizenship, and National Identity in the United States, 1908–1929, by Christina A. Ziegler-McPherson (2009)

Black Labor Migration in Caribbean Guatemala, 1882–1923, by Frederick Douglass Opie (2009; first paperback edition, 2012)

Migration and the Transformation of the Southern Workplace since 1945, edited by Robert Cassanello and Colin J. Davis (2009)

American Railroad Labor and the Genesis of the New Deal, 1919–1935, by Jon R. Huibregtse (2010; first paperback edition, 2012)

Seated by the Sea: The Maritime History of Portland, Maine, and Its Irish Longshoremen, by Michael C. Connolly (2010; first paperback edition, 2011)

Strike! The Radical Insurrections of Ellen Dawson, by David Lee McMullen (2010; first paperback edition, 2012)

New York Longshoremen: Class and Power on the Docks, by William J. Mello (2010; first paperback edition, 2011)

Life and Labor in the New New South, edited by Robert H. Zieger (2012)

Confronting Decline: The Political Economy of Deindustrialization in Twentieth-Century New England, by David Koistinen (2014; first paperback edition, 2016)

www.ingramcontent.com/pod-product-compliance
Lightning Source LLC
Chambersburg PA
CBHW021336230426
43666CB00006B/310